DAVID SOUTHWELL

THE HISTORY OF ORGANIZED CRIME

THE TRUE STORY AND SECRETS OF GLOBAL GANGLAND

THIS IS A CARLTON BOOK

This edition published in 2013 by
Carlton Books Limited
20 Mortimer Street
London W1T 3JW

First published in 2006

A CIP catalogue record for this book is available
from the British Library.

ISBN 978 1 84442 177 0

Printed and bound in Dubai

10 9 8 7 6 5 4 3 2 1

*For Stephen Grasso – one of the best partners
in crime you could ever hope to meet and a
true Sicilian gentleman of honour.*

*Salvatore Burzotta – anyone who first thinks
of the Mafia instead of hospitality and culinary
greatness when Sicily is mentioned has
obviously never enjoyed Sicilian wine or
food at one of his magnificent restaurants.*

DAVID SOUTHWELL

THE HISTORY OF
ORGANIZED
CRIME

THE TRUE STORY AND SECRETS
OF GLOBAL GANGLAND

CARLTON
BOOKS

CONTENTS

INTRODUCTION

> "For what are states but large bandit bands,
> and what are bandit bands but small states?"

St. Augustine of Hippo

Organized crime holds a constant fascination for many people. Outlaw mystique exists in folklore the world over. Whispered tales of the deeds carried out by the Garduna – a secret Spanish criminal society – were a staple of storytellers in the Middle Ages. The combination of secrecy, power and violence hiding in the shadows of our daily lives represented by organized crime is the stuff of countless newspapers headlines today. Why? Maybe it is because of our desire to know more about what is hidden from us, even if it is the underworld. Or maybe it is because we enjoy being scared.

I was certainly scared at times when writing this book. If I ever needed a lesson that the core power of organized crime comes from the threat of violence, I received it during the course of researching this project. Two serious threats against my life were made. I also got one, very thought-provoking warning against saying the wrong thing about a certain Triad group that involved a butcher's cleaver and maintaining the use of my hands because, as it was so indelicately put, "Writers need hands."

Organized crime is, by conservative estimates, a $1 trillion business that operates in every country in the planet. The keyword of the twenty-first century is globalization and no other human activity better illustrates international interconnectedness than modern structured criminality. Every nation has an underworld, but in today's global economy, a parallel global gangland has emerged where transnational criminal organizations (TCOs) control more economic power than some nation states.

Like legitimate global corporations, TCOs have utilized the system of international trade and advances in communication technology and travel. They have evolved complex alliances, connections and arrangements that mean, for example, that the activities of a Colombian cocaine cartel could have an impact on both the behaviour of a Brazilian street gang and a corrupt Chinese politician under the influence of a Triad society. The TCOs span the globe and their actions reverberate through the organized crime groups that are active in every territory and illicit activity found on the planet.

It is not surprising authorities have found tackling TCOs difficult when you learn that, even in the twenty-first century, law enforcement and other agencies have not even been able to agree on a single definition of what organized crime is. For the purposes of this book, however, organized crime is defined along the lines set out in the US Organized Crime Control Act of 1970 as any structured criminal group that comes together to further its unlawful activities. While some organized crime groups I cover have an element of political motivation, this book focuses primarily on those networks, syndicates and gangs whose main reason for existing is purely profit.

While their constantly changing and adapting nature may make organized crime groups difficult to define legally, the shared features of both ancient and modern groups are easy to spot. Throughout history, many bands of pirates, bandits, slave traders and drug traffickers have enjoyed direct state sponsorship. When those groups lost official sanction and protection, they began ensuring the support they needed to carry out their activities through bribery. This practice established a matrix of political influence and crime that has become one of the defining qualities of organized crime throughout history.

Other key characteristics of organized crime groups that have emerged over the last 4,000 years are that they challenge the state monopoly on violence; use fear as a method for controlling both their members and victims; and have a hierarchical system and internal code. Their tendency to derive from resistance movements or from immigrant communities, ghettoised by poverty and discrimination, is another common element. Although there are tens of thousands of organized crime rackets, they are usually a variation on the basic themes of theft, supplying the illicit, exploiting the human condition, utilizing fear to extract money and corruption.

Chicago gang boss Al Capone often claimed he was like any other businessman, saying, "All I do is supply a demand," and pointing out that, "Capitalism is the legitimate racket of the ruling class". The implication was clear: he like many other organized crime bosses wanted his activities to be thought of in purely commercial terms. Yet any company – aside perhaps from arms manufacturers – whose business involved fear, violence and adding to the total of human misery would be shut down. Today, however, many organized crime groups have invested so much of their revenue in legitimate businesses that half of their profits now come from non-criminal operations. The distinction between illegal and legal commercial organizations is becoming harder and harder for the authorities to determine.

Possibly the biggest lesson derived from studying organized crime is that it cannot simply be defeated by more police, harsher laws or greater scrutiny and monitoring of the whole population. If organized crime has been able to exist in the Soviet Union – the historical pinnacle of the police state – the idea that introducing new laws and more crime-fighting resources could ever totally eradicate the problem is clearly hollow.

The history of organized crime also shows us that there are three underlying and recurring sources of crime – poverty, prohibition and pure human greed. Given this, how can governments who wish, in the words of Tony Blair, to be, "Tough not just on crime but on the causes of crime," best serve their people? Surely it is impossible to legislate against the avarice that lies inside the hearts of so many of us? The only way forward therefore seems to lie in dealing with the other two prime criminal motivators – poverty and prohibition.

Hope can rest in re-examining the prohibitions and systems of taxation that inspire so much organized criminal activity. For example, when Canada tripled its tax on cigarettes, made major investments in extra police to tackle tobacco smugglers and introduced draconian penalties for anyone caught evading the duty, the end result was that its smuggling problem simply increased in line with taxation. The only

ones to benefit from the rise in taxes were the organized crime gangs involved in butlegging (underworld slang for the tobacco trafficking) who saw their profits boom.

However, in 1994, when Canada halved the tax on cigarettes, the government effectively starved the smugglers of the demand for their illicit goods and organized crime was deprived of a major source of income. The bravery to apply this principle to other areas causes more concern to major criminal networks than any government talk of harsher penalties for crime or increased police budgets.

Deprivation, hunger and hardship have always been the largest causes and sustainers of criminal activity. From the East End slum area of Dickensian London known as the Rookeries, to Matunga shantytown in modern Mumbai, the link between the underclass and the underworld is clear to see. As criminal networks have become truly transnational in reach, one of the only logical ways left to fight them is to tackle the privations of poverty at a global level. It is only if real change over its causes is achieved, that there will be any hope of its ever-growing, devastating grip on our world being defeated.

THE ITALIAN MAFIA

1

"Tutto è Mafia in Italia."

(Everything in Italy is Mafia.)

Traditional Italian saying

No organized crime group has more of a mystique than the Italian Mafia. Yet the Italian Mafia does not, in any concrete way, exist. At one level it is just a shorthand phrase to describe the wide range of very real Italian organized crime groups, ranging from the actual Sicilian Mafia to the 'Ndrangheta from Calabria and the less often mentioned Mala del Brenta of Venice.

In Italy, the phrase Mafia has become not only a synonym for all organized crime groups in the country, but also a term used to describe the web of collusion and corruption associated with them that reaches from the lowest to the highest levels of Italian society. In many senses, Mafia has become a brand name associated with everything of the underworld – violence, power, money, conspiracy, secrecy and blood. However, the Mafia "brand" also carries connotations of tradition, family, masculinity and, above all, honour.

Much of the aura that surrounds the Mafia in Italy stems from the fact that, although it has now become a nationwide criminal network, it is composed of organized crime gangs that have their roots in, and still often function as, age-old secret societies. This taps into the deep-rooted Italian belief in "potere occulto" (hidden power) – the idea that there is a clandestine group guiding the hand of those in visible authority.

The mythology of the Mafia has become so entrenched in Italian culture that it is almost part of the national heritage. Alongside the Mafia's money and violence, the folklore is a powerful tool for inspiring fear and promoting silence. You can tell that organized crime has achieved true power in Italy when the mere use of the word "Mafia" can silence those you are talking with.

THE ORIGINS OF THE MAFIA

Anyone who claims they can give a definitive and totally accurate history of the origins of the Mafia is mistaken. There is no fully comprehensive and perfect account of the genesis of the various Italian organized crime groups that have become collectively known as the Mafia. No one can even give a definitive origin for the word Mafia. Anyone who says otherwise is a fool and you would be even more foolish if you believed them.

Criminal organizations are not like town councils. They do not keep minutes and they do not do paperwork: that would be a guaranteed route to prison or execution. This, therefore, makes the job of the criminal historian, in trying to trace where, when and why an organized crime group came into being, exceptionally difficult. The problem is compounded when investigating the Sicilian Mafia and other Italian criminal networks, as many of them started out as secret societies that went to great lengths to keep not just their membership and activities concealed, but also the fact they existed at all. Given this, what follows is the best verifiable historical fact allied to the most accepted and reasonable speculation.

One defining and unifying characteristic of the longest established Italian organized crime groups is the use of ritual and ceremony, more commonly associated with some secret societies. While blood oaths are common across the Mediterranean, the complexity and shared elements of the rituals used by the Camorra, 'Ndrangheta and Sicilian Mafia suggest a common point of origin.

Some believe the rituals were imported and adapted from French Freemasonry into political groups opposed to the Bourbon regime based in Naples around 1820. However, this is almost certainly wrong. When Giuseppe Balsamo left Palermo in Sicily in the 1760s and travelled across Europe, styling himself as the adventurer, occultist and master Freemason Comte di Cagliostro, he took with him from the island knowledge of a set of rituals and ceremonies that are very close to some of those used by Italian crime groups today.

Cagliostro claimed the rituals came from the Knights of Malta, who had received them from the Knights Templar – Templar rituals also influenced the creation of Freemasonry. Given the large presence the Knights Templar had in Sicily and elsewhere on the Italian Mediterranean coast, it is more probable that the arcane oaths and ceremonies used by the Mafia today originated not in France, but in Sicily or Italy itself. It is also worth remembering that the earliest historical mentions of organized crime groups such as the Sicilian Mafia refer to them as "Sects".

While the origins of the early "Sects" that Italian organized crime groups sprung from may date back several hundred years, the direct link between them and the Camorra, 'Ndrangheta and Sicilian Mafia crime families probably dates back no earlier than the 1810s.

Organized brigands playing a role in the vicious politics of the Bourbon regime, and later Italian unification, helped create groups that sought a profitable place between the peasants and landlords in a country that was emerging relatively late from the bonds of feudalism. They adopted the trappings of established secret societies as a convenient cloak of camouflage and a useful tool for keeping members in line. The rapid growth in Italy of protection rackets, monopolies, exploitation of corrupt government power and provision of the illicit can all be traced to the years post-1860.

There is extensive positive mythologizing about the origins of Italian organized crime groups. The facts that the name 'Ndrangheta comes from the Greek word "andragathía" meaning "heroism" and "virtue" and that members of the Sicilian Mafia refer to themselves as

Secret chief – Jaques de Molay, last Grand Master of the Knights Templar. The inner rituals of the Templars influenced Freemasonry and provided the origins of the Mafia's ceremonial practices.

belonging to "The Honoured Society" give a strong indication of where most of the mythology comes from. This mythologizing can be seen in suggestions of where the word Mafia itself comes from.

Some Mafiosi claim it is a corruption of the Arabic "mu afah" meaning "a refuge" or "to protect", and refers to Sicilian resistance to occupation of the island by the Moors between 9 and 12 CE. Others claim it is an acronym of "Morte Alla Francia Italia Anelia" (roughly translated "Death To France Italy Cries"). The more prosaic truth, however, is that it probably comes from the Palermo dialect word "mafioso" meaning "self-confident" – something the earliest Sicilian gangsters most certainly were.

MAFIA RULES AND RITUALS

Part of the power of criminal networks in Italy comes from the mystique that surrounds them. In Italian consciousness they exist not just as criminals, but also as a people apart from the rest of the world.

Having rejected conventional morality and laws, there is awareness that members of organized crime groups are governed by a clandestine code. Beyond the obvious secrecy of criminality, below the separation that comes with living in the underworld, Italians know that members of the Mafia, Camorra and 'Ndrangheta inhabit a distinct, covert culture with its own words, symbolism and regulations that give such groups an intense atmosphere of mystery.

The rituals and ceremonies at the heart of many Italian organized crime groups may seem bizarre to most people, but to anyone who has been involved with Freemasonry they will seem reassuringly familiar. In both Freemasonry and Sicilian Mafia, 'Ndrangheta and Camorra initiation rites, the prospective member undergoes a symbolic death and rebirth. They "die" from their old life and are "reborn" into the organization, and make an oath to always obey the rules of their new family, knowing that disobedience will mean death.

To be eligible for initiation into the Mafia, the prospective member has to participate in a murder – this is known as "making bones". After this, the candidate will wait to attend a special meeting of the group he is to join. He will arrive to find his fellow members sitting around a table, or in some cases standing around a tomb or a shrine of a saint. After answering a series of questions, the process of being initiated, or being "made", in the Mafia will begin.

The ritual involves having to hold the burning image of a saint and reciting an oath of total secrecy and obedience. Next, his direct boss as a Mafia soldier, his capo, will take a knife and cut his hand. The burning is symbolic of the death of his old life and the blood signifies his birth into his new Mafia family. In the Camorra, the blood on the hand comes from the initiate trying to pick up a coin from the floor while fellow members stab at his hand with their knives. In the

Venetian organized crime groups that predate the current Mala del Bentra of the city, death used to be symbolized by the kissing of a skull.

The rituals not only vary between the different organizations coming from various Italian regions, but also between elements within the same overall organization. The localized differences can be seen clearly in the Sicilian Mafia, where each crime family has its own saint. Usually it is also the patron saint of the village or town from which the family originates. This explains why certain American Mafia groups place an importance on Saint Rosalia who is honoured in Palermo or The Three Saints, Alfio, Filadelfo and Cirino, who are central to life in Trecastagni in Sicily.

The rules a new initiate is expected to follow until his dying day, unless he wants to invite death, all revolve around obedience, honour and omertà (silence). Members learn that their crime family comes before their old family, God or the state. They must always obey the orders of the head of the family, or their capo. They must ask permission on all important matters and decisions – whether it is the starting of a new criminal enterprise or their choice of wife. They must never lie to another member of the family in any matter. They can never introduce themselves to another Mafiosi as a Mafiosi; instead a member who is known to both parties must introduce them, often using the code of "amico nostra" meaning "a friend of ours" (from which the name Cosa Nostra meaning "Our Thing" comes). They must never show disrespect to a member or their womenfolk and, above all, they must never speak of anything related to the family to anyone outside of it.

So successful have these rules been in ensuring a smooth-running criminal enterprise, that they spread not only throughout Italy, but also to America where they form the basis of the American Mafia's code of conduct. Some would say, however, that the Americans have had more problems ensuring omertà than the Italians.

THE SICILIAN MAFIA

In the nineteenth century, the British Consul in the Sicilian capital Palermo wrote about conditions on the island, saying, "Secret societies are all-powerful. Camorre and maffie (sic), self-elected juntas, share the earnings of the workmen, keep up intercourse with outcasts and take malefactors under their wing and protection". In 1877, an Italian government report concluded, "Violence is the only prosperous industry in Sicily".

So how did this domination of Sicilian life by the violent industry of organized crime come to pass? Two factors are usually cited. The first is Sicily's history of continual incursion and occupation, which started with the Greeks and was followed through the centuries by the Vandals, Byzantines, Arabs, Normans and Bourbons. This is held as being responsible for the creation of secret societies allied to resistance movements using the hierarchical structure of a capofamiglia (boss of a family), consigliere (counsellor), sotto capo (underboss), capodecima (one of a number of lieutenants responsible for up to 10 men) and soldiers often called uomini d'onore (men of honour), that is still used by the Mafia in Sicily and America today.

The second factor, used in most theories explaining the Mafia's domination of Sicily, is the existence of gabellotti – tax-collectors and estate managers, who acted as mediators between absentee landowners, who lived in the cities, and the rural peasantry. The immense power of the gabellotti effectively made them the rulers of their communities, being able to extort both the landlords and peasantry. When the gabellotti also came to control the network of Sicilian secret societies and take a role in politics, following Sicily's unification with Italy in 1861, they and their crime families became a form of shadow government, able to influence every aspect of life on the island.

Early on, the Mafia's rackets ranged from protection and extortion, to kidnapping and cattle rustling. They controlled to whom the farmers sold their produce and the markets in the towns where it was bought. They held monopolies on goods coming into the island and exerted political influence on the appointment of every state job, including police officers and judges. Attempts to crack down on this from the mainland only served to foster Sicilian nationalism. In 1922, the Fascist dictator Mussolini appointed Cesar Mori, "The Iron Prefect", as Sicilian governor. However, even Mori's thousands of arrests and widespread use of torture could not eradicate the Mafia or even break its power.

A deal struck between the American gang leader of Sicilian origin "Lucky" Luciano and the US military saw the Mafia assist in the Allied invasion of Sicily in 1943. This left the Mafia in an even stronger position in post-Second World War Italy. It also led to their alliance with leading figures in the Christian Democratic Party – the dominant political force in Italy for the four decades following the War. With political support in the highest echelons of government, they expanded their influence in Sicily and on the mainland. In 1957, a meeting arranged by Luciano between the Sicilian and American Mafias helped the Sicilians become a major force in the global narcotics trade.

The constant vendettas and power struggles between the various Mafia clans from different parts of the island continued, and if anything intensified, as the Mafia's profits and influence flourished post-1957. The level of warfare between the La Barbera clan from Palermo and the Corleonesi clan from the town of Corleone, led by Luciano Leggio, became so violent in 1963 that it led to a government clampdown that saw more than 250 Mafia leaders arrested. The

Corleonesi clan eventually came to dominate the loose federation of Mafia clans throughout Sicily, though occasionally major conflicts would still erupt – a trend that continues to this day.

Even the infamous maxi-trials of 1986, when Mafia supergrass Tommaso Buscetta broke the code of omertà leading to 475 senior Mafia figures being prosecuted, did little to reign in the Mafia's power. It was not until the Sicilian Mafia overreached and declared open war on the Italian state, through a series of car bombings, that the political and judicial system made a serious attempt to unravel its massive influence. However, by that point the Mafia was not only the dominant force in organized crime within Italy, but had also extended its illicit authority into a criminal empire that spanned the globe.

The Sicilian Mafia suffered a series of rarely experienced setbacks under an anti-Mafia campaign ordered by Italian fascist dictator Benito Mussolini, shown here.

EXTORTION

A common legal definition of extortion is: "obtaining money, behaviour or other goods or services from another by wrongfully threatening or inflicting harm to this person or property". As such, extortion of individuals and businesses by criminal gangs is one of the most widespread organized crimes, as it requires nothing more than the ability to inspire fear.

Huge criminal empires have developed from simple extortion rackets. The major criminal activity engaged in by the 'Ndrangheta and Camorra gangs who emigrated to the USA in the nineteenth century was the "Black Hand" extortion racket. Extortionists, such as Ignazio Lupo (Lupo The Wolf), would send any Italian American who obtained a measure of wealth, demands signed with the infamous black palm print. These demands threatened death or maiming if the money was not forthcoming.

When businesses are targeted for extortion, they are threatened with violence, vandalism or arson. This is ironically known as a "protection racket", as the victims are allegedly paying for defence against such acts. Even in well-policed cities, businesses such as street vendors are still vulnerable to this type of crime. However, size is usually no object when it comes to extortion – Russian Mafiya groups halted the progress of construction of England's new national soccer stadium at Wembley in London by threatening to use ex-Russian special forces snipers to shoot crane drivers if they were not paid thousands of pounds.

CAMORRA – THE NEAPOLITAN MAFIA

The term Mafia has become so synonymous with organized crime in Italy that other major organized crime groups often have to suffer the indignity of constant referrals to them as the "something Mafia". In the case of the Camorra, they have the annoyance of always being called "the Neapolitan Mafia".

The name Camorra means "quarrel". The group has always operated out of Naples, Italy's largest southern city and capital of the Campania region and evidence suggests the Camorra is Italy's oldest organized crime group. Although it may have an Arabic or piratical origin, many firmly believe it developed from the Garduna –
a secret Spanish criminal society from the Middle Ages. The Garduna specialized in contract killing, robbery and kidnapping. It is possible they moved to Naples when Spain controlled the city and deported large numbers of Spanish criminals to it.

Whether the Camorra grew out of the Garduna or not, it definitely existed in 1820. Raids carried out by the authorities in Naples that year against groups opposed to the Bourbon monarchy in Italy, discovered evidence of the Camorra's rituals and hierarchy. It was more structured

The Camorra trial of 1911 was one of the first in Italy to feature the mass prosecution of gang members (34 are in the large cage) thanks to the evidence being given by a supergrass, who is in the small cage.

than the early Sicilian mafia, having 12 families each run by a capofamiglia. These capifamiglia sometimes met together in a council to settle disputes and to elect a "Grand Master" to oversee its business. The families themselves were divided into divisions known as paranze, controlled by a caporegime who ran affairs on a day-to-day basis.

The group controlled life in the city's prisons, ran extortion, loan-sharking and gambling rackets in Naples and the rest of Campania, and even offered a murder-for-hire service. They were also powerful enough to set a "tax" that had to be paid by anyone who was unloading goods in the docks of Naples and by most legitimate businesses in the city. All revenues collected were given to the capofamiglia, who would then pay off corrupt officials, provide pensions for the wives of sick, dead or imprisoned camorristi (members of the group), take a cut for himself and then share the remaining profits with the rest of the family.

The Camorra was heavily involved in Neapolitan politics from the 1810s onwards, with its members often rising to significant positions within the police, civil service and army. However, this did not always protect it from clampdowns ordered by national government. In 1911, 35 of its leaders were convicted and imprisoned on murder charges after one member broke the code of silence. The severest challenge to its influence then arose when Mussolini took control of Italy in 1922. Under his regime, the power of the Camorra was effectively stripped,

Erminia Giuliano, the feared female head of a major Camorra family, refused to be arrested peacefully in 2000 until she had been given a chance to apply make-up and put on jewellery.

allowing the Sicilian Mafia and Corsican organized crime gangs to move into Naples.

After the Second World War, the Camorra enjoyed a revival in fortunes. Turning to cigarette smuggling as a new stream of income, it used the profits made from that activity to buy itself back into political favour and begin supplanting its rivals. It soon moved into heroin trafficking and gained control over most of the construction in Naples and Campania. It even showed a willingness to cut deals with the Sicilian Mafia, if mutual profits could be made, but aggresively pushed the Corsican gangs out of what it considered to be its territorry.

In 1970, some camorristi, under the leadership of Raffaele Cutolo, founded a faction of Camorra to fight against Sicilian influence within Naples. Cutolo's group amassed huge power during the 1970s, but it resulted in increasingly bloody conflict with other Camorra gangs. Between 1979 and 1983, it is estimated that inter-Camorra warfare led to over 500 camorristi deaths – ironically strengthening the Mafia's position. Camorra opposition to the Corsicans and Sicilians operating in Naples still leads to many assassinations in the city each year.

The Camorra used millions of dollars of stolen government funds, intended to rebuild Naples after the Irpinia earthquake in 1980, to invest heavily in legitimate businesses across Europe. However, the group's major sources of income still come from illicit activities, such as narcotics trafficking, vice and extortion. It has been suggested that the fact that women leaders of paranzes, such as Erminia Giuliano, have emerged in the Camorra reflects a higher level of adaptability to changing social conditions and attitudes than is found in other Italian organized crime groups. Adaptability is certainly a key characteristic of the Camorra. As Brigadier General Carlo Alfiero of Italy's military police has noted: "Where there is profit, there is always Camorra".

'NDRANGHETA – THE CALABRIAN MAFIA

The similarities between the Sicilian Mafia and the 'Ndrangheta organized crime group from the southern Italian province of Calabria are numerous and striking. They are also unsurprising, given that only a few miles – the Strait of Messina – separates Sicily from Calabria, the "toe" of Italy.

The geographical proximity suggests some common ancestry between the two different strands of southern Italian organized crime. The most obvious correspondence is the alternative name for both the 'Ndrangheta and the Sicilian Mafia – the "Honoured Society". Whatever the degree of cross-fertilization between them in the past, the analogous social, economic and political conditions in Calabria and Sicily during the last 200 years undoubtedly helped to shape both groups along similar lines.

Even today, Calabria remains one of the poorest, underdeveloped and crime-plagued regions of Italy. This makes it easy to understand how the 'Ndrangheta emerged from the same banditry, rural poverty and post-feudal conditions as those that helped form the early Sicilian Mafia. Records of clans of bandits operating in Calabria's Aspromonte Mountains go back several centuries and it is from these bandits that the early 'Ndrangheta was formed. Like the Sicilian Mafia, the 'Ndrangheta indulges in creating a positive mythology, portraying these mountain-dwelling criminals as resistance fighters against state oppression – hence the name 'Ndrangheta, which derives from the Greek words for "heroism" and "virtue".

Although the 'Ndrangheta has similar structure and rituals to the Sicilian Mafia, there are differences. In the nineteenth century, 'Ndrangheta families, or 'ndrina, were often blood families, with all the members coming from one extended clan of rarely more than 30 members. The head of a 'ndrina was called a capobastone (head stick). Regular councils of the capobastoni within a locale would meet to try and settle disputes and co-ordinate activities between the different clans.

Luckily for the 'Ndrangheta, they escaped the focus of Mussolini's clampdown on organized crime's activities and the penetration of regional government. After the Second World War, the 'Ndrangheta rapidly expanded the nature of its activities. While the old staples of extortion and kidnapping retained a central role, banditry was replaced with a push into tobacco smuggling and narcotics trafficking. It also began to move into urban areas and ally itself with key members of the Christian Democratic Party. With their help the 'Ndrangheta stole millions of dollars from government projects and was able to take control of most of the construction work in the region. The 'Ndrangheta has also spearheaded environmental crime in Italy and has been responsible for some of the worst illegal dumping of toxic and radioactive waste in Europe.

Like their Sicilian and Neapolitan counterparts, many Calabrian criminals emigrated to America, Canada and other countries between 1890 and 1920. As the Calabrian 'Ndrangheta became more heavily involved in global heroin and cocaine trafficking, they developed networks that linked them to the 'Ndrangheta groups that had formed in North America, South America and Australia. The 'Ndrangheta has also spread into a number of European countries, including Belgium, Holland, Austria, Germany and Spain. Between the 1950s and early 1970s, the 'Ndrangheta often closely co-operated with the Sicilian Mafia in drug trafficking and other activities. The co-operation has lessened over recent years, however, as 'Ndrangheta power has grown and their international ties have developed. Alongside its position as a major player in narcotics, it is now one of the largest global arms dealing organizations.

Although there have been notable police successes, including the capture of major capobastoni, such as Gregorio Bellocco in 2005, the strong family ties within the 'Ndrangheta have meant few members are willing to break the vow of silence. The fact that the 'Ndrangheta did not openly attack the state, when other Italian organized crime groups did, meant it avoided concerted police action until the 1990s. By this point it had consolidated its

Italian police scored a major victory against the 'Ndrangheta in February 2005, capturing Gregorio Bellocco, one of its most significant leaders.

power, having laundered its money through the purchase of real estate, retail chains and food production companies to give it a solid, legitimate income.

Infighting – such as when the bitter feud between rival clans led to the killing of six Italians in Germany and the arrest of more than 30 suspected the 'Ndrangheta members in 2007 – has begun to hurt the organization. However, the exposure of some its crime to public scrutiny, such as the revelation by a former member that the 'Ndrangheta had sank ships loaded with radioactive waste off the Italian coast, has brought them less problems than many in the international system wanted.

Italy's leading force fighting organized crime – Direzione Investigativa Antimafia – believes there are nearly 200 'ndrina currently in Italy with more than 6,000 members. They estimate their annual turnover at more than 23 billion Euros and admit that, "'Ndrangheta is now one of the most powerful criminal organizations in the world".

ENVIRONMENTAL CRIME

One of the most rapidly expanding areas of profit for organized crime in the twenty-first century comes from a raft of environmental criminal operations. As public concern over ecology has grown, so regulation has developed to protect wildlife, natural habitats and human health.

Major organized crime groups have, however, found a way to exploit these regulations by setting up complex schemes to circumvent environmental protection laws, using their networks of corruption to operate without detection. In Italy, Camorra groups bought land and created a string of artificial ponds and lakes to attract birds, allowing them to offer illegal hunting opportunities to those who wanted to shoot protected species. Bribery of local officials allowed the scam to run for several years without any problems.

The Russian Organizatsiya has devastated the sustainability of some marine species in the Bering Sea. Their illegal fishing and importation into the EU of $1 billion-worth of illegally caught fish may eventually eradicate some species and ruin the livelihoods of legitimate fishermen. Cosa Nostra and Triad groups have also earned a reputation for being major traders in banned CFCs and other environmentally damaging substances.

Possibly the most worrying trend is the illegal dumping, by organized crime groups, of toxic chemicals and other waste in developing countries. The Yakuza and the Sicilian Mafia are amongst the groups who have dumped deadly waste from their own countries in Africa, Brazil and the Philippines. In some cases, they have not even bothered to export the problem, merely putting it into their own country's waterways or abandoned mines.

MALA DEL BRENTA — THE VENETIAN MAFIA

Despite being one of the most powerful organized crime groups in modern Italy, Mala del Brenta is rarely written about in the English language. Some writers even talk about it in the past tense, assuming that the capture of its most infamous leader – Felice "Angel Face" Maniero – in 1993 spelled the end of the group.

Any such dismissal is disingenuous, however. The origins, nature and current crimes of Mala del Brenta (sometimes referred to as "Mafia del Brenta") provide a fascinating insight into the Italian underworld away from the confines of Naples, southern Italy and Sicily. Operating in Italy's north-eastern Veneto region and its capital, Venice, the organization has illicit interests in everything from art theft to arms trafficking. Despite its relatively small size, only a few hundred members, the Direzione Investigativa Antimafia estimate that it has the fifth largest income of any organized crime group operating in Italy, generating several billion euros per year.

Mala del Brenta takes its name from the still waters of the Riviera Brenta, the mainland area that became the retreat of many wealthy Venetians from the sixteenth century onwards. Felice Maniero formed the group in the early 1980s. His idea was to bring the existing Venetian and Veneto crime gangs together into a more unified structure. Maniero took his inspiration from the success the Camorra enjoyed thanks to its hierarchical arrangement and also from Venetian folklore regarding the city's "league of thieves".

Historical details of the league of thieves are sketchy, but may have been similar in nature and operation to the Garduna of medieval Spain. It seems to have developed from a prison gang, operating at the height of Venetian domination of European trade in the fifteenth century. The league of thieves has become entwined with the mythology surrounding the ancient practice of some Catholics in Venice of praying for intercession to dead thieves and saints associated with thieves such as St. Methodius and St. Nicholas.

Some of the Venetian crime gangs that Maniero melded into the Mala del Brenta claimed to have initiation rituals relating to the league of thieves. Elements of these were adopted and adapted, alongside an amalgam of Camorra and Mafia oaths and ceremonies, and used for bringing new members into the Mala del Brenta. From a core starting membership of around 40 members, the organization rapidly grew in size and power.

The vision of the organization was simple, but effective. With the various, previously competing, gangs co-operating and co-ordinated, greater profits could be made from old rackets relating to the city's casinos and water boat businesses. The profits were invested in new criminal ventures, such as arms smuggling. They were also used to heavily expand the previously limited narcotics trafficking operation and to pay bribes to key politicians, police and judges. Membership was not restricted to just those who came from the Veneto region – anyone who had a criminal speciality, such as fraud, forgery or money laundering, was eligible to join. Soon gangsters from southern Italy were brought into the fold. Mala del Brenta also attracted specialist thieves keen to benefit from its protection; theft of art and valuable religious items, such as the relics of saints, soon became one of its key crimes.

By the early 1990s, the Mala del Brenta had more than 400 full members and was fiercely and bloodily disposing of anyone who tried to operate in their territory without first making a profit sharing agreement. It established a loose alliance with the Sacra Corona Unita of the Puglia region and was able to hold its own against more established groups, such as the Camorra. Mala del Brenta also showed that it was not afraid to kill those in law enforcement who breathed too heavily down its back.

Neither the imprisonment of Felice Maniero, nor more recent raids against 33 gang members in January 2006 have dented the effectiveness of Mala del Brenta, and its grip on many Venetian casinos and legitimate businesses remains firmly in place. It has continued to carry out high profile crimes, such as art thefts and the arson that destroyed La Fenice, Venice's eighteenth-century opera house, in 1996. With growing international connections and profits flowing from narcotics and arms dealing, the twenty-first century may see the end of Mala del Brenta's English language obscurity.

Despite having his wings clipped by his 1993 arrest, Mala del Brenta mastermind Felice "Angel Face" Maniero has continued to have an incredible influence on organized crime in Venice.

SACRA CORONA UNITA – THE PUGLIA MAFIA

Italy's paramilitary police – Arma dei Carabinieri – are not short of senior officers with strong opinions on organized crime. One capitano working in the Puglia region located in the southern "heel" of Italy, told me "Puglia had crime, but nothing like the rest of the country until the Camorra bastards came. It is thanks to them we now have to fight the criminal army of Sacra Corona Unita."

Despite his venom toward the "Camorra bastards" and Sacra Corona Unita (SCU), he may have a valid point. While Puglia, like every place in the world, has always had an element of organized crime, the current size and shape of the problem in the area can be traced to events relating to Camorra groups based in Naples and the Campania region.

In 1970, Raffaele Cutolo had founded a new faction of Camorra known as Nuova Camorra Organizzata (New Organized Camorra). It quickly became a powerful crime syndicate, despite its conflict with other Camorra groups and the Sicilian Mafia. When the authorities seized the Nuova Camorra Organizzata's smuggling fleet in 1979, Cutolo sent some of his men to Puglia. His idea was to create a new crime group – Nuova Camorra Pugliese – that would carry out smuggling on behalf of the Nuova Camorra Organizzata.

However, by 1983, most of the initial men Cutolo sent over were inside Puglia's prisons in Bari or Lecce. While they were inside, one of Cutolo's lieutenants, Giuseppe Rogoli, formed a prison gang from both Camorra men and leading members of Puglia's native criminal fraternity. As its members returned to the outside, it became the genesis of the Sacra Corona Unita, with Rogoli as its head. He decided to use the organizational structure of the Camorra to provide coherent leadership to the then disparate organized crime groups existing in Puglia. At that time most of these groups were relatively small, some no more than extended family units specializing in small-scale smuggling and extortion.

Rogoli clothed his new group in religious meaning. Dropping the traditional initiation ceremonies of most other Italian organized crime groups, members of SCU were "baptized" into the family. The name itself also has mystical connotations. Sacra Corona Unita means "United Sacred Crown". The Sacred refers to the member's baptism, the Crown represents the rosary and individual elements working next to each other and the United is the chain linking the rosary and the strength of uniting two pieces of wood to form a cross.

Despite such spiritual imagery, SCU's core belief was making money. It did this through taking control of all smuggling operations within Puglia. Initially, this meant little more than just control over the profitable business of contraband tobacco. However, with the eruption

Camorra boss Raffaele Cutolo's strategy to establish a new Camorra faction in Puglia badly backfired and led to the establishment of rival organization Sacra Corona Unita.

Cupola leader Fabio Franco is pulled out of the boot of a car by Brazilian Federal Police after his capture in Sao Paulo in February 2004. His arrest was a major setback for the SCU.

of the Yugoslav wars in 1989, many traditional overland drug trafficking routes became closed and Puglia developed a central role in European narcotics. SCU fought hard to keep the Camorra, Sicilian Mafia and 'Ndrangheta out of its territory. Eventually most other groups recognized SCU's authority and agreed to pay a fee for landing contraband in their area. The massive profits from control over tobacco and narcotic trafficking were further boosted by the huge demand for illicit arms in the Balkans.

Another great gift to SCU came with the collapse of Communism and the boom in people smuggling. Forming alliances with the emerging Albanian Mafiya, SCU soon came to dominate the bringing of illegal immigrants into Europe via Italy. It also trafficked thousands of Albanian, Russian and Eastern European women into the misery of the forced sex trade in Western Europe. In co-operation with the Albanians, SCU now has a massive vice empire in Italy, Austria and Germany.

The Direzione Investigativa Antimafia believes there are currently 47 largely autonomous SCU clans working together in a loose confederation, but obeying the Cupola – the overall leadership body for the group, drawn from its top bosses. Although important Cupola members, such as Fabio Franco, have been captured within recent years, Rogoli's original pyramid command structure of one crimine (boss) supported by trequartini (three-quarters), evangelisti (evangelists), santisi (saints), sgarristi (enforcers) and cammoristi (soldiers) has proved incredibly resilient to police attack. Although it no longer commands the strong position it did in the late 1990s, it maintains an active membership of more than 1,200 individuals and remains an important player across the whole Adriatic area.

KEY CRIMES

How do you define key crimes? Are they purely the ones that produce the most profit, or is there another aspect that makes certain illicit activities worthy of the phrase? Many criminologists believe key crimes are those that define an organized crime group in the consciousness of the public and the law enforcement authorities. They argue that the killing of one young kidnap victim, whose image is beamed into homes across a nation, can shape the perception of a criminal body far more than 50 years of running protection rackets. If public concern caused by the crime then impacts on how the police react to an organized crime group, one particular crime can determine the shape of events far more than the earning of millions of illicit dollars.

If that is the case, there is no doubting what constitutes the key crimes in the history of Italian organized criminality. These crimes occurred on May 23 and July 19, 1992 in Sicily. The repercussions for all organized crime groups in Italy have been massive and are ongoing almost twenty years on.

The murder by car bomb of Italy's leading anti-Mafia magistrate Giovanni Falcone in May and then the killing of his friend and successor, Paolo Borsellino, in another car bomb attack in July, rocked Italy to its foundations. Both men had led the fight against the Mafia for more than a decade. Battling against a corrupt political and judicial system, they had worked together to secure the conviction of hundreds of Mafiosi at the famous Maxi Trial of the mid-1980s. With the

The twisted remains of murdered anti-Mafia magistrate Giovanni Falcone's car provide grim evidence of just how far the Sicilian Mafia were prepared to go to kill their victims' hopes of justice.

Firefighters work amidst the devastation and debris caused by the Mafia's detonation of a car bomb at the Uffizi Gallery in Florence in May 1993, one of many bombings in their all-out war against the Italian state.

support of new Justice Minister Claudio Martelli, the two crusading magistrates were gearing up for another campaign against the Sicilian Mafia. It was partly due to this that Salvatore Riina, also known as Totò "The Beast" Riina, the head of the powerful Corleonesi clan, ordered their deaths.

Riina was also motivated by revenge for the Maxi Trial. He considered the best way to win concessions against any government crackdown was by demonstrating the power of the Mafia. Riina's phrase describing this was "We must make war to best mould the peace". However, he had made a fateful misjudgement. The murders of Falcone and Borsellino led to a wave of public outrage and swept new anti-Mafia laws into effect. More than 7,000 troops were sent to Sicily and Riina was arrested in January 1993 after more than 20 years on the run.

The Mafia retaliated against Riina's capture and the attack on its power by launching a series of terrorist bombings. As informer Maurizio Avola would later reveal, the Mafia believed it could "Hold the state to ransom in order to force it to revoke the laws". Instead, the bombing of the Uffizi Gallery in Florence on May 27, 1993 and the bombing of two churches in Rome on the same day only hardened public and government resolve to tackle the Mafia menace once and for all. More than a decade on, the laws and new attitude to fighting organized crime from these events have impacted not just the Sicilian Mafia, but the Camorra, 'Ndrangheta, Mala del Brenta and Sacra Corona Unita as well.

If a key crime is defined as one that best illustrates the core nature of Italian organized crime, it may be that another tragedy needs to be considered. When a devastating earthquake hit Campania in Italy in November 1980, several organized crime groups actually stole from the government, charity and international funds that were meant to help with the relief effort. They then profited from the construction contracts for rebuilding the damaged areas. They would repeat the same crime when an earthquake hit San Giuliano in 2002. There can be no claims to honour in stealing from your own countrymen when they suffer such a terrible natural disaster.

In terms of key money-producing crimes, it is interesting to note that in the twenty-first century the prime profits for Italian organized crime stem from the smuggling of narcotics, people and tobacco, political and business corruption and extortion. Aside from developments in money laundering, arms dealing and financial fraud, there is little a Mafiosi from 100 or even 50 years ago would recognize in the key crimes of today's Mafia.

KEY FIGURES

Criminologists may debate the key crimes of Italian organized crime over the last 100 years, but there is little dispute as to the identity of the key figures behind these acts and Italian organized crime itself.

Speaking to members of the Italian paramilitary police, the Direzione Investigativa Antimafia, and leading experts on Italy's crime syndicates while I was researching elements of this book, the same names were mentioned again and again as the central shapers of organized crime over the last 50 years of Italian history.

Of the names mentioned, the one that has possibly cast the longest shadow over Italian organized crime is Luciano Leggio, "The Scarlet Pimpernel". In 1943, petty thief Leggio was brought into the Corleonesi Mafia clan, centred in the Sicilian town of Corleone, by its then leader and director of a local hospital Dr Michael Navarra. Leggio soon earned a reputation as the Corleonesi clan's most vicious enforcer and best hitman.

Unlike Navarra, the young Leggio had no time for many of the old Mafia values – he thought nothing of stealing a fellow member's farm by simply killing him, and refused to obey orders. In 1958 Navarra sent 15 of his men to kill the increasingly renegade Leggio. However, thanks

After more than 40 years on the run, police eventually captured Bernardo Provenzano, the head of the Sicilian Mafia, in 2006. He was found in a farmhouse just two miles from his hometown of Corleone.

Former hitman Tommaso Buscetta made history as the first senior Mafiosi to break the code of omerta and give evidence that condemned many of his ex-colleagues to huge prison sentences.

to his sharp shooting, Leggio escaped with no more than a graze, but the same cannot be said for some of his would-be assassins. Within weeks, Navarra was dead, gunned down by Leggio's two most trusted accomplices – Totò "The Beast" Riina and Bernardo Provenzano. Leggio then eliminated 29 men loyal to Navarra and seized control of the Corleonesi.

Under Leggio's leadership, the Corleonesi became the most feared group within the Mafia, winning bloody wars against other Sicilian Mafia clans such as La Barbera. As the bodies piled up and his power increased, Leggio

ensured that the Corleonesi dominated the most profitable areas of criminal enterprise, such as heroin trafficking. Even when the fugitive Leggio was finally captured and returned to the prison he had escaped from in 1974, he controlled the Corleonesi through his trusted lieutenants Riina and Provenzano, guiding the clan to greater influence, wealth and levels of fear.

Leggio's aggressive actions shaped not his clan's fortunes, but the whole direction of the Mafia in Italy. He died in 1993, the day after Riina was finally arrested. This left Provenzano as the head of the most powerful Mafia group. Provenzano proved to be far more elusive even than "The Scarlet Pimpernel" Leggio. He evaded capture from the 1950s up until 2006, when he was found in a farmhouse 3.2 kilometres (2 miles) from his hometown of Corleone.

One man who can claim to have had a comparable impact to Leggio on the Mafia is Tommaso Buscetta. The former La Barbera hitman became the first senior Mafiosi to break the code of omerta and become a pentito (penitent). Buscetta provided anti-Mafia prosecutors with the evidence they needed to arrest and try 464 Corleonesi, Greco and Bonate Mafiosi at the mid-1980s Maxi Trial. His actions not only led to the emergence of other supergrass pentiti, but also forced the Italian government to end decades of denial over the very existence of the Mafia.

If Buscetta was the man who exposed the inner working of the Mafia, several expert voices suggest Giovanni Brusca was the man who forever killed the idea that the Mafia had any honour left. Brusca was the leader of the "Fire Group" – the team within the Corleonesi responsible for the bombs that killed magistrates Falcone and Borsellino. He was also behind the Mafia bombings of the Uffizi Gallery in Florence and churches in Rome. Fellow Mafiosi called him "u Verru" (the Pig), because of his killing of an 11-year-old kidnap victim. When he was captured in 1996, Brusca did the unthinkable for such a senior Mafia figure and became a pentito, even telling

the police who his successor was and where to find him.

The arrest of Bernado Provenzano in 2006 sparked a wave of speculation over who would replace him as the new head of the Sicilian Mafia. In the following six years, no clear successor has emerged, but of all the names considered for the role, the one to get most attention from media and police was found on a slip of paper Provenzano had on him when captured – Matteo Messina Denaro. Nicknamed "Diabolik" after the cult Italian comic book character, Denaro has been a fugitive since 1993 when he became wanted for his part in a wave of bombings, including the attack on the Uffizi Gallery. Despite seizing more than one billion Euros worth of his assets in 2010, the authorities have not been able to find Denaro and it is believed likely that he will establish himself as ultimate boss of the Sicilian Mafia.

Masked police escort Mafia boss Giovanni Brusca into their Palermo headquarters after his arrest in 1996. His crimes were so bad that even fellow Mafiosi knew him as "u Verru" (the pig).

THE ITALIAN MAFIA TODAY

Until the 1980s and the shattering of the code of omerta by Tommaso Buscetta, the official position of the Interior Ministry and other Italian authorities responsible for fighting organized crime was that there was no such thing as an "Italian Mafia". Instead, they insisted that, despite all evidence to the contrary, what appeared to be the actions of highly developed criminal networks were simply the result of numerous unconnected gangs. Names such as 'Ndrangheta and Camorra were merely the descriptions certain groups of villains gave to themsleves. There was no Sicilian Mafia with a ruling council called the Cupola, there were only competing clans of criminals.

This rejection of established fact, history and evidence was a corrupt position bought by massive bribes to certain top politicians from organized crime. The denial helped the Italian Mafia in all its

guises to develop, free from the massive crackdown that many magistrates and senior police officers knew was needed to tackle the reality of Italy's incredibly powerful criminal syndicates.

Many asked how international figures suggesting organized crime in Italy made profits equivalent to more than 12 per cent of the country's Gross National Product could be ignored? How could the evidence of countless trials and investigations be forgotten? Most of all, people asked how the Interior Ministry could not notice the large numbers of corpses that resulted from la Mattanza (bloodbath) of the second Mafia war that raged between 1981 and 1983?

According to one senior member of the Direzione Investigativa Antimafia, it was la Mattanza that started the decline of the Sicilian

Police guard the crime the body of one of six men from Pelle-Romeo clan who were brutally slain in Duisburg, Germany in August 2007. The massacre caused the whole of the 'Ndrangheta crime organization to be subject to greater official scrutiny.

The massive anti-Mafia demonstrations that took place in Sicily and
Italy throughout 1986 and again in 1992 helped turn the tide of political
indifference against the problem of organized crime.

Mafia, a waning of power that has helped shape the nature of the wider Italian Mafia today. He told me, "The Mafia began to kill itself. All the death it managed turned back on itself. More than legal justice, it is the justice of blood that weakened it. Buscetta only gave evidence because as a member of La Barbera cosca [a Sicilian Mafia clan] he had lost two to Corleonesi gunmen. Through what he told Falcone the Mafia was made real – no one could deny it any more. More than making Buscetta break omerta, it was la Mattanza that created the thing that is now killing the Mafia. It was blood that created Stidda."

The Stidda (meaning "star") was formed when members of Sicilian Mafia coschi had to flee from Palermo and other northern Sicilian towns as their clans were massacred by the Corleonesi during La Mattanza. They, and even some renegade members of the Corleonesi, hid out in the hills of the southern Sicilian province of Agrigento. It was from these various orphaned Mafiosi that the Stidda was forged. Under the leadership of Giuseppe Croce Benvenuto and Salvatore Calafato it quickly became a more democratic and adaptable organized crime group.

The Stidda soon controlled the southern Sicilian towns of Gela, Caltanisetta and Agrigento. From this base it expanded into the areas of northern Italy with no traditional Mafia presence. Since 1983, the Stidda has emerged as the fastest growing Italian organized crime group and the main competitor to the Sicilian Mafia in many areas. It has been gifted by facing a Mafia weakened by the disbanding of the Christian Democratic Party – its strongest politcal supporter – and the public outrage caused by

The massive anti-Mafia demonstrations that took place in Sicily and Italy throughout 1986 and again in 1992 helped turn the tide of political indifference against the problem of organized crime.

the murders of anti-Mafia magistrates Falcone and Borsellino in 1992.

While the "Clean Hands" anti-corruption drives and the government anti-Mafia crackdown that began in 1992 hit the traditional Sicilian Mafia hard, it has had less impact on the other organized crime groups, such as the Camorra and 'Ndrangheta, allowing them to gain ground at the Sicilians' expense. In the Italian gangland landscape where there is success there is also death. As the other groups increased their power, the number of deadly in-fights rose as well. An example of this is the bloody war between the Strangio-Nirta and Pelle-Romeos clans of the 'Ndrangheta. What started out as feud over the throwing of an egg, developed into a sprawling, spiral of murders that exposed the whole of the 'Ndrangheta to unwanted international scrutiny. It culminated in 2007 when six unarmed members of the Pelle-Romeo clan were shot as they sat in their cars outside the train station in the German city of Duisburg. The massacre resulted in a strong police clampdown on 'Ndrangheta activity in both Germany and Italy.

Many criminologists believe that groups such as The Stidda and Sacra Corona Unita may have sown the seeds for their own future decline by having shown a willingness to hire out their territories to foreigners such as the Albanian Mafiya. Foreign challengers may mean the future of organized crime in Italy does not automatically belong to the Italian Mafia.

COSA NOSTRA – THE AMERICAN MAFIA

2

"Wherever there's opportunity,
the Mafia will be there."

Johnny Kelly, musician (1986)

Although organized crime is as old as civilization itself, the
image and mythology of Cosa Nostra – the American Mafia –
is so powerful that it almost seems as if the underworld
was invented in the USA.

Even in countries that have their own long-established
organized crime groups and traditions, the spectre of the Cosa
Nostra casts a shadow of inspiration that impacts all over the
world – from the dress sense of the Japanese Yakuza gangs, to the
kingpins of crime in Mumbai referring to themselves as "Dons".
At the most simple level this can be put down to the long reach of
Hollywood, but beyond this lies the special appeal of the criminal
fraternity that Cosa Nostra represents.

Despite its countless crimes and the mountains of misery
it has caused, Cosa Nostra has become symbolic of a system of
criminality that possesses a value system that prizes honour,
respect and family ties. It is seen as presenting a form of ordered
lawlessness – criminals who can be trusted to obey a set of rules,
which is typified by the infamous mobster Bugsy Siegel who
claimed "We only kill each other".

J. Edgar Hoover, Director of the FBI, even considered many
Mafiosi to be good American businessmen, who were impeccably
anti-Communist and truly patriotic. Today, some mob bosses
have their own fan clubs and are lionized by those who, years ago,
protested against the shame and stereotyping that their media
image brought to the Italian-American community. Yet for all
of this, the Cosa Nostra remains what it has always been: a cancer
growing inside the core of the American Dream.

ORIGINS OF THE AMERICAN MAFIA

The question of why the Cosa Nostra became established as the dominant form of organized crime in the USA is usually answered with: widespread Italian immigration, the pre-existence of organized crime in Italy and Prohibition. While all of these elements have played vital roles in the growth and success of the Mafia in America, they do not provide a complete explanation of why it came out on top of the Irish organized crime gangs that were already established in the USA.

The American Mafia partly owes its existence to what preceded it. Organized criminality in nineteenth-century America was dominated by Irish gangs. They represented an established network of criminal power that was entwined with political influence. In New York, street level gangs, such as the Roach Guards and Kerryonians, had started out protecting Irish immigrants from anti-Irish violence. However, they soon gravitated towards control of prostitution, extortion, armed robbery and control of the city's docks. The Democratic Party's political machine in the late nineteenth century in parts of New York developed links to the gangs, using them to ensure whole neighbourhoods voted the way they wanted them to. This collusion led to a corrupt system. It was a pattern that also occurred within at least two other US cities during the late nineteenth and early twentieth centuries.

When more than two million Italian immigrants left from the regions of Naples, Calabria and Sicily between 1880 and 1910, they

found themselves, along with the Jewish émigrés from Eastern Europe, at the bottom of the food chain. They also found a corrupt political system that was in the hands of the same Irish crime gangs that were busy preying on them, even on the streets of their own enclaves – what was to become New York's Little Italy.

In New Orleans, the city where the first Sicilian immigrants made their home, the Mayor, Joseph A. Shakespeare, openly called Southern Italians and Sicilians "The most idle, vicious and worthless people amongst us". He also threatened to "Put an end to these infernal Dago disturbances, even if it proves necessary to wipe out every one of them from the face of the earth". Given these statements, is it any wonder that the Italian communities accepted protection from criminal elements amongst them? Members of the Mafia from Sicily, the 'Ndrangheta from Calabria and the Camorra from Naples soon found a new role in protecting their countrymen from the Irish gangs, the corrupt police and others who wished to terrorize and exploit them.

This protection, however, soon turned to exploitation. In Italy, a form of extortion known as La Mano Nera (the Black Hand) had existed since the eighteenth century. Victims would receive a letter telling them to give the sender money or risk death from the secret Black Hand Society. The letters were always signed with a black handprint. Although there was no Black Hand Society in America, the terror that these letters provoked created the perfect cover for Italian immigrant crime gangs to work under. Soon the Black Hand racket was rife in America. Even famous Italian celebrities in America, such as the opera singer Enrico Caruso, were at risk – although unlike the majority of victims, he was able to call upon police protection.

The most infamous Black Hander was Ignazio Saietta ("Lupo The Wolf"). He had fled a murder charge in Sicily in 1898 and come to America where he worked for his brother-in-law Nicholas Morello. Morello had built the racket up into a thriving New York Mafia crime family that was eventually able to challenge the Irish and Jewish gangs for a piece of territory.

The growth of Morello's power perfectly illustrates the origins of the American Mafia and why it was so successful. Like other Italian gangs throughout America, it started out protecting its own community before exploiting them and turning the Italian immigrants' distrust of authority into an effective barrier of silence. It then used its Black Hand profits to expand into other criminal areas, benefiting greatly from the established gang structure and loyalty that had already been developed through hundreds of years of Italian history. It was these combined factors that gave not only Morello, but also the developing Mafia as a whole, an organizational edge over its ethnic rivals and the perfect launch pad for further success.

Italian immigrants celebrate their first glimpse of the Statue of Liberty, but amongst the poor huddled masses arriving to start a new life were members of the Sicilian Mafia and other organized crime groups.

PROHIBITION AND THE GROWTH OF THE MOBS

Most books dealing with the American Mafia start on January 16, 1920 – the day the Eighteenth Amendment came into effect and Prohibition descended upon the USA. There is no doubt that this day was probably the greatest day of all time for organized crime in America, but it more than just made the Mafia, it saved them from possible extinction.

Before the First World War, in 1914, the future of many organized crime gangs across America was already looking shaky. The reform movement sweeping the land had begun to end the link between the political machines and the bullyboy rackets of street gangs. Without political protection, many of the legendary gangs, such as New York's Eastman Gang and the Whyos, started to fall apart. Denied their previous lucrative political pay-offs, gang rivalry for a share of other criminal rackets, such as control of unions, gambling and prostitution, increased at the same time as infighting fragmented their power.

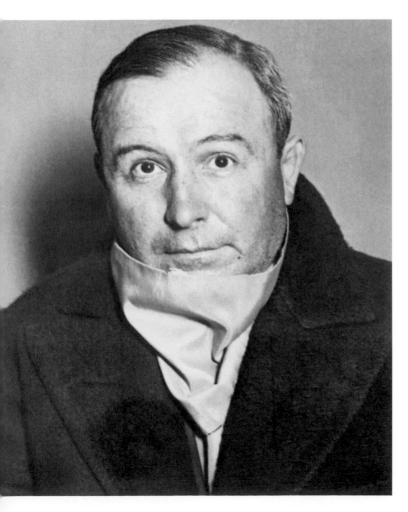

Not only were the traditional crime gangs inherently dependent on their symbiotic relationship with politicians, they also derived much of their power from the size of their membership. The Eastman gang, run by Monk Eastman, could call upon 1,500 men for a massed fight, but controlling such a large number of members on a day-to-day basis required a solid organizational structure that was completely absent and this made the gangs vulnerable if anything happened to their leaders.

The gangs also lacked any unifying philosophy, having been formed on a geographic and ethnic basis purely to operate rackets in just one neighbourhood. As economic conditions for immigrant groups improved over the years, new generations often moved out of the enclaves their parents had lived in. This meant the gangs often found that there were no new youngsters eager to fill the gaps left by the retirement, imprisonment or violent deaths of older members.

In the early 1900s, the most powerful of the traditional gangs was New York's The Five Points. Taking its name from the Carfax in Manhattan, where five streets converged, it was a predominantly Italian-American gang, with the likes of the young Al Capone and John Torrio, although it also had Jewish members. It reached the apex of its power in 1904 when its 1,000 members helped to elect George Brinton McClellan as Mayor of New York. However, like all the traditional gangs of the time, their power was waning in the face of political reform.

Ready to benefit from their downfall were the Black Hand operations that had spread into every Italian community nationwide. Desperate to move beyond the extortion game, their tight-knit nature and strong organizational structure, inherited from the Sicilian Mafia, Calabrian 'Ndrangheta and Camorra from Naples, gave them a strong edge. Countrywide they soon began to take over the gambling, vice, union and protection rackets that had previously belonged to other larger gangs. Italians who had previously not been Black Handers, such as Capone and Torrio, also began to recognize the benefits of the structured, traditional Italian approach to organized crime.

They flourished briefly, but these new Italian-American crime gangs were vulnerable because they lacked political influence. Soon their rackets came under attack by the authorities – several police forces even formed Italian squads to tackle them. With major clampdowns on vice in New Orleans, Chicago and San Francisco, and union racketeering in New York under pressure, a new source of income was desperately needed.

This new income proved to be the bootlegging and rum-running that boomed once the Eighteenth Amendment and the Volstead Act, banning the sale of alcohol, came into force in 1920. Suddenly, a massive, new, multi-million dollar, nationwide, illegal market had

John "the Fox" Torrio was a member of New York's Five Points Gang before going on to become Al Capone's mentor and the driving force behind the early days of bootlegging in Chicago.

opened up and the surviving crime gangs were in the perfect position to benefit by supplying the thousands of illicit speakeasies that sprang up overnight. It was Prohibition, therefore, that would lead to the growth of the mobs and rise of the Mafia.

The advent of Prohibition could not have happened at a more opportune time. If it had occurred just a few years later, the natural progression of Italian ethnic community and police harassment may have meant that the Mafia would have been a spent force within the American organized scene. As it was, Prohibition was to be their ticket to criminal glory and untold riches.

Philadelphia's Public Safety Director "Duckboard" Bill smashes kegs of beer after his agents busted an illegal alcohol operation. Despite thousands of such seizures, mobsters continued to keep the booze flowing during Prohibition.

CAPONE'S CHICAGO

The relationship between Al "Scarface" Capone and the city of Chicago was the perfect marriage and possibly the best example of right time, right place, right face in the history of crime. It might therefore surprise some to learn that Capone was not a native son of Chicago. He was, in fact, born to Italian immigrant parents who had settled in Brooklyn, New York, five years before his birth in 1899.

Capone was a graduate of New York's gang-filled streets. He had been a member of both the James Street Gang, alongside "Lucky" Luciano, and The Five Points Gang, whose members included John "Johnny the Fox" Torrio. In 1915 it was Torrio and his then partner Frankie Vale who gave Capone his first organized crime job as a bouncer in their brothel and drinking den the Harvard Inn. Later that year, Torrio left New York for Chicago – a move that would shape the destinies of both Capone and the city of Chicago.

Torrio made the move when his sister called him in to help resolve her husband Jim "Diamond Jim" Colosimo's problems with Black Hand extortionists. Diamond Jim and his wife ran a chain of more than 200 brothels in Chicago that earned them around $600,000 per year. His wealth made him a natural target for Black Handers. So when he received a demand for $50,000, Torrio was asked to help out, which he did by arranging for two New York gang members to kill the Black Handers when they turned up to collect their money.

Colosimo rewarded Torrio with a job helping to run his huge vice operation, which he used as a starting point for carving out his own empire. Torrio worked on the principle of supplying the three things he said people could never get enough of – gambling, alcohol and sex – and he soon had a chain of establishments that provided all three under one roof. In 1919, he called on Capone to come and join him in Chicago to help him run some of his joints.

When Prohibition hit, Torrio realized that the underworld was about to boom and that bootlegging was going to be the biggest and most profitable business to be in. Colosimo, however, forbade Torrio to get involved in the supply of illicit alcohol to the various speakeasies that were springing up all across the notorious Levee district on the South Side of Chicago. Other gangs were making fortunes and Torrio realized that Colosimo had to be eliminated if he wanted a part of the action. Capone arranged for some hired guns from New York to murder Colosimo, then he and Torrio set about transforming the dead Colosimo's vice empire into the most powerful bootlegging and organized crime outfit in the Windy City.

Between them, Torrio and Capone took control of a number of breweries, arranged protection for illicit shipments of alcohol that were coming into the city, and began to take over other Chicago gangs. Capone arranged for those who would not co-operate with them to meet a bloody end. A typical example of this was when Capone called

in his former boss, Frankie Vale, to act as the triggerman in the assassination of rival gang leader Dion O'Banion, who ran the mainly Irish North Side Gang, in 1924.

O'Banion's death led to a bitter war with the North Siders, and in 1925 Torrio was shot. Although he survived, he retired from his active role in crime and went back to Brooklyn to enjoy the $30 million he had already made. As he left the city he said to Capone, "Al, it's all yours". He had of course meant their criminal operations, but over the next few years Capone managed to build them up to the point where he practically controlled the whole city, its politicians, judges and even the police.

Through an ingenious mix of good business arrangements, alliances with gangs outside the Italian-American crime set-up, and brutal violence, Capone dominated Chicago's underworld. His combined booze, vice and gambling empire made more than $105 million a year and he proved time and again to be beyond the reach of both the law and the gunman's bullet. Between 1925 and 1931, when he was convicted of tax evasion charges, Chicago was truly Capone's city.

Between 1925 and 1931, Al Capone (left) was the kingpin of Chicago organized crime and held the whole city in his thrall through an astute mix of bribery, bullets and bravado.

The funeral procession of Chicago gangster and Capone rival Angelo Genna (above) brought the streets of the city to a halt in 1925, but did nothing to stop Capone's murderous quest for dominance.

THE ST VALENTINE'S DAY MASSACRE

Although Al Capone was Chicago's kingpin of crime, his position in the underworld was not without its rivals. In response, he had two ways of dealing with those who challenged him – peaceful co-operation or violent death.

Since he had taken over John Torrio's South Side Chicago operation in 1925, Capone had demonstrated magnanimity and fairness in dealing with those who had once opposed him. This brought many old adversaries into his outfit. He even employed Frank Galluccio, the man whose knife work in a fight had given Capone the legendary nickname "Scarface", as his bodyguard. As long as you bent to Capone's will and did not try to double-cross him, there was a profitable place in his empire, even for the most previously implacable enemies.

However, if as a rival gangster, you refused to make peace with Capone, you were choosing to go to war with someone who was notorious for ensuring enemies ended their opposition in a hail of bullets. It was war with a man whose criminal organization employed more than 1,000 men and had all the key politicians, police and judges in Chicago in his pocket. It was a choice to fight a war that few could possibly ever hope to win.

The brutal slaying of six North Side Gang members on 14 February 1929 bore all the hallmarks of a hit organized by Capone and has entered criminal folklore as an example of how he dealt with his rivals.

Capone's fair and generous approach to rivals had brought opponents such as the Saltis-McErlane mob from the West Side of Chicago and the Valley Gang into his outfit. One group that refused to do the same was the North Side Gang. Capone had been responsible for arranging the death of the North Side boss Dion O'Banion in November 1924 with the resulting escalation in hostilities that had eventually persuaded Torrio to retire and hand over the South Side to Capone.

Earl "Hymie" Weiss took over the North Side Gang after O'Banion's death and set about evening the score with Capone. In 1925 Weiss and his deputy George "Bugs" Moran used Thompson submachine guns on Capone's car. It was to be the first of many unsuccessful attempts they made on Capone's life. In September 1926 they fired more than 1,000 bullets into the Hawthorne Inn while Capone was eating his lunch there. After Weiss refused Capone's final offer of a peace deal, Capone had him killed by an out-of-town hitman.

Typically for Capone, he then offered Moran amnesty and a deal in which he could keep control of the North Side of Chicago. He accepted. In 1928, Al bought a huge estate in Florida and moved there with his wife and child. Moran used this as an opportunity to try and muscle in on Capone's territory. It was to be a fateful mistake. Outraged by Moran's treachery, Capone arranged for his right-hand man Jack "Machine Gun" McGurn to take care of Moran permanently.

Rival gang boss George "Bugs" Moran was late for the meeting that saw six of his North Side Gang stood against a wall and shot, so surviving one of the most infamous Mob murders.

On February 14, 1929, Moran was due to be at his gang's head-quarters – a garage at 2122 North Clark Street – to take delivery of a truckload of allegedly hijacked illegal drink from a Detroit gangster. It was a set-up. At the appointed time, several of McGurn's men, two dressed in police uniforms and arriving in a stolen police car, raided the garage and told the six North Side Gang members and a civilian associate to line-up against the wall. Thinking it was a police raid or shakedown, they complied. They were then machine-gunned, their dead bodies falling to the floor, pools of blood forming alongside the oil already on the ground.

Moran, who was late for the meeting, arrived just as the police car pulled up. By not entering the garage and fleeing when the shooting started, he survived. However, the power of his gang was broken. When he was later picked up by the police for questioning and asked who was responsible, Moran said, "Only Capone kills guys like that".

Although it consolidated his grip on the Chicago underworld and no one was ever charged for the St Valentine's Day Massacre murders, the massive bad publicity of such a large and brutal slaying hurt Capone. It brought the anger of the public, Federal authorities and even his fellow mob bosses outside of Chicago down on him. Many consider it his worst mistake and the first domino falling in the collapse of his empire.

THE CHICAGO OUTFIT

The decades since Al Capone's death in 1947 have done nothing to diminish his reputation as the most notorious American mob boss of all time and the embodiment of the rise of organized crime during Prohibition. Without doubt, he is the most infamous Italian-American gangster and member of the Mafia to have his blood-soaked name become part of both underworld folklore and US history. Except, of course, Al Capone was never an orthodox member of the Mafia and his mob, known as the Chicago Outfit and later just the Outfit, never started out as a traditional Mafia crime family. In fact, much of Capone's eventful career in organized crime saw him battling against elements of what would later be accepted as the American Mafia.

Although he had gone to school with and been a member of The Five Points gang with "Lucky" Luciano and other Sicilians, Capone's Neapolitan heritage prevented him from being accepted into the organized crime gangs in America that had links to the Sicilian Mafia. As his parents came from Naples, Capone could have become a member of an Italian organized crime group with links to the

Camorra, but he instead chose to go his own way. His reluctance to be a part of an established Italian-American crime group did not prevent Capone's rise to power within the underworld. His links to John Torrio, forged during his time as member of The Five Points, got him his first job as a bouncer and enforcer in Brooklyn, and later led to Torrio bringing him into his Chicago operations.

Amongst the rivals that Capone had to battle with for supremacy over Chicago crime, when he took control of Torrio's South Side vice, gambling and illegal drink operations, were the Terrible Gennas. This was a group of Sicilian brothers who dominated Chicago's Little Italy. They were originally Black Hand extortionists before getting into bootlegging, and had recruited an army of soldiers from their old village of Marsala. They were also the Chicago heads of the Unione Siciliane (or Unione Siciliana), a Sicilian-American political organization that had become the nationwide front for the growing network of Sicilian Mafia syndicates.

After Capone had brothers Mike and Tony "The Gentleman" Genna killed in 1925, he tried to have one of his own men, Antonio Lombardo, who was a Sicilian, appointed as the new President of the Chicago Unione Siciliane. This led Capone's Chicago Outfit into a bloody war with the city's last powerful Sicilian Mafia group, headed by Joseph Aiello, a former Genna ally. Aiello killed Lombardo and his Capone-backed successor Pasquale Lolordo. He also tried to bribe Capone's favourite chef to poison him. Despite the $35,000 on offer, the Chef told Capone what Aeillo was planning, which led to Capone declaring that Aeillo was going to "Get it real good!"

US marshals escort Al Capone from the courtroom during his 1931 trial for tax evasion that saw the start of his fall from power and eventual imprisonment on the island of Alcatraz.

Al Capone's wife Mae tried to stay out of the spotlight as much as possible and a $50,000 per year pension for life paid by the Chicago Outfit helped keep her silent even after her husband's death in 1947.

Jack "Greasy Thumb" Guzik (left) was Capone's most trusted aide. A Moscow-born Jew, he was a prime example of Capone's willingness to let anyone into the Outfit if they made him money.

Capone won the war against the Sicilian element in Chicago, which meant that when Salvatore Maranzano declared the creation of "Cosa Nostra" in 1931, he had to recognize Capone's Chicago Outfit as a separate family within the Cosa Nostra, despite its non-Mafia origins. Capone's Outfit had always been multi-cultural, his most trusted man being the Moscow-born Jew Jake "Greasy Thumb" Guzik, and Capone was happy to take anyone under his wing regardless of religion, nationality or race, as long as they made money and did as he said.

Even after Capone's fall from power due to encroaching syphilis and his imprisonment on Alcatraz, the Outfit retained its freedom from much traditional Mafia rule and ritual. Although Capone was still officially in control until his death and his wife, Mae, received a pension of $50,000 a year until her death, control passed first to Frank "The Enforcer" Nitti and then Paul "The Waiter" Ricca and Anthony "Big Tuna" Accardo.

After the end of Prohibition, the Outfit moved heavily into loan sharking, extortion, labour racketeering and attempting to shakedown Hollywood movie studios – a move outside of Chicago that would see both Nitti and Ricca facing prison time. Even post-1957, when Sam "Momo" Giancana took over the leadership of the Outfit and moved it to a more mainstream position in the American Mafia set-up, it still bore some of the character of Capone's cross-cultural approach.

THE BOSS OF BOSSES

The problem that Al Capone encountered, and successfully dealt with in Chicago, was the growing power of Italian-American organized crime groups with Sicilian roots. It was symptomatic of a growing criminal network that was spreading its power across America.

The Black Hand extortionists, who had been members of Sicilian Mafia groups before arriving in America, had begun to organize themselves along Mafia lines in the New World. Although originally few in number, their structure, traditions, unifying code of criminal ethics and rules soon gave them an edge over the established criminal networks that were beginning to fragment.

Although they faced opposition from similar groups to themselves forming from previous members of the Calabrian 'Ndrangheta and Neapolitan Camorra, the Sicilian gangs soon made their presence felt outside of Italian enclaves and the old Black Hand racket. Not only were they becoming major players in prostitution and gambling, they were even going up against the established Irish crime gangs for control of the docks and union rackets all across the Eastern Seaboard.

Using the front of the Unione Siciliane, a fraternal society originally designed to provide support and insurance for Sicilian immigrants, the groups developed a loose-knit, nationwide network of Sicilian crime gangs. When Prohibition came into effect in 1920, Sicilian organized crime groups were often in the strongest position to exploit the massive new opportunity that arose from the illicit alcohol business.

The Sicilian-American Mafia families enjoyed an incredible boom in profits throughout the Roaring Twenties. In many areas, especially New York, it was clear that they were now the strongest force in organized crime. Their remarkable rise and prosperity did not go unnoticed back in Sicily. The most powerful Sicilian Mafia boss on the island, Vito Cascio Ferro (Don Vito), had dreams of gaining control of the groups in America and organizing them into one all-powerful crime family, with himself as the "Boss of Bosses". When Don Vito was imprisoned by Mussolini's Fascists, his plan was taken over by one of his lieutenants, Salvatore Maranzano.

Arriving in New York in 1927, Maranzano set out to take over the Sicilian-American operation that was booming under Giuseppe "Joe the Boss" Masseria. Maranzano reasoned that if he controlled New York's Sicilian-American Mafia, he could also control those across the rest of the country. Maranzano recruited an army of Mafiosi around himself from his own hometown of Castellammare del Golfo in Sicily and was soon muscling in on Joe the Boss's rackets.

The original Godfather, Giuseppe "Joe the Boss" Masseria, controlled the majority of New York Sicilian-American Mafia until the outbreak of the Castellammarese War that challenged his underworld kingpin position.

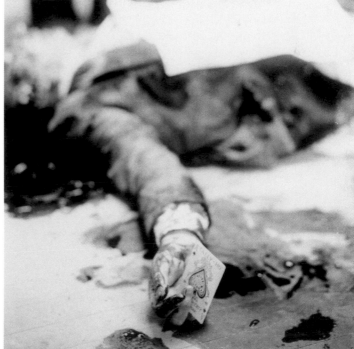

Giuseppe "Joe the Boss" Masseria's dead body still clutches the unluckiest card in the deck after his murder by Jewish gunmen working on behalf of "Lucky" Luciano.

By 1928, Maranzano had so many supporters that Masseria was forced to go to war with him. Between 1928 and 1930 the bloody conflict that would became known after September 10, 1930 as the Castellammarese War, had claimed more than 50 lives. Masseria's underboss "Lucky" Luciano saw the way it was going and brought the war to a swift end by arranging to have Masseria killed while he was playing poker with him at a Coney Island restaurant on April 15, 1931.

Maranzano declared the war to be over, made Luciano his second in command and called an extraordinary meeting of more than 500 gangsters from across the country to outline his plan. The Mafia in New York would be divided into five families, each with its own boss, underboss, lieutenants and soldiers, all reporting to the Capo di Tutti Capi (the Boss of Bosses), which was to be Maranzano. The new organization was called "Cosa Nostra" (meaning "our thing") and was intended to bring peace and profits to all.

Secretly, Maranzano was planning to ensure this peace, and that he stayed Boss of Bosses, by killing Luciano and his younger generation of gangster cohorts, including Frank Costello, Vito Genovese, Joe Adonis and Dutch Schultz. He also planned to kill "the fat bastard in Chicago", Al Capone. He hired Irish gangster and hitman Vincent "Mad Dog" Coll to kill Luciano and paid him $25,000 upfront.

The plan was for Maranzano to call Genovese and Luciano to a meeting at which Coll was to turn up and gun them down. However, before this could happen, Luciano arranged for four Jewish gunmen to burst into Maranzano's office and to shoot him instead. Maranzano's reign as the one and only Boss of Bosses had lasted less than four months. Coll turned up as Maranzano's killers were rushing from the murder scene – a situation that left him $25,000 up without even having to shoot anyone. No wonder he walked away whistling.

Giuseppe Antonio Doto was one of the leaders of Murder Inc. that helped ensure more than 500 men were murdered on behalf of the National Commission.

THE NATIONAL CRIME SYNDICATE AND MURDER INC

The reason why "Lucky" Luciano was so well prepared to survive the assassination attempt by self-styled Boss of Bosses, Salvatore Maranzano, in September, 1931, was that he had been making his own plans for seizing control of the Mafia for years. This was how Luciano could respond instantly by calling up a squad of four Jewish hitmen to smoothly wipe out his would-be killer the moment he got the fateful call to come to Maranzano's office.

Luciano had not been making those plans alone. He had been working on them with Meyer Lansky, a Jewish gangster and possibly one of the greatest criminal minds of the twentieth century. No one can definitively say how and when Luciano and Lansky and their joint friend Benjamin "Bugsy" Siegel had met. Underworld myths are legion about the fateful meeting. Most seem to revolve around Siegel and Lansky visiting one of Luciano's whorehouses or Lansky saving Siegel from a Luciano beating by smacking Lucky in the head with a wrench. Such details are much less important than the fact that the three became lifelong friends and broke down the existing racial barriers that prevented Italian and Jewish gangsters mixing and even working together.

Luciano did not merely want power. The vision that he and Lansky had was much grander than simply killing Maranzano and having Luciano replace him as Boss of Bosses. They wanted to create a lasting national organized crime network where Italian and Jewish gangs co-operated and that was administered by a board of directors. They wanted it to be a purely American operation with no loyalty owed to or control by the Sicilian Mafia and without all the old baggage of rituals, oaths and ancient blood vendettas.

Lansky and Luciano began to actively plan to seize gangland power and to usher in their scheme of a unified organized crime set-up in 1928, the year that the man who had inspired much of it – Albert Rothstein – was murdered. The original "Mr Big" (also known as "the Brain" and "the Fixer"), Rothstein was a criminal financier and mastermind who had bankrolled some of Luciano's early big drug deals and Lansky's acquisition of a trucking firm at the beginning of Prohibition.

With Rothstein's death, it was up to Lansky and Luciano to take their old mentor's dream, a national crime network, forward. During the Castellammarese War, Luciano recruited younger Mafiosi from both sides as allies in the secret scheme whilst Lansky secured support from key Jewish gangsters. When Lansky's hitsquad wiped out Maranzano in 1931 and Luciano took control of the newly formed Cosa Nostra, they were at last in a position to put their plan into action.

Arnold Rothstein was the original "Mr Big" of American organized crime and had the original vision of a National Crime Syndicate that Luciano and Lansky eventually brought to fruition.

Louis "Lepke" Buchalter, guarded by a Tommy gun wielding Federal Agent, is brought to trial in 1943 for one of the many murders he helped organize as one of the key players in Murder Inc.

They called it the National Crime Syndicate. At its head was the National Commission – a six-man advisory board of top Mafia and Jewish gang leaders that adjudicated over disputes. Reporting to the National Commission was the Chicago Outfit, the Mafia families in other US states and the New York Commission. They would act in the same way as the National Commission over the five families of Cosa Nostra that Maranzano had set up to control organized crime in New York. Luciano took over control of the Masseria crime family, but the other crime families remained intact and were allowed to keep their old rules and ritual.

To enforce the new order, keep the peace and guarantee that the word of the National Commission was always final, Lansky created Murder Incorporated – the name given to an elite group of hitmen that were only available for hire to mob bosses on Commission-sanctioned murders. Louis "Lepke" Buchalter, Albert Anastasia and Joe Adonis were put in charge of able lieutenants such as Abe "Kid Twis" Reles and Mendy Weiss. Between them, it is thought that they killed more than 500 men on the orders of the Commission between 1933 and 1940.

The new organizational structure of confederated gangs working across the ethnic divide that had once been dreamed of by Rothstein was made to work by Luciano, Lansky and the deadly muscle provided by Murder Inc. The fact that the same basic structure and the National Commission still exists and directs much of the American Mafia today is a testament to not only to its founders, but also to its basic strength as an idea.

THE SYNDICATE EXPOSED – APALACHIN 1957

One of the reasons Cosa Nostra and allied organized crime groups thrived under the structure and leadership provided by the National Commission was because it ensured the National Crime Syndicate and all Mafia families kept as hidden from view as possible.

The Commission strictly vetoed any hits on journalists, prosecutors or politicians that would have drawn massive, untoward attention to it. They also reined in any conspicuous activity by Cosa Nostra or its members that could potentially raise their public profile. Even leading Mafia members had to obey. "Dutch" Schultz was gunned down in 1935, when he had ignored the Commission and began planning the assassination of Special Prosecutor Thomas E. Dewey. Gang boss Albert Anastasia was murdered in 1957, partly as a result of his killing of an innocent civilian, while New Jersey boss Willie Moretti's violent end in 1951 had much to do with his loose-

Luciano-Masseria Crime Family boss Frank Costello (left) may have set up his rivals and colleagues when they met to discuss whether Vito Genovese should keep control of his old family.

lipped performance in front of the Kefauver Committee hearings on organized crime.

The rigorous enforcement of the code of omerta (silence) and the brutal clamping down on all who jeopardized Cosa Nostra's low profile was a great triumph. By staying below the radar of law enforcement and public concern, the National Crime Syndicate was able to expand without any concerted, co-ordinated attempt to fight its growing power. It was not until the Kefauver hearings, held between 1950 and 1951, that the public even heard the word Mafia. There was massive ignorance as to its structure and who its leaders actually were. In fact, up until Apalachin in 1957, when it all went wrong, their strategy of secrecy was so successful that even FBI director J. Edgar Hoover could claim there was "no such thing as the Mafia".

The National Syndicate's ruling body was the National Commission. It held meetings with wider leadership of the Syndicate's component groups at least once every couple of years. There was no fixed agenda, but the crime conventions provided an opportunity to resolve disputes, confirm changes of leadership within a family and agree the position on contentious issues, such as whether drug dealing was to be allowed as an acceptable Cosa Nostra activity.

In 1957, the National Commission convention was to be held on November 14 at the country home of Joseph Barbara in Apalachin, upstate New York. Barbara was a former member of the Buffalo crime family who had gone legit and was now running a successful soft drink distribution business. His home had previously been used for meetings of the New York Commission and the Buffalo family. One item of business that was going to be discussed was Vito Genovese's attempt on the life of Luciano-Masseria crime family boss Frank Costello, that had forced Costello into retirement. Genovese was hoping that the National Commission would grant clemency over the affair and agree to his continuing control of Costello's old family.

Almost 100 of the top Mafiosi descended on Apalachin. They were conspicuous in their expensive, handmade suits and luxury cars, but it may have been Barbara booking out all the motel rooms in the area that alerted the State Police to something unusual happening. It was, however, probably more likely to have been a tip-off from either Costello or "Lucky" Luciano – who had been invited to the meeting, but decided not to attend – as a way of getting revenge on Genovese.

Whatever it was that alerted the New York State Police, they sent representatives along with two officers from the Alcohol and Tobacco Tax and Trade Bureau to investigate. They turned up at Barbara's estate in the middle of a barbecue. When they saw the police car pull up in the driveway, the Mafia bosses fled the house and ran into the surrounding fields and woods. While Chicago boss Sam Giancana and nearly 40 others succeeded in getting away, a total of 58 were arrested. The captured men read like a Who's Who of the Mafia and included such top names as Joe Profaci, Vito Genovese, Santo Trafficante Jr and Carlo Gambino. Most explained their presence as being due either to visiting a sick friend or having experienced a car breakdown.

While all of them were eventually released, the exposure put the Mafia and the Syndicate firmly in the national spotlight. No one, least of all J. Edgar Hoover, could now deny the existence of the Mafia. The Apalachin fiasco's fallout was set to hurt Cosa Nostra for decades to come.

Mafia crime boss Sam Giancana (right) faced the spotlight and tough questions when he appeared before the Senate Labor Rackets Committee hearing in 1959 due to the Mob's increased public exposure.

extortion rackets that were carried out by the infamous Ignazio "Lupo the Wolf" Saietta. Lupo was part of his brother-in-law, Antonio Morello's crime family and set-up the "Murder Stable" in East Harlem, where extortion victims were taken to be tortured and killed. In 1910, Lupo and one of Antonio's brothers – Peter "the Clutching Hand" Morello were jailed for counterfeiting. When Antonio was killed in gang warfare in 1898, first his brother Joe and then his brother Nicholas Morello succeeded him as boss of the crime family. When Camorristas finally killed Nicholas in 1916, leadership passed to the ineffectual Ciro Terranova.

By 1922, what had been the Morello family was now under the control of Giuseppe "Joe the Boss" Masseria. When Peter Morello came out of prison, he recognized Masseria's power and joined forces with him in the position of underboss. Having arranged the murder of Salvatore D'Aquila, his main rival and then head of the Gambino family, Masseria was now the boss of the most powerful Italian organized crime group in New York. Amongst the members of what was now called the Masseria family, was "Lucky" Luciano.

In 1928, Joe the Boss started the Castellammarese War against the forces of the Sicilian Mafioso, Salvatore Maranzano. The War led to Luciano arranging the murder of Masseria, so helping Maranzano to create the Cosa Nostra and make the Masseria family one of New York's famous five recognized Mafia families. After Luciano had Maranzano murdered and established the National Crime Syndicate with Meyer Lansky in 1931, he kept the five family structure

THE GENOVESE FAMILY

One man held responsible for the Apalachin mess by many fellow Mafiosi was Vito Genovese. He had hoped the meeting of the National Commission in 1957 would officially ratify the coup that had brought him control of a crime family. It seems unfair, however, to blame Genovese for the fiasco just because he was one of the items under discussion – the police bust may have resulted from a tip off from Frank Costello, the man he had recently deposed.

The crime family that Genovese had seized control of, and which still bears his name, was previously called the Luciano-Masseria family. It enjoyed one of the most notorious pedigrees of any Mafia group in American history. It dated from the 1890s and the Black Hand

Vito Genovese poses for yet another police photograph as part of a criminal career that saw him go from small-time hood to leading player in Cosa Nostra politics and boss of his own crime family.

and control of the now-renamed Luciano-Masseria family.

Luciano's direct reign did not last long. In 1936 he was sentenced to 30 years on prostitution charges, whilst his underboss Vito Genovese fled to Italy to escape a murder charge. This left Frank Costello to take control of the family. Under Costello the family flourished, controlling profitable loansharking, gambling and union rackets and establishing interests in Las Vegas. When Genovese returned to America after World War Two, he set about trying to gain control. He eventually forced Costello to retire in 1957, but was set-up by Luciano and Costello on drug charges the next year and had to run the family that now bore his name from prison until his death in 1969.

Between 1969 and 1981, the Genovese family was run by Philip "Benny Squint" Lombardo who used a series of other men as front bosses, including Thomas Eboli, Frank Tieri and Anthony "Fat Tony" Salerno, to convince the FBI and other Mafia leaders that they were in charge. This was a useful strategy when it came to getting away with dirty jobs, such as the murder of Philadelphia Mafia boss Angelo Bruno. Upon Lombardo's death, Vincent "Chin" Gigante took over. He was a man that no one suspected at first due to his "mad act", where he faked mental illness by wandering the streets in his bathrobe and slippers. Upon his arrest in 1997, Dominick "Quiet Dom" Cirilo became the alleged day-to-day boss of the Genovese family working with Gigante who retained overall control from prison.

Upon his death on December 19, 2005, Gigante left a crime family in good shape. It has 275–395 full members and more than 1,000 associates. It retains control of labour and gambling rackets in Manhattan, owns shares in several casinos, controls street pitches across New York and enjoys a massive loan sharking empire. The twenty-first-century Genovese family remains one of the premier Cosa Nostra groups with an estimated illicit annual turnover of more than $500 million.

Genovese crime family boss Vincent "Chin" Gigante would often wander around New York in the day wearing pyjamas as part of his act to feign madness and escape prosecution.

The bloody body of Philadelphia Mafia boss, Angelo Bruno, who was assassinated in 1980, gives an indication of the type of dirty jobs the Genovese crime family were happy to undertake.

THE LUCCHESE FAMILY

While the Genovese family continues to be worthy of its position as one of the famous five powerful families that make up the Mafia in New York, the Lucchese family – also part of the legendary quintet – has definitely seen better days.

What would eventually become the Lucchese family started out as the Brooklyn branch of "Joe the Boss" Masseria's operations. It was run on Masseria's behalf by Gaetano "Tommy" Reina. When Masseria's campaign against Salvatore Maranzano led to the Castellammarese War, Reina secretly supported Maranzano, who had promised him his own family when Maranzano was "Boss of Bosses".

As part of his behind-the-scenes manipulation of the war, Masseria's underboss "Lucky" Luciano arranged for Vito Genovese to shoot Tommy Reina on January 26, 1930 as he left his Brooklyn apartment. Masseria believed Maranzano was behind the hit, while Maranzano thought Masseria had found out about Reina's treachery and had had him killed. Reina's replacement was Masseria loyalist Joe Pinzolo. He was a non-Brooklyn man whose appointment annoyed two men who had worked for and been close friends of Reina – Tommy Gagliano and Tommy "Three-Finger Brown" Lucchese (Lucchese had lost a finger in an accident in 1915 and took his nickname from the famous baseball player of the time, Three-Finger Brown).

Gagliano and Lucchese agreed with Luciano to secretly change sides and work as Maranzano insiders while they arranged for an unknown street thug to kill Joe Pinzolo – a move Masseria thought was the work of Maranzano. When Maranzano won the Castellammarese War and created the Cosa Nostra structure of five New York Mafia families under him as Boss of Bosses, he rewarded Gagliano with his own

MONOPOLIES AND LABOUR RACKETEERING

The practice of holding a monopoly on the supply of a commodity in order to inflate its price was originally pioneered by organized religions over substances that were required for sacrifice or sacred devotion. The Sicilian Mafia was profiteering from this basic idea in the early twentieth century, as anyone who wanted to buy a candle to light in church to symbolize his or her betrothal discovered.

In the 1930s, Cosa Nostra members held monopolies on everything from artichokes to ice and essential baking supplies. In only one case – the Chicago Outfit's monopoly on milk distribution – did Mafia control reduce the price that people ended up paying for their goods. Creating and maintaining monopolies remains a common and highly lucrative organized crime practice across the globe, with a focus on service industries, such as garbage collection.

With the growth of the union movement and the ability of workers to collectively withdraw their labour, criminal networks saw an opening to hold a monopoly on the provision of a workforce. Many of today's labour racketeering practices originated in America at the beginning of the twentieth century, as Jewish, Italian and Irish gangs took control of unions in the garment industry, trucking and docks.

Not only could they blackmail employers through strike threats, but they could also extort money from the workers, as employees often needed to be a union member to get a job. Organized crime's control of a union can also give significant political power, through the ability to direct the votes of its members, thus granting crime bosses considerable sway over corruptible politicians.

Mafia killer and crime boss Thomas Lucchese AKA Thomas "Three-Finger Brown" takes the oath at the Senate Labor Rackets Committee hearing in 1958.

Lucchese had strong sway with New York Mayor Vincent Impellitteri after the Mafia boss backed him heavily when he ran for office.

family to control the old Masseria Brooklyn rackets. Gagliano made Lucchese his underboss and they supported Luciano in his move to oust Maranzano and create the National Crime Syndicate.

Gagliano retained control of his family in the new order that was ushered in by Luciano and Meyer Lansky. He and Lucchese were powerful voices in the New York Commission, but wisely chose to stay out of the spotlight. They had a happy partnership that saw Lucchese lead the way in taking control of the Garment District unions and New York's Teamsters. They built up their illegal gambling, vice and drug operations and founded lucrative new rackets controlling Idlewild (now JFK) Airport and the garbage industry on Long Island. When Gagliano died of natural causes in 1954, he was replaced by Lucchese and the old family got the name it is still known by today.

Lucchese had made powerful contacts during his time as underboss. He had backed Vincent Impellitteri's campaign for mayor in 1950 and had strong sway with him whilst he was in office. He was also a close friend of the former US Attorney Thomas Murphy, who Impellitteri appointed New York City Police Commissioner. While Three-Finger Brown was running it, the Lucchese crime family was the most peaceful and fair Mafia set-up around – the mob every Mafiosi wished they worked for. The profits from the rackets were good and, unlike other families, generously shared around. Thomas Lucchese's political and police contacts kept convictions way below Mafia average and there was a notable absence of infighting and petty politics. Many put this down to the way that Lucchese genuinely seemed to care about the welfare of his men and went out of his way to resolve any problems they faced. They returned his concern with a loyalty that was rare in the annals of Mafia history.

When Lucchese died of a brain tumour in 1967, more than 1,000 mourners attended his funeral. Top Mafia men mingled with politicians, judges and senior policemen to say farewell to a well-loved kingpin of crime. After his death, Carmine Trumunti mismanaged the Lucchese family for few years before Anthony "Tony Ducks" Corallo took charge.

The political protection the family had enjoyed under Three-Finger Brown was gone and soon the family was hit by a series of police and FBI busts. Corallo went to prison himself in 1986, and the running of the family eventually fell to Vic Amuso and Anthony "Gas Pipe" Casso. Known as the "Kill! Kill! Kill! Boys", their slaughter of their own men soon put them behind bars and left the Lucchese family in a mess it has yet to recover from.

THE BONANNO FAMILY

Another of the famous five New York Mafia families, currently trying to recover from problems caused by law enforcement victories and a string of inept leaders, is the Bonanno family. It is due to the lousy performance of a number of ex-bosses that the family still goes by the name of a man who has not led it since the National Commission replaced Joseph "Joe Bananas" Bonanno as its official head in 1964.

What became the Bonanno family has its origins in the many Mafiosi who left the Castellammare del Golfo in western Sicily at the end of the nineteenth century to set up operations in New York. Between 1915 and 1920, one these Mafiosi was Stefano Magaddino. He eventually fled New York to escape a murder investigation and headed upstate to Buffalo where he formed his own crime family.

When Magadinno's young cousin Joseph Bonanno arrived in New York in 1924, he joined the Castellammare del Golfo gang. In 1927, Sicilian boss Salvatore Maranzano arrived in America with grand plans for a unified Mafia. He took charge of the Castellammarese and adopted Bonanno as his protégé. When Maranzano named himself the "Boss of Bosses" in 1931 and created Cosa Nostra and the five New York mafia families structure, he gave the 26-year-old Joe Bananas his own family to run.

When Maranzano was eliminated after just four months in charge of Cosa Nostra, Bonanno kept control of his family and played active roles on the New York and National Commissions. His was a small family, so he allied himself with cousin Magaddino's Buffalo family and the large New York family run by Joe Profaci. In the 1950s, finding the proximity of four other crime families in New York left him with little

Mafia boss Joseph "Joe Bananas" Bonanno walks away from the courthouse after being freed on bail in 1966, able to continue his campaign to try and keep control of the crime family that carried his name.

Haitian dictator Francois "Papa Doc" Duvalier was one of the many strange allies that "Joe Bananas" made while trying to expand his criminal empire outside of New York City.

room to expand his rackets in the city, Bonanno developed interests in other areas.

Much to the annoyance of his cousin, who sa Canada as his territory, Bonanno established his family in Montreal. Under trusted capo Carmine "The Cigar" Galante the "Montreal Connection" was soon bringing heroin with a street value of $50 million into New York. In the late 1950s and early 1960s, the profits from this were used to try and set up a gambling empire in Haiti to duplicate the success Meyer Lansky had in Cuba before the fall of Batista in 1960. Bonanno allied himself with Haiti's dictator, Francois "Papa Doc" Duvalier and the fearsome Tonton Macoutes, Papa Doc's secret police and organized crime force. A lack of American tourists to the voodoo republic, however, doomed his off-shore casino venture to failure.

Bonanno had more success invading the open Mafia territory of Arizona. By the early 1960s he had a strong and profitable network in place within the state. However, it angered his fellow Mafia bosses when it became clear he was planning his next move on California. When long-time ally Joe Profaci died in 1962, Bonanno went to his replacement, Joe Magliocco, with a plan to assassinate the heads of the Lucchese and Gambino families and to seize their power. When the plan was exposed, Magliocco and Bonanno were called before the Commission to explain themselves. Magliocco complied and begged forgiveness – for this he was allowed to retire gracefully. In 1964, however, Bonanno refused to appear so the Commission ordered his replacement as head of his family by Gaspar DiGregorio. As a result, Bonanno disappeared and began fighting a bloody war (known as the "Banana War") to try and regain control.

Although Bonanno eventually admitted defeat and retired to Arizona in 1968, the position of leadership over the Bonanno family was fought over for the next decade by, amongst others, Carmine Galante and Philip Rastelli.

Even the Commission-sanctioned murder of Galante did not bring unity to the family. The constant infighting eventually lost them their seat on the Commission in 1981.

Worse was yet to come when FBI agent Joseph Pistrone, who was undercover in the role of criminal Donnie Brasco, was able to worm his way close to the heart of the family. The prosecutions resulting from Pistrone's stitch-up helped place Joey Massino in charge of the Bonanno family in 1993. Under his leadership the family clawed back some of its lost power and even regained its position on the Commission. However, when Massino went to prison in 2004 for racketeering, seven murders, arson, extortion, loan sharking, illegal gambling, conspiracy and money laundering, the Bonanno family returned to its old ways of internal blood-letting and chaos. The current leaders of the family – Anthony Graziano and Vincent Badalamenti – pled guilty to racketeering and extortion charges in April 2012, further weakening the position of the family.

Boss Joey Massino rebuilt the Bonanno Family after its near destruction by an undercover FBI agent using the name Donnie Brasco, before being put away for seven murders, racketeering, arson, extortion and other crimes in 2004.

THE COLOMBO FAMILY

Another of the famous five New York Mafia families that has been blighted by decades of conflict over its leadership is the Colombo family. Even by Mafia standards, the infighting for the position of boss and control of the family's profitable collection of rackets has been bloody and treacherous.

The first don of what would later be called the Colombo family was Joe Profaci. By 1928, he and his brother-in-law and underboss Joseph Magliocco had transformed their band of Sicilian immigrants from simple Black Hand extortionists into a successful bootlegging, labour racketeering, gambling, counterfeiting and heroin dealing enterprise. Profaci and Magliocco were also key players in the Sicilian Mafia network that was developing countrywide under the cover of the Unione Siciliane.

When Salvatore Maranzano declared himself "Boss of Bosses" in 1931, and ruled that there would now be only five Mafia families in New York, it was inevitable that he would have to recognize the power of Joe Profaci and make him head of one of those five families. Profaci remained the boss of the Colombo family until his death in 1962. Under three decades of his leadership, despite the comparatively small number of members, his family became one of the most powerful in New York.

Towards the end of his reign, however, Profaci experienced open revolt from family members in Brooklyn under the leadership of the Gallo brothers: Albert, Larry and "Crazy Joe". When Profaci died, Magliocco took over the family and the on-going war with the Gallo brothers. When the head of the Bonanno family, Joseph "Joe Bananas" Bonanno, came to Magliocco with a plan to eliminate fellow New York bosses Carlo Gambino and Tommy Lucchese and take over their families, he agreed and gave the job of arranging the hits to his trusted capo Joe Colombo.

As is often the case, one bit of Mafia treachery inspired another.

Joey "Crazy Joe" Gallo (left) and his brothers Larry (right) and Albert were a constant problem for the Colombo family after splitting from the organization.

Colombo went straight to Gambino to tell them what Magliocco and Bonanno were planning. The Commission called upon Magliocco and Bonanno to explain themselves. Whilst Bonanno refused to co-operate and was stripped of his power, leading to the "Bananas War", Magliocco admitted his guilt, begged forgiveness and due partly to his old age and rapidly advancing cancer was allowed to retire peacefully. Carlo Gambino repaid his favour to Joe Colombo by ensuring the Commission installed him as the head of the old Magliocco family.

Within a few years of heading up what he had renamed the Colombo family, Joe was in trouble with the Commission himself for attracting massive publicity by running the Italian-American Civil Rights League. He formed the League to protest against what he claimed was FBI anti-Italian bias. His FBI picket-lines and appearances on national TV only enraged the Feds who stepped up their anti-Mafia activities. His fellow mob bosses decided he needed to be reigned in. They got the still discontented "Crazy Joe" Gallo to use his connections with black organized crime to arrange for Colombo to be shot by a Harlem hitman at a League rally on June 28, 1971.

After the shooting, Colombo was left, as Gallo callously remarked, "A messed up mind vegetable that can't even walk". Aged capo Thomas DiBella ran the family for a short time before capo Carmine Persico took over. With all the Gallo brothers eliminated by the time Carmine became boss in 1974, it should have been a time of peace.

However, with Carmine spending most of his time as boss in prison, internal warfare for control of the family raged. While he was in jail, Persico appointed Victor "Little Vic" Orena as underboss to run things. Orena used this position to try to gain permanent control of the family and prevent Persico's son Alphonse from fulfilling his father's wishes and becoming boss. This led to the "Colombo War" that raged on New York's streets in the early 1990s – so bloody that it even saw innocent bystanders dying in the frequent exchanges of bullets. Alphonse Persico emerged the

Joseph Colombo and his son Joseph Colombo Jr carried out a number of bizarre stunts, such as picketing the FBI, in a failed attempt to try and constrain the Fed's campaign against Cosa Nostra.

victor only to face a series of lengthy prison sentences.

With a solid base of 120–180 members and a profitable range of rackets including drug trafficking, pornography and stock fraud, many suspected the Colombo family would soon regain strength. However, in January 2011 Colombo street boss Andrew Russo, acting underboss Benjamin Castellazzo, consigliere Richard Fusco and other members of the family were charged with murder, narcotics trafficking and labour racketeering. Faced with information provided by the betrayal of capo Reynold Maragni who wore a wire for the FBI, Castellazzo and Fusco pleaded guilty to reduced charges. Their convictions and the nature of how they were obtained has greatly weakened the Colombo family.

THE GAMBINO FAMILY

Like its fellow New York Cosa Nostra families, the Gambino family can trace its roots back to a Sicilian Mafia gang operating in the city in the 1900s. What started as a collection of small-time Black Handers has now grown into a twenty-first-century organized crime empire, so large and profitable it's been called Gambino Inc.

The earliest leader of what developed into the Gambino family was Salvatore D'Aquila. His expert running of the gang saw it become one of the most powerful Sicilian crime organizations in 1920s New York. D'Aquila was murdered in 1928 on the orders of "Joe the Boss" Masseria by Joe Profaci and a team of three gunmen. Masseria then placed a gang member that was friendly to him, Al Mineo, as the new boss. Two years later, however, Mineo was wiped out by men working

Carlo Gambino transformed the fortunes of the crime family that came to carry his name and became one of the most powerful Cosa Nostra bosses in the history of the organization.

VEHICLE THEFT AND RESALE

Automobile theft is often thought of as a crime that is predominantly perpetrated by juvenile joyriders or solo thieves. However, the obtaining, modifying and transporting of stolen motor vehicles has increasingly become a large scale, transnational, illicit enterprise involving co-operation between criminal networks on different continents.

Although the sophistication of anti-car theft measures during the 1990s reversed an increasing trend in stolen automobiles, it did little to impact on the organized crime element of the problem. As it became more difficult to distribute stolen vehicles within national borders, gangs turned to illicitly exporting cars outside of their country of origin.

The America Mafia already had experience of stealing high-value vehicles, modifying them and taking them across the Canadian border for resale. However, the Gambino Mafia family pioneered the export of stolen luxury cars to Saudi Arabia and Kuwait, leading other US groups to follow it into what has become a valuable Cosa Nostra income stream.

More than 300,000 vehicles go missing in the European Union each year. Most of them travel to the unregulated car markets held in countries of the former Soviet Bloc. The Russian Organizatsiya now dominates the trade in stolen vehicles. Taking orders from customers in Moscow, it is able to guarantee delivery of a specific type of vehicle within three weeks.

Amongst the most stolen marques are BMW, Mercedes and Land Rover, with vehicles stolen in Britain reappearing in Pakistan or China, having been transported in container trucks over thousands of miles. Currently, one of the most profitable, growing global markets is the theft and resale of construction industry vehicles.

for Masseria's arch-rival, Salvatore Maranzano. This led to Maranzano-backed Frank "Don Cheech" Scalise becoming boss.

Scalise did not last long either. When Maranzano was deposed by "Lucky" Luciano in 1931, members of his own family decided they had to get rid of him if their family was going to continue to exist in Luciano's new National Crime Syndicate order. Rather than rub out Scalise, they gave him the chance to step down and to be replaced by Vincent Mangano. To keep in favour with Luciano, Mangano appointed Luciano's close ally Albert "Mad Hatter" Anastasia as his underboss, despite Anastasia's role as the "Lord High Executioner" of Murder Inc.

For the next 20 years, Anastasia worked faithfully for Mangano. In 1951, however, with the backing of Frank Costello, his close pal and boss of what was then the Luciano-Masseria family (known now as the Genovese family), Anastasia decided to get rid of Mangano and his brother Philip. No one within the Mangano family dared oppose Anastasia and with Costello's help, he was recognized as the new boss of the family by the Commission.

With guidance from Costello, Anastasia expanded the family's operations, moving into drug trafficking and securing a slice of the Cosa Nostra casino action down in Atlantic City. However, partly due to the power struggle between Costello and Vito Genovese for control of the Luciano-Masseria family and partly due to Anastasia ordering the murder of a civilian who had offended him by informing on a non-Mafia related bank robber, the Commission allowed a hit on Anastasia in 1957.

Anastasia's replacement was one of his capos, Carlo Gambino, who had been part of the plot to have him rubbed out. Until his health failed him in 1975, Gambino transformed the somewhat second-rate family into the most powerful of the five New York families. He increased his slice of Atlantic City action, practically took control of the construction industry in New York, augmented the family's labour rackets, diversified into a range of legitimate businesses to aid money laundering and became a major force in narcotics.

Gambino boss Paul "Big Paul" Castellano was murdered by members of his own crime family in December 1985 to pave the way for John Gotti to begin his reign as "King of New York".

He also pioneered the racket of stealing high-class US cars and reselling them in Kuwait and other Middle Eastern countries. With allies in all the other families, he was able to survive Joe Bonanno's attempts to remove him and became the most powerful Cosa Nostra boss in America.

Before his death from a heart attack in 1976, Carlo Gambino appointed his cousin and brother-in-law, Paul Castellano, as Gambino family boss with the powerful capo Aniello Dellacroce as underboss. Castellano was not popular with the soldiers and capos under him, who felt the family was declining under his leadership. The main member of the family who wanted to get rid of Castellano was John Gotti, a Queens-based capo. He was only prevented from assassinating his boss through pressure from Dellacroce, who in return stopped Castellano acting against his young rival. Within a fortnight of Dellacroce's death, from natural causes, on December 2, 1985, Castellano and his aide Thomas Billoti lay on the street outside a Manhattan steakhouse. Gotti was now the new boss and the reign of "the Dapper Don" AKA "the King of New York" began.

In 2009 several members of the family were arrested as part of the NYPD's "Operation Pure Luck" tackling loan sharking, bribery and illegal gambling on Staten Island. In 2010, 14 members were charged and pled guilty to racketeering, extortion and sex trafficking. However, despite such a setback, under the current leadership of Domenico "Italian Dom" Cefalu who became Boss in 2011, the Gambino family remains one of the most powerful, rich and resourceful Mafia families of any era

THE BUFFALO FAMILY

In an interview for this book, an ex-FBI agent said to me, "I blame Castellammare del Golfo. If it wasn't for the godforsaken place there wouldn't be a Mafia in America." The statement is somewhat of an exaggeration, but when you examine the number of founding godfathers of Cosa Nostra families that came from this western Sicilian town, some of the agent's bitterness begins to make sense.

One Sicilian Mafiosi who left Castellammare del Golfo and ended up helping to shape the face of organized crime in the USA was Stefano Magaddino, the founder of the Buffalo crime family. Magaddino left his hometown in 1902, when his brother Pietro was murdered during a vendetta against his family. He soon became part of the Black Hand and other extortion rackets that fellow ex-citizens of Castellammare del Golfo were running at the time in New York.

In 1921, the feud that had forced Magaddino to emigrate eventually caught up with him in America. He arranged for the killing of Camillo Caizzo, the man who had murdered his brother, but within days he was wanted by the police for questioning over the killing. He was also wanted dead by Caizzo's allies. When Magaddino and his friend Gaspar Milazzo were eventually shot at, they both decided it was time leave the city. Milazzo fled to Detroit, while Magaddino ran to Buffalo in upstate

Stefano Magaddino fled a Sicilian Mafia vendetta but soon established an American powerbase by founding the Buffalo crime family, which he ran until his death from natural causes in 1974.

New York. Both men went on to found major crime families in their new locations.

During Prohibition, Buffalo and Niagara Falls were major centres for the bringing across of illegal alcohol from Canada. The Sicilian Mafia that existed in Buffalo prior to Magaddino's arrival fought a bitter war with the Ontario-based 'Ndrangheta crime group that originated from Calabria in Italy. Magaddino quickly seized a slice of the bootlegging action and when the old Sicilian Mafia boss in Buffalo, Joseph Peter DiCarlo, died in 1922, Magaddino took over his operations.

Despite constant warfare with the Calabrians from across the border, the Buffalo family, under Magaddino, became increasingly profitable and powerful, thanks to its ability to guarantee the supply of alcohol to Sicilian organized crime groups across America. Magaddino, however, also had the foresight to see that Prohibition would not last forever and diversified the family into gambling, loan sharking and heroin trafficking. He also ensured the family gained control of the Labourers Local 210 union. The family's operations expanded into Ohio and Canada, even forcing the Ontarian 'Ndrangheta to recognize Magaddino's control over much of southern Ontario and Toronto.

Although some fellow bosses blamed him for the Apalachin fiasco in 1957 (it had been his idea to meet at Joseph Barbara's estate as he had for many other meetings), Magaddino kept his place on the National Commission and a key role in Mafia politics. However, his problems with his cousin Joe Bonanno, whom he was involved in kidnapping in 1964, as part of what became known as the Banana War

between Bonanno and the Commission, weakened his standing and he and his family began to fade in importance as the 1960s drew to a close.

Magaddino's longevity as a Mafia boss – he held on to power until he was over 80 – was an amazing feat given the number of assassination attempts he survived. However, his iron will to go on forever as boss of the family he founded created massive succession problems when he eventually died from natural causes in 1974.

With Magaddino gone, the Buffalo family quickly fractured. Magaddino's underboss Sal Pieri tried to take the reigns by rubbing out longstanding capo John Cammillieri, whilst another capo Joseph Todaro decided he was best man to fill Magaddino's shoes. The bitter infighting continued until Pieri's death in 1983 when the Genovese family, that now represented the Buffalo family on the National Commission, finally got recognition for Todaro as Buffalo boss.

Joseph Todaro Jr runs the Buffalo family today. A series of federal prosecutions for racketeering, however, have hit the family hard and it has lost its union rackets and most of its Ohio operations. The late 1990s saw Buffalo soldiers dying north of the border as the Ontario 'Ndrangheta started to battle for control of its Canadian rackets. Ironically, what was once the family's greatest asset, its proximity to the US-Canadian border, may now become its Achilles heel.

Federal Agents inspect one of the many customized vehicles of the sort used by the Mob for smuggling illegal booze from Canada into Buffalo during the Prohibition years.

THE NEW ORLEANS MAFIA

The disparate early organizations from which the Cosa Nostra eventually emerged went by different names in the various cities and states of America. In New England it was known as "The Office". In Chicago it was "The Outfit". In Buffalo, people simply referred to "The Arm". However, in New Orleans, right from the start, even the authorities referred to it as "The Mafia". Despite the mythology built up by hundreds of movies and TV shows, the Mafia's rise to power in America did not start in New York or Chicago. It started in the Deep South of America – New Orleans.

In the 1880s and 1890s, more Italian immigrants arrived in New Orleans than New York. Until the beginning of the twentieth century New Orleans boasted the largest and most poverty-struck Italian ghettoes in America. It is therefore no surprise that Sicilian Mafiosi had a strong, organized presence in the city by 1890. Two major groups who came from different towns back in Sicily – the Matranga and Provenzano families – fought for control of the Italian enclaves and of the city's docks.

In 1888, the Matrangas had forced the Provenzanos out of the docks and were growing rich by putting a "tax" on any boat wishing to unload its cargo. On May 5, a group of Provenzano hitmen ambushed and killed three Matrangas, including the brother of the group's boss, Charles Matranga. The killers got away with it, further convincing Charles Matranga that New Orleans Police Chief David Hennessey was in the pay of the Provenzanos. This conviction grew when Hennessey announced that he had proof the Matrangas were "part of a criminal society called The Mafia" and would soon be exposing them.

New Orleans Mafia boss Carlos Marcello repeatedly invoked the Fifth Amendment and avoided saying anything of importance when he was called before the Senate Rackets Committee in 1961.

Heart of Hoodoo – the French Quarter in New Orleans has long been the centre of both magical and Mafia-related activities that have impacted on the history of the city.

Hennessey was shot on October 15, 1890 – his dying words were: "The Dagos did it". Charles Matranga and 18 of his men were arrested the next day. When all but three of the men were acquitted at trial, a lynch mob, inflamed by a rabid press and New Orleans' virulently racist and anti-Italian Mayor Joseph A. Shakespeare, stormed the jail where the men were being held. Two of the men were hung from lampposts, one was shot and then hung and seven others were lined up against a wall and died in a shower of bullets. Matranga, however, survived, went into hiding and rebuilt his family into the dominant Mafia presence in New Orleans.

Charles Matranga died in 1922 and was succeeded by Corrado Giacona, who remained boss until his death in 1944. During his reign, the New Orleans Mafia became increasingly involved with key New York mob figures, most notably Frank Costello. After Giacona's successor, Sylvestro Carollo, was deported to Sicily in 1947, young capo Carlos Marcello took over the family. With backing and investment from the Luciano-Masseria family in New York, Marcello expanded operations not only in New Orleans, but also into territories, such as Dallas. He carved out a large narcotics, gambling, prostitution, pornography and union racketeering empire. Marcello also discovered a novel source of income – helping the CIA in their campaign against Fidel Castro.

Marcello was one of the Mafia leaders who faced severe problems from Robert F. Kennedy's anti-Mafia drive. As Attorney General, Kennedy got Marcello temporarily deported and was constantly breathing down neck of the New Orleans family. Marcello made threats against both Bobby and John Kennedy. Many believe – based on strong circumstantial evidence – that Marcello led elements of the Mafia in playing a key role in the assassination of JFK in Dallas on November 22, 1963.

Whether or not he played a part in JFK's murder, the accusation focussed further unwanted attention on Marcello, especially when he was named by a Congressional Committee in the 1970s as a suspect in conspiracies to kill both Kennedy and Martin Luther King. With such a high profile, Marcello and his operations were prime targets for FBI sting operations, and in 1982, he eventually was sent to prison for insurance scams and trying to bribe a judge.

Marcello's mind disintegrated in prison and he was released in 1993. He died soon after leaving a $60 million fortune to his heirs. Without his strong leadership, the New Orleans family has suffered badly and been significantly cut in size, due to pressure from both other Mafia families and non-Mafia organized crime groups.

THE DETROIT MAFIA

During the Roaring Twenties and the heyday of Prohibition, the Mafia was on the rise in almost every city in the US. One place where Sicilian and other Italian-American organized crime groups were relegated to second rank players, however, was Detroit. Between 1919 and 1931, Motor City crime was dominated by the Purple Gang – a ruthless mob of mainly Jewish gangsters.

The Purple Gang started out as a street gang from Detroit's lower east side. Up until Prohibition, their crimes were limited to extortion and armed robbery. The origin of the group's name is disputed, but many claim it comes from one of their victims who said, "They're rotten all the way, purple like the colour of bad meat".

When Prohibition came into force, the Purples quickly moved into bootlegging. A lot of illegal drink was flowing into America from Canada via the Detroit River. To ensure a steady supply, the gang

operated on both sides of the border, establishing a team to work out of Windsor, Ontario to provide security against the 'Ndrangheta gangs, who were powerful in Canada.

The Purple Gang dominated crime in Detroit through a body count that rivalled that of any other mob in the country. During their time in charge of Motown, they were responsible for more than 500 murders. Some of the bloodiest action revolved around a split in the gang that saw the formation of a rival mob – the Little Jewish Navy. However, many of those who caught the Purples' bullets were from Sicilian gangs who were also trying to get a slice of the bootlegging action. The Purples' reputation for death and proficiency with guns spread throughout the underworld. It even saw them being called upon by Al Capone, when he wanted an out-of-town team for a hit. Criminal folklore has it that Purple Gang members Harry Keywell, Philip Keywell and George Lewis were shooters for Capone at the St Valentine's Day Massacre.

When the Italian-Jewish partnership of "Lucky" Luciano and Meyer Lansky established the National Crime Syndicate in 1931, they immediately recognized the power of the Purples and asked them to join. This ushered in a new era of peace in Detroit with the Sicilian Mafia family that was established by Gaspar Milazzo, but at the time run by Joseph Zerilli, working closely with the Purples. As Prohibition ended, most of the Purples left Detroit to take up roles in the Syndicate

Leading Detroit Mafia man Anthony "Tony Jack" Giacalone (right) leaves the offices of the FBI with his attorney after refusing to cooperate with their investigation into the disappearance of Jimmy Hoffa.

elsewhere – many went to work for Lansky's gambling empire or found an outlet for their talents at Murder Inc.

With the effective end of the Purples in 1933, Zerilli's Mafia family became the underworld power in Motor City. Over the next couple of decades he expanded into narcotics, illegal bookmaking and loan-sharking. He built up a massive prostitution empire and dominated Detroit's powerful unions, especially the International Brotherhood of Teamsters and its leader Jimmy Hoffa.

Zerilli ran a tight ship. He and all of his trusted capos, such as William "Black Bill" Tocco, "Scarface Joe" Bommarito and Peter Licavolli, were said to have their roots in Terrasina, Sicily. There was almost no internal dissent, and unlike other godfathers, Zerilli had no problem ensuring his son, Anthony, became boss after he stepped down in 1975. His incredible four decades in control meant other Mafia bosses viewed him as an elder statesman and he was given a seat on the National Commission.

The Detroit Mafia's problems only really began on July 30, 1975 when the "disappearance" of Jimmy Hoffa put them in the national spotlight. A note found on Hoffa's desk read: "TG – 2pm – Red Fox". The Red Fox was the restaurant he was last seen alive at and TG was Anthony "Tony" Giacalone – a friend of Hoffa and trusted Zerilli family aide. In 2003, DNA tests proved that Hoffa had been in a car that, at the time, was owned by Giacalone.

With the FBI breathing down their necks over Hoffa and union control, the Detroit family had to pull out of some of its most profitable rackets, but even that did not help Anthony Zerilli and underboss Jack Tocco to avoid the racketeering and gambling charges that put them behind bars. Today, continuing FBI action against the Detroit family is constantly chipping away at its power and profits, leaving it a battered shade of its former influence and importance within Cosa Nostra.

THE L.A. MAFIA

Amongst their fellow crime families, the L.A. Mafia has a reputation for being small-time, ineffectual and something of a joke. Both fellow Mafiosi and crime fighters tend to refer to them as the "Mickey Mouse Mafia". When the Los Angeles police launched an operation against their bookmaking rackets in 1984, L.A. Police Chief Daryl Gates called it "Operation Lightweight".

Given the fact that California is one of the richest states in America, the Mafia should have been able to boom alongside the state's economy. There was nothing in the L.A. Mafia's origins to suggest they wouldn't follow the rise to power that the Mafia had experienced elsewhere. In the late 1920s, successful Sicilian bootlegging operations had been brought under the control of Anthony Rizzoti, better known

Despite his high profile and attention from the police, Jewish LA gang boss Mickey Cohen was still able to pose problems for the Cosa Nostra outfit in Los Angeles.

as Jack Dragna. Through the front of an organization he formed called the "Italian Protective League", his crime family had its fingers in all the usual rackets.

However, Dragna never seemed to find the strength to keep other families out of his territory – it was the Chicago Outfit that were notorious for attempting to put the lucrative squeeze on Hollywood's film studios. Dragna also seemed incapable of wiping out the independent L.A. organized crime group run by Mickey Cohen, whose set-up included both Jewish and Italian mobsters.

After Dragna's death, the family was run by lawyer Frank Desimone, who died in 1968, and then Nick Licata. When Licata died in 1974, the family came under the control of Jack's ineffectual nephew, Louie Tom Dragna. His weak grip on affairs allowed out-of-town mobster Jimmy Fratianno to come into the fold. Unfortunately, Fratianno was also an FBI informant and soon many of the L.A. Mafia were behind bars. In the 1980s, the family tried to rebuild under new boss Peter Milano, but were again weakened when Milano went to jail 1988 for racketeering. Today, the L.A. Mafia is believed to be a small, stretched organization with little influence outside of the vice, gambling, nightclub and narcotics operations it still controls in areas such as the notorious Sunset Strip.

Many top Mafia players have been caught on FBI wiretaps being openly contemptuous about the Mafia across the whole of California. Before he muscled his way into the Los Angeles Mafia, Jimmy "the

Weasel" Fratianno commented, "Them guys in San Francisco and San Jose wouldn't last two minutes if some real workers moved into their towns. Maybe we ought to move in and take over. Knock off a couple of guys. Scare the rest shitless."

Another mob figure once remarked about the L.A. Mafia, "The only thing they did was kill Superman". This is thought to be a reference to the suspicious death of actor George Reeves, in 1959, who played the Man of Steel in the 1950s TV series *The Adventures of Superman*. Although thought at the time to be suicide, forensic evidence strongly suggests murder and there are persistent underworld stories that Reeves was murdered by a Mafia hitman as a favour to a Hollywood producer whose wife was sleeping with the actor.

Another notorious murder that drew attention to the L.A. Mafia was the killing of Johnny Stompanato. Ex-Marine Stompanato had left the US Army and become a Mafia soldier in Dragna's L.A. crime family. The handsome, but brutal, thug became the lover of Hollywood actress Lana Turner in 1957. It was a tempestuous affair. In 1958, during a violent argument with Turner, her 14-year-old daughter Cheryl Crane rushed to her mother's defence and plunged a 10-inch kitchen knife into Stompanato's stomach. Such a high profile death brought the L.A. family under further media scrutiny at a time shortly after its then boss, Frank Desimone, had hit the headlines for being arrested at the disastrous Apalachin meeting. The manner of Stompanato's passing also brought further scorn from Mafiosi across the country, who said it was proof that "The L.A. guys can't even win a fight with a little girl".

Not everyone shares the conventional view that the L.A. Mafia has been, and always will be, small-time. One FBI agent told me, "They say the greatest trick the devil ever played was convincing people he didn't exist. It's the same with some of the L.A. crews. Being the 'Mickey Mouse' guys gets them a lot of incident room. And every time you underestimate these guys, that's when they hit you in the ass".

L.A. Mafia soldier Johnny Stompanato was murdered by the 14-year-old daughter of his lover, Hollywood star Lana Turner.

THE MAFIA AND LAS VEGAS

Bugsy Siegel (left) and Hollywood hard man George Raft (right) were close friends, explaining Raft's frequent trips to Las Vegas to help publicize Bugsy's casino The Flamingo.

The Mafia made Las Vegas. Even scraping away the vast mythology that has built up about Cosa Nostra's involvement in Nevada's "Sin City", the facts speak for themselves. Without the massive Mafia investment in Las Vegas, it is unlikely the obscure Nevada town would have become the globe's unofficial gambling capital.

The groundwork for what would become, for many years, the Mafia's biggest moneymaker since Prohibition was laid in 1931 when the Nevada authorities, desperate for revenue, legalized gambling. The only casinos that sprang up in the wake of the law change were small operations that had more in common with their Wild West forebears than anything approaching the luxury resort hotels Las Vegas is now famous for. The advent of plentiful electricity and water, thanks to the completion of the Hoover Dam, made expansion possible, but by the early 1940s, only two hotel complexes, both with less than 110 rooms, had been built. Las Vegas was still basically a dusty, backwater town in the middle of the desert.

"Lucky" Luciano and Meyer Lansky had sent out Benjamin "Bugsy" Siegel to Los Angeles in the 1930s. He was in California to run the

Syndicate's gambling operations on the West Coast and to set up a narcotics smuggling network bringing in dope from Mexico. In 1942, Lansky sent Siegel to scout out the possibilities for expanding into Nevada, given the legalized status of gambling in the state. While in Nevada, Siegel ran into a businessman called Billy Wilkerson and instantly shared his vision of what Las Vegas could become.

Siegel approached Lansky, Luciano, Frank Costello and other mobsters to loan him $2 million so that he could build a luxury resort hotel and casino. He planned to call it The Flamingo, after his mistress Virginia Hill's nickname. In 1943, the leading mobsters gave Siegel his loan, although most of the money came from Siegel's boyhood friend Lansky. Costs spiralled, however, during the building

Frank Sinatra and Rat Pack buddies Dean Martin and Sammy Davis Jr help celebrate the eleventh anniversary of The Sands Hotel in Las Vegas, owned at the time by Sinatra's friends in the Mafia.

ILLEGAL GAMBLING

Gambling has long been associated with the underworld. Criminal groups were usually connected to the collection of gambling debts and dishing out punishment to those who tried to evade paying. Some criminal networks, such as the Yakuza, even trace their origins to ancient guilds of gamblers that existed in the medieval period.

Illegal gambling itself has been a major source of income for organized crime groups ever since governments began to restrict and tax gambling, a notable trend in many countries from the end of the eighteenth century onwards. However, the public attitude towards operations such as illegal bookmaking and slot machines has been more tolerant than towards any other area of organized criminal activity.

Gambling rackets often revolve around the running of illegal lotteries within impoverished areas. The ability of those on low incomes to bet small amounts, even on credit, for potential tax-free winnings a thousand times their initial stake, continues to prove attractive across the globe. Known in America as the "Numbers Game" and believed to have originated in black neighbourhoods in the nineteenth century, they have grown into a modern-day illicit activity worth several billion dollars in the USA alone.

Criminal syndicates have always been keen to invest in legitimate gambling as it traditionally allows for a relatively easy way to legitimize illicit profits from other activities. Although forced out of most legal gaming and betting businesses in the Western world, organized crime has benefited hugely from the relatively recent proliferation of Internet betting.

of The Flamingo and Siegel eventually owed his Syndicate pals more than $6 million.

Once it was built, Siegel used his network of Hollywood contacts to attract famous people, such as actor George Raft, to The Flamingo in order to give it some publicity. This was desperately needed as it was losing money and Siegel was under pressure from his investors. By 1947 it was making a small profit and Bugsy thought he was in the clear. Unfortunately, Lansky and Luciano had already decided he had been stealing from them over construction costs. With genuine sorrow, they decided that he had to be punished. After his brutal slaying in June 1947, Lansky assumed control of The Flamingo and within a year it was making massive profits.

Lansky then invested heavily in the Thunderbird Hotel and bought a controlling interest in the Sands Hotel, while the Cleveland Mafia family bought into the Desert Inn and Frank Costello took a massive chunk of the Tropicana. With the millions they invested, the Mafia made Vegas boom. They were also responsible for bringing much of the entertainment talent to the resort. It is no secret that the Mafia helped bring Sinatra and the Rat Pack to Las Vegas in the 1950s and 1960s by giving him a cut of the Sands Hotel action.

The fortunes the Mafia made from Las Vegas were not restricted to the legitimate profits their investments in the casino made. Often, as secret investors, they used other means to collect on their capital. Most popular of these was "the skim" where millions a year were obtained without the IRS or anyone else ever having a clue. A percentage of the huge amounts of cash that went through the casinos counting rooms were never officially counted, but instead went straight to the Mafia. The casinos in Las Vegas also proved a great way of laundering money.

Although eccentric billionaire Howard Hughes notably failed in his attempt to clean up Las Vegas, he did put pressure on the FBI to clamp down on Mafia activities in the city. Through the 1970s, a series of wiretap and surveillance operations led to successful prosecutions and a massive clampdown on skimming and laundering, while Gaming Commission pressure led to the end of Mafia investment in the casinos. The Mob is still in Vegas, but these days they aren't earning a fraction of what they used to.

THE MAFIA AND THE MOVIES

If movies are America's true cultural jugular, then much of the blood pumping through it comes from the crimes of Cosa Nostra. Hollywood has enjoyed a very long and profitable love affair with the Mafia for two reasons. First, Cosa Nostra organized crime is so deeply rooted in the last 100 years of American history it would be difficult to ignore it and still accurately reflect life in the USA. Secondly, and more importantly to studios, people have an undying fascination with the underworld, and this means Mafia movies make money.

The love-in between Hollywood and the Mafia began in the 1920s. It has always been a two-way affair. Even the early Prohibition gangsters enjoyed what they perceived as the reflected glamour of seeing their crimes portrayed on the silver screen. Some of the earliest silent films depicting the mob even starred an actual former gangster – Joe Brown – who traded off his friendship with Al Capone.

Brown was not the last member of organized crime to be seduced by the idea of becoming part of Hollywood itself. Small-time hoodlum turned actor George Raft not only starred in massive Hollywood hits depicting gangsters, such as *Scarface* in 1932, but maintained close friendships with several mobsters. In the early 1940s, he even managed to get his good friend "Bugsy" Siegel a few screen tests.

The Godfather defined the image of the Mafia in the minds of the public for decades, but Mafia lobbying ensured the words Mafia and Cosa Nostra were not used in the film.

Throughout the 1930s, hundreds of movies about gangsters and the rising tide of organized crime were turned out by the leading studios, often making massive stars of their actors, such Edward G. Robinson. However, many filmmakers were frustrated by having to show the Mafia as anti-heroes. The Motion Picture Production Code even ensured the ending of *Scarface* was changed and that the movie had to carry the subtitle *Shame of the Nation*.

In an era where even the head of the FBI denied the existence of any organization called the Mafia, it was not surprising that movies never really touched on the origins and true nature of Cosa Nostra. All that changed in 1972 with the release of *The Godfather*, based on Mario Puzo's best-selling novel of the same name. After the exposés the Mafia had suffered since the 1950s, starting with the Kefauver hearings and the Apalachin fiasco, a truer picture depicting the mob was overdue. Mafia boss Joe Colombo's Italian-American Civil Rights League,

however, brought so much pressure to bear on Paramount Pictures ahead of the release of *The Godfather* that they agreed to cut out any use of the words Cosa Nostra and Mafia from the film.

Loosely based on many real life Cosa Nostra personalities and events, The Godfather was a massive success, especially with the Mafia. Undercover detectives have reported that Mafiosi looked to the film to gain inspiration and instruction on how they should behave. While attacked in some quarters as a massive exercise in creating a positive mythology for the Mafia, boss Joe Bonanno claimed the real reason the film was successful was because "It has to do with family pride and personal honour. It portrayed people with a strong sense of kinship surviving in a cruel world".

The Godfather and its first sequel *The Godfather – Part II* in 1974, unleashed a flood of Mafia movies. Two of the best of them – *Casino* (1995) and *Goodfellas* (1990) – were based on books by Nicholas Pileggi. While *Goodfellas* lacks any of the glamour of *The Godfather*, it did portray the real life story of Henry Hill with a high degree of accuracy. It neatly captured the treachery, petty politics, greed, casual violence and drudgery of life in the lower ranks of the Mafia. By the 1990s, the Mafia was even suitable as a subject for television. The hit drama show *The Sopranos* depicted the working and home life of the very believable New Jersey capo Tony Soprano.

The movies and more lately television, have both charted and shaped the American public's understanding of the Mafia as the dominant force in US organized crime. Cosa Nostra has always been more sympathetically portrayed than other organized crime groups (just compare Al Pacino's Cosa Nostra-based movies to his role as a Cuban Mafia boss in the 1983 version of *Scarface*). This is not the result of a media conspiracy; it merely reflects America's complex love-hate relationship with the mob.

COSA NOSTRA TODAY

Francis Ford Coppola is the only film director to have made a series of movies approaching a full, fictional history of Cosa Nostra from its roots in Sicily and New York's Little Italy to modern-day corporate boardrooms. Of the three films in The Godfather trilogy, it is the underrated *The Godfather – Part III* that best captures the essence of the American Mafia as it stands today – an organization in transition, struggling to both retain and transcend its origins.

Since the mid-1980s, many have predicted the fall of the American Mafia. Before he left his position as US Attorney for the Southern District of New York in 1989, the former New York Mayor, Rudolph Giuliani, predicted that the Gambino family, and the other New York Cosa Nostra families, would soon be "Reduced to the level of a mere street gang".

The Sopranos television series made a huge star of James Gandolfini (left) for his portrayal of fictional Mob boss Tony Soprano and redefined how movies and television show the Mafia today.

Others in law enforcement went even further, talking of a "Cosa Nostra free USA". The public and media thought they had good reason to believe them. Giuliani had spearheaded a campaign that saw the bosses and underbosses of the five major families of New York in jail. Elsewhere in America, the FBI used surveillance and numerous Mafia traitors to virtually imprison a whole generation of Mafiosi.

Yet declarations of victory were premature. What some in authority saw as Cosa Nostra's death throes were in fact the painful struggles of an organization that was evolving for life in the twenty-first century. Their recent policy of accepting new family members direct from the streets of Palermo, Corleone and Trapani in Sicily, instead of the streets of New York, was not an act of desperation – it was a clever recruitment shortage fix. It made tough Mafia soldiers available to work rackets that were unknown to the police and it also allowed for a massive replenishing of numbers that had been depleted through the jailing of original members. .

Their tight hierarchical structure and organizational methods have proved to be the most valuable part of Cosa Nostra's Sicilian heritage. Its resilience may be testament to its possible origins as a Sicilian resistance force, fighting superior aggressors. Wherever it comes from, however, it has certainly stood the Mafia in good stead with its ongoing war with the FBI. As one FBI agent told me "I don't think we realized, when we put the bosses and other leaders away, that the families would just carry on. New bosses, underbosses and capos just kept on emerging. We were taking out men, but not touching the structure."

A strong example of this is provided by the recent resilience of the DeCavalcante crime family – the New Jersey Cosa Nostra outfit that inspired hit TV drama *The Sopranos*. From 1999–2005, 45 of its members were convicted and imprisoned on charges ranging from murder to fraud and extortion. To avoid jail, even one of its acting bosses, Vincent "Vinny Ocean" Palermo broke the Mafia code and became an FBI informant whose information almost completely eradicated the DeCavalcante organization. Yet the hierarchical structure and methods of the Mafia quickly came into play. Joseph "Joe "Miranda, a soldier in the organization stepped up as acting boss and promptly recruited 12 new members into the family. By the time he stepped down to become the underboss and let Sicilian immigrant Francesco Gurraci become boss in 2006, the DeCavalante family was already back on its feet.

Future stories about Cosa Nostra crimes will have an increasingly global dimension, such as importing illegal human organs that have been culled from the street children of Brazil. There will also be headlines about their massive cyber-frauds and stock market manipulations. New bosses will emerge, college-educated but just as tough, callous and blood-soaked as the first Sicilian gang leaders of the 1920s, to lead their families in both traditional rackets and cutting-edge crimes. The growing trend of cross-family working teams may lead to new families arising and, within a few years, there may even

Vincent "Vinny Ocean" Palermo squealed to FBI and was placed in a witness protection programme. He came back into the daylight in 2008 when the strip-club he was running in Texas was busted for prostitution.

be war between the new Sicilian recruits and their established American bosses.

In 1931, when Salvatore Maranzano shaped the structure of the Sicilian Mafia in the USA and named it Cosa Nostra, he could have had no idea that he was helping to launch a specifically American Mafia that would endure well into the twenty-first century.

THE YAKUZA AND JAPANESE ORGANIZED CRIME

3

"Nowadays everyone is afraid of the Yakuza."
Juzo Itami, Japanese film director

With a history dating to the Samurai era, the Yakuza – Japan's notorious organized outlaw gangs and criminal clans – are one of the world's oldest and most strongly established criminal organizations. From the heart of government and multi-national corporations to shadow-filled city alleys, the influence of the Yakuza is felt across Japan. With its ancient ceremonies and bizarre sub-culture, there is no doubting the Yakuza are one of the most fascinating criminal groups in the world.

A few years ago, my brother designed, built and ran a nightclub in the neon Babylon of Tokyo's Roppongi district. It gave me a chance to ask someone I trusted, and who had experienced Japanese streetlife first-hand, if what the authorities had told me about Japanese organized crime was actually true.

Was it accurate that, despite the large number of Yakuza, there was very little street crime? Did some members of the Yakuza have business cards they would give out with rank, clan and contact information? Did they sometimes act as a form of shadow government and police in certain areas? Were they as lionized in popular culture in Japan as they were in the West?

THE ORIGINS OF THE YAKUZA

The estimated 150,000 members in the 2,500 criminal gangs that collectively form the Japanese Yakuza make it the world's largest organized crime network if the figures from Japan's National Institute of Police Science are correct. Yet for many in Japan, the size of the Yakuza represents not a source of shame, but one of pride.

One of the prime reasons for this sense of pride is the alleged origin of the Yakuza. Many organized crime groups across the word have tried to cloak themselves in the mythology of a noble and honourable history. Claims are often made linking a criminal syndicate to an old resistance movement or society that protected the poor from feudal lords. However, in the case of the Yakuza, such seemingly fanciful claims are not always without a degree of truth.

When Tokugawa Ieyasu became Shogun in 1603 and went on to unify Japan, many samurai found themselves without a lord to fight for. These masterless warriors were known as ronin. Some formed outlaw bands that preyed upon farming communities and smaller towns. Their outrageous behaviour, overlarge swords and exaggerated form of dress earned these bands the title of kabuki-mono ("the raving ones"). To protect themselves from the raving ones, peasants and town dwellers formed gangs – machi-yokko ("Servants of the town") or otokodate ("chivalrous commoners").

As only members of the warrior class were able to carry swords, many machi-yokko and otokodate employed ronin to help defend their towns and villages. Despite claims by police scientist Kanehiro Hoshino of the National Institute of Police Science that all ronin were wiped out by 1688, many Yakuza can produce complicated genealogies linking themselves to either ronin or noted otokodate. The Yakuza claim such illustrious ancestors eventually joined up with the bakuto (gamblers guilds) and tekiya (peddlers) to form the gangs that became the Yakuza. Most Japanese choose to believe the Yakuza version of their creation rather than the views of police scientists. The tradition of otokodate and ronin may be romantic clothing for the Yakuza, but many hold on to it as a link to what is seen as a nobler past.

The name Yakuza itself comes from the worst hand in the Japanese card game Oicho-Kabu, which is played with hanafuda or kabufuda cards. In Oicho-Kabu, as in baccarat, the value of three cards is added up to give a final number. The worst hand is made up of cards eight, nine and three. In traditional Japanese counting that sequence of numbers produces the phonetic sounds *ya*, *ku* and *sa* – hence the word *ya-ku-za*. In modern Japanese counting, eight, nine and three can be pronounced *hachi-kyu-san* – a name by which the Yakuza are sometimes now called. It is not known whether the term was first used as an insult, implying that they were "worthless hands", or because it represented the bad luck of somone who had problems with them.

Feudalism ended relatively late in Japan – it wasn't until the end of the Meiji Restoration in 1869 that there was rapid industrialization of the country. The Yakuza quickly became associated with control of prostitution and gambling, extortion and loan-sharking rackets and control of construction and labour forces. In 1879, Toyama Mitsuru founded the Gen'yōsha (Dark Ocean Society). The ultra-nationlist organization was dedicated to the expansion of Japanese power to mainland Asia and a return to traditional values. It was closely associated with the paramilitary and occult Black Dragon Society.

The surrender to the Americans by Japanese officials brought the Second World War to its final close but also provided the birth of a new golden era of growth for the Yakuza.

Both groups forged links with the Yakuza, using its members to murder left-wing politicians and carry out acts of terrorism, such as the assassination of the Empress of Korea in 1895. The association led to many of the secret society trappings still present in the Yakuza today and the tradition of support from right-wing political groups that would help the Yakuza thrive for decades to come.

However, possibly the biggest boost to the modern Yakuza arrived at the end of the Second World War and during the US occupation of Japan. The breakdown in the old social order coupled with the demand from American GIs led to a boom in the "floating world" pleasure districts under Yakuza control. Strict rationing led to a massive black market that was again Yakuza-controlled. With the US installing right-wing politicians as a bulwark against Communist influence, the Yakuza found their economy blossoming and old political friends coming into power. These two factors gave them the perfect starting position to grow into the world's largest organized crime network.

A member of the Yakuza who has lost fingers through yubitsome (the ritual severing of part of a finger) shows the cost of making mistakes and bringing dishonour to his crime family.

YAKUZA RULES AND RITUALS

Criminologists and Yakuza may disagree about whether their origins can be traced back to specific noble ronin and chivalrous commoners, but there is no denying that many of the rules and rituals that are central to the vast majority of Yakuza clans have an ancient ancestry that can be traced back to medieval Japan.

The ritual element of the Yakuza has deepened the sense of mystery they have inspired in some Western reports of their activities. However, it should not be forgotten that many aspects of life in Japan are highly ritualistic – in fact, it would be far more unusual if an organization such as the Yakuza did not have a series of rituals and complicated rules governing its operation. The Yakuza are not alone in their preservation of elements of medieval life in twenty-first century Japan, but, for their members, following the formal procedures and conventions can often be a life and death matter.

The Yakuza is structured to resemble a family and its defining element is the father-son and master-pupil relationship around which the hierarchy revolves. A Yakuza boss is called oyabun, which literally means "father role", and members below him are kobun, who take the

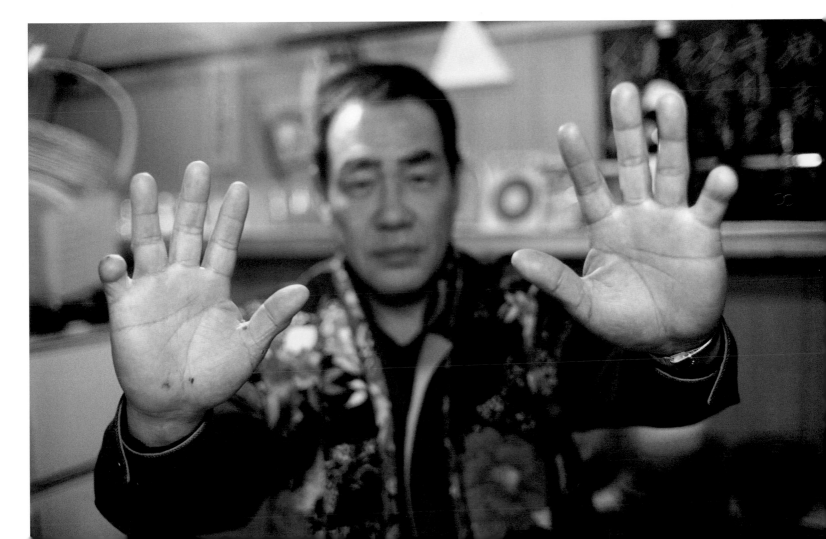

"child role". The oyabun is also sometimes known as kumicho (family head). The prospective member is introduced to the oyabun by azukarinin (guarantors) who are responsible for any problems the potential recruit causes. If the oyabun agrees to welcome the candidate into his family, a special "adoption" is held. This initiation ceremony is the most important ritual to any member of the Yakuza, forever defining the rest of their lives.

At his adoption, the fresh recruit sits facing the oyabun. His guarantors then prepare special sake by adding salt and fish scales to the rice wine and the oyabun's cup is filled to the brim to signify his status while the new boy's cup is half-filled to show his junior position. After making oaths to accept the oyabun as his new father, to obey him in every matter, to show loyalty to his new family and place it above all things, the two men sip the sake and then exchange cups. From this moment the initiate has become a kobun and is part of the family. His new father's other "children" then congratulate him. Even the oyabun's wife will now be known to the new kobun as one-san (big sister). With its stress on family, it is easy to see why the Yakuza have always been able to find recruits among orphans, bastards and outcasts.

Obedience to the oyabun is never to be questioned. Kobun are expected to go to jail for their boss and to always be prepared to be his teppodama (bullet). Any failure to carry out their duties or any act that brings dishonour to the family can result in the need for a formal apology and act of penance. This is usually carried out through yubitsume – the ritual severing of part of finger that is then presented to the oyabun. On the first offence, just the tip of the little finger is usually cut off, however, further offences can result in parts of other fingers being removed. Sometimes an azukarinin may have his finger severed instead, to atone for the mistake of the person he introduced to the family. It is thought the ritual dates to either a samurai practice of finger severing as a punishment, because it weakened a swordsman's grip, or as the traditional way the bakuto (gamblers guilds) used to mark out cheats.

Many Yakuza members revel in the notoriety of yubitsume, knowing the sight of a severed fingertip often produces better service in restaurants, bars and shops. However, many members operating abroad have taken to wearing prosthetic fingertips to hide the fact they are Yakuza from the authorities. Interestingly, when the British children's television characters Postman Pat and Bob the Builder were first introduced to Japan there were concerns that their four-digit hands could be misinterpreted and scare children.

Nearly all Yakuza clan headquarters and dormitories will display "Wakamono no Kokoroe" – a set of family rules that govern everything from how they must bow to non-Yakuza members to how to greet the oyabun. Police have noticed many of the lists now also include elements drawn from corporate employee manuals, alongside historic commandments on the correct posture to adopt when sitting on the floor.

YAKUZA TATTOOS

Contrary to what is seen in some Hollywood films, intelligence agencies do not employ heavily-tattooed operatives – they would be far too easy for any enemy to identify. The clandestine need of spies to pass undetected by the authorities is shared by criminals, a fact that only serves to make the Yakuza practice of tattooing even more puzzling to many Western criminologists. As one Scotland Yard detective once commented to me, "They cut off their fingertips and tattoo 70 per cent of their body. How easy do they want to make it for me to be able to spot a Yakuza member?"

However, to Japanese police scientists with an appreciation of the ancient art of irezumi or boshun (decorating the body), Yakuza tattoos are more than a tool to help determine membership – they are a window to the history, exploits and mindset of those involved in organized crime. Although there is strong evidence that irezumi was practised as far back as 300 BCE, the links between tattooing and the underworld in Japan date back to the Kofun Period (approximately 250–538 CE), when tattooing was practised as a form of punishment. The early criminals that received this form of punishment, however, subverted this form of branding by the authorities and turned the disfigurement into a form of bodily adornment.

It is not known for sure how this tradition was preserved into modern Yakuza practice, but it may originate from the kabuki-mono and the ronin. These brigands and warriors, who are said to have played a role in the origins of the Yakuza, were well known for sporting flamboyant tattoo designs. The tradition may have been transmitted through Yakuza interaction with the pleasure districts of the Edo period (1603–1867) – many of whose inhabitants were decorated with irezumi.

In 1868, due to their criminal connotations, the Japanese government outlawed tattoos. This merely increased their importance and appeal to the Yakuza while serving to send tattoo artists underground and into the sphere of criminal fraternities. In 1945, the US occupation forces legalized tattooing, but the stigma attached to them still remains. Even in twenty-first century Japan, many public swimming pools, bathhouses, fitness centres, steam rooms and hot springs still ban customers with tattoos from using their services.

The form of irezumi traditionally favoured by the Yakuza was either full back designs or "body suits". The body suit usually covers the arms, back, upper legs and chest, but leaves an untattooed space down the center of the body – it can cost the customer more than $30,000. While almost all Yakuza have some form of irezumi, many younger Yakuza, especially those who work outside Japan, are now wary of having large tattoos covering their bodies.

Taking more than 100 hours to complete, the process of tattooing the whole of the back is seen as a demonstration of masculinity and the ability to bear pain. The fabulous designs are not chosen purely for decoration; they have huge symbolic connotations. They are often passed from oyabun to kobun and can contain the complete history of a Yakuza family, representing its mythic lineage dating all the way back to the exploits of a noted ronin.

Many traditional Japanese tattoo artists remain quite secretive and unwilling to talk about the meaning of their art. There is, however, a famous tattoo museum in Tokyo run by Dr Fukushi, where full back skins are preserved in special flesh tanks. Japan's skin collectors, many of whom are Yakuza themselves, also have some of the best information on the meaning of irezumi. The collectors preserve the skins themselves, having often been willed them by Yakuza who want to know their tattoos will serve as a memorial to their exploits even after death. For their part, Japanese police photographically record Yakuza tattoo designs in massive books and online databases to help them identify criminals.

Alongside lineages, Yakuza irezumi often record specific crimes committed or notable victories a Yakuza member has experienced in his career. As one collector told me, "Some elements of design act like a resumé. They detail not only a Yakuza's family and rank, but also the enemies he has defeated and what deeds he has performed for his oyabun. A man's body can record more details of his activities than any evidence the police accumulate".

Members of the Yakuza take pride in their "body suits", which can act as both a living history book and criminal CV, as well as a demonstration of the wealth needed to have the body fully tattooed.

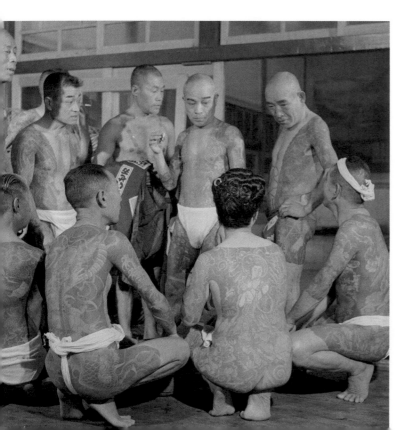

THE YAMAGUCHI-GUMI CLAN

The Yamaguchi-gumi is the largest Yakuza umbrella group in Japan. Although the actual Yamaguchi-gumi clan only numbers less than 200 members, with more than 1,000 gangs affiliated to it and tens of thousands of Yakuza under its control, it also qualifies as the world's single largest organized crime network.

Many in the Japanese law enforcement authorities are wary of providing an official estimate of the size of the Yamaguchi-gumi, for fear of being seen as alarmist. One expert at the National Institute of Police Science in Tokyo would only comment that: "It has no more than 45,000 members and a yearly income of no more than $50 billion". Whatever the exact figures are, it is certainly clear that the Yamaguchi-gumi clan deserves its reputation as the globe's premier criminal corporation.

The incredible rise of the Yamaguchi-gumi is largely down to one man – Kazua Taoka. It was thanks to Taoka that the original Yamaguchi clan went from a small gang operating in the docks of the southern port city of Kobe to an international business and criminal powerhouse with operations spreading into Asia and America.

Known in Japan as the "godfather of godfathers", there is no doubting that Kazua Taoka was one of the most important and brilliant criminal minds of the twentieth century. Like many who are recruited into the Yakuza, Taoka was an orphan. In the early 1920s, he made his way from his village to Kobe, hoping to get a job in the docks. As he was under 14, and therefore too young to be employed, he lived on the city's streets and earned a reputation as a ferocious street fighter. He came to the attention of Yamaguchi Noburu, who in 1925 assumed control of the Yamaguchi Yakuza clan founded by his father. Noburu nicknamed Taoka "The Bear" because of the way he fought. As soon as he was old enough, he was adopted into the clan and became one of Noburu's favourite "sons", working as the gang's leading enforcer for its dockland rackets.

When Noburu died in 1946, Taoka became the new kumicho (family head) of the Yamaguchi clan. A brilliant strategist and businessman, under his leadership his clan soon evolved from one of many in Kobe's docks to the city's largest gang. He accomplished this through acts such as the aggressive takeover of another city clan called Hondo-kai and the establishment of a construction firm that corruptly won all the contracts for rebuilding Kobe after the Second World War. When his domination of the local underworld was complete, Taoka set his eyes on Osaka – Japan's third largest city and its historic commercial capital.

During the 1950s, Taoka absorbed Osaka's leading Yakuza clans – Meiyu-kai and Miyamoto-gumi – into his own renamed Yamaguchi-gumi clan, and by 1964, Taoka was in control of 343 clans. He led them into new and profitable areas, such as narcotics and arms smuggling.

Alongside its massive prostitution, pornography and gambling empire, the Yamaguchi-gumi carved itself a large slice of the legitimate Japanese entertainment industry, taking over several film and record companies. Taoka's network of corrupt political contacts meant that the Yamaguchi-gumi went unopposed and also won many lucrative government contracts. By 1980, the Yamaguchi-gumi controlled more than 40 per cent of all underworld activity, laundering billions of illicit yen through its legitimate businesses, which ranged from golf courses to hospitals.

After Taoka's death in 1981, his widow, in her role as "big sister", ran the clan for a short period. It then appeared that the clan had fragmented, with Hiroshi Yamamoto taking up to 10,000 breakaway members to form the rival Ichiwa-kai umbrella group. Some, however, believe the split, and the subsequent war between the Ichiwa-kai and Yamaguchi-gumi, was nothing more than a complicated trick to make the authorities think that the clan had been weakened.

In 1989, Yoshinori Wantanabe emerged as the new, undisputed kumicho of the Yamaguchi-gumi. He showed excellent leadership skills and a flair for demonstrating the quality of ninjo (compassion) the Yakuza claim to value. When an earthquake hit Kobe in 1995, the Yamaguchi-gumi played a vital role in rescue efforts, providing relief for the survivors and pouring billions of yen into the rebuilding of the city (although the cynics say this was merely a public relations stunt). When Wantanbe retired in 2005, he passed on an even stronger organization to his successor Kenichi Shinoda, who quickly absorbed the Kokusui-kai gang from Tokyo along with its lucrative portfolio of criminal assetts. Under Shinoda, the clan continues to expand and strive towards even greater global crime and business domination.

ARMS SMUGGLING

The arms trade is one of the oldest technology-driven industries in the world. Conflict and warfare always creates a market for weaponry, especially where advances in weapon technology can give one side a dramatic advantage. During the twentieth century, the arms trade became increasingly regulated and controlled by nation states wishing to limit the spread of power that certain weapons could confer.

The demand for illicit arms from outside a country's own borders is heightened when one side of the conflict happens to be a rebel organization that is denied access to weaponry because they do not fit within the acceptable customer profile imposed by international law. Organized crime, however, has no qualms about selling weapons of any type to anyone, in some cases even supplying both sides in a conflict. Profit is their only motive.

From the Spanish Civil War onwards, the involvement of organized criminal gangs in arms smuggling has been crucial to the continuation of numerous conflicts across the world. However, it was with the collapse of Communism in the Soviet Union and the Balkan Wars in the early 1990s that there was a massive evolution in the nature of the market. Suddenly, it became easy for organized criminal gangs to obtain the latest sophisticated weaponry. Everything from combat helicopters, Scud missiles and nuclear material were added to their staple stockpiles of guns and explosives.

Alongside supplying terrorist networks and rogue states, organized criminal gangs also smuggle arms to countries such as Japan, where gun control inflates the cost of automatic weapons and bullets that are worth only dollars elsewhere.

THE INAGAWA-KAI CLAN

The only figure in twentieth-century Japanese organized crime whose story comes close to matching the remarkable success of Kazua Taoka is Kakuji Inagawa – the first head of the Inagawa-kai Yakuza clan. It is fitting, therefore, that Japanese cinema's closest equivalent to *The Godfather*, entitled *Shura no Mure* (*A Band of Daredevils*), is loosely based on Inagawa's colourful life.

Trying to sort the fact from all the fiction about Inagawa's rise to criminal power and his role as the "elder statesman" of the Yakuza, is not an easy task. All that can be said with any certainty is that he was born in 1915 to a well-educated, but poor, family from Yokohama. His father died while he was still a boy, and so the young judo student earned money to support his mother as an enforcer for a bakuto (Yakuza gambling gang).

During the Second World War, Inagawa formed his own gang, from street fighters and illegal gamblers, to take on the Korean and Chinese gangs that controlled Yokohama's black market. Legend has it that, after his gang forced all the others out of operation, Inagawa significantly lowered black market prices for food and other essentials as an act of compassion, while still ensuring a healthy profit was made. Inagawa came to the attention of Tsuruoka Masajiro, the leading Yakuza figure in the city, and Masajiro began to tutor him in strategy and organization.

By 1945, Inagawa's group – known as the Kakusei-kai – were one of the strongest Yakuza forces in the city. From an initial control over

The seedy dazzle of neon nightlife, peepshows and hostess bars in the Kabukicho, Roppongi and Shinjuku districts of Tokyo still provides a massive and steady income for the Inagawa-Kai Clan.

gambling, the Kakusei-kai branched out into prostitution, pornography and extortion. While the local police were acquiescent to Inagawa's growing power, the US Consul General stationed in Yokohama warned their superiors about his strength and potential danger, sending a cable to Washington highlighting that "The activities of this gang range from blackmail and intimidation to control and direction of bands of thieves".

In 1960, the Tokyo Metropolitan Police estimated that Kakusei-kai and its affiliated Yakuza clans controlled most of the gambling in Tokyo, Yokohama and the northern island of Hokkaido. Facing increasing pressure from the police, Inagawa changed the group's name to Kinsei-kai and sought to have it granted political status as an anti-Communist organization. He also tried to form alliances with other Yakuza leaders to bring about his vision of a unified Yakuza. However, his criminal career was interrupted by a prison sentence that saw him spend his years until 1972 behind bars in Fukushima Prison.

When he emerged, he found the Kinsei-kai a shadow of its former self. A lesser man may have retired as this point, but not Inagawa. He had spent his time in prison studying business culture and management techniques. He reorganized his clan to mimic the structure of a successful corporation and secured an alliance with his biggest competitor – the Yamaguchi-gumi clan. He moved heavily into legitimate business and narcotics and began an aggressive foreign expansion programme – especially targeting the US. By the end of the 1970s, the now renamed Inagawa-kai was once again one of the most powerful forces in Japanese organized crime.

With the emergence of the Japanese Red Army – a Communist terrorist group – in the 1970s, both politicians and fellow Yakuza bosses accepted Inagawa's idea that the Yakuza could be a bulwark against Communism. He told fellow crime bosses, "We bakuto cannot walk in broad daylight. But if we unite and become a wall to stop Communism we can be of service to the nation". There is no doubt his anti-Communist actions greatly enhanced both the Yakuza's political influence and its wider public reputation.

Inagawa was a man of great personal charm. He was known for his humour (not a common trait amongst men of his ilk and power) and seemed to many of his countrymen to represent a vanishing tradition of honour. He was also a modernizer, frowning on such traditional practices as yubitsume. He was succeeded by Susumi Ishii, who helped the clan to solidify its legitimate business empire throughout the 1980s.

Upon his death in 1990, Inagawa's son, Toi Inagawa, became the new head of the crime family. By the time of Toi's death in 2005, he had solidified an empire that mixed illegal enterprises with building hospitals, golf courses and hotels. The clan played a significant role in bringing relief to areas impacted by the 2011 earthquake and tsunami which hit Japan and continues to successfully blend being both a crime syndicate and a growing business corporation. If Inagawa's grandson, Hideki Inagawa, eventually heads the clan, he will be in charge of one of Japan's most powerful, if shadowy, enterprises.

BŌSŌZOKU BIKER GANGS

The noise is deafening. The sound of 25 specially adapted mufflers growl in a rumbling cacophony, as a fleet of black and silver motorbikes crawls along a Tokyo street at five miles an hour. The motorcyclists are all teenagers, dressed in the same black uniform, emblazoned with characters proclaiming: Black Ghost Squad.

Some of the troupe carries Japanese flags, to which ultra-nationalist slogans and even lyrics culled from Japanese-style mod songs have been added. Other riders carry spears and shout obscenities, daring anyone to come out and fight with them. As they drive by one business a Molotov cocktail is thrown. Suddenly the engines scream to life and the bikers roar away, driving in a street-wide formation at terrifying speed. This may sound like the panels of a manga cartoon, or a scene culled from some animé echoing the look of the hit movie *Akira*, but this is no cyberpunk fantasy, this is an everyday urban scene in cities across Japan in the twenty-first century. This is the reality of the bōsōzoku biker gangs.

Yet the bōsōzoku are not just a worrying trend in juvenile delinquency, they are a growing and increasingly important element of organized crime within Japan. Beyond their stylized and frightening façade, many bōsōzoku function as the Yakuza's drug distributors, enforcers and a prime recruiting ground for future kobun.

Bosōzoku means "running tribe" and describes a collection of rebellious teenagers with a passion for motorbikes and causing trouble. The first bōsōzoku biker gangs emerged in the late 1950s. They were originally called kaminari-zoku (lightning tribes), were few in number and did little more than indulge in their passion for fascistic uniforms and shinai bōsō – driving at high speeds down streets in formation.

Over the years, the gangs became more numerous and more extreme in behaviour. Whilst many bōsōzoku did little more than pose and develop new subset groups, such as the rolling-zuku (who specialize in driving fast on curving mountain roads) and the roulette-zuku (who ride around and around raised circular highways) a darker side began to emerge. By the 1970s, a thriving subculture existed, which can only be described as resembling the droogs from *A Clockwork Orange* on motorbikes. Gang warfare became commonplace, as did vandalism. It was at this point that the bōsōzoku began to interest the Yakuza.

The Yakuza had traditionally recruited the bulk of their ranks from the outcasts of Japanese society. They provided a home to orphans, a career path for burakumin (discriminated communities) who could not get work, and new fathers to those stigmatized by being bastards. By the early 1970s, state orphanages and new anti-discrimination laws had drastically cut the potential recruiting pool. However, in the bōsōzoku they saw young, impressionable teenagers who had already rejected conventional society and were gravitating to a role in

Whilst the Japanese youth biker gangs may read like something out of *A Clockwork Orange*, the bōsōzoku have become a major recruiting ground for the modern Yakuza.

organized crime. As one senior Tokyo Metropolitan Police officer rather indelicately put it, "The Yakuza have always taken in bastards. Where else do you find bastards these day but in bōsōzoku?"

As well as being the perfect subculture to scout for future tough fighters and law-breakers, the Yakuza also saw the potential of exploiting the age of the gangs. With the Japanese penal code not considering those under 20 years of age, they could be used to carry out acts of intimidation, harassment and other crimes with less fear of prosecution. The Yakuza also recognized that the bōsōzoku could be used as drug distributors – especially of methamphetamines, the most popular form of illegal drug used in Japan.

Instead of paying bōsōzoku to carry out these actions, the Yakuza decided to impose a "road tax" on bikers for riding within their territory. Thousands of yen a month could be charged, but they would give the teenagers a chance to pay off this debt by performing jobs for the Yakuza. In return for payment of the road tax, the Yakuza would use their law enforcement contacts to reduce police harassment of the bōsōzoku. While the bōsōzoku were not afraid of the law, they were afraid of the Yakuza and most gangs complied with the arrangement. This set-up also gave Yakuza head-hunters the perfect opportunity to spot any criminal talent among the biker gang members. It is an association that has brought fresh blood into the Yakuza and seems set to thrive as long as the bōsōzoku continue to ride.

KOREAN YAKUZA

Whether it originated out of purely practical need, or was part of the ancient code of the bakuto (gamblers guilds) or tekiya (peddlers), the Yakuza tradition of accepting those rejected by society into their crime families has proved one of Japanese organized crime's greatest assets throughout its history.

Alongside orphans, bastards and those disowned by their blood families, Yakuza have always shown a willingness to admit members of Japan's burakumin (discriminated communities) into their ranks. Even when the burakumin were more commonly called eta (full of filth) and faced discrimination of the worst kind, the Yakuza were prepared to call them "brother" and "son".

The largest burakumin community present in Japan over the last century has been composed of ethnic Koreans, who even today have to constantly fight against the racist attitudes of many Japanese people. Ironically, the Yakuza played a significant role in the conditions of history that mean that more than 620,000 Zainichi Koreans (resident Koreans) are living in Japan today. The allying of the Yakuza to the Black Dragon Society and Gen'yosha (Dark Ocean Society) in the nineteenth century helped to create the political climate that saw Japan annex Korea in 1910. The Yakuza had acted as terrorists in Korea for years before this on behalf of the Black Dragon Society, and had been responsible for the murder of the Empress of Korea in 1895.

Former Korean President Kim Dae Jung was kidnapped by the Yakuza in 1973 on behalf of politicians who were threatened by his left-wing views and support for striking workers.

The prostitutes behind the plate glass windows of the numerous brothels that line the streets of Seoul's red-light district are the visible element of the Yakuza's grip on Korean vice.

The annexation resulted in a large number of Korean economic migrants travelling to Japan, where they found themselves able only to work at the jobs that even the poorest Japanese despised. Although some of the Zainichi Koreans formed their own gangs that fought against the Yakuza – especially during the years of the Second World War – one area where Koreans found plenty of job opportunities was within organized crime clans.

Names such as Hisayuki Machii ("The Ginza Tiger") have become legendary in the Japanese underworld, despite the fact that Machii was an ethnic Korean born in 1923 with the name Chong Gwon Yong. Machii formed a Korean-based gang called Tosei-kai (Voices of the East) that grew to have more than 1,500 members by the 1960s. Under police pressure, he renamed the gang and it became the Tōa Yūai Jigyō Kumiai (East Asia Friendship Enterprise Association). Today it remains one of Tokyo's most powerful criminal groups, has many Japanese members and is fully integrated with other Yakuza groups. As one expert from the National Institute of Police Science in Tokyo told me, "Only in the Yakuza could ethnic Koreans like Kuniyasu Makino and Sin Myong U run enterprises such as the Matsuba-kai and Soai-kai clans. These groups are multi-billion yen businesses and they are the top men. This would not happen in other Japanese company boardrooms."

The Korean connection and membership proved exceptionally useful when Yakuza clans began to expand outside the Japanese mainland at the end of the 1960s. They were able to send Korean members of Yakuza over to mainland Korea to set up their first foreign branches. By the early 1970s, the well-financed Yakuza in Korea had managed to establish a firm grip on all the labour in the country's ports and construction. They also took control of vice in South Korea, making it a destination for Japanese sex tourists as well as arranging to send Korean women to Japan to work as prostitutes. Young Koreans who joined the Yakuza went to Japan to be trained, before returning to their native country to provide skilled soldiers for rapidly expanding Yakuza operations.

As in Japan, Yakuza in Korea supported right-wing politicians, often operating as strike-busters and anti-left-wing thugs. In 1973 they even kidnapped the future Korean President, Kim Dae Jung, at the behest of their political allies, who were having problems with growing support for Jung's left-wing views. With high-level support, Yakuza groups in Japan bought many legitimate Korean businesses and built up massive real estate portfolios. At the same time they have built up illicit empires with interests in narcotics and arms smuggling, extortion and corporate blackmail to complement their domination of Korean vice.

As one Japanese police scientist has commented, "What their old friends in the Black Dragon Society and Gen'yōsha dreamed of doing – creating a new Japanese empire on mainland Asia starting with Korea – the Yakuza have done".

KEY CRIMES

The post-Second World War economic recovery of Japan is often described as miraculous. The transformation from a war-ravaged, defeated nation into a global industrial and business giant brought new levels of prosperity to the citizens of the country. One group that benefited far more than the rest was the Yakuza.

Like a parasite embedded deep within the body of corporate Japan, the Yakuza has grown strong on the trillions of yen its has extorted, blackmailed and stolen from some of the country's most successful businesses. Preying on large corporations has become one of the Yakuza's signature crimes and is carried out by members known as sokaiya, quite literally "shareholder racketeers".

Sokaiya will threaten to disrupt a company's annual shareholder meeting unless they receive large cash payments or unsecured loans. As shareholder meetings are often the period of most scrutiny by a company's owners and the press, most businesses will pay to prevent trouble. A company who refuses can expect anything at their meeting from violent fights to the distribution of pornographic photographs of senior company executives with underage prostitutes.

Another ruse is for one group of sokaiya to forewarn a company that another group, paid by one of its business rivals, plans to cause a commotion. They then offer their protection services to prevent it happening. Sokaiya infiltration and intimidation at a shareholding meeting can also be used to shape company policy, vote directors off a board and replace them with ones reporting to a particular Yakuza clan. Even the largest Japanese corporate names are not immune to sokaiya, and a quiet, smooth-running shareholder meeting is usually a sign that a company that has made an arrangement to keep the peace. Some major Western companies, such as the American company Lockheed Martin, have also entered into deals with the Yakuza – in 1976, it was exposed as having paid millions of dollars to infamous Yakuza fixer Yoshio Kodama.

Other forms of corporate blackmail are also a key Yakuza crime. Top executives will be encouraged into compromising financial or personal situations so Yakuza have a hold over them. They will then be persuaded into making business decisions favourable to a Yakuza clan. In 1984, it became known that the Yakuza had kidnapped the president of Ezaki Glico – a major candy manufacturer. It did this to extort

Japanese film director Juzo Itami (right) was threatened, beaten and eventually driven to suicide by the Yakuza after speaking out against them in his 1997 movie *Minbo no Onna*.

Kaoru Ogawa (below) has admitted involvement with sokaiya and has tackled questions from journalists about sokaiya activities.

further funds from the company it was already blackmailing by threatening to poison its products. Unfortunately, the Ezaki Glico case was not isolated, but rather common Yakuza practice when dealing with a business that refuses to work with them.

According to the former head of the Organized Crime Division of Japan's National Police Agency, Raisuke Miyawaki, "Ties between corporate Japan and the Japanese underworld are so extensive it is impossible to even get a grip on where and how they are joined together". Miyawaki blames the Yakuza for the current weakened state of the Japanese economy, dubbing it, "The Yakuza recession". When the problems with the banking industry making forced bad loans to Yakuza threatened the stability of the whole country, the Japanese government took the unprecedented action of trying to reach a formal agreement with the Yamaguchi-gumi Yakuza clan for its help in policing and reducing the problem.

Traditionally, the Yakuza's most widespread and profitable rackets are related to illegal gambling. These days, the most prevalent activity for the Yakuza is the supply of the illicit – whether it is guns, drugs or pornography. The Yakuza supply more than two million regular users of methamphetamines in Japan and make billions a year from pornography that is more explicit than that permitted by Japanese law. Yakuza have always been associated with Floating World pleasure districts, but they have now achieved total domination of everything from vice to karaoke in the modern day equivalent areas such as Kabukicho and Roppongi in Tokyo.

It was the acclaimed Japanese film director Juzo Itami who said, "Nowadays everybody is afraid of the Yakuza," after making *Minbo no Onna* – a movie about Yakuza extortion. Itami faced Yakuza death threats, but refused to stop his criticism of their activities, despite being beaten and hospitalized by members of Goto-gumi clan. Juzo Itami apparently killed himself in 1997 after the Yakuza sent pictures of him and a young woman to certain magazines. His words ring even truer after his death.

KEY FIGURES

There is an expression that many Yakuza use when you talk to them, "Good for both sides of the street". It refers to a core idea within the Japanese underworld that is expressed by the dictum "There are two sides of the street, one clothed in sunlight, one in shade. The bakuto (gamblers) must walk in the shade and leave the sun for other citizens."

However, since 1945, many important Yakuza have left the shadows and emerged into the bright light of public scrutiny. In Japan, unlike many other countries, the exposure these key figures have received has often seen them met with as much acclaim as vilification. Of all the

Yoshio Kodama (above) was the ultimate kuromaku (black curtain), wielding power behind the scenes on behalf of the Yakuza, top politicians, secret societies and some of the world's biggest corporations.

Yamaguchi-gumi boss Masahisa Takenaka (right) was brought down in a hail of bullets whilst in bed with his girlfriend. The hit was carried out by a team of killers sent a by a rival faction within his own clan.

Yakuza figures who have walked both sides of the street, one name towers above them all – Yoshio Kodama.

As a youth living in Japanese-occupied Korea, Kodama became caught up in the murky world of occult secret societies, ultra-nationalist parties and Yakuza groups operating in the country. In the early 1930s, he formed his own right-wing paramilitary group that believed its patriotic duty was to export as many drugs as possible to Korea and Manchuria to weaken the resolve of the population to resist Japanese rule. His group also assassinated three prominent politicians for believing in peaceful co-existence with their foreign neighbours. Although Kodama was eventually jailed for plotting to kill the Japanese Prime Minister, he was freed during the Second World War so that his narcotic smuggling network could be used to help the Japanese war effort.

Kodama's freedom was short-lived, however. In 1945 the US prosecuted him as a Class A war criminal and he was sent to Tokyo's Sugamo Jail. It was this time in prison that helped him to become the most important Yakuza power broker and arranger of deals between the legitimate side of the street and the underworld. Living alongside him in Sugamo Jail were fellow Class A war criminals, who would become lifelong friends and important political and business contacts when they were freed by the Americans to help provide a bulwark against Communist intrusion into Japan. Among Kodama's new friends were the powerful businessman Ryoichi Sasakawa (the self-proclaimed "world's wealthiest fascist") and several leading members of the Liberal Democratic Party (LDP), including the future Prime Minister Nobusuke Kishi.

On behalf of his colleagues in the Yakuza, Kodama acted as a kuromaku (black curtain – one who wields unseen power). He arranged hundreds of corrupt deals and helped forge alliances between prominent Yakuza clans, politicians and corporations. Kodama fell from grace in the 1976 Lockheed Martin scandal, when it emerged that he was the channel for millions of dollars in illegal payments made by the company to try and win lucrative contracts to supply Japan Airlines with a new generation of jumbo jets. Many Japanese considered his major crime to be not bribery, but working for a foreign company.

Kodama's web of corruption became know as the kuroi kiri (black mist) yet his exposure did little to change the level of collusion between Yakuza, big business and the LDP. It was not until the 1990s "Hot Pot No Panties" scandal (which took its name from the restaurant where some Yakuza entertained their powerful political and police friends) that any serious attempt was made to try and curtail the activities of other leading kuromaku.

The most important Yakuza alliance brokered by Kodama was between Kazua Taoka and Kakuji Inagawa, the respective heads of Yamaguchi-gumi and Inagawa-kai clans. Taoka and Inagawa were the two most successful Yakuza bosses Japan had ever seen. Between them they controlled more than half of the underworld. The deal between the two, brokered by Kodama in the early 1970s, allowed for both to continue growing without wasting energy on fighting each other.

When Kazua Taoka was succeeded as head of the Yamaguchi-gumi by Masahisa Takenaka, his replacement was called upon by the Japanese government to help reduce Yakuza problems in the banking and financial industry, so becoming yet another Yakuza to walk in the light. However, Takenaka's time in the sun was short. In 1985, after two years as Yamaguchi-gumi boss, he was murdered by a team of hit men sent by a rival faction of his own clan – the Ichiwa-kai. Takenaka's killing led to the Yama-Ichi War, the most brutal infighting ever seen in Yakuza history. Even in death, Takenaka remained a key figure.

THE YAKUZA TODAY

When a society is so penetrated by organized crime that a government has to consult gangsters on how best to solve its problems, or when the police find leading politicians openly posting bail for the crooks they catch, it is hard to imagine the general population not protesting about the state of law and order. Yet Japan's citizens regularly top global polls expressing happiness on policing issues.

Outsiders find it hard to comprehend how a country that harbours the world's largest organized crime network does not have the dismantling of the Yakuza as one its top political priorities. Despite the series of scandals that have continued to unfold since the "Hot Pot No Panties" story broke in the 1990s – including one which saw a politician caught pushing his huge cash bribe away in a shopping trolley – there is no great public uprising on the streets demanding an end to corruption. No one is forcing the "black curtains" to be pulled down, no one is ensuring the "black mist" clears.

Some commentators believe that the reason the Yakuza continue to enjoy a position of so little opposition is their economic penetration of Japan. Alongside control of the trillions of yen that flow through the Japanese underworld, the Yakuza have established vast legitimate commercial empires that own everything from banks to hospitals and film studios. To dismantle the Yakuza would mean jeopardizing businesses that employ tens of thousands of innocent people.

Other experts believe this issue is not economic, but cultural. When Yakuza boss Masaru Fujii said, "We are the spirit of Japan," he was only enunciating a widespread belief. The Yakuza's nationalistic stance is well known, as is their support for many traditional values and aspects of Japanese life. To many, the Yakuza are a continuing representation of a nobler age.

Tales of ronin and chivalrous commoners, from which the Yakuza declare ancestry, have always been a favourite theme in Japanese art and literature. The manga and animé of modern Japanese culture continue this tradition. In the pages of comic books and on animated television shows, Yakuza are lauded as protectors of the common good. Popular action films are just as likely to feature the Yakuza gunmen as heroes as the cops. Film director Juzo Itami, who was beaten and harassed by Yakuza for making films that portrayed them as thugs and bullies instead of noble outlaws, was a rare voice in the Japanese film industry where the Yakuza themselves have massive investments.

The Yakuza appear to be such a success story that many journalists look for any angle that will show them losing their grip. Tales of them relinquishing control of the drugs, pornography, prostitution, extortion and gambling rackets to foreign rivals, such as the Chinese or Koreans, appear every year, but they always turn out to be over-hyped nonsense and the Yakuza remain firmly in control. They allow Nigerian, Russian and other foreign national organized crime groups to operate in return for a heavy share of their profits. This taxation system allows them to enjoy an income while concentrating manpower elsewhere.

It has also proved to be a good public relations exercise. The Yakuza have always acted out a ritual with many elements of the Japanese police. When tipped off in advance of a raid, they will leave some guns for the police to find so the law officers can declare a success. If enough local people complain about their activities, a junior Yakuza member is put forward for arrest to satisfy all parties. With foreigners now operating in some rackets, the police can arrest non-Yakuza and still be seen as being tough on organized crime. The Yakuza today remain on top.

Yet there is one cloud on the Yakuza's horizon. "Momentum is the problem," according to former police commander, Raisuke Miyawaki. He and many criminologists believe the key issue facing the Yakuza now is expansion. Like any other business that controls its home market, they must try to develop abroad or face the risk of infighting over an already swamped domestic underworld. While the Yakuza have had success in Korea, Hawaii and California, their other foreign operations have often floundered. As one expert told me, "The Yakuza need foreign partners to grow, but they can find no one as professional and big as them to do business with".

BLACKMAIL AND CORPORATE BLACKMAIL

Blackmail is a form of extortion where, instead of threatening to physically damage a person or business, the extortionist threatens to damage their reputation unless a demand is met. This is usually a threat to reveal information that would jeopardize a person's social or commercial standing, or in some cases lead to criminal charges being brought against them.

Argument rages as to where the word "blackmail" itself comes from. Some say it originates from the notorious Black Hand extortion notes of Italian organized crime, but it is more likely to originate from the "black rent" that was paid to Scottish and English brigands, known as Border Reivers, to prevent their raids.

Blackmail by organized criminals does not always involve financial demands. Often blackmail is used to achieve favours or concessions from politicians, civil servants, judges and the police. Director of the FBI, J. Edgar Hoover, was blackmailed by at least one organized crime boss between the 1930s and the 1950s over either his gambling habits or his sexual relationship with fellow FBI man Clyde Tolson.

Corporate blackmail targeted at large businesses is a speciality of the Japanese Yakuza. They often lure leading businessmen into "honey traps" to obtain evidence of sexual proclivities or infidelities, and then blackmail them with threats to distribute explicit photographs of their activities at shareholder meetings. Yakuza clans have also successfully blackmailed leading food companies, such as Ezaki Glico, not by threatening to actually poison its products, but by leaking rumours merely suggesting that they have done it. Businesses have paid up, knowing the mere suggestion of such a thing could ruin their sales and their brand's reputation.

In 1945, Tokyo's Sugamo Jail was home to a host of Class A war criminals and leading Yakuza, who would go on to become Japan's top politicians and leading businessmen upon their release.

THE TRIADS AND TONGS — CHINESE ORGANIZED CRIME 4

"They've been around for 2,000 years and no one has put them out of business. That tells you everything you need to know about Triad power."

John Leung, Hong Kong and Shenzhen private detective

It is sometimes hard to know exactly what the Chinese organized crime groups known as Triads and Tongs believe themselves to be — secret societies that take part in criminal activities, or criminal organizations that occasionally choose to operate as ancient clandestine orders? The naked facts of their criminal enterprise, however, is the most eloquent statement of the frightening and pervasive power they possess. Truly trans-national, with flourishing branches on every continent, the Triads dominate criminal activity in Chinese communities across the globe. They only fail to qualify as the world's largest official crime network because investigators admit that they can no longer track their spectacular growth.

The Triads are firmly at the forefront of organized crimes such as drug and people trafficking. Fluid, adaptable and sophisticated, the Triads have survived for centuries despite the efforts of many governments to end their influence. It is no wonder they have been called "the immortal society".

Throughout history, the Triads have also been used as an excuse for anti-Chinese prejudice. The racist villainy of Sax Rohmer's fictional Si-Fan organization and Dr Fu Manchu ("the yellow peril incarnate in one man") has often been applied to Chinese people in general. While some of the facts revealed in this chapter may read like pulp fiction, the evil of the Triads and Tongs should reflect only upon the organizations themselves.

THE ORIGINS OF THE TRIADS AND TONGS

A global secret society that has a role in most criminal activities, from white-slaving to trafficking heroin with the CIA, and which could date back as far as 25CE? It sounds like something that could only exist in the confines of a good comic book or a bad Hollywood movie. Throw in the Shaolin monks who created kung fu and groups with names such as the Red Dragon Society, and it begins to sound like a ridiculous film script.

Yet this is no juvenile fantasy, but a mere hint of the amazing and often credibility-stretching history of the Triad and Tong syndicates, who are behind the colossal power of Chinese organized crime. While many organized crime groups claim an ancient lineage and dress their crimes up in mystic trappings, the Triads and Tong are, as one Scotland Yard detective colourfully told me, "The real deal. The only thing they lack is a secret volcano base".

The earliest group that some experts have linked to the origins of the Triads are the Chih Meh, or Red Eyebrows. They were a secret society of warriors, dedicated to the overthrow of the despot Wan Mang in 25CE. They gained their name from the practice of painting

their eyebrows red, to look like demons, in order to inspire fear in their enemies. The Chih Meh operated in the Shangdong province of China and exhibited all the characteristics of the later groups that evolved into modern Triads – a resistance movement with mystical beliefs that eventually turned to crime.

One group that had a definite impact on the creation of the Triads was the White Lotus Society, which emerged at the end of the Tang Dynasty in the tenth century. A Buddhist sect with many similar spiritual beliefs to the current day Falun Gong movement, it was suppressed by the Chinese authorities and led the revolt against Mongol rule over China in the thirteenth century. Its actions helped former Buddhist monk Hung Wu become Emperor and found the Ming Dynasty in 1368.

When the Qing Dynasty (sometimes known as Manchu Dynasty) conquered all of China in 1644, the White Lotus Society once again became the focus of a resistance movement dedicated to removing the Qing from the Imperial throne and restoring the Ming Dynasty. According to the Triad's own accounts of their origins, prominent in the resistance were the monks of Shaolin monastery. The Manchu Emperor sent troops to destroy the monks and burn down the monastery. However, 18 monks managed to escape, of which five managed to make their way to a hidden sanctuary and form the Heaven and Earth Society.

Dedicated to the overthrow of Qing and restoration of Ming, it quickly became a form of regional shadow government and inspired numerous rebellions. Each time the Qing dynasty suppressed it, new offshoots of the Society would form, with names such as the Hung Family League and the Harmonies Society. With each crushed rebellion, resistance members tended to flee further, even moving outside the Chinese Empire and joining Chinese trading communities across South East Asia. They also turned to extortion, smuggling and other illicit enterprises to fund the fight against the Qing Dynasty. One group reformed under the name of the Fists of Righteous Harmony. Known as the Boxers to foreigners, they were the force behind the Boxer Rebellion of 1899–1900 that tried to expel Western influence from China.

The political activities of the various groups were not fully understood by the authorities in countries to which the groups had spread. This led to them being called Tongs in America (due to the names of their meeting halls) and Triads in the British Empire, because of the triangular emblem used in their rituals. However, the authorities certainly understood their criminal activities, which included opium trading, prostitution, extortion and illegal gambling. The authorities tried to clamp down on them, but met with little success.

Members of the Fists of Righteous Harmony, known more commonly in the West as the Boxers, after being captured by the U.S. Sixth Cavalry during the failed Boxer rebellion of 1899–1900.

The HQ of a Triad front organization in London's notorious Limehouse district at the start of the twentieth century. Few in Scotland Yard at the time understood the secret nature of many Tongs.

By the time the Qing Dynasty was finally overthrown in 1912, thousands of members of different, but interlinked, groups, sharing the same philosophy, mystical beliefs and way of operating, had spread into every Chinese community across the globe. From the streets of San Francisco to the opium dens of London's Limehouse district, there now existed an established secret society and criminal network robbed of its core purpose. It was at this point that the modern Triads and Tongs were born.

TRIAD RULES AND RITUALS

Despite more than 100 years of investigation by the authorities, it was not until 1960 that any clear picture of the extraordinary rules and rituals used by the Triads emerged. Although an account of some of their beliefs was published in the 1925 book *The Hung Society*, it took years of detective work by senior Hong Kong police officer W.P. Morgan to expose a reality that no one outside of the Triads had ever known.

Morgan's book – Triad Societies In Hong Kong – was formed from his groundbreaking interrogations of captured Triad members, made while he was fighting their influence in the British-controlled Chinese territory. What he detailed in his groundbreaking book seemed so far-fetched that the bizarre occult practices of Sax Rohmer's fictional Si-Fan organization, based upon the Triads, suddenly stopped looking like spurious fantasy. Morgan's work also explained the mystical

numerology used as code by Triads and the meaning of emblematic tattoos, such as the green dragon or the white tiger, that are sported by many Triad members.

The research carried out by Morgan showed that all of the numerous, and often competing, Triads shared a belief in a largely mythological account of their origins. The most important aspects related to the escape of the five monks from the destruction of the Shaolin monastery. The monks were known as the Five Ancestors and it was the trials and events they were said to have gone through that underpinned Triad belief. This legendary history shaped the ceremonies and symbolism that was a common feature of all the disparate groups.

Whereas the Sicilian and American Mafia have initiations of fire and blood, the initiation of a new member of a Triad involves fire, blood, swords and water. A prospective member must pay a joining fee to the organization and to the person who sponsors him for membership. Both fees must be some variation of the number 36 and could range from $3.60 to $36,000, or an even higher amount. The joining ceremony takes place in the Triad's headquarters in an oblong room known as "City of Willows", which represents the new monastery founded by the fleeing monks.

The initiate has to walk through a serious of symbolic gates, meeting various challenges ranging from having to give a secret ritual handshake to passing under an archway of swords held by other members. The Triad leader – the Shan Chu (Master of the Mountain) – dressed in red and an official known as Heung Chu (Incense Master) dressed in white, then guide the initiate through the next stage.

Whilst the warrior monks of the Shaolin Temple are famous in the West for creating Kung Fu, the ancient order also features heavily in the Triads' account of their origins.

Approaching an altar on which symbolic magical objects are placed, the neophyte is given a piece of paper on which the 36 Oaths a Triad member must vow to keep are written. After making the 36 Oaths, the paper is burned and its ashes put into a cup of spiced wine. A cockerel is then beheaded and its blood added to the cup. Finally, the initiate's finger is cut and his blood joins the brew of wine, ashes and cockerel's blood. He is now given a membership certificate with his own unique code number and a feast in his honour is held. A symbolic water cleansing ritual, three days later, signals his final rebirth as a new being and a full member of the Hung Society.

Amongst the 36 Oaths, the last one relates to the professed purpose of the Triad: "To avenge our Five Ancestors and endeavour to overthrow Qing and restore Ming by joining my efforts to those of my sworn brothers". Many of the other Oaths relate to expected behaviour in the society, which ranges from a promise not to seduce a fellow member's "wife or concubine", to the fifth Oath: "I shall not disclose the secrets of the Hung Society… if I do so I will be killed by a myriad of swords".

The Oaths are not mere window dressing. The death by "a myriad of swords" is more commonly known as "the death of a thousand cuts" and is a form of Triad punishment still used today. Anyone considered a traitor faces being slowly killed by having every muscle severed by butcher's cleaver until he slowly dies from loss of blood. Despite the mystical trappings, the Triads are a serious and deadly affair.

THE 14K TRIAD

Although almost all Triads and Tongs share the same basic rules, rituals and beliefs, they are not part of one grand united force with one recognized leadership. Since the unifying aim of overthrowing the Qing Dynasty was achieved in 1912, the various Triad societies have not only become increasingly criminal, they have also evolved into distinct and rival branches under which hundreds of individual gangs are affiliated.

One of the largest and most notorious of these Triad branches is known as the 14K Triad society. It is origins date to 1945 when the Chinese nationalist forces, under Chiang Kai-shek, were fighting a bitter civil war against the Communist forces of Mao Zedong. A senior Triad member and Lieutenant-General in the Kuomintang Nationalist Army, Kot Siu-wong, was asked to put together a league of all Triad societies operating in the Guangdong province to help fight against the Chinese Red Army.

By 1947, Kot had merged several Triad groups into the Hung Fat Shan Loyalty Association, with himself as its leader in the traditional position of Shan Chu. For organizational reasons, the Triads were split into 44 different groups, all given coded names that included the number 14. The number was chosen because of the address of

Police in Macau launched a massive hunt of possible Triad hideouts in 1997, after a campaign of assassination and fire-bombings carried out by the 14K brought chaos to the island.

Kot's headquarters – 14 Po Wah Road, Canton. The letter K was also added to the group's code, either as a reference to the carat mark on Chinese gold or to honour Kot's name. It was not long before the various crime gangs reporting to Kot were known collectively as the 14K Triad society.

When Mao Zedong led the Communists to a successful takeover of mainland China, members of the 14K fled to Hong Kong, Taiwan and Macau to avoid Zedong's brutal clampdown on nationalist sympathizers and the criminal activities of the Triads. With their role of anti-Communist fighters over, the 14K began to concentrate on criminal activities. Despite facing heavy competition from other Triads already established in the areas it fled to, the 14K began building up an illicit empire focussed on illegal gambling, prostitution, smuggling, loan-sharking and extortion.

Through its old allies in the Kuomintang, who now controlled Taiwan, the 14K began to receive funds in return for fomenting anti-Communist feeling in Hong Kong and Macau. Most of the money originated from the US government, but instead of being used to build an anti-Communist network, the 14K used it primarily to bribe corrupt officials in the government of Hong Kong and Macau. It also helped the 14K to buy the services of the police. At one point in the late 1960s, they even had Hong Kong's Chief Superintendent of Police,

Peter Fitzroy Godber, working for them. One group the 14K did foment feelings against, however, were the British, inspiring several major riots against them in Hong Kong between 1956 and 1968.

The level of political corruption the 14K achieved in Hong Kong helped it become the second largest Triad society in the territory, with more than 8,000 members and up to 20 different gangs. Although it had branches in Taiwan, competition with the United Bamboo Gang constrained its growth on the island. However, the place where the 14K was best able consolidate its powers was Portuguese-administered Macau. Until China took control of the area in 1999, the 14K's reign of fear allowed it to dominate the underworld and everday life in Macau. It controlled not just vice and gambling throughout the territory, but openly used it as an international base for heroin trafficking. The police were unable to make any dent in 14K activities and any journalist investigating them received death threats.

Many people in Macau welcomed the handover to Chinese rule as a way of reining in the 14K. Within months, the Chinese-administered Macau Security Force had imprisoned the 14K's leader Wan Kuok Koi ("Broken Tooth") and instigated a massive clampdown on their activities. Despite this, the 14K continues to flourish. In the twenty-first century, it is increasingly becoming dominant in the trafficking of drugs and people and the problems it has encountered in Macau have not had any impact on its massive network of international operations. Nor has their occasional high-profile exposure, such as when they were revealed as being behind a major kidnap plot in New Zealand in 2008. It continues to be one of the fastest growing Triads in several major cities across the globe including Los Angeles, Vancouver, Sydney and Johannesburg.

THE SUN YEE ON TRIAD

The Sun Yee On Triad is synonymous with Hong Kong. The biggest Triad group in the area today, it has been a factor in the teeming Hong Kong underworld for more than 150 years, often acting as a hidden hand shaping the territory's destiny.

Hong Kong was home to Triad societies long before the British seized control of the territory from China during the Opium Wars in 1842 – it had been a base for Triad smugglers, pirates and fugitives since the eighteenth century. Triads were quick to recognize the advantages of British rule, as they brought a boom in trade and protection from the Chinese authorities who wanted to root out anti-Qing Dynasty rebels.

The British outlawed secret societies in the territory in 1849, but the Triads continued to flourish, establishing a firm grip on the labour market, opium distribution, gambling and prostitution. As the British colony grew, so did the Triads who were able to extort increasingly larger sums from anyone in the Chinese community conducting legitimate trade in the region. By the early 1930s, there were eight main

Triad societies operating in Hong Kong – one of the most significant was called the Yee On.

To escape the prohibition of secret societies they registered themselves as everything from the To Shui Boxing Club to the Yee On Commercial and Industrial Guild, a front for trade union control. The Yee On's main criminal activities were labour racketeering and vice. When the Japanese occupied Hong Kong during the Second World War, the Yee On actively collaborated with the invaders. In return for a free hand in vice, the black market and other activities, they helped police the territory and fight against the Dongjiang guerrillas that were opposed to Japanese rule.

Although siding with the Japanese meant that the Yee On enjoyed success between 1941 and1945, the post-war situation proved challenging. When the Communists took control of mainland China, the resulting inrush of new Triad groups unsettled the Hong Kong underworld and vicious warfare for control of territory and rackets broke out. Despite assimilating some of the recently arrived gangs, rival Triads provided the authorities with information on the Yee On and its top leaders were deported. This led to the society splitting into two warring factions in 1953.

Yet the Yee On refused to die. Within years it had re-emerged as the Sun Yee On and was soon dominating two prime criminal activities in Hong Kong – vice and opium. Sun Yee On specialized in buying girls and women

The tough and highly-trained forces of China's Public Security Bureau are tasked with waging war against organized crime, but the Sun Yee On Triad has close ties with its leading officers.

US Homeland Security Secretary Michael Chertoff meets his Chinese counterpart in the Public Security Bureau, Zhou Yongkang, despite fears the PSB are soft on Triads.

from their families and forcing them into prostitution. It was also quick to establish itself amongst Chinese émigré communities in Europe and the British Commonwealth, quickly becoming one of the biggest trans-national Triad operations with a booming narcotics network.

As the Hong Kong cinema industry boomed in the late 1960s and 1970s, the Sun Yee On moved in and seized control. Soon, no film could be made without some form of payment going to the Triad who owned film studios, cinemas and distributors. Despite attempts by directors and actors, including Bruce Lee and Jackie Chan, to break the power of the Triads in Hong Kong film, the Sun Yee On remain firmly in charge. Leading Hong Kong actor and businessman Charles Heung is the son of one of Sun Yee On's founders, and is widely believed to be a leading player in the society today, and does not appear to have taken any action to quell these rumours. The continuing dark side of Sun Yee On's control of the movie business was demonstrated in 2002. *Eastweek Magazine* published a topless picture of the actress Carina Lau, who had been abducted and abused in an attempt to pressurize the star's actor boyfriend into co-operating with Sun Yee On plans for him.

The Chinese takeover of Hong Kong in 1997 has done nothing to stem the power of Sun Yee On. A recent violent Hong Kong turf war over vice establishments involving the Sun Yee On saw 222 people arrested in 2012, but no one of any significance to the organization served any jail time. A series of scandals over recent years have exposed the Triad group's ties with top members of China's Public Security Bureau. There is little doubt that this corruption explains Sun Yee On's growing power in the Guangdong province of mainland China, especially its domination of the city of Shenzhen. With its actions on its home turf appearing to meet with only the most muted official punishment, it is unsurprising that the Sun Yee On has the energy and resources to continue its worrying expansion across Asia.

THE WO SHING WO TRIAD

The oldest established Triad in Hong Kong is the Wo Shing Wo. Originally known as the Wo group, it has survived more than 300 years of bloody history to emerge as one of the major trans-national Triad groupings active in the twenty-first century. Evidence suggests it had members operating in Hong Kong, involved in extortion and opposition to the Qing Dynasty, as far back as the 1680s.

The Wo was one of the first Triad societies encountered by the British forces in Hong Kong in the 1840s. They were partially responsible for the British placing a ban on secret societies in the territory in 1849. By the 1930s the authorities recorded that the Wo Shing Wo Triad society had arisen from the Wo Triad. It had criminal operations covering everything from rickshaw monopolies to pickpocket gangs and illegal gambling. Wo Shing Wo were notorious for buying peasant girls from their parents in mainland China in exchange for food and shipping them into Hong Kong to work as unwilling prostitutes. They dominated the Kowloon Peninsula and were rated as the largest and most troublesome of the eight major Triads operating in Hong Kong before 1939.

After the end of World War Two, the Wo Shing Wo was soon beset with problems. The invasion of Hong Kong by Triad groups such as the 14K, fleeing from the Communist takeover of mainland China in 1949, upset the underworld balance of power. Alongside this threat to Wo Shing Wo supremacy, it had to deal with a full-scale attempt by the

The infamous Walled City of Kowloon belonged to no nation and was not governed by any law, so it was no surprise it helped give birth to the powerful Wo Shing Wo Triad.

British authorities to wipe it out. While many Triads had collaborated with the Japanese invaders of Hong Kong during the war, the Wo Shing Wo were remembered and hated by the British for having shot and killed scores of its retreating soldiers. The Wo Shing Wo also worked for the Kempetai – the Japanese political police – arranging for the rounding up of many rival Triad members, British sympathizers and Allied spies.

In the face of ever-increasing police clampdowns and territorial warfare, the Wo Shing Wo did what it had always done in times of trouble – it retreated into the infamous Walled City of Kowloon. The Wo Shing Wo had evolved from the Walled City and after 1956 it became the main base of operations for its climb back to power. The city's reputation as the most crime-ridden and law-impenetrable ghetto the world has ever seen was well deserved. It was the one place in Hong Kong where Triads never feared the police. This was due to a dispute over whether Britain or China controlled the 61-acre site. As the Hong Kong police had no authority to act within the Walled City, it soon became a zone with no law except for that of the Triads.

After 1949, the walled City became home to thousands of refugees from mainland China. This transformed it into a labyrinth of miniscule homes, making it the most densely populated place on earth. The 50,000-plus inhabitants were all prey to the Wo Shing Wo, who dominated the city. Anything could be bought on its black market and its main thoroughfare was charmingly known as Heroin Alley. By the time the authorities started to pull it down in 1988, the Wo Shing Wo had already rebuilt its power.

In the early 1990s, the main Wo Shing Wo Triad had 10,000 members across the world, while its nine main subdivisions, such as the Wo On Lok

Police remove the body of one of the 21 illegal cockle pickers drowned at Morecambe Bay in England. Behind the scenes of the tragedy lay the Wo Shing Wo and its role in bonded labour.

and Wo Shing Tong, became more specialist and autonomous, with a combined membership of more than 12,000. The constant crackdowns it faced in Hong Kong encouraged the Wo Shing Wo to expand abroad and in the early years of the twenty-first century it had flourishing operations in Amsterdam, Macau, New York, London and Sydney. Key Wo Shing Wo crime activities now involve the trafficking of heroin and designer drugs, illegal immigration and worker exploitation, forced prostitution, money laundering and restaurant extortion. Within Hong Kong it is highly focused on extortion. In 2010, its control over minibus routes in the territory was highlighted when police arrested a Wo Shing Wo member known as "Broken Mouth Bun" for extorting HK$14 million per year from bus drivers.

The group is particularly strong in the United Kingdom. It operates from London, Manchester and Southampton, but has small pockets across the whole country. Preying mainly on the Chinese community in Britain, Wo Shing Wo involvement in crimes has ranged from the casual murder of Hok Wan Leung in Essex, for failure to repay a loan, in 1999, to the tragedy of 21 drowned, illegal cockle pickers in Morecambe Bay in 2004.

UNITED BAMBOO GANG

There are few organized crime groups that can ever claim to have been government sponsored. Yet Taiwan's largest Triad society – Chu Lien Pang, or the United Bamboo Gang – is one of them. Its special relationship with the Taiwanese authorities was born out of the violent conflict for the soul of China, fought by the Mao Zedong's Communists and the Kuomintang (Chinese Nationalist Party), which raged during the Chinese Civil War of 1927–1949.

Even during the Japanese occupation of much of China during World War Two, many Triads had remained loyal to the Kuomintang cause. Unfortunately for them, they had backed the wrong side in the Civil War. By 1949, their allies were in retreat, forced to abandon cities such as Shanghai that had long remained in Nationalist control thanks to the fact that they were also major Triad bases. With Communist victory guaranteed, many Triad members allied with the Kuomintang joined the more than two million Nationalists who fled mainland China and set up on the island of Taiwan. It was a wise move. Mao ruthlessly suppressed those Triads who did not flee, killing tens of thousands of them in the years after the Civil War was concluded.

Taiwan in 1950 was awash with ex-Triad members and Kuomintang soldiers. However, instead of arising from a generation of defeated men, the United Bamboo Gang arose from among the teenage sons of senior Kuomintang officials and various ex-Triad leaders. The gang took its name from the Bamboo Forest Road area on the outskirts of the Taiwanese capital, Taipei, where its members lived. With many of their fathers in senior political positions, the United Bamboo Gang

Thousands fled Shanghai as Communist forces closed in on the city. Among those who escaped were Triad members and Kuomintang whose sons would form the United Bamboo Gang.

This disaster exposed the end result of political corruption, revealing how Triad-backed businessmen were being given key government construction contracts and then failing to complete the work to any reasonable level of safety. After the trial of United Bamboo Gang member Chen Ti-kuo for his company's role in the Hsipin disaster, the Taiwanese government launched a major crackdown on all Bamboo Gang activities. Many of its top leaders, such as Zhang, had to flee abroad. Ironically, they often headed for mainland China where the United Bamboo Gang had begun to extend its criminal network.

Despite the arrest of Chen Chi-Li ("Dry Duck"), the current spiritual head of the United Bamboo Gang, in Cambodia in 2001, the group continues to go from strength to strength. It is now one of the largest Tongs in Canada and America and has again become the dominant force in Shanghai's underworld. To protect its position in Taiwan against further government crackdowns, it has become deeply involved in politics, opposing its old Kuomintang allies and supporting the reunification with China. Already a multi-billion dollar global business, thanks to its heroin, vice, extortion and gambling interests, White Wolf Zhang recently boasted: "Sweeping United Bamboo out of construction or one place matters little. Brothers are already in stock, finance and new business elsewhere".

The current spiritual head of the United Bamboo Gang, Chen Chi-Li ("Dry Duck"), sits behind the dock in a Cambodian court during extradition proceedings to return him to Tawian in 2001.

soon enjoyed government sponsorship under the title of the United Bamboo Society.

With this level of top support, it was relatively easy for the United Bamboo Gang to quickly become the dominant force among Taiwanese Triads. Within a decade they had built up an empire controlling the majority of prostitution, drug dealing, illegal gambling and loan-sharking in the country. When United Bamboo Gang members were recruited to work for the Taiwanese intelligence and security services, it only helped strengthen their heroin trafficking network and foreign operations. By 1974, Taiwan had become so notorious as a major Triad base that the government asked the United Bamboo Gang and the two other main Taiwanese Triads – the Four Seas and the Celestial Way – to take a lower profile for fear of international political ramifications.

However, the withdrawal of official government sponsorship did little to hurt the United Bamboo Gang. In the 1980s, the society had more than 10,000 members worldwide and 24 sub-groups with names such as the Bamboo Union and Bamboo Alliance. Its honorary leader was Zhang An-lo ("White Wolf Zhang"). He was regularly publicly consulted by high-ranking Taiwanese politicians and was a frequent guest on TV chat shows. However, the United Bamboo Gang's cosy government relationship started to fall apart with the tragedy of the collapse of a tunnel on the Hsipin expressway in northern Taiwan in 1996.

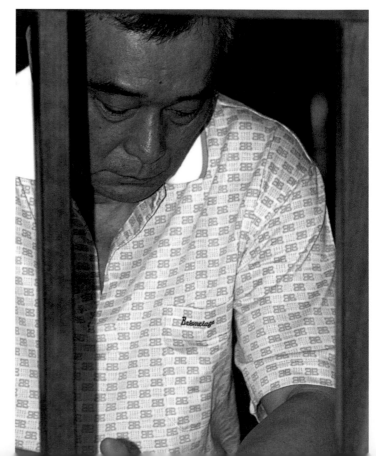

VIETNAMESE TRIADS

Since the 1970s, a new major trans-national Asian organized crime network has emerged. The authorities have consistently labelled its crimes the work of "Vietnamese Triads". In recent years, the various groups operating under this title have begun to rival established Triad societies, such as the 14K, Sun Yee On, Wo Shing Wo and United Bamboo Gang. By 2001, many criminologists believed them to be the largest Asian crime threat at a global level.

However, the Vietnamese crime groups are not true Triads, having a completely different origin to the ancient Chinese secret societies. The roots of what law enforcement call Vietnamese Triads belong in the horrific conflict that raged in Vietnam in the 1960s and early 1970s. Upon the fall of Saigon (or liberation of Saigon depending on which history books you read) in April 1975, millions of non-Communist Vietnamese tried to flee the country in a bid to escape the "re-education camps" or "new economic zones" set up by the Communist rulers of the newly unified Vietnam.

Many who attempted to escape became "Boat People", risking the cruelty of the open seas in an attempt to find a better life. Those reaching the relative safety of a foreign country, however, found themselves prisoners in a string of refugee camps. Over the next few years, more than a million Vietnamese refugees were resettled in foreign countries, with the United States, Canada, Australia, Hong

The tough conditions experienced by Vietnamese "Boat People" made it easy for some of them to be recruited as ma jai (horse boys) by the established Triads.

The partner of murdered Australian MP John Newman is overcome with grief at his funeral in 1994. Newman was assassinated because he spoke out against the power of Vietnamese crime gangs in Sydney.

Kong, France, Germany and the UK taking most of them.

The vast majority of these refugees were totally law abiding, however, the resettlement program also gave global distribution to a worrying new crime network that had emerged in the refugee camps. Among those that had escaped were members of the South Vietnamese army, some of whom were formerly involved in heroin trafficking. The camps also contained a number of ethnic Chinese who had fled their homes in Vietnam, including some Triad members. Within the camps, individuals from both groups quickly organized many of the young male orphans into gangs who were able to terrorize and exploit their fellow countrymen.

Once released from the camps, and in their new countries, the gangs quickly established their organized crime credentials. They dominated extortion, loan-sharking and prostitution rackets within the recently established Vietnamese communities, who often felt isolated and unable to turn to the law enforcement authorities for help. Gangs with names such as Born To Kill, Red Dragons, Saigon Cowboys and Thunder Tigers were soon operating in every country the Boat People had found new homes in. Family and village-based links remained in place, allowing groups such as the infamous Born To Kill or Black Dragons to develop and maintain intercontinental crime links between cities as far apart as Los Angeles and East Berlin.

It was not only as a mark of the traditional domination of Asian-organized criminality by the Triads that the Vietnamese gangs had the title applied to them. In the early stage of their development, established Triads employed many of the Vietnamese groups. They referred to them as ma jai (horse boys) – a source of cheap, expendable labour, useful for the dirty crime jobs, including murder and drug running, that the Triads preferred not to risk their members in.

It did not take the horse boys long to throw their riders, however. Comprised mainly of a generation brutalized by war, the Vietnamese street gangs showed few compulsions when it came to violent crime. From New York to the Cabramatta district of Sydney, bloody wars erupted over areas previously dominated by the Triads, such as heroin distribution. Unlike the Triads, who traditionally tried to keep a low profile when operating in the West, gangs such as the 5T had no compunction about killing those in authority who stood in their way, including Australian MP John Paul Newman whom they assassinated in 1994.

Hopes that, as successive generations of Vietnamese immigrants prospered, the menace of Vietnamese Triads would decrease, have not materialized. Each year of the twenty-first century has seen increasing numbers of suspects bearing distinctive gang tattoos being arrested. Whether the Red or Black Dragons or the five dots representing 5T's five Ts of Tinh, Tien, Tu, Toi, Tho, (love, money, prison, crime, revenge), increasing police familiarity with these tattoos is a sure sign of the continuing spread of Vietnamese Triads.

KEY CRIMES

Throughout the centuries of recorded criminal activity by various Triad societies, there cannot be a form of organized crime the Triads have not participated in. As far back as the seventeenth century, their revolts against the Qing Dynasty were being financed by a range of crimes, including extortion, piracy and prostitution.

However, there is one key crime above all others that is forever associated with the Triads and Tongs – opium dealing. From pulp novels to rabid newspaper reports of the Tong Wars that flared sporadically in New York and San Francisco between 1899 and the 1930s, the one thing always guaranteed a mention is "the vile evil of the Tongs' opium den".

The role of opium in Chinese history began in the ninth century, when Arab traders paid for Chinese goods in the infamous sticky brown resin of the Papaver somniferum (opium poppy). The widespread problems caused by opium addiction were recorded in China as early as the sixteenth cenutry, but this did not stop later European and American merchants from continuing the practice of bartering opium rather than gold for Chinese products. Despite their declared hatred of foreigners, Triad groups from the eighteenth century onwards took a leading role in the distribution of imported opium within China.

In the nineteenth century, with the US and European desire for

The broth of oblivion served up by the Triads at opium dens across the world in the nineteenth and early twentieth centuries helped establish them as the dominant force in today's $700 billion global heroin trade.

Chinese spices, tea, silk and porcelain, China became awash with opium. Chinese attempts to combat this situation led to the Opium Wars that were fought primarily by the British against China between 1834 and 1843. Britain eventually seized Hong Kong and forced China to accept opium as Britian's prime trading commodity with the country. Despite it leading to what the Chinese call a "century of shame", the Triads encouraged the import of opium, believing they benefited from the problems it caused the Qing Dynasty as well as the profits they made as distributors.

The illegal opium trade developed by the British has been described by the eminent Harvard historian John K. Fairbank as: "The most long continued and systematic international crime of modern times". When the British eventually pulled out of opium importing in 1917, the Triads filled the vacuum they left, supplying the needs of an estimated 180 million opium addicts in China. The Triads also provided opium for the Chinese émigré communities that were scattered across the globe. From New York's Chinatown to the Limehouse district of London's East End, Triad-run opium dens sprang up, providing the broth of oblivion to both Chinese and Westerners.

This well-established involvement in international narcotics provided a head start in the booming heroin trafficking business of the twentieth century. Already market leaders in this area, they received a massive boost to their drug smuggling empire in the 1970s, when the CIA chose the Triads as a key partner in exporting heroin from Cambodia during the Vietnam War. By the 1990s, the UN estimated that the Triads controlled up to 75 per cent of the world market in illegal opium derivatives, which was estimated to have a value in excess

Chinese police use dogs to sniff out human cargo hidden in one of the hundreds of container ships leaving China every day, used by the Triads to smuggle people into the West.

of $700 billion. Even with increased international co-operation, Triad domination of the drugs trade has continued unabated into the twenty-first century.

Despite also being the dominant players in wildlife smuggling and increasing moves into cyber-crimes, financial fraud and stock market manipulation, the illicit activity for which the Triads are most likely to become notorious these days is people smuggling. Benefiting from decades of experience, gathered from covert transportation of large quantities of opium across the globe, the Triads were quick to utilize their drug trafficking networks for the purpose of illegal immigration. Working in conjunction with local Snakehead gangs in China, the Triads charge fees of up to $60,000 to transport illegal immigrants to Europe, America or Australia.

If the person paying for these services actually survives the journey without suffocating or being thrown off a container ship in the middle of the ocean, they will often have to work off their debt as a bonded labour slave in a Triad-controlled enterprise in their destination country. Many women who are trafficked end up being forced into prostitution. Making profits second only to their narcotics operations, and with conservative estimates putting the number of people Triads transport per year in excess of 175,000, people trafficking looks set to remain one of their key crimes for decades to come.

DRUG TRAFFICKING

Drug trafficking can claim credit for spawning the first truly international criminal networks, and the illegal trade in narcotics currently produces the greatest source of revenue for organized crime. The United Nations estimates that the activity is worth more than $300 billion per annum and is continuing to grow. Other agencies believe that the figure is between $500 and $550 billion per year.

Drugs that are today socially frowned upon and outlawed, such as opium, coca leaf, assorted psychedelics and hashish, have been used for medicinal, religious and recreational use since the dawn of human civilization. Prohibition of such substances has historically always created a trade in their illicit supply. Until the twentieth century, the largest drug smuggling activity revolved around the supply of opium, with the British government even willing to fight wars against China to ensure that British opium suppliers could carry on their business.

In America, before the Harrison Act criminalized a range of substances in 1914, there were up to two million dependent users of opium, morphine and coca leaf derivatives. As Western nations began to ban narcotic substances in the 1910s and 1920s, organized crime groups already had an established base of addicts to supply. As the illicit trade grew, it transformed not only the fortunes of the drug traffickers, but also shaped the nature of major-drug producing countries, such as Colombia, Afghanistan and Laos. As new substances such as amphetamines and ecstasy started to become popular, and were subsequently banned, lucrative new markets developed for the traffickers to move into and these show no signs of diminishing in the twenty-first century.

KEY FIGURES

A struggle between two men shaped the history of twentieth-century China. There can be no doubt that the battle between the Chinese Nationalist Army of Chiang Kai-shek and Mao Zedong's Communist Party of China, during the country's Civil War of 1927–1949, forged the fate of a nation. However, the epic struggle for China's soul also had a massive impact on the nature and direction of Asian organized crime.

The aim to overthrow the Qing Dynasty was one of the prime reasons the Triads had come into existence. In 1912, it was the actions of the Nationalist leader and Triad member Sun Yat-sen that led to the final Imperial Edict that brought about the abdication of the child Emperor, Puyi. The fall of the Qing ended all pretence that the Triads existed for a higher political purpose, finally exposing them as the purely criminal networks they had become. However, Puyi's abdication did nothing to end Triad strength, nor did it bring a hoped-for era of peace to China.

Sun Yat-sen's fragile political alliance with the Communists was already failing when he died in 1925. His role was taken over by Chiang Kai-shek and a course towards the Chinese Civil War was set. From the outset, Chiang recognized the value of being able to call upon the Triads as a military, intelligence and financial resource in the fight against Mao. The secret society and criminal network nature of the Triads made them the perfect covert force. They also helped to generate much needed war funds through opium trafficking.

For his part, Mao was initially hopeful of bringing in the Triads on the Communist side. He wrote in 1926: "Outlaws are under the control of secret societies in various places, such as the Triad society of Fujian and the Triad Green Gang in Shanghai… These people are capable of fighting very bravely and, if properly led, can become a revolutionary force". Mao's vision of a Triad Communist vanguard did not come to pass, however. Although Mao enjoyed support from a handful of Triad groups, the majority of them saw the best future for themselves with the Nationalists.

One of the most important factors behind the Triad alliance with Chiang's Kuomintang army was the key triad boss, Tu Yueh-sheng ("Big-Eared Tu"), who lent his support to the cause. The leader of Shanghai's infamous Green Gang since 1910, the Triads under Tu's control dominated the city and the opium business for hundreds of miles around, and had effective control of the Yangtze River. The efforts of Tu and his men helped prop up the failing Kuomintang in Shanghai until 1949, when even he was forced to flee the Communist advance.

Mao ruthlessly punished the Triad members who did not manage to escape to Taiwan or make it Macau or Hong Kong with Chiang and

Chinese Nationalist leader Chiang Kai-shek forged an alliance with the Triads in his fight against Mao's Communist forces, which led to the creation of many new Triad gangs.

Tu Yueh-shen, better known as "Big-Eared Tu", was the leader of the Green Gang and kingpin of Triad crime in Shanghai. He used his opium smuggling network against Mao's Communist forces.

the remnants of the Kuomintang, for backing the wrong side. Post-1949, Mao's campaign against the Triads led to tens of thousands of executions. Few of those who were not hanged survived the horrors of the "re-education camps". This "iron fist" approach decimated the Triads in mainland China and it has been only in recent years that they have begun to claw back their dominance in its underworld once again.

The actions of both Mao and Chiang continue reverberating through the history of the Triads, shaping their destiny even today. Those Triad members who fled with Chiang to Taiwan saw their sons form new Triad societies that flourished under Kuomintang control of the island. Other Triads that had arisen out the Chinese Civil War, such as the 14K, survived their exile and began to prosper as never before, upsetting the established balance of Triad power across the world.

In recent years, a new generation of key Triad leaders has emerged, such as the notorious Wan Kuok Koi ("Broken Tooth" Koi) of the 14K

Key Triad boss Wan Kuok Koi, also known as Broken Tooth, also known as Broken Tooth Koi, remains determined and defiant despite his capture by the authorities in 1999.

and Chen Chi-Li ("Dry Duck") of the United Bamboo Gang. While they have inherited organizations forged in the heat of the Chinese Civil War, they are far too young to have been part of it themselves. Mao and Chiang are merely dead names to them. Their politics are governed by greed and desire and by business and illicit advantage. The only Triad traditions and history that they cling to are those of a purely criminal nature.

THE TRIADS TODAY

The last 100 years have seen massive changes around the Triads. Their ancient purpose for existing has disintegrated. Their country of origin has gone from being run by an Emperor to control by a Communist oligarchy, and they are no longer unique in being a trans-national organized crime network with branches spanning several continents.

Yet none of this has impacted on their reputation as the "Invincible Triads" and the "Immortal Triads". By adapting, they have retained everything from their domination as a theme in Asian action cinema, to a continuing global spread. From San Francisco to Vancouver and

Johannesburg, the Triads remain the biggest organized crime threat in many Western cities.

Whether fleeing mainland China due to Mao's takeover or surviving a twenty-first-century police crackdown, Triads have shown their adaptability and flexibility time and time again. While the names of societies, rackets and bases of operation remain fluid, all of the groups preserve the essential Triad and Tong structure, which allows them to organize for criminal enterprise wherever they find themselves. Society officers, with odd-sounding titles such as White Paper Fans and Straw Sandals, have never been as important as many outsiders believed. The basic arrangement of an overall head called the Shan Chu (Master of the Mountain to whom the Red Poles – local commanders responsible for between 15–50 basic soldiers known as 49s – ultimately report) is the key, and allows for considerable flexibility.

A Red Pole can be highly autonomous, whether his men control a single street or a multi-million dollar heroin trafficking operation. By being a collection of individual units in a loose network that can come together for massed strength if needed, Triad societies can operate effectively at the level both of a small gang and an international collective of more than 10,000 men. Removing one unit or one major boss rarely affects the whole syndicate, while the shared trappings of a secret society provide cohesion across distant and wildly disparate elements of the same Triad.

The rapidity of change that accompanies autonomy has also been reflected in the Triad societies' ability to move quickly into any new criminal enterprise. Triads have been amongst organized crime's pioneers in cyber-crime, credit card fraud and piracy of intellectual property. They have added luxury car theft and advance fee fraud to their common repertoire of illicit operations by learning from the success of Russian and Nigerian organized crime groups in these areas.

While still retaining their Chinese ethnicity, many Triads are now willing to enter into deeper alliances with foreign crime syndicates. In recent years, the Russian Mafiya (whom the Triads call "the walking bears") have become trusted collaborators in massive people smuggling, narcotics trafficking and prostitution networks requiring partners in the countries of the former Soviet Bloc. Triad groups operating in Southern Africa have linked up with local crime gangs for drug and wildlife crime purposes, while some Triad members have even travelled to South America to see whether the Colombian cartels could branch out into heroin production for them.

Triads are increasingly facing some of their toughest challenges from rival Chinese organized crime groups with non-Triad origins. Prime amongst these are the Dai Huen Jai ("Big Circle Boys"). They appeared in 1970 and were at first composed of ex-members of the Red Guard who had survived Mao's purges and subsequent imprisonment in the re-education camps, to flee to the West. The Big Circle Boys are now a major Triad competitor in both mainland China and North America.

Several criminologists predicted that China regaining control of Hong Kong and Macau in the late 1990s would signal a massive Triad exodus from the territories. As ever, the Triads adapted and stayed; they now use the regions as bases for a move back into mainland China. The Wo group and 14K now regularly work for the Second Department of the General Staff (the Chinese version of the CIA) and even the Premier of the People's Republic has referred to the Triads as "patriots" and "part of tradition". Therefore it is not surprising they have found it easy to forge a new web of police and political corruption in their old homeland. Many commentators are already calling the twenty-first century "the Chinese Century". If this is the case, then the twenty-first century may also be the Triad Century.

Despite a host of predictions, the Chinese authorities have not turned their massive power against the Triads and continue to prioritize targeting political protest rather than organized crime.

THE ORGANIZATSIYA – THE RUSSIAN MAFIYA

5

"The gates to a dangerous new world are open. Nobody will have the resources to stop them. You people in the West don't know our Mafiya yet, but you will."

Boris Urov, former Chief Investigator for the Russian Attorney-General

No country can claim to be free from organized crime. Any appearance that the former Soviet Union had of being relatively devoid of it was largely the result of propaganda. Even at the height of the Communist police state, the vory-v-zakone (thieves-in-law) ran sophisticated syndicates covering everything from a black market to extortion. "Western vices", such as drug addiction and prostitution, were rife and the Ministry of Internal Affairs fought a constant war against what was known as the "thieves' world".

However, under the repressive conditions of a police state, the fight against criminal networks was brutal and effective. Despite widespread poverty and the opportunities for extensive corruption in a one-party system, Russian organized crime was held firmly in check and within the borders of the USSR. After the fall of the Communist system and the removal of the Iron Curtain, however, there was nothing to prevent its rapid development and spread into the West.

When the first stories of the "Red Mafiya" surfaced in the West, many thought it was journalistic hype. Some even believed the stories were inspired by security services trying to invent a new Russian menace, since the Cold War was over. Yet soon bodies began to mount up in the streets of New York and London, just as they were in Moscow and St Petersburg. These deaths were only the visible tip of a deep-rooted organized crime problem that has gone on to shape not only the underworld, but also the politics and economy of Russia in the twenty-first century.

THE ORIGINS OF THE RUSSIAN MAFYA

The Russian Mafiya – often called the Organizatsiya – is not one homogenous group. In many ways it only exists as an umbrella term used to describe the myriad organized crime networks operating within the former Soviet Union. Given this, it is obvious the Mafiya does not have one single point of creation. The Ukrainian Bratva started in a different time and place to the Chechen Mafiya or the Solntsevo Syndicate. Yet there are many aspects of shared history between all elements of the Organizatsiya.

Organized crime societies existed in pre-Revolutionary Russia. The concept of the "thieves' world" was a part of Russian folklore, but had a strong basis in fact. Called the staryi blagorodnyi vorovskoi (old noble thieves), the early crime groups had a set of regulations by which members had to agree to live. They also had an initiation ritual and secret signs for recognizing each other. They lived in the vorovskoi mir (thieves' world), beyond the usual laws of the land and norms of society, but with its own form of courts and justice for those who broke its rules.

Seeing beyond the usual criminal myths of outlaws who gave some of the proceeds of their crimes to the poor, we can catch glimpses of early Russian underworld groups in the old noble thieves. They were enough of a reality to later give birth to the vory-v-zakone (thieves with a code of honour or thieves-in-law). The vory were a prominent part of life in Soviet gulags, instantly recognizable as a separate group

by their tattoos and shared dress code. Much more than a set of mere prison gangs, secret documents from the Ministry of Internal Affairs, which came to light after the fall of the Soviet Union, talk of the vory as, "A national fraternity spread in all places of imprisonment and in highly populated areas".

Once outside prison, evidence shows that ex-prisoners, who had become vory while in the correctional system, operated as part of a highly structured network. The vory certainly provided a national framework for co-operation between organized crime groups as far apart as Siberia, the Ukraine, the Baltic States and the Soviet Central Asian Republics. Taking advantage of official corruption, the vory were much more than the mere thieves their name suggests. They played a massive role in the black market, illegally sourcing both luxury and essential goods, that were not available in state shops, and selling them under the noses of the authorities.

The term Mafiya was first used in the Soviet Union to describe a vory scam where a factory owner had been persuaded by a gang to order more raw materials than he needed in order to manufacture surplus goods that the vory could sell. The type of organized exploitation of the Soviet economic system was one of the most common ways of generating illicit revenue, alongside illegal gambling and prostitution that the vory heavily controlled. Despite the levels of surveillance in the Soviet police state, the vory also handled the distribution of illegal drugs within the USSR. The market for heroin boomed in the 1980s after the Soviet invasion of Afghanistan, when many soldiers returned home hopelessly addicted to opium. Vory gangs were quick to exploit the growing market and to recruit former soldiers who were living in poverty into their ranks.

The vory groups grew in power throughout the duration of the USSR, but with the fall of the Soviet Union between 1989 and 1991, the constraining power of the police was lifted. When the statue of the secret police's founder Felix Dzerzhinsky was pulled down from outside the KGB headquarters in Moscow in 1991, it was a symbolic sign that the brakes were off and organized crime would now be able to grow unopposed.

However, it was the collapse of the post-Soviet economy that provided an even bigger benefit. Almost everyone in Russia had to become involved in some aspect of crime in order to survive. When the state could no longer afford to pay all of its police, and with many KGB officers out of work, it was only the vory and other emerging organized crime groups that offered them alternative employment. Poverty stricken government and local officials were also cheaply bought and a vast web of corruption was quickly established. By 1992, it was estimated that more than 75% of businesses in Russia were paying some form of protection money and that the only growth industry was crime.

The pulling down of the statue of Felix Dzerzhinsky, founder of the Soviet state's secret police, outside the KGB's headquarters in 1991.

THE STRUCTURE AND SECRETS OF THE RUSSIAN MAFIYA

Despite the fact that the Russian Mafiya is not one united group, shared elements of Organizatsiya history mean that from Moscow to Vladivostok, disparate gangs often enjoy a common heritage that is reflected in their structure, rules and even tattoos. While this collective culture has done little to stop the fierce, constant warfare between Mafiya gangs, it has helped the vorovskoi mir (thieves' world) continue into the twenty-first century.

The thieves' world is more than just another term for the Russian underworld; its mutual customs mean a loose Organizatsiya network can exist that allows rival gangs, thousands of miles apart, to recognize and work with each other with relative ease. Although the thieves' world existed in Tsarist Russia, it was in the gulags of the USSR that it became a unifying force among criminals across the hundreds of nationalities and regions of the former Soviet Union.

Within the Soviet prison system, it did not take the authorities long to recognize the existence of the vory-v-zakone (thieves with a code of honour), even across ethnic groups that would never normally mix. Their shared uniform made them instantly apparent – a stylized beard, home-made aluminium crosses and customized waistcoats. Members had to undergo an initiation and agree to follow a code that carried across into the world outside the gulag. Failure to follow the rules meant risking trial at the vory's own court system, called skhodki. The courts were held both inside and outside of prison, and an offending vor faced mutilation or death if he was found guilty.

In the 1950s, a Ministry of Internal Affairs investigator put together a secret report on vory-v-zakone. In it he described a "crowning" – the initiation that a prospective vor had to go through. The first element was swearing an oath, after which he would receive a special vory tattoo and a klichka (nickname), by which he would be known by all other vory. Among the codes he agreed to live by were commandments such as: "A vor should support another vor in any circumstances" and "All vory are obliged to attract and win sympathy from clever youth in order to replenish the group".

One of the rules was that no vor should serve in the army, which led to the Suka Wars or "Bitch Wars". During the Second World War, Stalin offered pardons to prisoners willing to fight against the invading Germans, which led many vory to join the army. However, at the end of the war, Stalin reneged on his promise and sent the prisoners back to the gulags. A massive split in vory ranks, between the suka (bitches)

Members of Russia's tax police clamp down on small fry black market traders. Unlike established vory, petty operators rarely have powerful police friends to protect them.

who had fought against the Nazis and those vory who had kept to their code, erupted. After hundreds of killings, the suka gained the upper hand and the code was altered to allow for collaboration with the state if it benefited the vory.

Elements of the vory code and variations of the initiation ceremony are still present in the majority of Russian Mafiya groups, even among members who have never been to prison. The system of secret symbolic tattoos the vory developed to enable them to recognize fellow vory and known traitors is also still used. Prisoners who are informants or who have committed sex crimes are forcibly tattooed using needles and a mixture of soot and urine, while vory themselves elect to have tattoos showing the crimes they have committed and how long they have served in prison. A skull on a finger, for example, will allow a member of the Mafiya to know that someone he has met for the first time is a murderer; a tiger on the arm signifies he is meeting a gang's enforcer. It has become the Mafiya equivalent of an exam certificate, combined with a calling card.

The vory have also been responsible for the most common structure used in the Organizatsiya. Most groups have a boss called either a pakhan or krestnii otets (leader of the families), under whom will be at least four brigadiers running specialist cells known as brigady (brigades). These can often have more than 200 individual boyeviky (soldiers) working in them. While staying in the shadows, there is evidence to suggest many Mafiya groups participate in the bratski krug (circle of brothers) – a policy-making and dispute-settling body, acting like a skhodki for the elite Organizatsiya bosses.

THE SOLNTSEVO CRIME SYNDICATE

In the fast-paced and violent world of the Russian Mafiya, what holds true one week can be overturned the next in a blast of bullets or by the discovery of a grisly, mutilated body. Suggesting one individual is a powerful pakhan (crime boss) or a certain group controls a particular racket does not just carry the risk of being outpaced by events, it can often put you in the line of vengeful Organizatsiya fire.

However, one thing all Mafiya specialists agree about is that the Solntsevo crime syndicate is the largest, most influential and wealthiest Organizatsiya group operating not only in Russia, but across the world. Its meteoric rise to power, both in its homeland and in other countries, provides a perfect illustration of why the "Red Mafiya" has become many international police authorities' gravest cause for concern.

The group that today launders billions of dollars in the West each year has its genesis in the Moscow suburb of Solntsevo. Although not as rough as many of the harsh concrete housing estates that surround

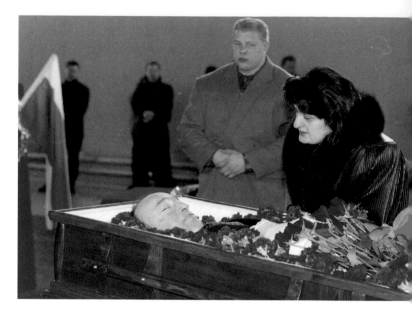

The widow of gangland leader and former Soviet Olympic Wrestling Coach Otari Kvantrishvili, pays her respects to her husband who was shot outside a Moscow bathhouse in 1994.

Moscow, Solntsevo had a reputation for being home to a large number of Moscow's most notorious vory-v-zakone. Their main areas of operation were the black market, vice and the distribution of drugs.

During President Mikhail Gorbachev's introduction of free market enterprise in the Perestroika economic reform programme, the Solntsevo vory were able to rapidly expand and extensively penetrate both state enterprises and Moscow's local government. It was during this period that the name Solntsevo or Solntsevskaya Brigada started to be talked about as a major Moscow underworld player. When the fall of the Soviet Union began in 1989, the Solntsevskaya Brigada was well placed to benefit from the ensuing chaos. With access to a pan-Soviet Union smuggling network, good political and business contacts and an experienced leadership, by the time of the USSR's official demise in December 1991, the Solntsevo syndicate had grown to a membership of more than 1,000 "soldiers".

The early 1990s saw Moscow become a Mafiya murder park. All of the city's Organizatsiya factions jostled for control of the lucrative protection, prostitution and gambling rackets that were a prominent feature of Russia's capital. The Solntsevo were engaged in an ongoing battle with their Moscow-based rivals, the Orekhovskaya Brigada as well as Georgian and Chechen Mafiya groups. The violence averaged more than two murders a week between 1991 and 1994.

The Solntsevo effectively announced their victory and undisputed domination of the Moscow underworld in April 1994 with the assassination of Otari Kvantrishvili. A former Olympic wrestling coach, convicted rapist, politician, leading Georgian Mafiya member and arranger of deals across the whole Organizatsiya, Otari Kvantrishvili was Moscow's kingpin of crime. He often entertained President Yeltsin at one of his "gentlemen only" clubs, and had recently been given a two-year tax break which included all his business interests. By arranging for his death using a former Russian special forces sniper, the

Solntsevo's path to power in the city was greatly smoothed.

With Moscow under their control, Solntsevskaya Brigada was able to concentrate on foreign expansion. It was already a partner of the Colombian cartels, selling them weaponry – including ex-Soviet military helicopters, but its plan to sell them a Soviet submarine had been uncovered and stopped – in exchange for cocaine. It had also made links with Triad and Italian Mafia groups, thanks to its major role in heroin and people trafficking, and was keen to consolidate its extensive operations in America and Israel. To this end, in 1994, it split itself into 12 sub-groups with a total of more than 9,000 members. Among the key leaders were Sergei Mikhailov (Mikhas), Viktor Averin and Yurii Esin, with V.K. Ivan'kov (Yaponchik) running the American side of things and Semyon Mogilevich running Israel.

The Solntsevskaya Brigada has continued to maintain its position not only as Moscow's prime Organizatsiya group, but also as a rapidly growing international crime syndicate. This is testament to its firepower, financial muscle and political connections that extend to the highest reaches of the Russian state. It is no surprise, therefore, that the FBI describes the Solntsevo syndicate as "A significant and sophisticated threat at a global level".

THE CHECHEN MAFIYA

Across the globe there are many organized crime gangs that began life as resistance movements. Launching an armed campaign against the established government of a nation is a costly affair and such groups often turn to crime in order to fund their operations. Once they have established illicit revenue streams through rackets such as extortion, drug trafficking and robbery, the profit motive often overtakes the political cause. This makes the Chechen Mafiya unusual in underworld terms – they began purely as organized criminals and have evolved into part of a major terror network.

In the 1980s, when organized crime in Russia started to emerge from the shadows to openly participate in the economic changes that were occurring due to Perestroika, the Moscow police became aware that the number of gangs composed of ethnic Chechens operating in the city was growing at an alarming pace. The blatant evidence for this was the number of bodies executed in what they called "Chechen fashion" – shot in the back of the head, mutilated and displayed near the victims' homes.

The increasing murder rate led to a series of investigations into the origins, structure and activities of these Chechen crime groups. Tsarist Russia had conquered Chechnya in the nineteenth century, but it took a century of warfare against Chechen Muslim guerrillas before control was total. During the Second World War, Stalin was so worried the Chechens might aid Nazi invaders that he deported hundreds of

FUNDING TERRORISM

For centuries, organized crime groups have been entwined with the sort of extreme resistance movements that we now call "terror networks". Many of today's premier criminal syndicates, notably the Triads, began as secret societies dedicated to the overthrow of a particular regime.

The Triads have long since lost any political motivation for their criminal activities, but the pattern they followed – an underground revolutionary movement turning to crime to fund its rebellion – is still repeated across the globe. Launching a terrorist campaign against the established government has always been a costly business that has often led terrorists to turn to arms smuggling, kidnapping, robbery and extortion to produce an income.

Once the initial CIA funding of al-Qa'eda ran out, it turned to organized crime to fund itself. Specializing in arms smuggling, heroin trafficking, counterfeiting and DVD piracy, al-Qaeda amasses millions of dollars a year, which then moves across international borders through the Islamic hawala money transfer system. Al-Qaeda receives additional financial support from the Chechen Mafiya, who plough some of their profits into Islamic, anti-Russian terrorism. Some terror groups, including the Colombian FARC movement, receive funding from organized criminals in return for providing specific services, such as guarding drug plantations.

As can be seen from the trajectory of terror groups, such as the IRA, enjoying criminal profits can become more important to some members than using them to actually fund terrorism. For many in the IRA, their original cause developed into a mere cloak for a criminal empire, taking in duty trafficking, drug dealing, pornography and prostitution alongside the usual sources of terrorist earnings.

In October 2004, the Russian capital was placed on a state of emergency and troops flooded the streets, after terrorists funded by the Chechen Mafiya took more than 700 people hostage in a theatre.

thousands of its citizens to other parts of the USSR. As a result, the Chechen communities that sprang up across Russia fell back on traditional clan ties and loyalties in an attempt to survive. This provided the perfect breeding ground for organized criminal groups to emerge.

Moscow had a large ethnic Chechen element and its crime gangs used links to family members in Chechnya and in Chechen communities elsewhere in the USSR to set up a smuggling network specializing in drugs and guns, separate to the one that was operated by the vory-v-zakone. As the Soviet police state began to fail, the Chechen gangs used their propensity for violence to carve out a criminal empire in Moscow, centred on the control of stolen car

markets, protection and narcotics. Profits were ploughed into buying political and police support in the now more independent Chechnya and among local government in Moscow.

The breadth of their operations was exposed in 1992 when the Chechen Mafiya undertook a massive swindle on Moscow's major banks that netted them more than a billion roubles (then the equivalent to $700 million). Through corruption in Chechnya they had obtained promissory notes that allowed them to take out huge amounts of cash in roubles; this was then converted into dollars for easier laundering. The investigation into the "billion rouble affair" also brought to light the fact that that the Chechen Mafiya in Moscow was responsible for the flow of an estimated 10,000 firearms a month into Chechnya. In return, vast amounts of opium flowed into Russia from Afghan warlords via the Chechen paramilitary groups of Wahabist Islamists, who were opposed to Russian influence in the country.

This tide of weaponry allowed the rebels in Chechnya to fight an open war against Russia between 1992 and 1996. The total breakdown of order in Chechnya benefited the Chechen Mafiya elsewhere in Russia without interfering with their still close political links to Russia's ruling elite. The Mafiya even played a role in facilitating President Yeltsin's ceasefire negotiations with the rebels in 1996. However, continuing terrorist activity led to a second Chechen War starting in 1999. Widespread atrocities by the Russian army in Chechnya and a massive Russian crackdown on all Chechen groups, whether political and criminal, throughout Russia, brought the Chechen Mafiya fully into the sphere of the rebels.

Whilst still making hundreds of millions of dollars through extortion, car theft, narcotics and arms trafficking, the Chechen Mafiya has become fully integrated into the struggle for Chechnya's independence. Known Chechen Mafiya leaders have participated in the planning and execution of terrorist attacks, such as the Beslan school siege and Moscow subway bombing of 2004, and its criminal network now launders money and provides weapons for Taliban leader Mohammed Omar. The Chechen Mafiya's transformation from organized crime syndicate into a terrorist group is complete in the eyes of the CIA who described it as "An integral element of Al-Qa'eda, providing access to a global smuggling operation, high-grade weaponry and financial support".

Supreme leader of the Taliban, Mullah Mohammed Omar, enjoys a successful arms dealing and money laundering relationship with the Chechen Mafiya according to the CIA.

TAMBOVSKAYA GRUPPIROVKA CRIME SYNDICATE

Asking around about the influence of the Tambovskaya Gruppirovka crime syndicate in Saint Petersburg produces strong reactions. One local councillor told me, "You want to know how powerful the Tambov bastards are? They even steal monkeys and tigers from the zoo and no one catches them!" This is the most unusual way of gauging criminal influence I've ever come across, but it is not entirely inaccurate.

Throughout the late 1990s and early twenty-first century, Saint Petersburg Zoo has suffered several raids in which rare animals were taken, by members of Tambovskaya Gruppirovka syndicate, for sale to private collectors. The authorities have a good idea of who is responsible, but no action was taken against them. The pattern of successful Tambov crimes and police failure to prosecute extends way beyond zoological theft, however. It even includes fatal shootings that have been captured by television cameras, but whose perpetrators remain untouched by the law.

The Tambovskaya Gruppirovka (or Organizatsiya Tambov) comes from the small Russian town of Tambov, 200 miles south of Moscow. The town was home to a group of vory-v-zakone who built up power by supplying the thriving black markets in Moscow and Saint Petersburg. Although the leadership remained in Tambov, they had brigadiers in Moscow and Saint Petersburg to look after their interests. As the profits rolled in, the brigadiers recruited large numbers of enforcers and moved aggressively into prostitution and extortion rackets in both cities. By the time of the collapse of the Soviet Union in 1991, the Tambovskaya Gruppirovka was a major underworld player.

The leadership in Tambov took the decision that stiff competition from the Chechen Mafiya and Solntsevskaya Brigada in Moscow made Saint Petersburg a better place to concentrate their efforts. They then flooded the city with Tambov soldiers, pulled from Moscow to ensure they could outman every other Mafiya gang. They also took steps to ensure that they had the largest "roof" in Saint Petersburg. In Organizatsiya terms, the roof is the protection that those you pay in politics and the police can extend to you, "so that when it rains you don't get wet".

With domination of Saint Petersburg achieved through a mixture of influence over local politicians and the police and traditional gangster firepower, the Tambovskaya Gruppirovka were able to bring about alliances with Saint Petersburg's other major Organizatsiya groups, including the brigady Malysheva and Vorkutinskaya. This, however, did not stop the number of Mafiya-related murders in Saint Petersburg averaging more than 700 a year from 1992 to the present. No wonder the city became known as "Russia's crime capital" or "Chicago on the Neva".

rapid growth in the twenty-first century has been in its legitimate interests in oil, gas, minerals, food and alcohol importation. Reported to own many of the top 100 companies in northwest Russia, the Tambov is now a commercial as well as a criminal empire.

The extent and continuing growth of the Tambov overseas empire can be judged by the increasing number of arrests of its members made in foreign countries. In 2008, Spanish police arrested 20 of its members and seized $307,000 in cash, 23 luxury cars and froze bank accounts with a total of more than 12 million them. As part of the operation, arrests were also made in Berlin for money laundering. Also in 2008, Bulgarian prosecutors made arrests and claimed a Tambov money laundering scheme had ran more than $1.4 billion of dirty money through the various businesses within the country. However, such arrests have done nothing to dent Tambov's dizzying record of criminal growth which continues to go from strength to strength.

THE ORGANIZATSIYA IN ISRAEL

Until the end of the 1980s, Israel hardly ever featured in any expert analysis of global organized crime. Aside from a few reports in criminology journals looking at the gangs based around the country's prominent role in the worldwide diamond trade or how vice prospered in the Jewish state, it was rarely mentioned. Organized Israeli criminal activity was judged to be small-scale, localized and without a significant international dimension.

However, the Organizatsiya changed the situation in Israel within the space of a few years. From the mid-1990s onwards, reports by the UN, the FBI and a raft of police agencies around the world were all pointing towards Israel as a "hot zone of international organized criminality". Even by the rapid growth typical of the Russian Mafiya, this was an incredible illicit success story for the Organizatsiya, and a miserable misfortune for the majority of law-abiding citizens of Israel.

The swift and deep penetration of Israel by elements of the Organizatsiya and its transformation into one of their key strongholds outside Russia was largely down to a fundamental concept of Zionism – aliyah (ascent). Embodying the sense of return to the Biblical "promised land", aliyah led to the enshrinement in Israel of the Law of Return, which afforded every Jew in the world the guaranteed right of assisted immigration. Even when Jewish emigration from the Soviet Union was heavily restricted in the 1950s and 1960s, many vory-v-zakone paid heavy bribes and provided forged documents to prove Jewish descent and escape from Communism.

When Israel and the Soviet Union reached a secret nuclear spying agreement in the 1970s, the number of Jews allowed to emigrate from Russia each year greatly increased. This also meant a higher number of Soviet criminals – with both genuine and fraudulent Jewish ancestry –

The Tambov crimes range from the commonplace, such as vice, murder and narcotics, to the slightly surreal theft of monkeys, polar bears and tigers from Saint Petersburg's zoo.

The favourable conditions the Tambovskaya Gruppirovka enjoyed in Saint Petersburg had to be defended from new rivals through a constant flow of bribes and violence. In 1995, when one of the top Tambov Brigadiers in the city, Mikhail Bravve, was caught by an ambush that left him and his four bodyguards wounded from the blasts of several Kalashnikovs, more than 30 gangsters from rival gangs were shot in a fortnight of retaliation. When the rivals hit back by killing the brother of Tambov Brigadier Victor Gavrilenkov and making an attempt on his life, the word went out: "Kill more of them". By the end of the year, the truculent Kazanskya gang run by former Olympic boxer Artur Kzhizhevich was firmly back in line minus many of its members.

Although dominating Saint Petersburg rackets ranging from burial spots at cemeteries to vice and extorting money from more than 70 per cent of businesses in the city, Tambovskaya Gruppirovka's most

setting up shop in Israel. Until 1988, these Russian criminal émigrés were too small in number to work effectively with their comrades back in the Soviet Union and pose much of problem to Israeli law enforcement. However, between 1988 and 1995, more than 750,000 Jewish émigrés left Russia for Israel.

According to Israeli police intelligence officer Brigadier General Dan Ohad, in a briefing to his American colleagues, more than 30,000 of those were related to elements of the Organizatsiya. An Israeli police sting entitled "Operation Romance" caught a senior Israeli Interior Ministry official taking payments from Russian Mafiya members in exchange for approving Israeli passports for known criminals without genuine Jewish ancestry. Even at the time, the police admitted it was "only the tip of the iceberg".

Although some established Mafiya leaders, such as Gregory Lerner, who was wanted for defrauding four Moscow banks of $106 million,

An Israeli police intelligence officer checks the nationalities of prostitutes working in Israel and suspected of having been smuggled illegally into the country by elements of the Organizatsiya.

were eventually prosecuted, hundreds escaped any action at all. In 1995, US State Department official Jonathan Winer commented, "There is not a major Russian organized crime figure who we are tracking who does not also carry an Israeli passport". Aside from Israeli citizenship affording a safe base to flee to if problems emerged in Russia, with so many ex-Russians and Mafiya members living in the country, the leading Organizatsiya groups were soon setting up rackets across Israel.

The favoured area was vice. According to Commander Meir Gilboa, Chief of the Israeli Serious Crime Unit, the Organizatsiya would buy East European women for $10,000–$15,000, smuggle them into Israel

DIAMOND, GEM AND PRECIOUS METAL SMUGGLING

Diamonds, gems and precious metals, such as gold and platinum, have an established role as an internationally accepted alternative to hard currency. Therefore, they have always played a major part in the modern underworld – when organized crime gangs are not interested in stealing them, they can still make a profit from the clandestine transportation and importation of them.

The evasion of taxation on the importation of precious metals by smugglers is as old as the imposition of duty itself. Before the growth of global banking, gold and other valuable metals were the best way for organized criminal groups to move resources across national borders. Today, in countries where exchange and capital flight regulations are in place, criminal networks derive an income from turning assets into gold, platinum or gems that can then be smuggled abroad to evade such economic controls. Before 9/11, al-Qa'eda converted more than $20-million-worth of currency into diamonds, knowing that they would prove untraceable, despite any restrictions applied to the group after its terrorist outrage.

The difficulty of transporting metals has led organized crime to increasingly focus on the smuggling of conflict diamonds, also known as "blood diamonds". These gems derive from countries such as Angola, Congo and Sierra Leone, where they are often obtained through forced labour and are used to fund warfare, armies of child soldiers and the continuation of war crimes. Organized crime networks, especially the Russian Mafiya, Israeli groups and Nigerian syndicates, currently help smuggle more than $10-million-worth of these illicit stones per week to major diamond dealing centres, such as Antwerp and Tel Aviv.

and force them to work as sex slaves in the red light districts of Haifa and Tel Aviv. Alongside this appalling trade in human misery, an extensive Mafiya-controlled pornography, drug distribution and extortion network soon sprung up. By 2012, experts estimated that Israel had also been used to help launder up to $25 billion of Russian Mafiya illicit profits. The situation was not helped by the fact that, for many years, Israel did not have any prohibition against many common forms of "washing" dirty money or membership of an organized crime group. The Israeli police dubbed it "Local international crime".

According to frontline law defenders, such as Commander Gilboa, the Russian Mafiya is a key threat to Israel's future, "They have the means at their disposal to corrupt government and whole economic systems". With growing evidence that they are doing just this, and with criminal profits booming from their various rackets, it is no wonder many Organizatsiya bosses continue to call Israel "the second country".

THE ORGANIZATSIYA IN AMERICA

In the early 1990s, when many crime writers in the US were writing stories that earned headlines such as "Red Mafiya Scare" and the "Secret Soviet Invasion", the US Justice Department was quick to dismiss worries about the Organizatsiya in America. In private briefings, they accused some writers of "hype" and of "producing stories on the Russians as it's sexier than the old Mob". In public, it went as far as to say it did not consider "the Russian criminals as organized crime".

However, by 1995, the Justice Department had ensured the arrest of Vyacheslav Ivan'kov, one of the brigadiers of the Solntsevo crime syndicate, for running rackets in America, and the FBI was talking about "broad connectivity" between the various Organizatsiya groups operating illegal gambling, extortion, drug smuggling, money laundering and vice operations on both the East and West Coast. One of the reasons that the Justice Department got it so wrong to begin with was because many Mafiya members coming into the US had been carrying out a criminal process called "identity shuffling".

The Justice Department had been tracking criminals through the Immigration and Naturalization Service, but they had failed to account for the fact that many Russian criminals had obtained the identities of dead Jews to first emigrate to Israel before heading to America. This shuffling of identities across countries allowed them to launder their criminal history and sneak into the US under the law enforcement radar. A number of Organizatsiya had used this tactic to enter America before the fall of the Soviet Union, but they had not brought much attention to themselves, usually preying only on Russian émigré communities in areas such as Brooklyn's Brighton Beach.

Before his arrest in 1995, Vyacheslav Ivan'kov, known to his Red Mafiya colleagues as Yaponchik (Little Japanese) was sent to the USA to expand the operations of the Solntsevo Syndicate.

However, post-1991, other American organized crime groups were quick to notice the large numbers of Mafiya coming into their territories. FBI and police wiretaps on Cosa Nostra began to pick up on talk of groups the American mob nicknamed "the Odessa Gang", "the Moscow Gang", "the Saint Petersburg Gang" and "the Russian gypsy gangs". Until this point, Cosa Nostra had only had one significant encounter with a Russian competitor, back in 1985, when the Gambino Family had murdered Evesi Agron to muscle in on his diesel tax fraud. Now they were running into them "all over the place". It was clear in New York, Philadelphia, Los Angeles, San Francisco and Toronto, that the Organizatsiya groups were carving out a piece of the extortion, drug and vice rackets. As far as the American mob were concerned, the Russians were in the US and they were organized.

The more recent Russian Mafiya arrivals hooked up with those who had been in America since the 1970s in order to speed up their US expansion plans. Many Cold War émigrés with criminal backgrounds, such as Monya Elson, were only too eager for the chance to team up with powerful groups like the Solntsevo syndicate. Elson was a hitman with more than 100 admitted kills to his name and the motto: "Don't show pity or regret when you kill, don't even think about it". He was arrested in 1993 after a bloody shoot-out with members of a rival syndicate. Months later, in 1994, expert financial fraudster and money launderer Marat Balagula was arrested. Faced with $85 million of tax evasion charges, Balagula is believed to have provided evidence that detailed Organizatsiya operations and helped lead to the arrest of Vyacheslav Ivan'kov in 1995. Known to fellow Mafiya members as Yaponchick (Little Japanese), Ivan'kov had been sent by the Solntsevo to America in 1993 to expand and run their US operations.

Despite the run of high-profile Mafiya-related arrests, the US-based Organizatsiya continued to grow. It soon boasted over 5,000 members and was heavily involved in the forced sex trade, illegal gambling and stock market manipulation. It was also blamed for crimes ranging from the murder of world cruiserweight boxing contender Sergei Kobozev in Brooklyn in 1995, to channelling $15 billion through the Bank of New York in 1997.

With more than 60,000 Russian residents, Brighton Beach in Brooklyn, known locally as Little Odessa, has become the centre for the Organizatsiya's US operations. Any doubt that the Russian Mafiya is doing well on American soil is abruptly ended with a visit to Little Odessa's nightclubs, where it is impossible to miss the Mafiya men flaunting their ill-gotten wealth. No surprise then that some in American law enforcement call the area "the most notorious Russian satellite since Sputnik". By 2012 it was reported to Congress that several Russian Mafiya groups were now firmly established on both the East and West Coast and estimated to be laundering several billion dollars a year through American financial institutions and businesses. The once promised "Red tide of crime" could finally said to be flooding America's gangland.

KEY CRIMES

Among the key instigators of the attempt to seize control of the USSR and reintroduce strong Communist party control in the coup of August 1991, were senior members of the KGB. One of the public reasons they gave for their actions was to tackle the rising tide of crime sweeping across Russia and its satellite countries.

Although the coup leaders and their supporters did not use the terms Organizatsiya or Mafiya, they did neatly catalogue their key crimes up until that point. They spoke about the Soviet Union being "to the neck in drugs" and "assailed by prostitutes, pimps and pornographers". They also spoke of all businesses facing extortion, banks "under criminal control", "murder after murder", and massive collusion between politicians and "thieves with guns". The failed August putsch was possibly the last time that the Organizatsiya faced a serious attempt to rein in its power. In its aftermath, the key crimes that the coup plotters had pledged to tackle went from bad to uncontrollable.

If Russia was "up to its neck" in drug problems in August 1991, by 1993 it was in way over its head. Although some of the vory-v-zakone had dabbled in drug distribution during the most severe days of the Soviet police state, it had never been their major source of income. The vory had, however, an established pan-Soviet smuggling network for

black market goods, and they were quickly able to convert this into a narcotics network when they saw the potential profits and low risks of being caught.

The Organizatsiya began working with foreign partners to turn the former Soviet Union into a major Eurasian narcotics transit corridor. The Mafiya undertook heroin transportation from Asia to Europe for the Triads and moved cocaine for the Colombians. The Chechen Mafiya quickly started to control opium coming through Afghanistan and the Central Asian Republics. By 1993, hard drug seizures were at a record high for Russia, with more than 50 tonnes seized in that year, but police admitted this was merely a fraction of the amount going through the country each month. Alongside their role in international drug transit, the Mafiya developed a domestic market for illegal drugs, finding thousands of users amongst the young and the poor. By the twenty-first century, Russia had one of the largest number of drug addicts in the world and correspondingly high levels of HIV infection.

AIDS has swept across Russia in recent years – just one of the many devastating side-effects brought about by the incredibly high number of Russian users of Organizatsiya-supplied heroin.

The Organizatsiya's culpability for the crisis levels of HIV in Russia is not purely down to their domination of drug distribution. Another major source of Mafiya income is vice. Experts estimate that the number of prostitutes working in the former Soviet Union has grown a thousandfold since 1991. As well as control of the domestic vice market, the Mafiya has become a major player in the global trafficking of women for use in the sex trade. Young Russian and East European women are sold into forced sex operations in America, Israel, Australia and Europe. The Mafiya also run vice rings in Japan, Thailand and other parts of Asia, where European women can command a price premium. In 1998, the Mafiya used the FIFA World Cup in France as an opportunity to flood the country with both drugs and prostitutes, knowing the French authorities would be stretched to cope with the

The huge numbers of visitors to Paris for the 1998 World Cup overwhelmed the authorities, providing the perfect cover for the Organizatsiya to flood the country with drugs and prostitutes.

massive surge of visitors to the event. It is no surprise, therefore, that the Russians now dominate vice in France.

Despite earning billions a year from narcotics and vice, the main source of the Mafiya's illicit revenue remains the extortion of businesses. In 1993, it was estimated that more than 75 per cent of businesses made some form of protection payment to Organizatsiya groups. Despite a concentrated effort by the authorities, this figure has not fallen in the twenty-first century. However, many Western businesses can at least now buy their protection from state-approved "legitimate" security firms that are solely run and manned by Mafiya members.

Although the major Organizatsiya groups have established their own legitimate business empires (experts believe the majority of the top 100 Russian companies are under criminal control) they have not abandoned the chance to make money through simple stealing. The last decade has seen Russia ravaged by art theft – from precious religious icons to modern art, thousands of the best pieces are now missing. As leading artist and theft victim, Sergei Bugayev, commented, "The Mafiya even dominate contemporary art".

KEY FIGURES

There is a Russian police joke that goes, "How do you tell whether someone is a pakhan (crime boss) or one of the simple boyeviky (soldiers)? Easy, if we catch him and he goes to prison, he isn't important enough to be a pakhan".

While Russian humour is often lost in translation, the underlying point here is clear – the key figures in the Organizatsiya rarely find themselves behind bars.

When Moscow politician Viktor Novosyolov was killed on the orders of the brigadiers of the Tambovskaya Gruppirovka crime syndicate, the police failed even to uncover a motive for the crime. It was journalists who discovered the identities of the two men who carried out the bombing on Novosyolov. Their finding led to the bombers' arrests, but the Tambov boss, known as Kostya Mogila (Mogila was a nickname meaning "the grave"), escaped prosecution,

despite good evidence linking him to the crime. It is a pattern that is repeated on a daily basis in the Russian justice system.

If you ask the police why this is, the same answer comes back at you from all ranks: "The top men have wide roofs". It is beyond disheartening when even senior law enforcement officials are resigned to explaining that the web of police and political corruption Mafiya leaders have bought themselves does indeed seem to shelter the most important of them from police action.

Semyon Mogilevich (below) was described by his university teachers as able to "add, divide and multiply seven digit numbers in his head", so it is no wonder he masterminded billions of dollars' worth of financial crime.

Organizatsiya leader Sergei Mikhailov (right) at the time of his arrest, in 1996, in Switzerland. The death of several key witnesses and protection by the Russian government meant he eventually escaped Swiss justice.

While this holds true for key Organizatsiya figures in Russia, justice is more likely to catch up with them when they operate abroad. An example of this is Vyacheslav Ivan'kov, who is also known as Yaponchick (Little Japanese). A key leader of the Solntsevo crime syndicate, he was arrested in Switzerland on suspicion of money laundering. The Russian authorities requested his extradition on murder and fraud charges and within weeks of returning home he was a free man – even able to travel to America in 1993 to supervise Solntsevo expansion in the US. For the next two years he developed vice, gambling, extortion and drug rackets in New Jersey, Philadelphia and Brooklyn, instigating up to 70 Mafiya-related killings in America. When the FBI eventually caught him, he received a nine-year sentence for extortion and the Justice Department was understandably unwilling to send him back to Russia.

The Swiss authorities learned their lesson with Ivan'kov. In 1996, when they arrested the overall pakhan of the Solntsevo, Sergei Mikhailov, they decided to try him in Switzerland. It looked like an open-and-shut case – when they raided the castle near Geneva that Mikhailov had bought in 1995, they found evidence of the millions of dollars he had laundered through front companies in Israel, America and Switzerland. By the time Mikhailov came to trial in 1998, however, several key witnesses were conveniently dead and the Russian government had decided to refuse to aid the prosecution. Mikhailov was freed and continues to run the Solntsevo crime syndicate. Under his leadership it has become the leading Russian Mafiya group with a criminal empire operating in America, Europe, Israel, Asia, and Australia, as well as Russia.

Mikhailov has been greatly aided in becoming the most powerful Russian Mafiya boss operating in the world today by a skilful alliance with one key figure – Semyon Mogilevich. Although his name did not make headlines in the West until 1999, when he was linked with the Mafiya's laundering of billions of dollars through the Bank of New York, Mogilevich had been part of the Russian underworld since the 1970s. Described by his former university professor as "Brilliant – able to add, divide and multiply seven digit numbers in his head instantaneously and see a panoramic picture of national and world economies," he fell in with a Moscow vory group known as Lybretskaya.

By the time he emigrated from Russia to Israel in 1990, Mogilevich had already masterminded crimes worth billions of dollars. Always one step ahead of the authorities, he moved to Hungary in 1991 and set up a global money laundering and vice network. Immensely powerful and respected across all Organizatsiya groups, Mogilevich was approached by Mikhailov in 1992 to become part of the Solntsevo ruling council and run its Israeli operations. Mogilevich was arrested in Moscow in January 2008 for suspected tax evasion. However, he was released in July 2009 after the Russian Interior Ministry stated: "The charges he faced were not of a particularly grave nature." Despite the protection he seems to enjoy in Russia, abroad Mogilevich is regarded as one of the world's most dangerous mobsters and in October 2009, the FBI placed him on their infamous Ten Most Wanted List.

THE ORGANIZATSIYA TODAY

Historians rarely agree. Even on something as basic as the date of the fall of the Soviet Union there are camps and divisions. Some argue the USSR ceased to be an effective state on November 9, 1989, when the Berlin Wall started crumbling. Others hold that the USSR continued until December 8, 1991, when the official declaration of ending it was signed. However, there is one thing that everyone agrees upon and that is that as the political superpower fell, a criminal superpower – the Organizatsiya – came of age.

Whether this is due to a relatively flexible structure, geographical position or its network of corruption, the Russian Mafiya has proved that it is usually able to move into the provision of anything that is prohibited and not sufficiently policed faster than any other competing criminal network. The Organizatsiya has earned an internal reputation not just for brutality, but also for pioneering. From cyber-crime and designer drugs, to new money laundering scams, Russian criminals have got their first. They have also shown no bounds to their daring – stealing Scud missiles and even attempting to obtain nuclear material for sale to terrorists.

Within five years of the disintegration of the Communist system, and the demise of the only superpower able to challenge American hegemony, the Organizatsiya emerged from the Soviet ashes as a force that was capable of redefining the face of the global gangland. While the Russian Interior Ministry is currently tracing Organizatsiya operations in 28 foreign countries, the FBI believes it is actually operating in more than 50 nations. From America to Holland, Switzerland to South Africa it has set up shop and is slowly expanding beyond its current role in the forced sex trade, drugs, extortion and gem smuggling operations. In Israel it has already become the dominant organized crime network, while in France it is heading in the same direction, having pushed many of the established forces in the French underworld into a secondary, subservient role.

In countries such as Italy and Japan, where the native organized crime network is too strong for the Russian Mafiya to challenge, they have developed mutually beneficial arrangements. In return for permission to operate vice and smuggling rackets on Italian Mafia and Yakuza territory, they agree to pay a percentage of their profits in "tax" to the other groups. Through the narcotics and arms trafficking, the Organizatsiya has developed strong alliances with the Colombian cartels, Turkish gangs and Triads.

This book is now in its second edition. One of the most generous sources of information on the Organizatsia and the links between Russian politicians and criminal networks for the original edition was a man that many suspect was murdered by the Mafiya. That man was Alexander Litvinenko, sometimes known by the tabloid title "the radioactive Russian spy" after his dying days as victim of

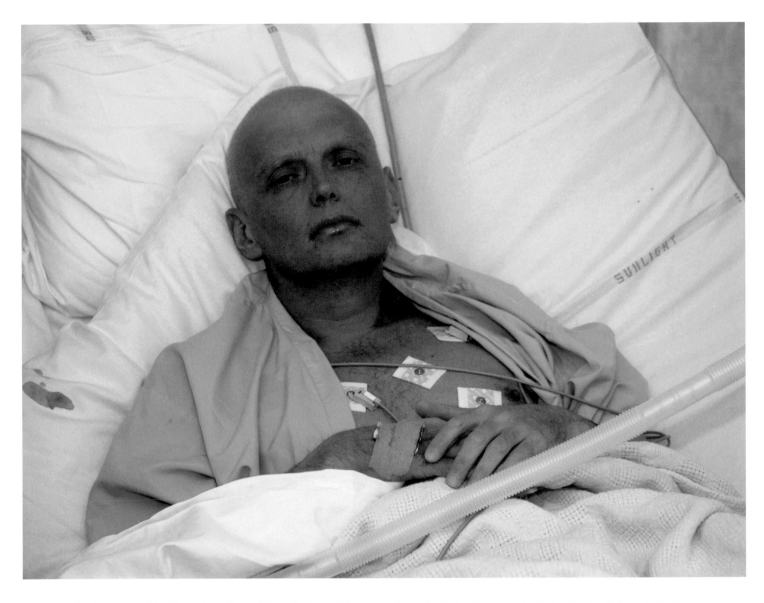

poisoning by the rare and highly toxic radionuclide polonium-210 were seared onto global consciousness in November 2006.

Although some have portrayed him as raving conspiracy theorist, Litvinenko had been a lieutenant-colonel in the Federal Security Service of the Russian Federation (FSB), the successor organization to the Soviet KGB. In 1998, after more than 12 years loyal service in the KGB and FSB, Litvinenko had fled Russia after claiming the then head of the FSB – future Russian President Vladimir Putin – had ordered him to assassinate billionaire businessman Boris Berezovsky.

Litvinenko, was an expert on the workings of the FSB and linkage between the security services and elements of the Russian Mafiya and had earned the hatred of the Solntsevo crime syndicate. Although he drafted a statement before his imminent death in which he blamed President Putin for the conspiracy to silence him through the 'beating wings of the angel of death', many believe the actual mechanics of his

Alexander Litvinenko pictured suffering the deadly impact of radioactive poisoning at the Intensive Care Unit of London's University College Hospital on November 20, 2006. The picture was taken shortly before his death as Alex wanted the world to see what his murderers had done to him.

bizarre radioactive murder were carried out by Mafiya members.

That it seems entirely possible and plausible that members of an organized crime group could kill with impunity on the international stage, have access to radioactive material and potentially collude with presidents, is a testament to the power the Organizatsiya has achieved in today's Russia. It top leaders launder billions through London, the Dutch Antilles and Israel on a yearly basis and have legitimate business empires that stretch across the globe. They have bribed their way to safe positions and, while their political allies remain in power, seem truly untouchable.

GANGLAND AMERICA

6

"The only way out is death."
Outlaw Motorcycle Club motto

The strength of the American Mafia in the USA creates an impression in most people's mind that Cosa Nostra rules organized crime unchallenged. This notion has been strengthened by the entertainment industry's love affair with the American Mafia that usually portrays them as the top dogs in all areas of criminal enterprise.

Despite its formidable power and size, Cosa Nostra has never been the only player in organized crime in the United States. More than 50 years before the wave of immigration from Sicily brought leaders of the Black Hand to the USA, cities such as New York, Chicago and New Orleans all had thriving organized criminal networks linked to numerous street gangs and top politicians. From the earliest organized Anglo-Saxon criminal gangs, who later became associated with the anti-immigrant political movement the Know-Nothings, to infamous Irish gangs, such as 40 Thieves and The Kerryonians, America has always been a gangland.

Journalists often write about new organizations replacing the American Mafia as the dominant criminal power in the USA. These stories invariably prove as over-hyped and false as the claims that were made in the 1980s that the Cuban Mafia was poised to seize control of the US underworld. However, the success of the FBI in clamping down on many Mafia activities has helped to create a power vacuum into which other organized criminal gangs have moved. As we shall discover, recent years have seen the emergence of new players who are shaping the ever-changing face of gangland America.

THE OUTLAW BIKER GANGS

The dominant, non-Mafia force in gangland America today is without doubt the outlaw biker gangs. If you were to listen to the publicists employed by the Hells Angels and other motorcycle gangs, you would be forgiven for thinking that they are all merely lawful organizations that unfortunately have criminal members within their ranks. This may be true for some of the gangs but not all of them. The hired spin-doctors also claim that the various outlaw biker gangs have been the victims of smear campaign by governments who wish to portray them as one of the growing powers within organized crime in North America. However, no amount of paid-for advocacy can disguise the number of contract killings believed to have been carried out by some members of these groups in many American states, or the evidence of the vice-like grip of some gangs on the multi-billion dollar illegal methamphetamine trade across the USA.

As in many criminal organizations, the early origins of the outlaw biker gangs remain contentious. Most informed, neutral authorities agree that one of the most significant starting points was the POBOB (Pissed Off Bastards Of Bloomington), a Californian biker gang formed from Second World War veterans. In 1946, a July 4 race meeting in the small town of Hollister in California between the POBOB and other gangs saw 4,000 bikers rioting after one biker was arrested and the others stormed the jail to free him.

Over the next few years these early motorcycle clubs – immortalized by the 1953 Marlon Brando movie *The Wild One* – set the pattern for the emergence of outlaw biker gangs across America. In California the Hells Angels established themselves as the dominant gang, while groups such as the Pagans, the Outlaws and Bandidos sprang up across the rest of the country. One thing they all had in common however was that they saw themselves as "1 per cent-ers", after the American Motorcyclist Association made the statement, "99 per cent of motorcyclists are law-abiding citizens and only 1 per cent are not." For outlaw bikers, this has translated into the idea that they represent the 1 per cent of citizens who believe the law has no meaning for them.

The crimes the public tend to associate with bikers are gang rapes, intimidation and occasionally fatal acts of violence, such as the infamous slaying of black Rolling Stones fan Meredith Hunter at the Altamont music festival in 1969, when Hells Angels were hired by the band as security. However, as reports by the President's Commission on Organized Crime and others have shown, the reality is that the outlaw biker gangs have evolved into a sophisticated, well-disciplined and powerful element of structured criminal activity in the USA.

To prevent infiltration by law enforcement officers, membership today is strictly controlled. Not only do prospective members have to be nominated by an existing gang insider, in-depth background checks are also run. The "prospect" then has to serve a one to three

Many members of the Hells Angels and other outlaw biker gangs are now at the forefront of non-Mafia-related organized crime across the United States and Canada.

year apprenticeship. It is believed that some gangs, although not all of them, require that recruits must "roll their bones" (commit a gang-ordered murder) before they earn their "colours" (the leather or denim patched jacket that shows the club's name, logo and location) before they become a full member. Once in, loyalty is ensured by strict enforcement of gang rules with punishments that range from the burning off of club tattoos, to execution for any infringement.

Outlaw biker gangs' main criminal activities are drug-related. Although playing a role in cocaine and heroin dealing, especially in more isolated areas, they hold effective control over the trade in meth-amphetamines, being the largest players in production and distribution. Drug profits are often reinvested in massage parlours, escort services and pornography production. Law enforcement authorities have identified that the traditional US Mafia often use outlaw biker gangs as loansharking enforcers and assassins. The Pagans are the outfit most favoured by the Mob after successfully rubbing out men like Philip "Chicken Man" Testa, the Philadelphia Mafia boss, in 1981.

With hundreds of chapters and thousands of members across the USA, the various outlaw bikers are a fearsome, powerfully organized criminal element nationwide. Like Cosa Nostra before them, they are increasingly making attempts to legitimize themselves. According to the President's Commission on Organized Crime, the future will see the biker gangs increasingly "abandoning their outlaw image, wearing suits and driving luxury cars: in essence, becoming an outlaw motorcycle gang without motorcycles".

PORNOGRAPHY

In modern times, pornography comes in many different forms of media – from films and photographs to cartoons and audio recordings. All of them, however, depict human sexual behaviour and are designed to bring about sexual arousal. Using this definition, the first recorded piece of pornography is the figurine that archaeologists call Adonis von Zschernitz, which dates to 7,200 BCE. Pornography was common in the Roman Empire and in Japan, in 1808, more than 800 shops selling pornography were recorded in Edo and Osaka.

However, as laws reflecting cultural taboos concerning sexual behaviour were introduced, the creation and distribution of pornography increasingly became a prohibited activity, allowing organized crime to move into the market to satisfy a continuing demand for it.

A significant source of revenue for many crime gangs in the nineteenth century, the creation of new technologies, such as photography and film, led to a massive boom in criminal pornography in the early years of the twentieth century. The first countries to produce large numbers of pornographic movies were France, Germany and Argentina. They supplied a global demand for early pornographic hits, such as the 1910 German film, *Am Abend*.

As cultural taboos on so-called "softcore" and "hardcore" pornography relaxed in the latter half of the twentieth century, adult entertainment became a mainstream industry from which organized crime investments are estimated to make billions of dollars in legitimate profits. They continue to make illicit profits from pornography by supplying its most extreme forms, such as child pornography, bestiality and extreme sexual violence, that are still prohibited, or by supplying pornographic material to countries such as Saudi Arabia, where a total ban remains in place.

LA EME

La Eme has gone from being a 13-strong prison gang in 1957 to a massive and blood-drenched modern organized crime group controlling an increasing amount of the US narcotics trade.

Prison is meant to be one of the answers for organized crime. However, in America, during the last 40 years, the high security establishments of the US correctional system have ironically become the incubation chambers for a whole raft of new organized crime networks. The largest of these is La Eme – commonly called the Mexican Mafia or MM (it is also known as El Eme, La Hafia and Mafioso).

There has been a tradition of Hispanic street gangs on the West Coast of America dating back to the 1920s, when Mexican refugees fled the political violence resulting from the Mexican Revolution and settled in what became the barrios of East Los Angeles and other Californian cities. By the mid-1950s, infamous gangs such as the El Hoyo MaraVilla and the Black Angels had a number of members within the correction system serving long sentences for crimes such as murder.

In 1957, a group of 13 Hispanic gang members were incarcerated at the Deuel Vocational Institution in Tracy, California. Finding themselves in a minority and facing violence from the guards and white prison gangs, they bonded together across their old gang rivalries to form La Eme, or the Mexican Mafia. The ability of La Eme to defend its members became legendary and as its core members were moved to other prisons in the state, the gang spread and grew.

Originally formed to provide protection, within a decade they were the most feared and aggressive organization within the Californian penal system, operating extensive extortion rackets and controlling homosexual prostitution and drug distribution within all of California's prisons. La Eme even took out contract murders within the prisons on behalf of other external criminal organizations. Ironically for an organization with a rule that makes homosexuality punishable by death, many La Eme prison intimidations involve the threat of male rape as well as mutilation and death.

The La Eme structure involves a general taking overall command of captains, who in turn each have up to 10 lieutenants, who are in charge of the foot soldiers of the group. Membership of La Eme is restricted to chicano prisoners, who fulfil the first part of the gang's motto "In by blood, out by blood". Prospective candidates must kill or at least shed the blood of another prisoner or guard in an attack. After this, three existing Mexican Mafias must agree to vote them in and they must swear an oath to follow four rules. These are that they must never be an informant, a coward, homosexual or disrespect another Mexican Mafia member.

From its earliest days, when part of its reason for forming was to protect Hispanic inmates from the dominant Jewish prison gangs, the Mexican Mafia has been strongly anti-Semitic. It is also strongly anti-black. Therefore, when it began to struggle in its long war with rival Mexican prison gang La Nuestra Familia they formed an alliance with the Aryan Brotherhood, a prison-based white supremacist gang.

The loyalty that La Eme created within the Californian penal system was translated to the outside world when members were released. Old gang rivalries had been dissolved in prison through Mexican Mafia membership, and uniting against the common enemy of La Nuestra Familia allowed the Mexican Mafia to form alliances with Hispanic gangs throughout Southern California. By the early 1980s, Mexican Mafia leaders still inside the prison system had effective control of many gangs on the outside, organizing them into a focussed criminal enterprise that was able to begin collecting a "tax" on all illegal narcotic activity taking place on the streets of Southern California. Despite recent internal leadership rivalries, the Mexican Mafia continues to grow in strength as an external criminal organization. With thousands of members and associates, it now also specializes in extortion and the siphoning of government funds meant for community projects.

In January, 2012, federal authorities indicted 39-year-old crime boss Rudy Espudo for running a criminal network that forced drug dealers in San Diego to pay taxes in tribute to the Mexican Mafia. One Drug Enforcement Agency official told me: "Catching Espudo gives a glimpse into the reach and organization the Mexican Mafia has over narcotics in their areas. They are gangsters who run a vast amount of drugs in prisons and on the streets. What they do not run, they tax. That gives them real power."

LA NUESTRA FAMILIA

La Nuestra Familia hold the distinction of being the only known organized criminal network formed because of an argument over a pair of shoes. The nexus point occurred in San Quentin State Prison on September 15, 1968. Hector Padilla, an inmate associated with Norteños (Mexican-American street gangs located in Northern California), discovered that his cherished shoes had been stolen by Robert "Robot" Salas, a leader of La Eme (AKA the Mexican Mafia). When he tried to retrieve them, Padilla was stabbed 17 times and died. This was the third murder in recent weeks by La Eme members, who came mainly from Sureños (Hispanic street gangs from Southern California).

To protect themselves from further attacks and to show that the Mexican Mafia could not carry on its campaign of violence against northerners with impunity, the nascent Nuestra Familia (meaning "Our Family") banded together the Norteños in San Quentin and launched a reprisal on September 16 that left 11 La Eme members severely wounded and one dead. From that day forward, the bloody war between La Nuestra Familia and La Eme had begun.

Throughout the California penal system, the Nuestra Familia began to attract members from Norteños, sick of suffering abuse from their Sureños rivals. It was also soon able to offer protection services against Mexican Mafia extortion and male rape rackets across the state. They even sold protection to non-Hispanic inmates and began to challenge the Mexican Mafia for its control of prison drug distribution.

The late 1960s and early 1970s was a time of intense political conflict across America and this was reflected heavily in the California penal system. Alongside incarcerated black nationalists and left-wing terrorists, labour movement hero César Chávez was also jailed for standing up to strike-busting, anti-union thugs who were attacking striking members of his Californian United Farm Workers. Partly inspired by his example and also by views on chicano pride and the strength that poor Mexicans could achieve through proper organization, the Nuestra Familia adopted a written constitution and began an education programme for its members. As a result, this political edge made the black, radical-based prison gang, the Black Guerrilla Family, ideal allies in Nuestra Familia's continuing fight against the Mafia, an association that continues to this day.

Since the formal structure and written constitution was developed under Robert Rios "Babo" Sosa's leadership while he was in Folsom State Prison, membership has been open to any Norteños or Mexican-American opposed to La Eme. Junior members must agree to the 14 Bonds of the Nuestra Familia constitution detailing conduct in prison and the usual gang stipulations about secrecy, loyalty and following orders. Gang advancement is dependent on following the education programme. The curriculum includes learning how to establish a chain of command in any new prison an inmate may be transferred to, mastering secret communication with more senior Nuestra Familia leaders in prison, and

Labor rights leader Cesar Chavez (third from right) inadvertently helped inspire the rise to power of La Nuestra Familia when he was in jail for standing up to anti-union thugs.

writing essays on Nuestra Familia and the struggle for chicano justice. It also includes an hour of intense physical exercise that is designed to build muscle and keep inmates "combat ready". Nuestra Familia symbols revolve around the colour red; the number 14 (often written as X4 or X and four dots) as "N" is the fourteenth letter of the alphabet; a star to represent the North Star; and the huelga bird or eagles.

As with other prison gangs, freed Nuestra Familia members took their new allegiance back to the streets. They began co-ordinating the disparate Northern California Hispanic gangs into an organized criminal network, reporting back to La Messa, the Nuestra Familia's ruling body that is currently formed of members imprisoned in the high-security Pelican Bay State Prison in California. Alongside drug dealing, embezzlement of community funds, extortion and fighting a bloody war against Mexican Mafia-affiliated gangs, Nuestra Familia has become a significant player in credit card theft and fraud.

The sophisticated level of organization means that it has been able to spread outside California and is now known even to have members in Europe. It has also become a major target for FBI anti-racketeering investigations. Operation Black Widow saw an FBI undercover operation against Nuestra Familia that led to 13 of its leaders in prison being indicted for murder, drug dealing and racketeering. It also saw the rapper Sir Dyno charged with conspiracy after he put out a pro-Nuestra Familia CD called *G.U.N. – Generations of United Norteños*, that was funded by Nuestra Familia as part of a money-laundering operation. April 2010 saw Federal and local law enforcement agencies again try to dismantle the leadership of Nuestra Familia with Operation Knockout. However, despite months of investigation and raids which saw the authorities arrest 37 alleged gang members, the seizure of 18 kg (40lb) of cocaine and several jail sentences, Nuestra Familia remains a significant player in West Coast gangland.

ARYAN BROTHERHOOD

Over recent years, a number of new organized crime organizations have sprung directly from prison gang members taking their loyalties from jail with them when they are released and begin engaging in criminal activity back on the streets. Of these, the one with the most fearsome reputation for violence is the Aryan Brotherhood, shortened to AB.

The Aryan Brotherhood developed out of two Irish prison gangs operating in the California penal system in the 1950s – the Bluebirds and the Diamond Tooth Gang (so-called because of the piece of glass that the members wore in their front teeth). In response to increasing victimization of white prisoners by the Mexican Mafia and black prison gangs, the two Irish gangs amalgamated and were joined by a number of inmates with neo-Nazi beliefs and has-been outlaw bikers.

The gang began operating under the name of the Aryan Brotherhood for the first time at San Quentin State Prison in 1967. Accordingly, it did so well in terms of hospitalizing Mexican Mafia members in early battles that within a few weeks it was recognized as a significant force within the facility. It also earned an instant reputation for barbaric brutality and extreme violence – even by harsh prison standards.

Despite having been formed to offer protection to white prisoners, it was soon heavily involved in the usual prison rackets of drugs, prostitution and extortion. Alongside these profitable criminal enterprises, members increasingly became focussed on race hate and white supremacist ideas, believing themselves "at the vanguard of the coming race war".

The Aryan Brotherhood saw themselves as a racially pure elite. Membership was originally restricted to those of Irish descent, but within a couple of years the requirement to have Irish ancestry was expanded to allow potential members to have German, English or Scottish roots. The need to increase the number of gang members to further develop Aryan Brotherhood criminal enterprises and combat threats from groups such as La Nuestra Familia and the Black Guerrilla Family eventually led to associate membership being open to any white, non-Jewish prisoner who could prove themselves useful.

When the Mexican Mafia began to lose ground to an alliance that had been struck up between La Nuestra Familia and the Black Guerrilla Family, peace talks were held between the Aryan Brotherhood and the Mexican Mafia. The origins of the Aryan Brotherhood as a defence against the Mexican Mafia were forgotten and an alliance between the two formed.

To become a full member of the Aryan Brotherhood and earn the right to wear the Aryan Brotherhood brand – a tattoo of a swastika within a shamrock containing three sixes – an associate member of the gang had to receive a unanimous vote from all other full Aryan

The tattooed right hand of a Death Row inmate clearly shows his membership of the fearsome Aryan Brotherhood. Such a tattoo is usually only obtained by shedding blood for the gang.

BLACK GUERRILLA FAMILY

The most intriguing of the new organized crime networks that have evolved directly from the US justice system is the Black Guerrilla Family.

In 1966, George L. Jackson became a member of the radical black power group the Black Panthers while serving a potential life sentence in San Quentin Prison for the theft of $71. Inspired by the Panthers' revolutionary Marxist and Black Nationalist message, he founded a prison gang known originally as the Black Family (it was also known as the Black Vanguard). The Black Family had higher aims than other prison gangs. It was dedicated to eradicating racism, maintaining dignity in prison and to the overthrow of the United States government.

The political nature of the gang meant that it attracted members not just from jailed Black Panthers and other Black Nationalist movements, but also from members of terrorist groups operating in America in the late 1960s and early 1970s, such as the Symbionese Liberation Army and the Weather Underground Organization (also known as the Weathermen).

In the late 1960s, Jackson swelled the ranks of the gang by accepting the "Black Mafia" – upstart crime syndicates that began operating in US cities such as Philadelphia and New York – as members of his now renamed Black Guerrilla Family. The Black Mafia had formed from street gangs that had organized around extortion and drug distribution activities in predominantly urban African-American neighbourhoods.

Those who had once been in the Black Mafia taught the political members of the Black Guerrilla Family about the potential profits to be made from street rackets. In return they learned from those imprisoned for politically motivated crimes about the benefits of tighter organization and discipline. The loyalties formed and lessons learned while in prison, meant that as members of the Black Guerrilla Family were let back out on the streets, they stuck together and began to function as an organized crime network.

The rules of joining the Black Guerrilla Family are that prospective members must be black, nominated by an existing member, make a lifelong pledge of loyalty and receive a Black Guerrilla Family tattoo. This is usually a dragon surrounding a prison tower and holding a correctional officer in its clutches, but it can also be a crossed rifle and machete with the letters BGF.

Although relatively small in numbers, the Black Guerrilla Family has become a major player, both within the gangland of the US correctional system and out on the streets. This has been achieved through the careful formation of alliances. The Black Guerrilla Family has allied itself with the powerful Mexican prison gang and organized crime network La Nuestra Familia. It has also formed alliances with numerous black street gangs, including Chicago's Black Gangster Disciples, the Los Angeles based Bloods and Crips and the 415s that originated in San Francisco.

Justice Department intelligence reports suggest that the Black Guerrilla Family has organized itself around the cell structure traditionally favoured by terrorist groups. This involves a few members working in a tightly knit

Brotherhood members within a prison and to be prepared to "make his bones". This involved committing a murder or a disabling assault on a victim that had been selected by the Aryan Brotherhood. Anyone wearing the Aryan Brotherhood brand without having met this requirement was subject to the threat of execution by the gang. However, in recent years, membership requirements have been marginally relaxed in an effort to keep the strength of the gang up.

Full membership of the Aryan Brotherhood is seen as a life commitment. Members who leave prison are expected to further the Aryan Brotherhood cause on the outside by financially supporting Aryan Brotherhood members who are still in the penal system. This requirement is one of the factors that has led to the Aryan Brotherhood becoming a fully-fledged, organized criminal network operating in several US states. The close-knit, cohesive mindset of the supremacists has allowed them to make inroads into bank robberies, weapons dealing, contract killings and narcotics, where they are known to have co-operated with outlaw biker gangs in wide-scale marijuana and methamphetamine dealing. Inside prison walls, the Aryan Brotherhood continues to play a significant role in prostitution, protection and extortion. However, it has relinquished all but a secondary role in drug distribution and the contract killing of prisoners to its allies in the Mexican Mafia.

The Aryan Brotherhood has spread outside California, both in the prison system and on the streets. It is known to have links with other white supremacist groups, such as Aryan Nation, and some race-hate organizations that portray themselves as factions of the neo-Odinist faith. Despite recent internal power struggles and losing battles against the Black Disciples and the Black Guerrilla Family, it remains a growing threat to law, order and racial harmony.

unit and following orders given to them by the "Chief" of the cell. Contact to the wider organization is restricted to the Chief. The leaders who remain in the prison system supervise the overall direction of the Black Guerrilla Family.

Secrecy and discipline are firmly maintained and Black Guerrilla Family groups are encouraged to form joint enterprises with street gangs operating in predominantly black neighbourhoods. The Black Guerrilla Family is the only known US organized crime network to have developed and named its own intelligence agency. Called the New Afrikan Revolutionary Nation, or NARN, its function is to gather data and undertake analysis to improve Black Guerrilla Family security and criminal performance.

The discipline and secrecy of the BGF is at odds with the style of some other Black American crime groups. One particular example is the Black Mafia Family (BMF), which was established in the 1980s by brothers Demetrius and Terry Flenor. By 2000 they had built a multi-million dollar cocaine distribution syndicate with cells in most cities across the United States of America. However, the Flenors and their associates led a high-profile "bling" lifestyle, attempting to legitimize their operation through entering the hip-hop music business by setting up a company called BMF

Entertainment. The lavish lifestyle of the Flenors and their presence in hip-hop brought them the scrutiny of the justice system. In 2005, the Drug Enforcement Administration indicted the brothers and other members of the BMF for running a continuing criminal enterprise. Demetrius and Terry were both convicted and given 30-year jail sentences. By 2009, 150 members of the BMF had been arrested and indicted for their roles in a drug gang which was estimated to have made more than $1 billion during its life.

The lower profile and carefully considered tactics of the Black Guerrilla Family may not have seen it make the rapid expansion of the Black Mafia Family, but its members have received a far lower level of indictments – the largest single number was ten in Baltimore, Maryland in 2010 for crimes committed in both prison and on the streets. It has made wise allegiances with other crime gangs such as the Zoe Pound Haitian Mafia, MS-13, the Vice Lords and the Crips, allowing it to continue to grow and remain an emerging force in American organized crime.

The radical politics of the Black Panther party became integral to the formation of the Black Guerrilla Family although there is no link between the organizations today.

GANGLAND GB – ORGANIZED CRIME IN THE UNITED KINGDOM

7

"The English love a good villain."
Charlie Richardson, London crime gang boss and businessman

Some of his contemporaries – usually the ones who didn't find themselves with electrodes attached to their private parts – have called Charlie Richardson one of the cleverest English criminals of the twentieth century. When it comes to understanding the English psyche and its fascination with crime, his insight is very accurate.

In Britain, there has always been a strong tendency to romanticize crime. A gang of robber bandits, led by a local outlaw, became the folk heroes Robin Hood and his Merry Men. In just over 250 years, since his hanging in York, the sadistic highwayman Dick Turpin has become the hero of a television series and been used to sell everything from beer to porcelain.

This mythologizing is not restricted to historical figures, however. Just two decades after his release from prison for an assortment of violent crimes, "Mad" Frankie Fraser is enough of a celebrity to appear on television game shows and has joined the ranks of iconic names in British organized crime from the second half of the twentieth century, who, like the Krays, hold a firm grip on the public's imagination. This British love affair with outlaws has often obscured the vicious and horrific nature of organized crime in the United Kingdom.

Dave Courtney is another insightful ex-gangster who has benefited and commented on the nature of organized crime's celebrity status in Britain. He, however, claims that this love affair may be well and truly over in the twenty-first century – the transnational, pervasive and increasingly violent nature of crime in Gangland GB leaves no room for romance.

THE ORIGINS OF ORGANIZED CRIME IN GREAT BRITAIN

Organized gangs of Essex criminals bringing in contraband from the continent; under-age girls from Europe being shipped to London and forced into prostitution; widespread corruption amongst the police; high-placed professionals consorting with street thieves to commit fraud; groups of foreign thieves making London their base – the current state of organized crime in England has uncanny echoes with the past 500 years of British criminal history.

In 1739, a group of criminals organized under the name of the Essex Gang were smuggling contraband liquor and tobacco. Led by Dick Turpin, they also engaged in highway robbery and housebreaking. Today, organized gangs of Essex criminals are still heavily involved in duty trafficking, the only real change being that they are also likely to be involved in smuggling narcotics.

Victorian Britain was rife with child prostitution. The common belief that sex with a virgin cured syphilis was a significant element of this sickening trade, the import of young girls from France by foreign criminal groups. As in many modern-day cases, the girls, usually aged around 12, were either sold by their parents or persuaded to leave home with the promise of well paid jobs as maids in England. Once across the Channel, they were raped, beaten and terrorized into working as prostitutes. The only difference with twenty-first-century Britain is that the girls are now usually older and come from Eastern Europe, Russia and Africa.

The rampant collusion with criminals exposed as existing in certain sections of Scotland Yard in the 1970s and more recently amongst certain detectives in the West Midlands is just a shadow of the activities of Jonathan Wild. In eighteenth-century London, Wild was known as the "Thief-Taker General". His public image of a successful "policeman" hid the fact that for many years he was running one of the largest professional criminal gangs in English history. He eventually went to the gallows at Tyburn on May 24, 1725.

Current newspaper stories of how professional criminals use street gangs to obtain credit cards and other documentation that allows them to steal people's identities and commit massive fraud, are old hat. James Townsend Saward, an outwardly respectable barrister, used gangs of child pickpockets to steal chequebooks in order to perpetrate a raft of frauds until he was transported to Australia in 1857.

Tight-knit immigrant groups often face a hostile local populace – this has a tendency to breed criminal networks within their communities. England has never been short of convenient groups of immigrants to blame for their crime problems, even before the hanging of French "gentleman highwayman" and gang-leader Claude Duval in 1670. Sicilian secret societies with criminal elements operated in London in the 1850s. From the Victorian period right up to the trial of Brilliant Chang in 1924, the Limehouse area of east London was notorious for Chinese Triad activity that centred around opium and "white slavery". Recent waves of immigration have brought with them both new organized crime groups and new scapegoats.

When you examine the origins of organized crime in England and the other parts of the United Kingdom, it is impossible to ignore the self-evident truth that wherever Britain has created prohibition and a repressive tax regime, it has created organized crime. Whilst British legislators missed out on anything like the grand mistake of the Eighteenth Amendment that brought Prohibition to America, the advent of the Second World War created the perfect conditions for organized crime to flourish in Britain.

The influx of American GIs saw the vice and pornography trade, especially in Soho, boom, while rationing and countless prohibitions

The notorious "Rookeries" and slum areas of nineteenth-century London gave rise to numerous crime gangs that helped set the pattern for crime in the capital during the next 100 years.

created a massive black market. Add to this the fact that the majority of the established police were called up into the armed forces and it was a perfect time for those in the British underworld to expand their criminal operations. Infamous gangster "Mad" Frankie Fraser summed up the wartime experience by saying, "The war years were the best years of my life. Paradise. I'll never forgive Hitler for losing the war".

The echoes of the past create the future. Despite how little has changed at many levels, it is the historical absence of an already dominant ethnic-based Mafia and the failure of a single, effective home-grown organized crime syndicate to emerge during the post-war years that created the ideal environment for today's range of trans-national criminal gangs to make Britain their European base.

Dodgy gear – a potential customer examines a black market camera, just one item amongst millions that were offered for sale during the black market boom of the Second World War.

THE SABINIS

Our Lady of Mount Carmel is taken on a procession through the streets of London's "Little Italy" in the 1920s. The area was the home turf of the notorious Sabini crime family.

Britain may never have seen the Sicilian Mafia take a firm hold on its shores, but with the Sabinis it did have its own "Italian Mob" that dominated the criminal scene in England in the 1920s and 1930s.

The organized crime gangs of the Krays and the Richardsons were not the first to be led by sharp-suited brothers who ruled London's underworld through an unhealthy combination of violence and fear. The Sabini brothers, all five of them, came from Saffron Hill in London, an area that had been known as the Italian Quarter or Little Italy since the 1840s.

Born of a Scottish mother and an Italian father, the Sabinis grew up in the late 1890s and early 1900s. The area they lived in was already infamous for its gangs of up to 30 thieves and villains, each of which was led by a "Captain" who put together a crew made up of both muscle and specialist criminals. Gang warfare was rife with many of the clashes over the control of illegal street bookmaking pitches and protection of local businesses. With good money to be made from these rackets, it is not surprising that a life of crime was such an enticing prospect to poverty-stricken boys short on legitimate opportunities, but endowed with natural strength and cunning minds.

Ullano "Darby" Sabini was born in 1889. He was a talented boxer, but gave up his career in the ring to provide protection to bookmaker Harry Sullivan. He quickly formed a gang around himself and began offering protection and debt-recovery services to other bookmakers. At the core of the Sabini gang were his four brothers – Harry Boy,

Joseph, Fred and George. They gained a reputation for extreme violence and became known both to their gangland enemies and the police as the Italian Mob.

In England in the 1920s and 1930s, bookmaking was illegal anywhere other than at a racetrack. The vast sums that were bet at racecourses attracted gangs of organized criminals. Running protection rackets against the legitimate bookmakers at racetracks could net a gang up to £5,000 a day – a princely sum in the 1920s. It is no surprise, therefore, that the Sabini brothers' Italian Mob wanted some of the action. Referred to by the police as "racecourse terrorists", the razor-wielding Sabinis began to carve themselves a territory.

To begin with, they didn't have things all their own way. Since 1910, even the southern racetracks, such as Newbury, Kempton Park and Epsom, were considered the turf of gangs originating in Birmingham. These gangs were led by Billy Kimber and Andrew Townie and were known as the Brummagen Boys. Despite their Birmingham origins, by the 1920s, the Brummagen Boys drew much of their membership from the tough streets around the Elephant and Castle area of south London in which Kimber had originally been born.

In 1921, fierce battles between the Sabinis and Kimber's gang raged across the racetracks, with Darby Sabini having to shoot his way out of trouble on more than one occasion. Even teaming up with a gang from Leeds and bringing in the feared London gang the Titanics could not save Kimber. After being shot outside Darby Sabini's house, Kimber gave up and returned to the Midlands, allowing the Sabinis to dominate the racetrack rackets throughout England.

Not satisfied with this source of income alone, they moved into running nightclubs and gambling dens in London. As a result of this, in 1922, they fell out with former allies the Cortesi gang in a feud that came to a head when one of the Cortesi brothers tried to assassinate Darby but only succeeded in wounding Harry Boy Sabini. Despite such rivalries, the Sabinis remained kings of organized crime until 1936, when they lost the famous "Battle of Lewes" against another London gang led by the White family. Even importing Sicilian thugs to swell their ranks could not keep them on top after this defeat, despite masterminding a huge gold bullion robbery from Croydon Airport in the same year.

While the Second World War created the biggest opportunity for making money that British villains had ever been given, for the Sabinis it marked the end of their criminal enterprises when they, like many other Anglo-Italians, were interned as enemy aliens. The Italian Mob's time was over and new organized crime gangs began to take their place.

Police called the razor-wielding Sabini brothers "racecourse terrorists" as they conducted a vicious battle for gangland control of England's racecourses during the 1920s and 1930s.

JACK SPOT AND BILLY HILL – THE KINGS OF GANGLAND

The two men who would eventually claim the top title in English organized crime, when it had been vacated by the Sabinis, were Jack Spot and Billy Hill. Like many professional criminals, Jacob Colomore had more names than most men have suits – Jacob Comacho, John Comer, Jack Corner and the name by which he became an English gangland legend, Jack Spot, self-proclaimed "King of the Underworld". Born in 1912 to Polish immigrants living in Whitechapel in the East End, the nickname Spot came not as he later claimed from "being there whenever there was a spot of trouble that needed sorting out", but from the mole on his left cheek.

By the age of 15, he was running protection rackets and preying on the Jewish stallholders in London's Petticoat Lane market. By 18, with a gang around him, he saw off rivals to the illegal bookmaking rackets and declared himself "King of Aldgate". He continued to build his empire and became a local hero when he led the attack against Oswald Moseley's fascist Blackshirts when they marched against Jews in the

Billy Hill's attendance at the funeral of fellow gangster Billy Blythe in 1957 marked his retirement as London's top crime lord and a sign that a new generation of trouble was on the rise.

East End in 1936. Spot was sentenced to six months in prison for assault on a Blackshirt and this proved to be the only time the police managed to put him away.

It was said that he saw his prison sentence as a badge of pride, an underworld medal for standing up to fascists. It was, however, the only medal Spot did receive for standing up to the jackboots that were marching across Europe at the time. He, like many of his colleagues and rivals in organized crime, did everything within their power to ensure that they were not called up to fight for their country during the Second World War. Instead, Spot was one of the hundreds of villains who made vast fortunes from the black market and the range of criminal opportunities that opened up while the majority of the established police force was away fighting. In Spot's case this included the theft of 100,000 ration books worth more than £500,000 from Romford in Essex.

In the aftermath of the Second World War, England's underworld was awash with weapons and men who had been trained to fight. Bolstering the ranks of his Aldgate gang from these men, Spot went to war with the White family, who had taken over the racetrack rackets from the Sabinis. In 1947, a climatic battle, involving more than 100 men armed with coshes, razors, knives and guns, was won by Spot's mob, and he declared himself "King of the Underworld".

Jack "Spot" Corner, the self-styled "King of Soho" and "King of the Underworld", after his run-in with Italian-Scottish gangster Albert Dimes on a Soho street corner.

The other gang leader who had enjoyed a profitable war thanks to the black market and organized thieving was Billy Hill. Born at Seven Dials near Leicester Square, he grew up in Camden. One of 21 children, his family already had a criminal reputation – his sister Maggie was "Queen of the Forty Elephants", London's most notorious gang of female shoplifters. Hill also went to war with the White family to gain control of their racecourse and London club action. With the likes of the vicious fighter and thief "Mad" Frankie Fraser at his side, he too had the Whites on the run by 1947. Hill was soon calling himself the "Boss of Britain's Underworld", but instead of going up against the self-proclaimed "King", Hill formed an alliance with Spot that saw them share control.

The profitable Hill-Spot axis was not destined to last and, in 1955, a feud between the two men spilled out into bloody confrontation. Spot knifed one of Hill's associates, the respected Italian-Scottish gangster Albert Dimes, on a street corner in Soho, and Dimes fought back, badly slashing Spot. Open gang warfare broke out. Spot bribed Parson Basil Andrews into giving evidence that freed him from police charges, only to receive vengeance from Hill in the shape of an attack by Frankie Fraser in 1956, who attempted to carve a noughts and crosses pattern on Spot's face. When a few months later, Spot's nightclub, The Highball, was burnt down, he threw in the towel and retired from the scene.

Hill's reign as undisputed "King" did not last long, however. His courting of publicity had earned him constant police attention and new gangs, notably the Krays, were on the up. Rather than face the same fate as Jack Spot in 1957, Hill announced his retirement from crime and went to live in Spain where he died in 1984.

THE KRAYS

More than 50 years after he retired, underworld king Billy Hill is still considered by many of the English gangsters I've interviewed as a criminal mastermind. This reputation rests not just on putting together his organized crime network or pulling off such heists as the £287,000 Eastcastle Street Great Mailbag Robbery in 1952. It persists because he was smart enough to avoid confronting a violent new breed of criminal, symbolized by the Kray twins, who would have challenged him for his crown.

Identical twins Ronald and Reginald Kray were born in 1933 to a classic East End family of legally somewhat shady characters, Petticoat Lane market stallholders and boxers. Despite the matriarchal grip of their mother Violet on the family home in Bethnal Green, by the time the boys were 17 their reputation for violence was not limited to their official jobs as professional boxers.

The crowds attending Reggie Kray's funeral in October 2000 demonstrated how the once feared gangster had made the transition to adored working class hero.

The criminal cliché of thugs being model sons when it comes to looking after their mothers held true for Reggie (left) and Ronnie Kray who idolized their mother Violet.

In 1954, the boys took over a run-down snooker hall called The Regal, off the Mile End Road in Whitechapel. A gang of Maltese extortionists was plaguing it, but the twins saw them off in a bloody confrontation involving cutlasses. Within a year, their underworld standing had grown, as had their illegitimate business empire. By 1956, the Krays were heading a gang they called "The Firm", were considered valued associates of Jack Spot and had control of unlicensed gambling clubs and bookies across a swathe of East London. They also began to enforce the collection of a tax on illicit profits made by any criminal operating on their patch.

Seen by many as the natural successors to Jack Spot, many believed it would only be a matter of time before the Krays went up against Hill, but his resignation in 1957 as "Boss of the Underworld" avoided the need for any conflict. Instead, the twins began to expand into the power vacuum created by Hill's abdication, especially in London's West End clubland where, in 1960, they forced businessman Stefan De Fay to sell them his interest in the Knightsbridge gambling club Esmeralda's Barn for £1,000.

Between "long firm" frauds, receiving protection money from more than a third of London's illegal gambling clubs and taxing fellow criminals, the brothers were wealthy enough to be treated as equals by the celebrities and politicians they mixed with. They were also easily able to afford to pay the ever-increasing number of members of The Firm. Alliances were made with gangs in Glasgow, clubs in Birmingham were taken over and they even began to court the American Mafia.

By the mid 1960s, things should have been gloriously easy for the Krays. They ruled the East End and were treated like celebrities in the West End. Their main gangland rivals, the Richardsons, had been jailed

Even notorious rival of the Krays, "Mad" Frankie Fraser – known to the police as "gangland's A-bomb" – turned up to see that Reggie Kray was given a proper East End send-off.

and the police always met with a wall of silence when enquiring after them. Even the press were too afraid to tackle them after the *Daily Mirror* newspaper was forced to offer an "unqualified apology" for a story it ran linking them to the politician Lord Boothby. However, the empire of violence and fear they had built contained an inherent weakness: Ronnie Kray, the self-styled "Colonel", who modelled himself and his outfit on the 1930s American gangster films he loved.

When Ronnie was imprisoned for grievous bodily harm in 1957, he was diagnosed as a paranoid schizophrenic and declared insane. While this is not always a handicap in a criminal career, as the years went by his strange behaviour grew to the point where it threatened The Firm. In 1966, his personal love of violence saw Ronnie execute Richardson gang member George Cornell by shooting him in the head while he was drinking at the Blind Beggar pub. Cornell had called him a "fat poof". He then egged on his twin Reggie to kill Jack "The Hat" McVitie in September 1967. By this point, some members of The Firm were so worried about Ronnie's irrational behaviour, they began making plans to assassinate him.

Loyalty to the twins began to crumble and so did the fear they generated. In 1968, their long-time police nemesis, Inspector Leonard "Nipper" Read, was able to secure witnesses. The twins were sentenced to life imprisonment, with the judge recommending that they serve at least 30 years, for the killings of Cornell and McVitie. The self-mythologizing of Ronnie, the courting of publicity and unnecessary violence all played a part in ensuring that Ronnie died behind bars on March 17, 1995, and Reggie only saw 36 days of freedom before his death on October 1, 2000.

The Krays ruled the East End like feudal lords and were feted like celebrities in the West End, but their empire of fear crumbled due to Ronnie's insanity.

THE RICHARDSONS

The naturally memorable nature of identical twins being crime lords and the publicity surrounding them may have made Ronnie and Reggie Kray the most iconic English gangsters of the twentieth century, but two other brothers will go down in history as having headed London's most feared and respected organized crime family in the 1960s.

Charlie and Eddie Richardson ran what even Ronnie Kray later called "a mightily powerful and feared organization". The Krays might have held the East End of London in their grip and been a major power in West End clubland, but the Richardson gang ruled the underworld roost in South London. According to former Billy Hill gang member Frankie Fraser, who would eventually join the Richardsons, "Comparing the Krays and the Richardsons, the Richardsons were miles in front on everything – especially brain power".

I was brought up on family tales of the Richardsons. The comic cliché of them being good to their mother was even given credence by my own mother, having attended both family picnics and weddings with them. The widespread mythology that the Krays made the streets of the East End of London safe from petty crime is much less pronounced around the Richardsons. However, in reality it seems to hold much more truth, as I've met more than one South London villain who received a "smack" from Charlie Richardson and was told to "Piss off up to the West End and steal from some fucking rich bastards".

Charlie was born in 1934, his brother Eddie in 1936. The sons of a former prizefighter, they grew up in Camberwell, South London. Charlie's early career in petty crime was interrupted by his call up for National Service, during which he received a court martial for his attitude and insubordination and served time in Shepton Mallet military prison alongside the Krays. He founded a legitimate and profitable scrap business that had a chain of five yards across South London, and a string of drinking clubs. He fled to Canada in 1959, when he was charged with receiving stolen goods, but returned in 1961 (having set up, run and then sold a legitimate company during his time away) and managed to avoid the charge against him.

With his brother Eddie on board, Charlie set about expanding his business interests, both legitimate and illegal. By 1966, the brothers, and the gang they had built up around them, were running one of the most successful and sophisticated criminal networks England had ever seen. They had interests in everything from airport ticket machine fraud to fruit machine rackets, "long firm" swindles with added arson to clubland extortion and diamond smuggling. Charlie always hated the word "gang", seeing his organization only as a group of business associates, and saying, "Gangs are what kids have – or big kids in American films".

Charlie Richardson attends the funeral of fighter Lenny MacLean in 1998. Even today, England's underworld figures accord him legendary status and massive respect.

They ruled through fear of the violent retribution that would be dealt out to anyone who crossed them, and yet it was this retribution that brought about their downfall. In 1966, a squad of 100 Scotland Yard detectives seized the Richardson brothers and 11 of their associates. They were charged with torture and other violent crimes against an assortment of criminals who had tried to cheat them. The police may have overstated tales of the Richardsons' system of kangaroo courts and torture, but there was certainly sufficient evidence of electrodes being attached to certain delicate body parts and other bits being removed without anaesthetic for Charlie to receive the longest sentence for grievous bodily harm – 25 years – ever handed out in a British court. His brother got sent down for 10 years.

Eddie Richardson was released in 1976. However, in 1990 he received another 25 years for smuggling cocaine. On his release from prison in 1984, Charlie Richardson went to work in the City of London, carving out a successful career in the financial markets. His universally well-regarded brain helped him to reap legitimate rewards on the stock exchange. Interestingly, Charlie has commented that "The City is far more dishonest than anything I did before", and perhaps jokingly that "the biggest organized crime in Britain was performed by the Government stealing something the British people already owned and selling it back to them" – the privatisation of nationalized industries under Margaret Thatcher.

OPERATION COUNTRYMAN

Of the many insights former organized crime leader Charlie Richardson has made since becoming a widely respected and purely legitimate businessman, the most controversial is possibly his suggestion that "The most lucrative, powerful and extensive protection racket to ever exist was administered by London's Metropolitan Police".

What could sound like a meaningless jibe at the honesty of Scotland Yard's officers is unfortunately supported by a sordid history of fact. It shows not only police extortion from criminals, but also active collusion between many in the Metropolitan Police and the organized criminal underworld, and goes back more than 50 years. Research has proved that some Met officers were drawing two salaries – one official and one from Billy Hill – while others were known to have colluded in major heists, such as Hill's infamous Eastcastle Street job in 1952.

Richardson's claim that he made "regular payments to the police" and that it was "a sort of taxation on crime" may have seemed fanciful at the time of his arrest in 1966, but it later became clear he was speaking from a position of knowledge. In 1969, the *Times* news-paper revealed there was a "firm within a firm" – corrupt police officers within the Metropolitan Police who could arrange for charges to be dropped in exchange for large cash sums. Following this eye-opener, three officers were charged, but bigger scandals were yet to come.

In 1972, the Sunday People newspaper printed pictures of the head of the Flying Squad, Commander Ken Drury, holidaying with noted Soho villain and pornographer Jimmy Humphreys. When Humphreys was charged with a severe slashing in 1973, he revealed that the Dirty Squad (the nickname for the Obscene Publications Squad responsible for tackling illegal pornography) really were dirty cops. His evidence showed Commander Wally Virgo and Detective Chief Superintendent Bill Moody received thousands of pounds to turn a blind eye to organized crime in Soho. Both men were convicted while a host of junior officers also received prison sentences.

In the wake of the judge's statement that elements of the police had been operating a "vast protection racket", the Commissioner of the Metropolitan Police, Sir Robert Mark, ironically remarked "A good police force is one that catches more criminals than it employs." In 1978, he instigated Operation Countryman.

Costing four million pounds and involving a taskforce of more than 200 officers working for four years, despite massive obstruction, Operation Countryman saw the mainly rural Dorset Police Force investigate Scotland Yard for corruption. Their report has never been made public, but it is known they recommended that nearly 300 officers should face criminal charges for corruption and colluding with organized criminals. However, only four officers were eventually prosecuted. In 1994, Metropolitan Police Commissioner Sir Paul Condon told Parliament that his force contained "250 bent officers." A decade on, only a handful of these had been successfully charged.

Former head of the Flying Squad, Kenneth Drury, attending Bow Street Magistrates court in 1976 to face corruption charges relating to the "firm within a firm" run by senior officers.

Retired Scotland Yard Commander, Wally Virgo, received thousands of pounds from crooks and was condemned by the judge sentencing him for running a "vast protection racket".

Writing in academic papers several years after the Operation Countryman debacle and the earlier scandals at Scotland Yard, several noted criminologists have suggested that police corruption within the Met played one of the most significant roles in the spread of organized crime in England.

Of course, there are many other reasons why the police have found it difficult to proceed against organized criminal groups in Britain. The back-of-the-mind belief amongst many of the police and general public that criminal networks operating in England were little more than gangs of Jack-the-lads, created an air of complacency. The absence of a strong ethnic-based Mafia or apparent unified, organized crime syndicate controlling criminal enterprise, allowed more than one police chief to comment that "gangs like the Mafia could not happen here".

The police often also had to face walls of silence. In areas like London's East End, there was a natural, historical distrust for the police that had grown stronger since they were used as brutal strikebreakers against the area's dockers on several occasions. This pattern of "them and us" between the public in poverty stricken districts and the forces of law and order was repeated in many places across the country. In areas outside London where there has been no taint of police corruption, this factor may have been much more important in the establishment of thriving gangs of organized criminals.

THE GLASGOW GANGS

One area of Britain where distrust in the forces of law and order, sharpened by the strike-busting activities of the police in the shipyards and rampant sectarianism, helped organized criminal groupings thrive was in Glasgow, Scotland's largest city.

Gangs had been part of the culture of the Catholic-Protestant sectarian violence that had plagued Glasgow since the Irish Potato Famine between 1845 and 1849 led to widespread Irish emigration to the city. In the 1880s, these gangs were known as Penny Mobs, in that members had to pay a penny subscription to help clear the fines of any member caught by the police.

In 1916, the local press was still reporting on a thriving, brutal gang culture that dominated the city's underworld. Mobs such as the Beehive Boys, Hi-Hi, Death Valley Boys, Baltic Fleet, Tim Malloy and Calton Entry Mob clashed in ultra-violent street battles involving hundreds of men, that often left behind a road littered with razors, swords, bayonets, axes and lengths of metal pipe.

Gangs like the Redskins spread from isolated districts to become citywide and developed a dress code. Reminiscent of the street gangs in Anthony Burgess' *A Clockwork Orange*, all members of the Redskins had to wear a light-coloured tweed cap. Other gangs followed suit with their own bizarre sartorial posturing. While at first the gangs and their

The religious rivalry that fuelled the bloody violence often seen in clashes between Glasgow's Celtic and Rangers football teams also inspired much of the city's gangland conflict.

attendant violence were almost purely territorial and anti-Catholic or anti-Protestant, they soon developed their criminal enterprises.

In the 1930s, mobs competed to run protection rackets at local racetracks and even extended their extortion activities to menacing the public as they left dance clubs. Gang members were held in so much dread that they could drink for free in many public houses and steal from shops and businesses without fear of anyone informing on them. The notorious Glasgow loan sharks often used them as their debt collection agency, while many gangs were also involved in prostitution.

Neither bringing in gang-busting English police chief Sir Percy Sillitoe in 1931, nor the impact of the Second World War, dented Glasgow's gang menace. The massed knife fights of Protestant Billy Boys versus the Catholic Norman Conks remained as numerous and deadly as ever. By the 1960s, the gangs had renamed themselves "teams", but they were still as violent and strange as ever. Prominent teams included the Calton Tong (named after the 1961 film *The Terror of the Tongs*), the Fleet, The Toi and Possilpark Uncle – this team was named after the television show *The Man From U.N.C.L.E.* and famed for its razor-wielding members' habit of dressing like their television heroes Napoleon Solo and Ilya Kuryakin.

The gangs retained their links to organized crime, but beneath the street fighting scene, more sophisticated criminal groups were claiming an ever-bigger share of the illicit economy. Most significant of these was the Thompson crime family. Led by Arthur Thompson and run from two council houses that he had knocked into one, his family and associates carved a huge slice of Glasgow's underworld riches. From extortion to drugs, if it went on, Thompson was involved in it and was demanding his cut of the profits. He started out as a street gang member and feared money-lender in the 1950s, but soon diversified into a range of legitimate and criminal enterprises. Before his death in 1993, it was estimated that he earned £100,000 per week just from his protection rackets, so it is not surprising he often bought long-serving and loyal "family soldiers" a pub to run as a retirement present.

Thompson was so feared that when his son, Arthur Thompson Junior (AKA "Fatboy" Thompson) was murdered in a gangland hit in 1991, the suspected killers went straight to the papers to declare their non-involvement. This didn't stop two of them, Joe "Bananas" Hanlon and Bobby Glover, being found dead shortly afterwards in a car, having been shot in both the head and anus. Thompson prophesied that after his death Glasgow could become a "criminal Bosnia" of killings. With the retirement and subsequent death of fellow crime boss Thomas "the Licensee" McGraw in 2007, those words seem to have been borne out, as the now top dog Daniels crime clan finds itself competing with nearly 150 other crime gangs for a significant slice of the estimated £3 billion per year made by organized crime in Scotland. With an increasing amount of guns being reported in circulation in Scottish cities, it seems as if the pattern of ever-escalating turf wars established since 2008 may soon begin to become more deadly.

IRISH TERRORISM AND ORGANIZED CRIME

Glasgow is not the only place in the British Isles where the sectarian divide between Catholic and Protestant communities has helped to promote the development of organized crime networks. The ethnic and religious divisions in Northern Ireland that have fostered so much hatred and violence also created the perfect breeding ground for organized crime, allied to terrorism, to thrive.

Early Irish secret societies and nationalist groups dedicated to overthrowing British rule in Ireland, such as the Fenian Brotherhood and the Irish Republican Brotherhood, funded their terrorist activities through crime. If the crimes they regularly engaged in, such as theft, armed bank robbery and kidnap, were against British businesses, citizens or state enterprises they were viewed as acts of legitimate attrition against the enemy.

Being seen as freedom fighters often means the community that is being operated within offers a shield from detection and capture. This has certainly been the case for organized crime elements linked to the Irish Republican Army (IRA) operating within Northern Ireland. In the traditionally poor Catholic districts of cities such as Belfast and Derry, the natural antipathy towards the police that poverty engenders was strengthened by the sectarian nature of the Royal Ulster Constabulary (RUC).

As the conflict deepened in Northern Ireland and British troops were sent into Ulster in 1969, the Nationalist community became increasingly hostile to the police. Lacking public support and in fear of terrorist attacks against them, the RUC retreated to fortress-like police stations, making only occasional, army-backed raids in Nationalist areas, which they saw as enemy territory. This abdication of providing effective law and order in certain areas of Northern Ireland allowed paramilitaries to step into the power vacuum – the groups with organized crime elements now policed themselves and the communites in which they were based.

The IRA quickly established control over drug dealing within their communities, rapidly expanded extortion and protection rackets, created monopolies and secured control of legitimate businesses, such as bookmakers and taxicab firms, to help in money laundering. The borders between Northern Ireland and the Republic of Ireland, in places such as Antrim, became known as "bandit country" and were impossible for the police or army to control. This allowed not only the movement of weapons, men and bomb-making equipment over the now porous demarcation between the two countries, but it also meant the IRA could easily move into wide-scale duty trafficking of commodities, such as petrol and cigarettes.

What had started out as supplements to more traditional money-spinners, such as armed bank raids and wage snatches, grew into a sophisticated criminal empire producing vast revenues. It funded not only the armed Nationalist struggle at home and abroad, but also luxury lifestyles for those who were involved. The criminal network was defended with punishment beatings, bullets in kneecaps and regular disappearances of anyone who got in the way or who was even suspected of betrayal.

The funds generated were also used to buy massive amounts of arms,

The massive amount of firearms acquired by the IRA through profits from crime helped propel them into the position of the UK's most significant force in illegal arms dealing.

including hundreds of tonnes of guns, explosives and rocket launchers from rogue states, such as Libya. Excess weapons were sold to criminals in the UK, an activity that the IRA had been involved in as early as 1916. While Loyalist terror groups are also involved in organized crime, they have never matched the IRA's sophistication or reach. The Republican foreign political fundraising network was an ideal additional route for laundering money and the IRA also used its arms smuggling network to import drugs into Europe, forging links with the Cuban Mafia and the Colombian Cartels.

With the peace process of the late 1990s, the reform of the RUC and the IRA's commitment to end the armed struggle, many commentators hoped terrorist involvement in crime would diminish. Some even talked about the £26.5 million raid on the Northern Bank headquarters in Belfast in December 2004 as being an "IRA retirement job" to help stop its members continuing criminal activities. Whilst independent observers have noted a reduction in IRA and Unionist involvement in organized crime, unfortunately the old link between Irish terrorism and crime remains intact. Dissident Irish Republican groups such as the Real IRA and Óglaigh na hÉireann continue to engage in both terrorist attacks and a pattern of organized criminal activity to fund it.

The £26.5 million raid on the Northern Bank headquarters in Belfast in 2004 was thought to be an IRA "retirement job" to help keep its members in luxury lifestyles during a period of peace.

DUTY TRAFFICKING

The role of organized crime in duty trafficking – the smuggling of contraband goods to avoid paying duty on them – dates back to at least 1780–1750 BCE, when Babylon and the other city-states of ancient Mesopotamia introduced taxation on the trade of certain commodities. As a consequence, it also created the first organized groups to make a profit from evading this duty.

It set a pattern that has continued throughout history. Wherever there has been a significant difference in the cost of a particular item in different countries due to tax, organized crime has exploited the situation by engaging in smuggling. In previous centuries, wool and spices were amongst the top items smuggled; today the two most commonly duty trafficked goods are alcohol and cigarettes – referred to in criminal slang as bootlegging and butlegging.

In the USA, differential taxes on cigarettes between states have led Cosa Nostra to control the selling of more than 400 million duty-trafficked packs of cigarettes per year in the New York metropolitan area alone. This costs the state of New York more than $100 million annually in lost taxes and produces a solid Mafia income.

Butlegging is also a pronounced problem in Europe, where billions of dollars' worth of cigarettes from countries such as Moldova, Russia, Andorra and Morocco are trafficked into EU countries with high tobacco taxes. In Great Britain alone, the cost of tobacco trafficking to the government is more than £4 billion. The illegal trade is a major revenue source for the Italian Mafia, Russian Organizatsiya groups and Vietnamese crime gangs, who all see it as a low risk, high profit activity.

THE COSTA DEL CRIME

Retirement is an important consideration for anyone who has spent their entire professional life working in organized crime. In an industry where just surviving to old age is problematic, pension planning often amounts to putting together one last big deal or pulling off a major heist – such as the £26.5 million Northern Bank raid. Large sums of money are needed, not only to pay for a life of ease, but also to stay one step ahead of the law and any old enemies with a grudge to settle.

In 1957, former "Boss of Britain's Underworld", Billy Hill, was the first leading English gangster to announce that he was leaving organized crime to spend his retirement in Spain. Hill's retirement saw him not only enjoying a good exchange rate for his illicit fortune, but also a much lower level of police scrutiny than if he had stayed in Britain. This allowed him to act as a financier for villains back in Britain, without being a potential target for rival gangsters or investigation by the British authorities. Many commentators believed that Hill's retirement set the model that most in the British underworld aspired to. If this is true, Hill may have unintentionally played a role in creating the "Costa del Crime".

Although often mocked as a British tabloid newspaper creation, when you look at the various Interpol, Europol and Scotland Yard files, there is no doubting the fact that the Costa del Sol, which is made up of coastal communities in the western part of Malaga in the south of Spain, has become home to a vibrant community of former major names in the London underworld and a host of dubious characters whose status within British organized crime is obviously far from retired. Therefore, its nickname of Costa del Crime appears well-earned.

One of the prime reasons why the Costa del Sol became a mecca for those retiring from involvement in organized crime in Britain, or merely those who wanted to leave the country, is easy to understand. In the summer of 1978, the 100-year-old extradition treaty between Spain and England collapsed. Suddenly, for those involved in British organized crime who were on the run from the police or feared the long arm of the law, there was a safe haven in an attractive European country. As more than one gangster who has retired has noted, "The only bars were ones serving alcohol". It was also close enough to Britain to make it easy for family and criminal associates to visit.

Within a few short years it was home, or temporary refuge, to more than 50 British criminals who were wanted in connection with organized crime, including such infamous names as Howard Marks, Ronnie Knight and Freddie Foreman. While the legal loophole against extradition was sealed in 1985, and many of the criminals were eventually returned to Britain's shores, at the time of the signing of a new extradition treaty in 2001, there were still 35 fugitives at large in Spain.

Puerto Banus near Marbella on the Spanish coast has earned a reputation as the retirement destination of choice for a host of multi-millionaire British and Russian gangsters.

By this time, however, it was more than just the sun and staying out of jail that attracted elements of British organized crime to the Costa del Crime. The villains who had been living there had set up a vast hashish smuggling network, bringing the drug in from Morocco to the Spanish coast. This exceptionally profitable business expanded in the 1990s to include the distribution of ecstasy to Britain and the Spanish Balearic Islands.

The large sums of money this involved brought one thing that the semi-retired villains didn't want in their paradise – gang-related murder. Since the death of ex-Great Train Robber Charlie Wilson in 1990, there have been a series of drug-related killings, including that of drug trafficker Michael McGuinness whose body was found in a Range Rover at Malaga airport car park in 2000. Many of these murders are thought to revolve around Mickey Green, who ran the "Wembley mob" in London in the 1970s. Nicknamed "The Pimpernel", he and his Costa del Crime drug-dealing outfit are not alone in turning Spain into a new battlefield for British organized crime. However, as one ex-gangster told me, "It's still a lot safer than London. When the foreign gangs moved in it became a potential bloodbath for the likes of me".

FRANCE-PROSTITUTION
NOUS-VOULONS-GAGNER
NOTRE-VIE......
LE-SEXE-EST-
UNE-THÉRAPIE

GANGLAND EUROPE 8

"I used to run the crime in only one village.
Now Europe is my playground."

Zef Nano, Albanian mobster, 2006

In the last two decades, Europe has undergone the type of radical
political and economic transformation that many predicted would
take a century of history to bring about. Since the fall of the
Soviet Union, the continent is often seen as a land without many
of the old borders – one European market, one European people.
The drive to ever-closer integration seems, for many, to be an
inexorable process. The New Europe is increasingly viewed as one
territory not just by politicians, but also by Europe's numerous
organized crime gangs. For years, criminals have dreamed of
bigger markets, fewer barriers to trade and free movement of
people and goods.

It was not just the forces of democracy that were unleashed by
the crumbling of the Soviet state. From the ashes of the Eastern
Bloc came a host of organized criminal groups looking to expand
into rich Western European markets. Without the Warsaw Pact, it
was only a matter of time before the museum of conflicts in the
Balkans erupted into bloody fighting. One result of those wars
has been new criminal empires emerging from countries such as
Serbia and Albania.

The established criminal networks in countries across Europe
now have to face these fresh, brutal rivals. As one gangster told me,
"Western Europe is like a constant party with free food in a rich
person's house. Did you ever think you could keep the poor and
the bad men with guns from such a feast?"

THE CORSICAN MAFIA

Caught between France and Italy, the strategic position of the island of Corsica has gifted its people a history of blood and violence that almost eclipses that of its near neighbour Sicily. The constant struggle against whoever was ruling the island has produced a legacy of secret societies and resistance movements that helped create the Corsican Mafia. Even today, the main terrorist movement fighting to free Corsica from French rule, Front de Libération Nationale de la Corse (FNLC) is closely linked with organized crime both on and off the island.

The Corsican Mafia is structured along similar lines to the Sicilian Mafia. It is made up of several different families who compete and sometimes co-operate in various organized criminal activities. The Corsican Mafia is most famous for its role in the heroin trade and its part in the infamous "French Connection".

From the 1920s onwards, the Corsican Mafia largely controlled the supply of heroin to Europe and America. It ran vast laboratories in Corsica where Turkish opium poppies were processed. The heroin was then sent to the French port of Marseille and from there into Europe and the Americas. Raw opium from the French colonies in South-East Asia also arrived in Marseille for processing in Corsica. A deal with "Lucky" Luciano in 1946 radically grew their American export market.

The network went almost undisturbed until 1960, when Mauricio Rosal, Guatemalan Ambassador to Belgium, The Netherlands and Luxemburg, was caught smuggling 440 pounds of heroin a week for the Corsican Mafia. At the time, the French authorities were only seizing 200 pounds of the drug in a year. This discovery eventually led to more than a decade of international co-operation in trying to dismantle Corsican drug trafficking.

When President Nixon declared his "war on drugs" in 1971, one of the first to feel its effects was Corsican Mafia kingpin Auguste Ricord, who was running the South American end of a heroin distribution operation. Nixon ensured Ricord was extradited from Paraguay to face charges in the US, despite opposition from some in the CIA who had links with the Corsican Mafia operating in South America.

Italian, Sicilian and American mobsters respected Corsican Mafiosi as trustworthy and efficient assassins. Their reputation for keeping their mouths shut outdid what was usual under the rule of omerta. Those who had fought with the resistance movement against the Nazis in the Second World War were among the most inventive and skillful killers available for hire in the underworld. The American Mafia, especially in Montreal and New Orleans, regularly used Corsican hitmen up until the late 1970s.

A Corsican bank is reduced to rubble by a separatist bomb; on the troubled island, the links between separatists and the Mafia mean that one man's terrorist is another man's organized criminal.

President Nixon was not always a crook – when he declared a "War on Drugs" in 1971, the Corsican Mafia was one of the first criminal organizations to face his personal anti-narcotics wrath.

Due to the established link between the American Mafia and Corsican Mafiosi being used as shooters for the Mob, some researchers and elements of the American intelligence community have given credence to claims made by the writer Stephen J. Rivele. In 1988, he revealed research that suggested Corsican hitmen were used in the assassination of President John F. Kennedy in 1963.

The long held view by many that Carlos Marcello and the New Orleans Mafia family were involved in JFK's death is supported by some interesting circumstantial evidence. Rivele put forward research that seemed to suggest members of the American Mafia had recruited three Corsican Mafiosi to carry out a hit on the President. One of the men named by Rivele was Lucien Sarti, a well known Corsican assassin and member of the Ricord drug cartel. His role, if any, in the killing of Kennedy remains cloudy, but the fact that some in US intelligence consider it possible, underscores the Corsican Mafia's reputation for exporting hitmen and their links with the American Mob.

The power of the Corsican Mafia has waned since its peak in the late 1960s and early 1970s. Cross-country cooperation against its drug network hit it hard, as did increased competition from the Italian Mafia and the emergent South American powers in drug distribution. It has lost its previous major role in prostitution in France and is rapidly diminishing in importance in North Africa. Being pushed more and more back to its Corsican homeland has led to increased infighting amongst the rival Corsican Mafia groups. Since 2008, there have been more than 60 murders of its members in Corsica, further weakening what some observers now see as a twitching corpse instead of one of Europe's top gangland forces.

THE ALBANIAN MAFIYA

Established organized crime groups such as the Corsican Mafia may have seen a decline in recent years, but for newer players in gangland Europe the last decade has been a time of unprecedented boom. The Albanian Mafiya has been one group to have grown considerably since the fall of Communism in its homeland in 1991.

As the statues of Marx and the Albanian Communist dictator Enver Hoxha were pulled down, law and order began to collapse in the north of Albania – an area that had always been regarded as bandit country. The political chaos of a country trying to emerge into democracy finally loosened the restraining bonds on the local criminal clan chiefs and northern Albania quickly became a virtually autonomous and lawless region. These were already perfect conditions for the emergence of a new criminal network, but added to this, in 1991, was the outbreak of war in neighbouring Yugoslavia.

The war disrupted one of the major pathways for heroin entering western Europe. Italian and Sicilian Mafia groups seeking alternative routes seized on the opportunity presented by an increasingly unregulated Albania. Alliances with the 15 Families – a grouping of Albanian criminal clans operating out of the north of the country who

The Kosovan Liberation Army was funded by the organized crime profits of the 15 Families that grew up mainly from heroin distribution and trading in forced sexual slaves.

had been dabbling in drug trafficking since the 1970s – were forged. Within months, the Italian Mafia had a huge prescence in Albania, especially the port city of Vlorë.

The Albanians learned quickly from their Italian colleagues, adopting the traditional Mafia organizational structure, and within a couple of years they were no longer happy being the junior partners in the heroin trafficking operation. The 15 Families expanded, forcibly assimilating criminal groups in other areas of Albania and emerging as the force in organized crime that was quickly dubbed "the Albanian Mafiya" by European police officers. After asserting their position over their former Italian allies, the Albanians were quick to expand their role in heroin distribution. By 1999, Interpol estimated that the Mafiya controlled 60 per cent of the European heroin trade.

With the aim of extending the zone of lawlessness in which their criminal empire flourished, the Albanian Mafiya began to heavily fund armed secessionist movements for the Albanian communities in the neighbouring countries of Kosovo and Macedonia, including the Kosovo Liberation Army. The full-scale war they helped foment in Kosovo in the late 1990s was incredibly good for business. New

The presence of UN military forces in Kosovo has not slowed the growth of organized crime in the area and some UN personnel have even been involved in trafficking women and children.

fortunes were made smuggling thousands of fleeing refugees, and with the flood of armaments in the region, the Mafiya became a major player in arms dealing.

When the United Nations took political and military control of Kosovo in June 1999, the Albanian Mafiya became their effective partner in running the country. Corruption amongst UN personnel and the military in the NATO-led Kosovo Force was so endemic at one point that NATO vehicles were used for smuggling and UN administrators colluded in the trafficking of women and children.

The Kanun clan law of Albania sees women and children as property that can be bought and sold. This partially explains the massive part the Albanian Mafiya now plays in prostitution across Europe, especially in Great Britain where they control vice networks in most parts of the country. A young girl bought for a few hundred pounds in Albania can be smuggled into the UK and sold to a new "owner" for at least £5,000. She will be expected to generate an income through forced prostitution of at least £30,000 per year.

A strong alliance for the trafficking of women and prostitution rackets in Italy, Austria, Germany and Switzerland has grown between Italian Mafia grouping the Sacra Corona Unita and the Albanian Mafiya. Other Italian Mafia groups have allowed the Albanians to run the prostitution, hash and people smuggling operations on their territory in return for collecting a "tax" on the illicit trades and the understanding that the Mafiya will not expand into any other areas on Italian soil. Through Albanian refugee and émigré communities, the Mafiya has established operations not only across

Europe, but in America too.

Bloody conflicts with Turkish and Kurdish gangs in Germany and the exposure of Mafiya controlled prostitution and drug-rings across Europe hugely increased international police attention on Albanian crime groups. However, this uncovering of the extent of their operations and even the high profile arrests of 15 Family bosses such as Dayt Kadriovski have not seemed to dent their growth. In April 2012, an Interpol contact told me: "The Albanian Mafiya keeps extending its reach, developing its networks. We have yet to see the apex of their power."

THE SERBIAN MAFIA

The Albanian Mafiya were not the only organized crime network to thrive on the wars that were unleashed by the fall of Communist rule. As 1,000 years of bottled-up ethnic, religious and political prejudice exploded across the map of Yugoslavia in 1991, Serbian organized criminals began a rise to power that not only saw them enter the gangland of Europe as a significant new player, but also finance war crimes and assassinate a Prime Minister.

During the days of Tito's Communist rule over Yugoslavia the tensions that would later destroy the federation of states were kept in check, and organized criminal activity was heavily policed. Despite this, smuggling groups operated on the Croatian coast and on the unruly borders between Kosovo and Albania, while the most powerful organized crime gangs operated out of the capital Belgrade.

The backbone of the "Naša Stvar" (one of the names given to the Serbian Mafia) were the five major gangs operating in Belgrade, each taking its name from the district in the city in which it was based. Of these, the Voždovac and the Zemun gangs were regarded as the most powerful, with interests in prostitution, smuggling and blackmail. "The Business", as some gang members refered to it, managed to survive under Tito, due to heavy police corruption and its ability to meet the needs of the populace that the state could not.

However, with the disintegration of the Socialist Federal Republic of Yugoslavia in 1991, and the subsequent wars between the various states that had once been a part of it, the brakes were taken off the Serbian Mafia just at the time when myriad opportunities to profit from the misery of armed conflict were arising. The imposition of harsh economic and trade sanctions on Serbia also created massive profits for those who had already established smuggling networks.

Various elements of the Serbian Mafia poured a portion of their massive illicit profits into forming paramilitary units that were meant to protect Serbs in areas outside the Republic of Serbia. However, in reality these Serb volunteer units became an unofficial part of the Serbian war machine and were implicated in some of the worst war crimes of the Yugoslav wars. The paramilitary forces welded the Naša Stvar to the highest ranks of Serbian government – it was often difficult to work out where the regime of President Slobodan Milošević ended and The Business began.

One of the most notable figures that blended his role of leading "The Tigers" (a paramilitary group that had started with 20 Red Star Belgrade soccer club supporters and became a force of 10,000 men), with organized crime, was Željko Ražnatović. More commonly known as Arkan, a name he gave himself after a character in the comic *The Avengers*, the career criminal was intent on maintaining his political and underworld power in peacetime.

Arkan's death was just one of many high-profile killings as the Voždovac and Zemun gangs openly operated death squads on the streets of Belgrade. They made it clear they had no intention of giving up any of the power they had acquired during the war years. The killing of police chief Major-General Bosko Buha in 2002, just days after he announced he would clamp down on organized crime, was a clear show of the true power of the Serbian Mafia. However, with the killing of Prime Minister Zoran Đinđić, in 2003, their utter contempt for the official leaders of Serbia backfired. A massive

Zvezdan Jovanović, AKA "Snake", stares impassively during his trial for his role in the assassination of Serbian Prime Minister Zoran Đinđić, who was shot by the Mafia in 2003.

crackdown followed the assassination, with more than 300 suspected Serbian Mafia members arrested, including Ceca Ražnatović. She was held in custody for four months on charges of illegal weapon possession and harbouring wanted felons before being released without being convicted.

Despite the high-profile action that has been taken against organized crime post-Đinđić's death, the Serbian Mafia is so entrenched in the Serbian economy and politics that its influence makes it appear almost a vast shadow government. Alongside billions of dollars already laundered in the West, interests in cigarette smuggling, arms dealing, people trafficking, cyber-crime and extortion now extend its reach across all Europe. Unfortunately, the fall of Yugoslavia will not be the last time war and the bloody politics of power help to spread the blight of organized crime.

THE TURKISH AND KURDISH GANGS

Century-old ethnic, religious and political divisions were not just restricted to Yugoslavia. They also existed in the nation that arose from the fall of Ottoman Dynasty – Turkey – and the Kurdish people who wanted their freedom, from first Ottoman and then Turkish rule. Just as in the former Yugoslavia, the divides eventually helped to foster organized crime groups that would eventually spread across Europe.

For the first half of the twentieth century, the raw material for most of the heroin consumed in Europe and America came from Turkey, making its way through Corsican refining laboratories and the port of Marseille. Originally it was legal for Turkish farmers to grow opium poppies for medicinal purposes, but the huge illegal demand led to the creation of a thriving black market. Co-ordination of village-level enterprises was overseen by the figures that eventually evolved into the "Babas" (the godfathers of the Turkish drug underworld). In the 1970s, after American pressure ended the legal growing of opium poppies in Turkey, the Babas adapted. They began importing raw opium from Afghanistan and Pakistan, refining it themselves and using Turkish émigré and "guest worker" communities to create a street-level distribution system in countries like England and Germany, on top of supplying their traditional Italian and Sicilian Mafia partners.

The vast profits earned by Babas brought massive political influence at the highest levels of government. Figures such as "Heroin Emperor" Huseyin Baybasin and the legendary godfather Inca Baba enjoyed a large degree of tacit military and intelligence community support for the criminal networks. They were even helped to diversify into people trafficking and cigarette smuggling and businesses such as casinos and hotels by elements of the army, security services and government.

During the late 1970s, members of the armed militant sections of Kurdish liberation movements, such as the Kurdistan Workers Party and Dev Sol, began to see the vast profits that could be made from heroin trafficking and organized crime. In an effort to fund their terrorist campaigns, they began to challenge the established Turkish organized crime gangs for a share of the multi-billion dollar business. As a result, the line between freedom fighter and gangster blurred to the point of invisibility. The age-old ethnic, religious and political divides exploded into a bloody gang war between Turkish and Kurdish organized crime gangs, which still rages in many countries across Europe to this day – as shootings and frenzied street battles in the Green Lanes area of North London will attest.

The raw opium that is grown and extracted by warlords in Afghanistan fuels the massive profits and bloody conflicts that rage between Turkish and Kurdish organized crime gangs.

During the last decade, an even bigger occupational hazard has emerged to threaten members of Turkish and Kurdish organized crime gangs than the usual inter-gang murders. A violent turf war with the Albanian Mafiya has now developed over the control of heroin distribution in several European countries. The roots of the conflict go back to the Balkan Wars (1991–1996) that disrupted one of the major routes used for heroin entering Europe from Turkey and Kurdistan. Because of this, the Italian Mafia and other groups changed their suppliers to the Albanians, and as a result the Kurds and Turks lost a considerable slice of their income. Worse was to come when the Albanians began to challenge them for their street-level operations thanks to the swelling of Mafiya ranks through the diaspora of ethnic Albanians fleeing the conflict in Kosovo.

In a pattern that is being repeated everywhere from Britain to Belgium and Scandinavia, this attempted takeover by the Albanians has resulted in an ongoing violent underground battle for dominance. The battles, however, have been bloodiest in Germany – the traditional stronghold of Turkish and Kurdish organized crime in Europe, with numerous shootings and murders. A contact at Europol described to me how he and other experts view the escalating war between the Albanian Mafiya and the Turkish and Kurdish gangs, likening it to "Two animals, who have evolved in similar environments, suddenly coming face-to-face and having to fight for the same evolutionary niche in the crime jungle".

The rivalry with the Albanian Mafiya has stripped the Turkish and Kurdish gangs of much of their previous strength. However, for some Turkish gangs at least, other people's misery has been a boon. The ongoing conflict in Afghanistan has seen a vast increase in poppy production, with much of the product being trafficked via Turkey. This has led to an increase in revenue and many alliances with the most powerful force in gangland Europe today – the Organizatsiya.

THE ORGANIZATSIYA IN EUROPE

The alliances between the Organizatsiya, the umbrella term for the various criminal syndicates that form the Russian Mafiya, and Turkish and Kurdish organized crime gangs, is symbolic of the revolution in European organized crime following the collapse of the Soviet Empire. In just 15 years, the Russian Mafiya in Europe has achieved a level of power that has made some of the oldest established criminal networks mere junior partners within their own nations.

With the disintegration of the Communist system in 1991 and with no effective force to combat it on its home territory, the Russian Mafiya was able to thrive. Like any booming business that dominates its own native marketplace and has amassed billions of dollars, its natural evolutionary path was to diversify, develop new operations and expand into new foreign markets. In a happy coincidence for the Organizatsiya, this desire to extend its reach occurred at the same point in the early 1990s that Europe was increasingly becoming one vast economic territory. With huge illicit fortunes available to set up new enterprises and the personnel and firepower to remove all opposition, the Russian Mafiya could not fail to benefit from a move into Europe.

Not surprisingly, the first countries to feel the brunt of this Russian invasion were the Baltic States. They had been under Soviet control and were also ex-members of the Warsaw Pact that had long-standing political, cultural and economic ties to Russia. However, by 1995, just over five years after the fall of the Berlin Wall, Interpol and other police intelligence was reporting Russian Mafiya related killings and activity in every major European nation. The initial activities of the Organizatsiya saw them ally themselves with the Colombian drug cartels to carve a huge role in the trafficking and distribution of cocaine into and around Europe. They also developed a prostitution network that extended from the Urals right up to the Republic of Ireland's Atlantic coast.

However, the Organizatsiya showed a degree of sophistication that caught the police and more established rival criminal groups completely by surprise. In many European countries, once a bridgehead into the criminal underworld via prostitution and drug dealing or smuggling was established, profits would be channelled into diversifying into other areas, rather than having to recruit the muscle required to become the dominant player in already crowded illicit areas, such as vice.

This tactic has seen the Russian Mafiya become Europe's dominant force in the blackmail of big business, institutional corruption and financial fraud. Using former KGB agents, the Organizatsiya has indulged in wide-scale industrial espionage and even highly visible enterprises – for example, the building of England's new national soccer stadium, Wembley, has suffered from attempted Mafiya extortion. Organizatsiya schemes have become increasingly more audacious, such as French-based Russian Mafiya boss Alimzhan Tokhtakhounov using the French judge to fix the result of the 2001 Winter Olympics ice skating competition. It robbed Canadian ice skaters Jamie Sale and David Pelletier of gold medals and earned him and his colleagues millions of dollars in a global betting scam.

The Organizatsiya's ability to evolve new crimes is legendary among European authorities. An often-quoted example of this is the way that the Russian Mafiya moved into illegal fishing. The World Wildlife Fund blame the Mafiya for devastating fish stocks in the Bering Sea to satisfy a demand in Europe that exceed the levels that can be met by fishing within legal quotas. The massive poaching, smuggling and fraud involved earns the Mafiya more than a $1 billion a year and is pushing some marine species towards extinction.

Uzbekistan-born Organizatsiya boss, Alimzhan Tokhtakhounov, was arrested in Italy in 2002 for his role in fixing the result of the 2001 Winter Olympics ice skating competition.

Different European countries have developed different roles within the Organizatsiya network. Britain and Switzerland are its favoured places for money laundering and fraud; Spain plays a vital role in drug trafficking operations; Poland is the hub of its duty trafficking and smuggling empire; and France and Germany are at the heart of its vice profits.

In tandem with their criminal enterprises, Mafiya bosses have invested heavily in legal businesses and now own everything from football clubs to casinos and vast commercial property portfolios in cities across the continent.

Despite the move into legitimate business, Europol figures show that the number of Russian Mafiya related deaths continues to rise each year. No nation in Europe is free from the taint of the Organizatsiya and there isn't a rival organized crime group that doesn't fear the newest European criminal superpower.

ORGANIZED CRIME IN FRANCE

One country that has felt the massive impact of the rise of the Organizatsiya in Europe, and has seen its traditional organized crime networks suffer at its hands, is France. It came as little surprise to many in the French police that when, after 50 years, they finally nailed one of the last established godfathers of the French underworld, it was for his role with the Organizatsiya.

In November 2004, 74-year-old Jacques Imbert was sentenced to five years for tobacco trafficking and trying to establish an underground cigarette factory near Marseille, alongside members of the Russian Mafiya. Imbert was one of the infamous "Marseille bosses" and had evaded prosecution in a dance through the French underworld that spanned 50 years. Also known as le Matou (the Tomcat), Jacky le Fou (Mad Jacky) and Jacky le Mat (the Death Cheater), Imbert became something of a French folk hero, known for out-foxing the authorities and enjoying the highlife with friends such as actor Alain Delon. That he was sentenced for being in partnership with the Organizatsiya was symbolic of the way that the Russians had overtaken previously established groups in many areas of the French underworld.

The Corsican Mafia and Marseille Caïds (an Arabic word implying "King of Crime") had dominated French organized crime since the 1920s. Profits from drug trafficking were diversified into gambling and vice empires across the whole of France. Even the Paris underworld was alleged to be controlled from the Mediterranean coast. Underpinning this power was the infamous "French Connection" that made Marseille the global hub of heroin distribution. However, the concerted international effort to dismantle the international drugs trade operating out of the city significantly weakened the

Hundreds of masked Parisian prostitutes took to the streets in Paris to protest against new laws and the growing domination of prostitution by the Organizatsiya.

Corsicans and Caïds. A reduced market caused increased rivalry and a new eruption of the "100 Years War" between the various Marseille-based gangs in the 1970s. The blood-letting led to the death of Caïds, such as Gaetan Zampa, an old rival of Jacky Le Mat, and continued through the 1980s and 1990s until the assassination of the legendary Caïd, Francis "the Belgian" Vanverberghe in Paris in 2000.

The 100 Years War weakened the established order, making it vulnerable to incursions by other criminal syndicates and it became a prime target for Organizatsiya expansion in Europe. They quickly made their presence felt in drug dealing and the trafficking of women to work within the sex industry. When France hosted the 1998 FIFA World Cup, the Russian Mafiya used the vast increase in foreign visitors that overwhelmed the immigration and customs authorities as the perfect cover to flood the country with thousands of illegal immigrants acting as drug mules.

Within a decade of the Soviet Union's collapse, they were acknowledged to be dominating cocaine distribution and vice across most of France. In 2000, hundreds of prostitutes took to Lyons' streets to protest about the Mafiya's impact on their business by importing thousands of women from the former Soviet Union and Eastern Europe into the country. In Paris in 2002, more than 500 prostitutes wearing white porcelain masks rallied outside the French Senate, partly against the increased violence and exploitation that Organizatsiya control of vice had brought.

The Russian Mafiya is not the only trans-national organized crime network operating in France. The country's history as a former colonial power has resulted in several ethnic-based criminal groupings having a presence on the streets of Paris and other major cities. The Haitian community contains a criminal network formed from former members of the Tonton Macoutes – the death squad of the Duvalier dictators. They exploit a reputation for using voodoo to bolster the violence they use within the drug, fraud and extortion rackets they operate. Despite France being one of the leading players in international co-operation against global organized crime, it has ironically become the favoured home of many foreign crime bosses when they "retire" to enjoy their illicit fortunes. The Côte d'Azur has proved so popular with Organizatsiya bosses that one of its resorts – Antibes – has even started being referred to as "the Mediterranean Odessa". The continuing rise of the Mafiya and other trans-national groups in France is never likely to be reversed whilst its home-grown crime gangs bleed themselves to the point of destruction with internecine conflict. In 2008, the

The old port in Marseille was home to the legendary "French Connection" that saw Corsican and Marseille Caïds supplying heroin across the whole of the Western world.

gang de la Brise de Mer, one of the most powerful remaining Corsican outfits, lost four of its most important members in attacks by rival Corsican groups. As one Mafiya member told me: "In France, there is no national team to play against. All their own players cut each other's throats."

PROSTITUTION

Prostitution is often referred to as "the oldest profession", making organized crime the second oldest, as it has always been entwined with the provision of sexual services for money. In every country, control of the illicit sex trade has generated, and continues to generate, vast incomes for the criminals who are intrinsically linked to it.

The selling of sex remains a cultural taboo in most countries. Turning commercialized sexual liaisons into something shameful and prohibited by law has always robbed prostitutes of the official protection enjoyed by others. This makes the women and men who, often because of poverty, have to make money this way, easy prey for the underworld: pimps who extort a share of the earnings of streetwalker prostitutes and brothel owners who charge exorbitant sums for providing a place of work are symptomatic of this.

The unending demand, cash nature and illegality of prostitution has turned it into a huge profit magnet for organized crime networks that control the pimps and own or "tax" the brothels and escort services. While sexual slavery has always been part of prostitution, modern organized crime has developed a global network where women are trafficked and sold into the misery of forced prostitution.

In Africa, Asia and Eastern Europe, millions of girls each year are tricked or forced into prostitution and smuggled into the world's richer countries to work. Although it is impossible to fully gauge the problem, the UN estimates put the value of sexual slavery as high as $15 billion per year. Worryingly, figures also suggest that an increasing number of children are getting involved in prostitution.

ORGANIZED CRIME IN SPAIN

France's Mediterranean resorts might be developing a reputation as a favoured destination for retiring Mafiya bosses, but they have some way to go before they can rival the Costa del Sol's status as having more multi-millionaire criminals per capita than anywhere else in Europe. However, organized crime in Spain does not begin and end solely with the drug traffickers and assorted villains who choose to spend their illicit gains in the playboy paradise of Puerto Banus – the heart of the Costa del Crime.

Any exploration of Spanish organized crime must take into account the impact that nearly 40 years of authoritarian rule under the dictatorship of Generalissimo Francisco Franco had on the nature of society in Spain. After his victory in the Spanish Civil War in 1939, his allying with the Catholic Church meant pornography, prostitution and homosexuality were all prohibited under the severest of legal penalties. As a result, the profits to be made from these activities radically increased as they were forced further underground and into the tighter grip of the Spanish underworld. Homosexual and hetrosexual prostitution and pornography flourished under a vast network of collaboration between the organized criminals and the Guardia Civil – the Spanish police force, with both military and civilian functions, that dominated Franco's Spain.

The economic and political isolation Spain suffered at the hands of the international community, post-World War Two, created a situation of severe consumer rationing. The demand for the illicit was soon met by a

The Fascist, pro-Catholic regime of General Franco created the perfect circumstances for corruption and massive markets in pornography, prostitution and black market goods.

Basque separatist group ETA has funded its terrorist activities through its involvement in organized crime and has developed close links with the Medellin drugs cartel from Colombia.

vast black market of smuggled goods. A shadow economy known as "Estraperlo" emerged that forged fundamental links between the organized crime gangs involved in the smuggling and corrupt officials. This entwinement between Spain's native organized crime networks and the authorities was so strong that even three decades of democracy following Franco's death have not been enough to dismantle it completely.

Franco's harassment of Spain's gypsy population set up conditions that led to the creation of a new organized criminal network. Increasingly marginalized, many gypsies turned to criminal activities, especially smuggling, where their closed society and nomadic lifestyle gave them a strong advantage. In the early 1990s, gypsy patriarch Tío Casiano led a campaign against allegations that Spanish gypsies were heavily involved in heroin distribution. However, in 1995, Casiano was arrested for his personal involvement in heroin dealing – when busted, he was in the process of counting out $320,000 in cash.

The oppression of the Basque language and people under Franco played a large role in the formation of Euskadi Ta Askatasuna (ETA), the Basque separatist terrorist group. To fund their armed struggle for an independent Basque state, ETA turned to drug smuggling, armed robberies, extortion, kidnap for ransom and arms dealing in Spain, Portugal and France.

Upon the death of Franco, Spain once again became integrated into the international community. As a result, the illicit networks that Franco's regime had unwittingly helped create suddenly had to deal with an influx of foreign organized crime groups. By the late 1970s, the Colombian Cartels had formed alliances with Galician smugglers, who had previously been focussed on supplying the Estraperlo economy, switching them from consumer goods to cocaine. Rivalry between the Colombian Medellin and Cali cartels saw the former develop links with ETA, moving its cocaine through ports in the Asturias and Cantabria regions of the Basque country.

It was the presence of English gangsters on the Costa del Sol that helped turn Spain into a major hub for European hash distribution, with vast Moroccan cannabis plantations established to meet the huge demand. English mobsters also control the lucrative distribution of ecstasy on the Spanish Balearic Islands. The vast profits to be made in

drugs has led to Spain becoming an increasing area of interest to the Russian Mafiya and to Moroccan-based crime gangs no longer willing to be just junior partners.

Until the financial crisis that began in 2008 one of the biggest areas of growth in organized crime in Spain was money laundering. An estimated $5 billion per year was cleaned through Spanish construction companies, casinos and investment groups. However, like many other major business players, international crime groups have withdrawn from investing in the Spanish economy, limiting their exposure to more reliable generators of income such as drug trafficking.

ORGANIZED CRIME IN GERMANY

Despite a growth in organized crime in West Germany post-Second World War, partly related to the vast black market that opened up in a country recovering from the ravages of war, many in the German police and government refused to believe that Germany had an organized crime problem. This attitude became a contributing factor to the relatively unimpeded growth of Turkish and Kurdish organized crime gangs in West Germany. The criminal elements amongst the large Turkish and Kurdish immigrant communities in West Germany also benefited from the natural cohesion of the ethnic community and a "them and us" antipathy to the German police.

Many gangs were based around geographical and family ties to villages in Turkey and Kurdistan, from which the immigrants had originally come. Some were quick to make use of the links to home to forge alliances with already established narcotic trafficking groups in their home countries. By being able to source drugs, especially heroin, at prices that were way below the usual German market rates, they were quickly able to grab as much as 80 per cent of the drug action in the country. This position was fiercely guarded and quickly earned the Turkish and Kurdish gangs a reputation for extreme violence and bloody retribution.

The most significant event in the development of organized crime in Germany in the last 60 years occurred in 1989, with the fall of Communism and the pulling down of the Berlin Wall. Almost overnight, West Germany went from having one of the most heavily guarded borders in the world to being wide open to an influx of East European criminal gangs, determined to use Germany as a backdoor into the rest of Europe. With Unification, the apparently simple picture of limited domestic German crime groups and the activities of the Turkish and Kurdish gangs was blown apart. Within a few years Russian, Albanian, Serb, Polish, Romanian and Vietnamese organized crime groups were all active within Germany.

There had been a significant Vietnamese community in East Germany since 1975, when the Communist government of Vietnam had sent several thousand workers to the German Democratic Republic. Socially isolated, the lack of policing in the Vietnamese communities was soon exploited after the fall of Communism. Forging alliances with Polish criminals, Vietnamese gangs soon had control of the huge black market in illegally smuggled as well as counterfeit cigarettes that was created by the high levels of taxation on tobacco in Germany.

Recent years have seen evidence of the Vietnamese gangs expanding outside of this lucrative business. They are becoming more tightly organized and are hooking up with established Vietnamese trans-national crime groups, such as the US-based BTK (Born To Kill). This is charted by the increasing number of criminals caught with the tattoos or three dots on the hand that signify membership of the Triad-like gangs. These alliances have seen the German-based Vietnamese gangs diversifying into the supply of heroin and the trafficking of women and children for prostitution.

The two organized criminal networks that dominate the illegal German sex trade are the various elements of the Russian Organizatsiya and the Albanian Mafiya. Although prostitution is legal in designated areas in Germany, both the Organizatsiya and the Albanian Mafiya have been responsible for flooding the country with thousands of women, illegally trafficked from countries such as Albania, Bulgaria, Moldova, Romania and Ukraine. Recent raids on forced-prostitution enterprises have shown that Albanian gangs based in Germany are beginning to work closely with the Italian Mafia group Sacra Corona Unita in this despicable crime.

Another area of organized illegal activity that all the criminal networks in Germany are currently vying for more control over is the growing

An X-ray shot of a HGV reveals that it is carrying more than officially listed in its cargo manifest. People trafficking is now one of the largest growth areas of organized crime in Germany.

business of people trafficking. Turkish, Albanian and Russian experience of smuggling drugs and women into the country is now being used to create routes into the EU via Germany for thousands of illegal immigrants from across Asia, China and the Indian subcontinent.

The Organizatsiya also has a strong grip on the theft of vehicles in Germany, but during the last five years there has been increasing evidence that the Organizatsiya is now focussing on extorting money from large German companies and the theft of industrial and commercial secrets. Competition in this and other illegal activities is intensifying and some organized crime experts are predicting a massive upswing in violence and deaths related to organized crime in Germany over the coming years.

ORGANIZED CRIME IN THE BALTIC STATES

Nothing could dim the joy of the people in the Baltic States of Estonia, Lithuania and Latvia, when the start of collapse of the Soviet Union in 1990 allowed them to reclaim the independence and freedom so long denied to them. Yet freedom came with an unexpected price as the newly re-established states quickly found themselves in the grip of organized crime.

With their geographical proximity to Russia and large ethnic-Russian communities, it is no surprise that the Organizatsiya play a dominating role in organized crime across the Baltic States. Yet in Estonia, the Nõukogu and Obtshak networks have managed to hold the major Organizatsiya groups at bay. The Nõukogu (meaning "council") acts as a ruling body of native Estonian organized crime groups, preventing territorial disputes and encouraging co-operation along the lines of the US Mafia's National Syndicate. The Obtshak (meaning "common treasury") acts along similar lines for Estonia's ethnic-Russian criminal gangs and those native Estonian groups excluded from the Nõukogu. The Obtshak even levies a "tax" amongst member groups to provide a central fund for foreign expansion.

Between them, the Nõukogu and Obtshak have maintained control of gambling, nightclubs and prostitution in Tallinn and other cities. They have become heavily involved in the transportation of young women from the Baltic States to work in the Western European illegal sex trade, and expanded to be a major force in drug distribution and prostitution in neighbouring Finland.

Lithuania's borders with Poland and Belarus have given it a pivotal role in Organizatsiya drug, duty and people smuggling and the Mafiya have invested heavily to protect their operations within the country. Lithuania is now so dominated by organized criminal networks that the killing of Vitas Lingys, deputy editor of the second-largest daily newspaper in Lithuania in 1993, was an almost inevitable consequence of his paper

CYBER-CRIME

It is estimated that the cost of cyber-crime in 2005 was in excess of $50 billion. With such potential for vast illicit revenues, it is no surprise that the Internet has become one of the most hotly contested criminal territories of the twenty-first century.

Different organized crime networks have already begun to specialize and dominate within certain cyber-crime activities. Nigerian crime syndicates are the acknowledged global leaders in advance fee fraud (where victims pay sums of money in the hope of obtaining a share of some non-existent wealth) and identity theft. Although the cost of such crimes to private individuals totals tens of millions of dollars per year, Nigerian syndicates have also netted hundreds of millions from businesses through the same scams, including $242 million from the Brazilian bank Banco Noroeste, in 2004.

The Russian Mafiya is known to specialize in the online protection racket called "network-based denial of service". In this type of operation, firms relying exclusively on Internet customers, such as online betting operations, face demands for money if they wish their clientele to have access to their website. If they refuse, the cyber-crime gang overloads and brings down their system, thus paralyzing their business.

The Organizatsiya are also global leaders in profits derived from activities such as extortion through threats of unleashing viruses on corporations and hacking. Organized crime hacking activities increasingly focus both on stock exchanges and other financial institutions and private individuals. In 1994, customers of New York's Citibank lost more than $11 million through a successful hacking manoeuvre.

opposing the growth of criminal gangs. The 2004 deposition of Rolandas Paksas, the President of Lithuania, after it was revealed that he was believed to have had links with prominent Russian Mafiya figures, provides even further evidence of the grip that organized crime has on this country.

One area where the native organized crime groups of the Baltic States have developed a legendary reputation within the global underworld community is cyber-crime and money laundering. The Latvian capital Riga is home to more than 20 national banks, as well as significant foreign banking enterprises. In 2004, the US government issued a report singling out Latvia as a "primary country of concern" with regard to money laundering, on account of the country's "failure to prosecute money launderers", the "strong presence of active organized crime networks in the country" and suspected corruption, leading to the "inconsistent application of policies by banks to prevent financial crimes".

Even though Latvia was one of the first states in the former Eastern bloc to bring in new cyber-crime laws in 1998, it is still seen as a global leader in hacking, denial-of-service-attacks and cyber-extortion against multinational businesses and institutions. The nature of the cyber-extortion tends to mean that successful instances of the crime go unreported, as even when a company does inform the police, the incident is not made public in an attempt to limit the possibility of copycat crimes.

When I asked among policing circles in Riga, I was told that Latvian organized crime gangs have obtained millions of dollars from British betting firms, a German telecoms company and on-line banks through cyber-extortion in recent years. Europol sources confirmed this. The US Justice Department believes that up to 85 per cent of US corporations have

been subject to some form of threat. FBI Director Ronald L. Dick has spoken of the potential nature of these crimes – "To destabilize a country's whole economy" – while his agents continue to confirm a large proportion of these crimes originate in Latvia and the other Baltic States.

In 2005, the US Securities and Exchange Commission took legal action against an Estonian firm it accused of electronically stealing confidential business information from press releases before they became public, and using them to make stock market deals netting them millions of dollars. One US financial investigator commented that those accused must have felt "Very unlucky to have been singled out as it's a crime rife across the Baltic States with organized crime groups heavily involved".

The former Lithuanian President, Rolandas Paksas, was forced from office in 2004 after his links with prominent Russian Mafiya figures were exposed and he was impeached.

ORGANIZED CRIME IN SCANDINAVIA

Members of the Bandidos outlaw motorcycle gang at the 1999 funeral of Morten Viggo Laursen – a casualty of the Scandinavian Bandidos vs. Hells Angel war.

I've had some interesting threats made to me in the course of doing the research for this tome. The most surprising of them came from a Norwegian biker who suggested that something unpleasant involving a shotgun could be arranged to happen to me if I implied anywhere in the book that Finland was part of Scandinavia. Not only is it an unexpected issue to be threatened over, but it goes against the common perception of the Nordic countries, Norway, Sweden, Denmark, Finland and Iceland, as relatively free from the violence that is associated with organized crime. However, no country is totally free from the influence of criminal networks, and despite this international perception, none of the Scandinavian nations is an exception to the rule.

Even a cursory investigation of crime in Scandinavia will quickly show that outlaw biker gangs dominate it. Although under-reported internationally, there has been a prolonged and bloody war fought amongst the Hells Angels and Bandidos for control of drug distribution in Denmark, Norway, Sweden and Finland. The origins of the conflict date back to 1980, when a Hells Angels chapter was founded in Copenhagen in Denmark. It quickly established itself as the dominant player in heroin, cocaine and methamphetamine distribution and led the way to the establishment of Hells Angel chapters across Scandinavia.

At the start of the 1990s, however, one of the Hells Angels' greatest rivals, the Bandidos outlaw biker gang, expanded from its only other European chapter in Marseille, France, by turning the existing Danish biker gang the Undertakers into Bandidos. Within months the first shoot-outs between the two organized criminal networks over drug and vice territories were being reported in Sweden, and the Bandidos clubhouse in Marseilles had been bombed. The fact that this was an actual war was underpinned when members of the Bandidos stole 12 anti-tank missiles from an army base near Malmo in Sweden in 1994.

By 1996, the war had escalated to the point where Danish Bandidos leader Uffe Larsen was shot in an open shoot-out at Copenhagen airport. The Bandidos responded with missile attacks on the Hells Angels, which including blowing up their headquarters in Helsinki, Finland. Bombs, hand grenades, machine guns and anti-tank weapons were regularly used, until a shaky truce was called in 1997, as the overt violence was becoming increasingly bad for business.

Less blatantly violent, the Albanian Mafiya used the inter-gang warfare between the bikers to bolster their position within the Norwegian and Swedish underworld. They control much of the importation of the drugs that the outlaw biker gangs distribute and have increasingly taken control of the vice trade, illegally trafficking women and children from Albania to be used as sexual slaves. Anti-immigrant feeling has led to a growth of the Swedish neo-Nazi movements, some of which have turned to crime to fund their activities. They were organized enough, in 2004, to raid the army base Camp Jøstadmoen in Norway and steal more than 90 weapons.

In Finland, the Estonian-based Obtshak organized criminal network dominates the distribution of narcotics. Called the Yhteiskassa by the Finnish police, Obtshak groups have also used extreme violence to remove Finland's previously established vice kingpins and now dominate organized prostitution in the country. They are responsible for illegally trafficking high numbers of young girls from the Baltic States, Belarus and Russia into Finland.

Even Iceland, the country perceived to be one of the least corrupt and most lawful in the world, has an element of organized crime. Despite the country's zero-tolerance of narcotics, Norwegian organized criminals still manage to supply and distribute drugs on the isolated island state. However, concerns expressed by Britain's Serious Fraud Office and other international authorities that Icelandic businesses and financial institutions were being used to launder Russian organized crime proceeds diminished after the collapse of Iceland's banking system during the financial crisis of 2008–2012.

Scandinavia is renowned for innovative attempts to combat organized crime through different legislative approaches. Some, such as the Swedish law decriminalizing the selling of sex but criminalizing the buying of sex as an aspect of male violence against women and children, have been judged successful. However, no experiment remains more controversial than Freetown Christiania – a self-governing region of the Danish capital, Copenhagen. After years of zero tax, open drug dealing and self-policing, the authorities began to clamp down on the free state in 2005, citing the fact that it was a base for some organized criminals as one reason for the crackdown.

Danish police launched a brutal crackdown on the citizens of Christiania in 2004, claiming its libertarian policies made it a haven for organized criminals.

GLOBAL GANGS – ORGANIZED CRIME ACROSS THE WORLD

9

"The state is the biggest criminal for making us poor."

Red Command graffiti, São Paulo, Brazil

We live in an era of corporate globalization, which impacts on the lives of 6 billion people daily. When Marshall McLuhan coined the phrase "Global Village" in 1962 he was describing how electronic mass media was collapsing the barriers of space and time in human communication. He imagined the whole world being turned into a village, where everyone could interact on a global scale. Today, globalization at every level of our lives is a reality.

It should not surprise anyone that one of the word's largest, oldest and most profitable industries – organized crime – has also become a global enterprise. The tradition of criminal groups being limited to controlling and fighting over territories only in their native countries became outdated with the success the Sicilian Mafia and the Chinese Triads enjoyed when they left Europe and Asia and expanded their illicit networks into America and other territories in the nineteenth century.

The truly global economy that we have witnessed forming in the last 40 years has allowed organized groups to benefit from technology and ease of travel in exactly the same way that legitimate business has. New alliances on an epic scale have emerged. Established criminal organizations are now linked to newly emerging gangs in a network of criminality that, for the first time in human history, really does encompass the whole globe. No country is free from the taint of organized crime – what happens today on the streets of São Paulo can have implications for organized crime and its victims half a world away.

THE COLOMBIAN CARTELS

Many organized crime groups started out as movements trying to overthrow an established government. Originally dedicated to protecting the poor or oppressed, they eventually mutated into criminal gangs committed to nothing more than making money. It is ironic, then, that the Colombian drug cartels started out as ventures of pure criminal greed, but ended up giving millions of dollars to the poor and trying to bring down a government.

Since their formation in the 1970s, the Colombian cartels have changed the global face of organized crime by controlling the world supply of cocaine. From Yardies in London to Yakuza operating in Tokyo's Roppongi district, US Mafia families to Danish bikers – if a criminal group distributes cocaine it is, at some point, doing business with a line of narcotics production and transmission that is linked to the Colombian Cali or Medellin Cartels.

The Cali Cartel was the first of the Colombian drug cartels to be formed. It began in 1970, when master strategist and visionary criminal mastermind Gilberto Rodriguez Orejuela, the "Chess Player", realized the demand for cocaine was increasing on a yearly basis. He could see the vast profits that could be made from reorganizing the small-scale cottage industry approach to cocaine distribution in Colombia that then purely focussed on producing it for domestic demand and exporting a small surplus to America.

Orejuela could see that Colombia's geographical position, bordering Panama, Ecuador, Venezuela, Brazil and Peru, and with access to both the Pacific Ocean and Caribbean Sea, gave it the potential to become the hub of cocaine production and distribution. With the help of his brother, Miguel, and fellow visionary, José Santacruz Londoño, Orejuela put together a global network of cocaine production and distribution. It started as simply smuggling cocaine from Peru to the USA and became a vast empire that, at one point, was behind 80 per cent of the export of cocaine from South America to the rest of the world.

Taking its name from the Colombian city of Cali, out of which its leaders operated, the cartel was organized to mimic a terrorist cell structure – groups of up to 10 soldiers working for a commander who reported, via a chain-of-command, directly to the cartel leaders. Orejuela believed this was the most robust set-up for foreign expansion and would prevent infiltration by the authorities. He also set up alliances with the New York Mafia, Jamaican Yardies and other organized crime groups, which still stand today and became a model for international co-operation in trans-national organized crime.

After Orejuela's capture in 1995 and the police shooting of Londoño in 1996, the Cali Cartel lost much of its power, but it still remains a global factor in organized crime and drug trafficking. It has moved away from its old practice of buying power within the Colombian government and now gives funds to the country's growing rebel army – the Revolutionary Armed Forces of Colombia. Although the Cali Cartel is more splintered, it appears to be on solid comeback trail.

The Cali Cartel's main rival in Colombia and abroad was the Medellin Cartel, which took its name from the Colombian city of Medellin near the border with Panama, from which its leaders operated. It was formed in the mid-1970s by the co-operation of drug traffickers Carlos Enrique Lehder Rivas, Pablo Escobar-Gavira, Jorge Luis Ochoa, Gonzalo Rodriguez Gacha and the Ochoa brothers –

Despite his arrest in 1995, Gilberto Rodríguez Orejuela, known as "the Chess Player", remains regarded by many as the king amongst the Cali Cartel's infamous array of cocaine barons.

Medellin cocaine kingpin, Jorge Luis Ochoa, in a 1991 interview he gave before entering jail. His release just five years later angered the US and showed just how much power and influence Ochoa maintains.

Fabio, Jorge and Juan David. At its height in the 1980s, it controlled 50 per cent of cocaine distribution in the USA, was earning between 2 and 4 billion dollars per year, and thought nothing of running a campaign of bombings and terror that culminated in the assassination of the Colombian Minister of Justice, Lara Bonilla, in 1984.

Escobar and Lehder poured millions of dollars into philanthropic projects aimed at alleviating poverty and were seen by many as heroes when the Colombian government began a major crackdown on the Medellin Cartel after Bonilla's killing. Even an offer by the Medellin gangsters to pay off Colombia's entire $13 billion national debt could not resolve their fugitive status. Nearly a decade of conflict between the authorities and the Cartel followed until the death or capture of most its leaders. However, surviving former members and associates have spent the time since Escobar's death in 1993 rebuilding their power and once again the Medellin Cartel is becoming an active and influential power on the international drug scene.

THE MEXICAN CARTELS

One element of international organized crime that owes much of its current power and size to the rise of the Colombian cartels is the Mexican drug trade. Although the drug trafficking networks of Mexico always played a role in illegal drug distribution in North America, it was the cocaine boom created by the Colombians that launched the Mexican cartels as a major force in the global narcotics business.

Prior to the explosion of cocaine production and demand, the majority of Mexican organized crime revolved around the trafficking of heroin into the USA, the smuggling of illegal immigrants across the US border, providing Mexican women for US vice networks, and the wide-scale cultivation and export of marijuana to the United States. By the late 1960s, the assorted enterprises of Mexican drug barons, such as former policeman Jaime Herrera Nevarez (the "Drug Lord of Durango"), had become so large that the US President at the time, Richard Nixon, made them the first targets in what became the unofficial start of America's "War on Drugs".

In September, 1969, Nixon sanctioned "Operation Intercept" which effectively closed the border between Mexico and the US, but did little to prevent the organized drug traffickers. After three weeks and a major diplomatic row with Mexico, the US scrapped Operation Intercept and changed tack by offering the Mexican government millions of dollars to destroy the marijuana plantations and dismantle the drug rings within Mexico. It was also an approach that failed.

Despite the highly-publicized burning of some marijuana crops by the Mexican army, the traffickers continued to thrive. It took until 1988 for the Mexican police to arrest Jaime Herrera Nevarez. By this point, the US Drug Enforcement Administration (DEA) estimated that his

Mexican investigators explore one of the trans-border tunnels (some are more than 20m (65ft) deep and 457m (1,500ft) long) that have been found in Tijuana and are used by the cartels to smuggle drugs and people.

"farm-to-arm" heroin operation was responsible for exporting 746lbs (338kg) of pure heroin into America each year – this equated to more than eight tonnes of cut-down, street level heroin and annual profits for the Herrera Family in excess of $200 million.

However, after the cocaine boom of the mid-1970s that coincided with disco, then later fuelled the excess of "Reaganomics", and is still going strong in the twenty-first century, the DEA's real concern was the Mexican organized crime groups trafficking cocaine. The loss of power that the Colombian cartels experienced in the 1990s with the death and arrest of their major leaders, such as Pablo Escobar and José Santacruz Londoño, provided all three main Mexican cartels with the perfect opportunity to expand their operations and emerge as more than just the Colombians' junior partners.

By 1997, the Mexican cartels had expanded their empires into America, forming alliances with the La Nuestra Familia and La Eme in

California and even Yardie gangs in New York. The three major cartels also had effective control of the 1,951 mile (3,140km) US–Mexican border. Where they were unable to actually cross it, they went under it, as the discovery in 2003 of two tunnels running beneath the border between Tijuana in Mexico and Otay Mesa in California highlighted.

With the Juarez Cartel controlling smuggling in the centre of the US–Mexican border area, the Tijuana Cartel the north-western area and the Gulf Cartel focussed on the east, and with profits of up to $200 million a week for each group, there should have been enough money and space to go round. However, with the murder of the Juarez Cartel leader, Amado Carrillo Fuentes, (known as the "Lord of the Skies" due to his use of jets to transport cocaine) in 1997, a bloody territorial war broke out amongst the three groups.

The protracted war has allowed the Mexican authorities to make some progress against the organizations, scoring notable victories, such as the shooting of the Tijuana Cartel leader, Ramon Arellano Felix, in 2002, and the capture of the Gulf Cartel's leader, Osiel Cardenas, in 2003. Cardenas continued to effectively play a large role in running the cartel from prison until 2010, when his brother Antonio Cárdenas Guillén, better known as "Tony Tormenta", was killed after an eight-hour battle between more than 650 Mexican marines and gangsters loyal to him. The Los Zetas, a unit of ex-Mexican special forces soldiers that Osiel had formed to support his leadership also broke from his command in 2010, allying to the New Juárez Cartel and the Tijuana Cartel.

It was the New Juárez Cartel, the name given to the old Juárez Cartel operations that emerged after years of infighting, which was responsible in 2010 for bombing the cars of federal police officers and in 2011, for the execution of several police officers in the Ciudad, Juárez and Chihuahua districts. However, one of the most notorious incidents of recent years – the dumping of 22 mostly beheaded bodies in Acapulco in January 2011 – was the work of the Sinaloa Cartel, just one of eight major cartels currently carrying on a blood-soaked war for dominance of the Mexican drug trade

JAMAICA'S YARDIES AND POSSES

One set of organized crime groups that has a reputation for bloody violence and inter-gang warfare, that even manages to outstrip that of the Mexican cartels, are Jamaica's Yardies and Posses.

Although Yardie is a term often used by the police and journalists when talking about Jamaican organized crime groups, the term most gang members use themselves is Posse. Yardie originates from the government yard tenement of Trenchtown and Jamaican patois, where yard means home. The gangs adopted the term Posse from the spaghetti westerns they loved whilst taking their structure from gangster movies, hence the use of Don for a Posse's leader, underboss for his second-in-command and soldiers for average gang members.

The Posses sprang from the "rude boy" culture prevalent in the poverty stricken districts of Kingston and Spanish Town. In the late 1960s, Jamaican politicians began to co-opt the gangs as enforcers and bodyguards. This involvement of the heavily-armed Posses ensured that every Jamaican election resulted in hundreds of shootings. When the government of Michael Manley's People's National Party was defeated in 1980, many Posse members fearing a crackdown fled to the large Jamaican émigré communities in Britain, Canada and America.

Back home in Jamaica, the gangs had been heavily into organized robbery and marijuana distribution; abroad they quickly carved out a territory based on cocaine dealing. This stemmed from Jamaica's geographical position in the Caribbean, which had seen it become a favoured staging post of the Colombian cartels for exporting cocaine to America and Europe, via Britain. With high levels of poverty, the Posses found no shortage of willing drug mules in Jamaica, and quickly moved into specializing in crack cocaine, with its higher profits.

The Posse gun culture meant that, in Jamaica, the army regularly had to be called in to match their firepower when the police wanted to take action against a Posse "garrison" (base). Since the late 1970s, the gang-related murder rate in Jamaica has averaged nearly 1,000 per year, according to figures provided by international policing bodies. Posse gun violence was also soon seen on the streets of Manchester and London in Britain, where Posses fought blazing gun battles over drug turf. In New York, the Shower Posse, Dunkirk Boys Posse and Spangler Posse quickly earned a reputation, according to one former senior New York policeman, as the most "gun-crazy, stone-cold killers dealing in NYC".

Bodies, including that of cartel leader Ramon Arellano Felix (right), lie in the streets of Mazatlan in Mexico after a 2002 skirmish in Mexico's ongoing bloody drug warfare.

Scotland Yard display a small fraction of the illegal firearms seized after a number of successful raids on Jamaican Posses operating across the English capital.

Roy Ramm, former head of Scotland Yard's Yardie Squad, infamously called the Jamaican crime groups operating in Britain, "disorganized organized crime". Some in the black community see the comment as symptomatic of a police structure that not only does not understand Jamaican culture, but has singularly failed to penetrate the Posse network and therefore fails to appreciate just how well-organized it actually is.

Although Ramm meant no racial implication to be taken from his remark, rival organized crime groups have taken it up as an oft-repeated slur against a supposed Jamaican lack of organizational skill. By the time of the formation of Operation Trident by Scotland Yard in 1998, to tackle what they referred to as "black-on-black gun crime" following an ever-increasing number of Posse related shootings in London, the fallacy of Ramm's words were clear.

The Posses across the world are clearly highly structured, sophisticated and resourceful. Alongside the vast drug trafficking and dealing operations, they have established an efficient contract killing network. Members of a Posse will travel from Jamaica to a city in America, Canada or Britain to conduct a hit and will then be moved on to another country before police forensic experts are even finished at the crime scene.

Complex webs of extortion, blackmail and corruption have also been established, to ensure key airline staff and customs officials turn a blind eye to trafficking activities. Certain Dons operate headhunting programmes to recruit banking and computer graduates into their Posses to assist in money laundering. Instead of casinos and nightclubs, illicit profits are invested in the type of low-key legitimate businesses, such as supermarkets, that are never usually subject to police scrutiny.

The true level of complexity behind Posse violence has done nothing to

dent their public image of drug-fuelled, kings of bling gunmen. Yet even their well-deserved reputation for ending every argument with a bullet has not prevented them from facing increasing challenges to their turf from other emerging global gangs.

NIGERIAN ORGANIZED CRIME GANGS

One emerging force in global organized crime that has tended to work with, rather than oppose, the Posses on the streets of Britain has been the various Nigerian organized crime gangs that are also at work in the country. Police intelligence experts have noted that when the Albanian Mafiya or Turkish gangs have threatened the Nigerians over their interests in prostitution or heroin in the UK, the Nigerians have brought the Posses in to back them up. This mercenary arrangement is merely an extension of the relationship between the two groups that already sees Nigerians selling the cocaine they bring into the country to the Posses, as well as providing them with assistance in frauds and money laundering.

For many people, the idea that Nigerian organized crime exists and plays a strong role in activities such as drug trafficking is surprising. The common view of Nigerian crime is that it consists of isolated, advance fee fraudsters with no real organization or presence abroad. This is not the case. Intelligence from the FBI, Interpol and the US Secret Service has indicated that there are more than 500 organized Nigerian crime gangs operating in between 60 and 80 countries worldwide.

When a 1996 FBI investigation into a trans-national Nigerian crime gang involved in heroin trafficking led to arrests in Bangkok, Pakistan, Chicago, New York and Detroit, US Attorney General Janet Reno was quick to comment: "This demonstrates that Nigerian criminal organizations are no longer just couriers, but have developed into a major force in their own right". This statement also seems to apply to their role in slavery, child prostitution, complex trans-national frauds and identity theft.

The South African government has complained of Nigerian gangs penetrating the entire region of southern Africa, controlling heroin and cocaine distribution, document fraud, car theft and business extortion. In North African and southern European governments there is increasing concern about the Nigerian role in the smuggling of aliens across the Mediterranean. Nigeria, the centre of the slave trade until 1850, has once again earned a terrible reputation as a focus of international trafficking of children for sexual exploitation and a new form of slavery – "bonded-labour".

The rise of Nigerian syndicates, and Nigeria's role as the hub of organized crime in Africa, date to the oil price crash of the 1980s. With 90 per cent of its earnings coming from oil exports, the result was a collapse in the country. The economic turmoil heightened political instability and corruption to the point that effective policing in Nigeria broke down. Many well-educated

Nigerians turned to crime to support themselves, safe in the knowledge that they could bribe their way out of any trouble if caught. They developed criminal networks that could seemingly engage in drug and bush meat smuggling from Lagos and Port Harcourt with impunity, as well as operating trans-national fraud with hardly any fear of prosecution

Many Nigerian syndicates operate advance fee frauds where people in other countries are asked to send money or provide bank account details in return for receiving a cut of an immense fortune that is allegedly held within the international banking system. The gangs recruit young men known as "yahoo-yahoo boys", who are apprenticed to the gang's leaders, given special training and then set loose in the Internet cafes of Lagos and other cities. The trial in Abuja in 2004 for a 419 fraud (so named after the relevant section of the Nigerian Criminal Code), which targeted the Brazilian bank, Banco Noroeste, for $242 million, was only unusual because very few prosecutions ever result from the millions of dollars fraudsters operating in Nigeria manage to obtain on a weekly basis.

Cross-dressing Nigerian governor, Diepreye Alamieyeseigha, won the "Golden Trophy of Good Governance" despite skipping bail for laundering money.

NOTICE
• 419 MAILS
• SPAM E-MAILS
• E-MAIL EXTRA...
are NOT ALLO...

NOTICE
• 419 MAILS
• SPAM E-MAILS
• E-MAIL EXTRACTORS
are NOT ALLOWED

Nigerian crime syndicates are infamous for running gangs of young men, known as yahoo-yahoo boys, from Internet cafes, who work 419 and phishing scams that bring in millions of stolen dollars.

The splintered cultural identity of Nigeria may mean it will never develop a national crime structure. However, although its organized crime gangs may not follow conventional models, they have flourished in Nigeria, and play an increasing role in trans-national organized crime activities. In a country described by many international politicians as a "failed state", the pandemic political and police corruption has allowed organized crime to thrive. The corruption extends to the highest levels. In 2005, governor of the Nigerian State of Bayelsa, Diepreye Alamieyseigha, won the "Golden Trophy For Good Governance" despite having skipped bail by dressing as a woman when arrested for allegedly laundering more than $3.2 million. When it seems that almost anyone can be above the law, the rule of law borders on meaningless.

ANIMAL AND BUSH MEAT SMUGGLING

The smuggling of rare animals is, by its very nature, a trans-national crime, best suited to organized gangs collaborating across international borders. A multi-billion dollar illicit business, the trafficking of endangered wildlife is one of the most profitable smuggling activities, after the illegal transportation of narcotics and arms.

Usually, a criminal group in the animal's country of origin obtains live or dead specimens from poachers. They then co-operate with an organized crime network in another country to arrange for the prohibited wildlife importation. Live animals are sold to private collectors or scientists, and there is also a huge demand for pelts, ivory and body parts (for use in traditional Asian medicine) from beasts such as tigers, rhino and gorilla.

Some crime gangs have even tried to use the Internet in order to find their own buyers and cut out crime syndicates in destination countries. As a result, these syndicates have responded by sending their own representatives to the illicit animal markets in Nigeria, Thailand, Vietnam, Cambodia and Brazil to ensure that they can continue to source their horrendous criminal commodity.

Alongside the devastating impact smuggling has on endangered animals, the killing of internationally-protected species for use as "bush meat" is also a rapidly increasing problem that threatens biodiversity. Thousands of tonnes of bush meat are illegally transported to Europe, Asia and America each year by African crime syndicates. While they can make huge profits selling bush meat outside Africa, their vile trade risks spreading disease as well as pushing some species ever closer to extinction.

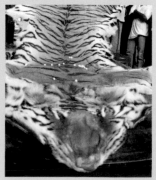

THE COMMANDS – BRAZIL'S ORGANIZED CRIME GANGS

The type of endemic political and police corruption that provides a fertile breeding ground for organized crime where a large number of the population are fighting for economic survival is not restricted to Nigeria. It is a story that is repeated across the globe, though few countries illustrate how poverty and a lack of social justice can lead to the creation of organized criminal gangs better than Brazil.

Brazil has always been a country where the divide between fabulous wealth and crushing poverty has been dramatic and only separated by the distance of a couple of streets. The opulent beachside penthouses and skyscrapers of Rio de Janeiro have always been uncomfortably close to the slum conditions of the city's favelas, first established as a community of squatters by freed slaves in the 1890s. The 25 million people that live in poverty in Brazil have believed for decades that the police only exist to protect the wealthy. The police were even seen as a predatory force – the numerous cases of police massacres of favela residents and unprovoked shootings of street children are testament to this.

Between 1964 and1985, Brazil was under a military dictatorship. Members of political resistance groups were sent to the same prisons as criminals from the favelas. In the infamous maximum security prison on the island of Ilha Grande, members of street gangs known as falanjes and convicted robbers learnt about revolutionary justice, terrorist cell organization, solidarity and Trotsky from the socialist prisoners. This led to the formation of the "Red Command" prison gang, which protected members from guards and other convicts. When the prisoners returned to the favelas they took the Red Command structure and ideals with them, forming new criminal networks called "Commands".

In the lawless favelas which the police made no attempt to keep in order, the Commands first seized control of drug distribution within the communities and then took charge of the communities themselves. In return for providing them with a base for their cocaine dealing and organized robbery operations, that targeted only the wealthy, the Commands used some of their profits to fund basic amenities and social welfare programmes, including general health and emergency medical clinics. They also acted as an unofficial police force, giving out violent punishments for crimes such as domestic violence and rape. To start with they were regarded by many as heroes, but problems soon arose as their criminal activities began to dominate and the Commands began to fight amongst each other to take control of various favelas.

Before the Commands evolved, organized crime in Brazil had been mainly limited to corruption, murders conducted on behalf of big business, foreign groups such as the American and Sicilian Mafia using it as base, and numerous rural outlaws. Now there was open street warfare between groups such as the Third Command, the Red

Rioting inmates at the Urso Branco prison in Brazil protest over moving one of their leaders to another prison, highlighting the organized structure of the Commands both in and out of prison.

Command and the Friends of Friends Command. It often involved combat with rocket launchers in an area where innocent civilians were at risk and an official police force was entirely absent.

In recent years, many of the Commands – especially the most political of them – have forged links with the Revolutionary Armed Forces of Colombia (FARC). Established in 1964 as the military wing of the Colombian Communist Party, FARC has now grown into a large-scale rebel army that controls up to 30 per cent of Colombia's territory. Backed by many of the Colombian drug cartels, FARC is now the major cocaine and weapons supplier to many of the Commands. Their criminal ties have also blossomed into an ideological alliance with FARC's teachings on fighting poverty, land rights for the poor and championing social justice, which has helped reignite some of the ideological fire that first led to the formation of the Commands.

In 2003, Brazilian Federal Police Superintendent Marcelo Itagiba warned that things had moved beyond simple organized crime claiming: "Rio de Janeiro is immersed in a urban guerrilla war, promoted by armed and organized terrorist groups." Many in the Brazilian government were privately afraid that the Commands links to FARC would inspire them to seek to form a grand coalition between themselves and militant elements of the Brazil's Landless Rural Workers' Movement. However, these fears have not been manifested and there is no sign yet of a countrywide revolutionary criminal network developing. Yet in a country where some sections of the police have formed militias to enact their own protection and extortion rackets, control of organized crime continues to seem beyond the reach of the state and rampant criminality may yet play a huge role in destabilizing Brazil.

ORGANIZED CRIME IN CANADA

One country that does not have Brazil's looming problem with a crime network high on the rhetoric of Leon Trotsky, but which does have a problem with foreign organized crime groups and outlaws, is Canada. The outlaws in this case are the biker gangs, while the foreign element of organized crime revolves around both the American Mafia and Triads, who have established a strong role in the Canadian underworld.

When America became "dry" on January 16, 1920, it was obvious that Canada was going to play a significant role in the bootlegging of booze across the border. With alcohol still legal, no shortage of breweries and distillers and 6,414 kilometres (3,985 miles) (not including Alaska) of unfenced border, Prohibition proved as much of a boon to Canadian organized crime as it did to American mobsters.

Although the Buffalo crime family, under the legendary Stefano Magaddino, represented American Mafia control of booze coming in from Ontario, elsewhere Canadian gangs such as Montreal's Irish-based West End Gang played a significant role. However, it was Rocco Perri, known as "Canada's Al Capone" and "King of the Bootleggers", who gained the most. He diversified into prostitution and gambling long before Prohibtion ended in 1933 and probably would have succeeded in keeping the American Mafia out of his territories if he had not been interned during the Second World War due to his Italian origins.

With the decline of Perri's power, the American Mafia, in the shape of the Bonanno crime family, hooked up with Montreal boss Vincent "The

Egg" Cotroni to form what became known as the Montreal Connection. With its well-established French links, Montreal was the perfect staging post for heroin, shipped in by Corsican and Sicilian gangsters from Marseille. It was smuggled across the border in specially converted cars and by the mid-1950s the operation was transporting heroin with a street value of $50 million into New York each month. Despite the Montreal connection being busted open by the Royal Canadian Mounted Police in 1961, drug trafficking remains a large part of Cosa Nostra's Canadian action, and the Bonanno family and the Cotroni gang still wield immense power in the Canadian underworld.

Today, the biggest players in Canadian organized crime are not the American Mafia operations, but the outlaw biker gangs. Cosa Nostra, Triads and increasingly the Nigerian syndicates may import heroin and cocaine into Canada, but it is the biker gangs who control its distribution across the country. With their own massive methamphetamines production network and their role in hash and ecstasy dealing, there is no element of the illegal drug trade in Canada that they do not dominate. The vast profits made have been invested in the vice trade, making them the biggest players in prostitution and pornography in every Canadian province. Some gangs boost profits further by running sophisticated contract killing services that even use databases to track their victims.

Despite engaging in publicity stunts, such as a 6,000-strong annual Vancouver Christmas Ride that brings presents to underprivileged children, Canada's outlaw biker gangs are still finding it hard to portray themselves as they want to be seen – lawful motorcycle clubs with a few, unfortunate criminal members. The failure is largely down to the highly visible gang warfare that has raged since 1984, when the Hells Angels fell out with the Quebec-based Rock Machine. The war claimed the lives of dozens of bikers and also innocent victims, such as 11-year-old Daniel Desrochers, who was killed by a bomb in Montreal, in 1995. The absorption of Rock Machine into the Bandidos in 2000, has done little to create stability, and fear of another massive upswing in violence has led to increased anti-biker activity by the Canadian authorities and police.

The outlaw biker gangs are not without challengers to their position as the most powerful criminal network operating in Canada today. The Triads have an ever-growing presence on Canada's Pacific coast. Heavily involved in narcotics importation, people trafficking, extortion, environmental crime and forced prostitution, groups such as 14K and Wo On Lok are increasing their profits and numbers on the ground on a weekly basis. Vietnamese groups such as the Big Circle; Jamaican Yardies and a growing number of home-grown Indo-Canadian and neo-Nazi crime gangs are all flourishing in major Canadian cities. With such ongoing developments, it seems organized crime's grip on the nation looks stronger than ever.

Key Triad figure and mastermind of a multi-billion dollar smuggling racket, Lai Changxing, is brought to trial. He is just one of the growing number of Triad members operating in Canada.

ORGANIZED CRIME IN AUSTRALIA

The growth of Triads and Vietnamese organized crime gangs in Vancouver, Canada is only part of a pattern of rapid expansion across the whole Pacific region. One country that has been particularly targeted has been Australia.

For the majority of Australians, the menace of Asian organized crime groups is seen as something restricted to the growing inter-gang warfare in Sydney's Cabramatta district, where the violence of Vietnamese gangs such as BTK, 5T and the Black Dragons has made the problem increasingly visible. However, as the gang-related shooting of MP John Paul Newman in September 1994 showed, the bloodshed is not a problem that is limited just to members of the gangs or their immediate community.

In contrast to the obvious street level carnage linked to the Vietnamese crime organizations, the Triads have made efforts to keep a lower profile. They have focussed on crimes such as people smuggling, illegal gambling and infiltration of the Australian financial community to facilitate money laundering. As key global players in heroin trafficking they have attempted to expand their share of the Australian market, but have found the way blocked by a longstanding alliance between Australia's indigenous organized crime groups and the American Mafia.

Prior to the expansion of air travel to Australia in the 1960s, the continent had been relatively isolated from the global criminal underworld. With no equivalent to Prohibition, organized networks developed from street gangs such as Sydney's Surry Hill Mob or the Melbourne gang members who were under the influence of the notorious political fixer John Wren. The main rackets revolved around illegal betting, prostitution and grog (drink) shop protection. Competition came from family-based outfits or criminal members of the Painters and Dockers Union. The largest and most sophisticated operations developed from the Italian immigrant community from Calabria, and formed what was known as the 'Ndrangheta or L'Onorata Societa (the Honoured Society).

By the mid-1960s, routine airline travel to and from America helped to bring Australia to the attention of Cosa Nostra. They saw it as an underdeveloped market that was ripe for them to expand their operations into – especially narcotics. In 1965, the Chicago Mafia sent out Joe Testa to hold exploratory talks with Australian organized crime groups. Relationships were forged with both Calabrian crime groups, Lennie "Mr Big" McPherson (the godfather figure of the Sydney underworld) and later with Robert Trimble.

Things started slowly, but under the direction of Jimmy "The Weasel" Fratianno, the Chicago mob persisted. Despite competition from Australian Greek and Lebanese ethnic-based crime networks, by the mid-1970s the Mafia and their Australian partners had developed an effective drug importation and distribution operation.

Since the 1980s, Australian organized crime has been beset by a series of bloody, ongoing battles. They may have begun as a fight for control of territory, but they have often degenerated into murderous vendettas beyond the confines of logic. Many killings stem from the 1983 bombing of a boss of the Calabrian Honoured Society, Liborio Benvenuto. He survived the blast on his vehicle and started a campaign of revenge on his rivals that, according to one police source, saw "More dead bodies dumped in the Yarra and Murrumbidgee Rivers than kittens in sacks".

One of the men suspected of killing Frank Benvenuto was Victor Pierce, part of the notorious Melbourne-based Pettingill crime family. Pierce had been tried for his part in the execution-style murder of police officers Steven Tynan and Damian Eyre, who were gunned down on Walsh Street in suburban South Yarra in 1988. Along with Melbourne's Moran crime family, the Pettingills have been blamed for many of the 30-plus organized crime-related killings that occurred in Melbourne between 2000 and 2005. However, with a share of the $5 billion amphetamine and party drugs market at stake, it is clear that other factions are also at work, including members of the newly arrived

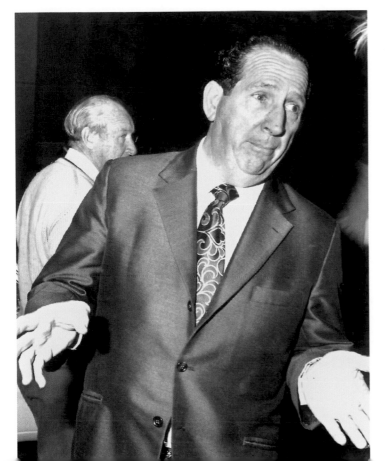

Lennie "Mr Big" McPherson was front-runner for title of kingpin of the Sydney crime scene and one of those the American Cosa Nostra formed an alliance with.

The four sons of vice queen Kath Pettingill (from left to right: Victor Pierce; Trevor Pettingill; Dennis and Peter Allen) who were wanted by the police for murder, gun dealing and running a drug empire.

Serbian and Albanian Mafiya.

After many years of being swept under the political and media carpet, Australian organized crime has moved into the forefront of the national psyche thanks to the high profile TV drama series *Underbelly*. Telling the stories of Melbourne drug wars, the Mr. Asia drug syndicate and police corruption in New South Wales, the controversial show has at times almost seemed to celebrate Australian gang crime. With organized crime still continuing to expand in Australia, it seems unlikely that future series will be short of new crimes to dramatize.

ORGANIZED CRIME IN NEW ZEALAND

It is perhaps of little surprise to learn of the deadly inter-gang warfare that rages amongst organized criminal groups in Melbourne. Yet the fact that Australia's neighbour New Zealand also has a growing problem with battling organized crime groups is something of a revelation. The majestic landscape of the country highlighted in *The Lord of the Rings* films has helped to make New Zealand one of the world's top tourist destinations, something enhanced by its continuing reputation as a tranquil and almost crime-free destination.

However, like every other country in the world, New Zealand has always had its underworld. Before the Second World War, it was dominated by ethnic Irish gangs, who fought for control of the docks and its lucrative union, theft and smuggling rackets. With only two cities being home to substantial populations, the rest of organized crime was in the

control of small, family-based groups who knew better than to focus police attention on themselves through public disputes over territory.

As the global demand for heroin and cocaine boomed in the 1970s, New Zealand became a key part of the notorious Mr Asia international drug syndicate which also operated in the United States, Europe, and Australia. Sophisticated enough to regularly spy on New Zealand customs officials to find out if any of its couriers were suspected, Mr Asia dominated the New Zealand drugs scene until the arrest of its key member, Terry Clark, in Britain in 1979, toppled the organization.

In the wake of its collapse, Mr Asia's role as a hard drug importer into New Zealand was taken over by a number of Asian crime gangs that were starting to establish themselves in the country. Triads such as the 14K and the Yee On led the way, but rival Vietnamese and Thai operations soon joined them. All of the groups grew on the base of a police force that lacked both the resources and the experience to tackle organized crime. They also enjoyed the added bonus of the difficulty the police found in gathering intelligence from the Asian community. These factors allowed, the groups quickly built up a complex and robust drug trafficking network in New Zealand, which remains in place today. Many of the Asian organized crime groups have expanded into people smuggling, identity fraud, prostitution and gambling, and they have made use of New Zealand's bikers and Maori gangs to distribute the drugs they bring into the country.

The oldest Hells Angel chapter outside of the USA is the Auckland Hells Angels Motorcycle Club, formed in 1961. The Angels, alongside Highway 61 (the other major biker group in New Zealand that recently announced plans to merge with the Bandidos), claim to be a lawful organization. However, the New Zealand police rate the bikers as the most influential organized crime groups in the country, and also, notoriously, the hardest to catch.

Both bikers and Maori gangs have moved into drug production. The bikers run hash plantations in isolated rural areas and operate methamphetamine and LSD laboratories, while the Maori gangs specialize in lower scale hash farming. The bikers have the largest share of drug distribution, especially in rural and smaller communities, but in New Zealand's two major cities the distribution and dealing role has increasingly become the province of Maori gangs.

All the major Maori groups, notably the Mongrel Mob, Black Power, Nomads and King Cobra, sprang from the same well of poverty, poor living conditions and state neglect of the Maori community. Mixing Maori warrior traditions, initiation rites and a dislike for the government, they were originally only of interest to the police because of inter-gang violence, especially a longstanding feud between Black Power and the Mongrel Mob. However, as elements of the gangs moved into organized crime, pooling welfare payments to buy weapons and drugs, the violence escalated into drug turf warfare and the number of killings radically increased.

Whilst the home-grown Maori and motorcycle gangs remain rated by the New Zealand police as the most significant organized crime threats in the country, the country's Pacific placement has seen it suffer

A member of the fearsome Maori gang, the Mongrel Mob, displays both his traditional tattoos and his gang colours. Many Maori gangs have moved into organized crime during recent years.

from increasing targeting by Indian and Chinese crime groups across the region. Recent trends have also seen an increasing of Nigerian and Ghanaian crime groups operating in its two major cities, especially in the areas of drug and illegal firearm importation. Below the nation's apparent tranquillity, international organized crime is gaining a stronger grasp on New Zealand.

ORGANIZED CRIME IN INDIA

One country that does not share New Zealand's current, rather overstated, image of being relatively free from organized crime is India. Regular surveys from independent bodies consistently place India close to the top of a list of nations perceived to be the home of a corrupt government that is penetrated and compromised by organized crime networks.

In India itself, it is hard to find anyone from any social or economic stratum who isn't able to relate at least one example of how organized crime has some daily impact on the life of the nation. One element of Indian organized crime that stands out is the strange mixture of revulsion and popstar-like adoration that is given to some of its most notorious criminals. No case better demonstrates this than that of Dawood Ibrahim, the head of D-Company – India's most powerful and most feared criminal network. Regarded by the CIA and the Indian government as a "global terrorist", in India he has legions of supporters and has even been the subject of several glamorous Bollywood films.

The son of a police constable, Ibrahim started his career as a member of a Mumbai gang. Run by respected underworld leader Karim Lala, the gang specialized in drug trafficking and dealing. Within a few years, Ibrahim was challenging for leadership of the gang, against Karim Lala's two sons Amirzada and Alamzeb. After winning a bloody showdown that killed his main rivals, he emerged as the most powerful "Don" in Mumbai. By the time Ibrahim fled the city for the United Arab Emirates in 1985, to avoid arrest for the rackets he had masterminded, he had already turned D-Company into a major trans-national criminal network responsible for smuggling hundreds of millions of dollars' worth of narcotics into Europe.

Over the next few years, he maintained his grip on organized crime in Mumbai, while overseeing D-Company's rise to prominence as possibly one of the most important international arms trafficking networks, as well as drug operations. However, in 1993, the Indian intelligence services accused Ibrahim of masterminding a series of bombings in Mumbai that killed 257 people. Forced to flee the United Arab Emirates, his control over the underworld in India was weakened. Mumbai became gripped by a vicious gang war as rival Dons, such as Chhota Rajan and Don-turned-Member of Legislative Assembly (the lower house of state legislature) Arun Gawli, carved out new powerbases. Ibrahim's power in India was further weakened, when his links to Osama bin Laden started to put the whole of D-Company in jeopardy.

Even at levels below that of the superstar Dons, the hold of organized crime on Indian politics and business is immense. Political corruption and a lack of resources have a severely detrimental effect on the police's ability to combat the variety of gangs that operate in every state in India. Kidnapping and extortion from India's huge cinema industry are two crimes where the police have had some success – however, the police admit that these activities are still rife. While many of the crimes favoured by the gangs, such as protection rackets, prostitution and illegal gambling, are localized, some of their biggest operations cater for a Western export market.

Counterfeiting of luxury goods and copyright piracy are well-established and major money-spinners, a situation that international business pressure has done little to challenge. India also remains the centre for illegal trafficking in human organs. Alongside legitimate avenues where the poor can sell parts of their bodies, some gangs run scams where the poor are tricked into operations to remove a kidney and never paid. In Bangalore, some were even tricked into thinking they were giving blood, but were drugged and woke up missing much more. Without doubt, the most heart-breaking organized crime export to the West is the large number of children that are sold into sexual slavery and trafficked out of the country.

As India continues to develop as one of the powerhouses of the twenty-first century global economy, so its organized crime gangs have benefited. Where once its power was from obtaining sensitive details from call centres based in the country, it is now from the vastly increased money laundering opportunities and economic extortion. The suspected links between some elements of Indian organized crime and the Indian security forces have been criticized by Western security services who fear it will serve to help entrench organized crime at the heart of Indian politics and economic expansion – both at home and abroad.

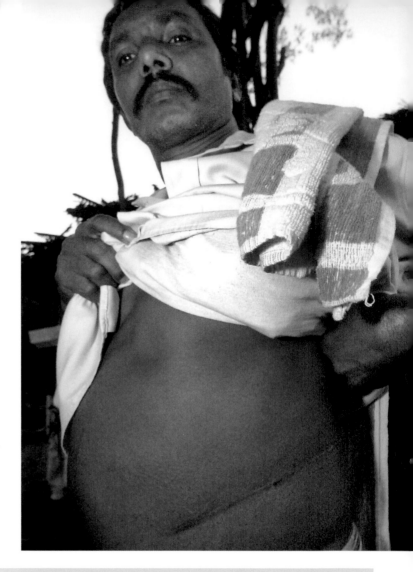

A victim of a scam that saw one of his kidneys stolen by organ traders for an Indian organized crime gang working out of Bangalore, shows his scar.

COUNTERFEITING

Counterfeiting of currency is a crime as old as money itself. Traditionally it has been a specialized area of criminal activity, requiring a group to successfully carry it out. The advent of paper banknotes meant that counterfeiting could pose a potential danger to a nation's economy. As a result, counterfeiting has often been used as a tactic in conflicts, such as the United States' production of Confederate currency during the American Civil War.

As organized crime networks developed in the nineteenth and twentieth centuries, they often incorporated existing counterfeiting gangs – who benefited from the additional cash distribution channels. As advances such as computers and laser printing have spread, so counterfeiting has become a more accessible activity. However, organized crime continues to take a strong role in counterfeiting everything from currency to shopping coupons, food and postage stamps. It also has a strong focus on the forgery of specialized financial documents, such as stock certificates.

One of the largest growth areas in organized crime at the end of the twentieth century and in the early twenty-first century has been the counterfeiting of consumer goods, such as CDs, DVDs, computer software, designer label clothes and accessories, perfume, cigarettes and alcohol. Worryingly, counterfeiters are also increasingly producing fake pharmaceutical products and medicines. Up to 8 per cent of global trade now consists of counterfeit products.

Smuggling networks developed by criminal syndicates to traffic narcotics have now been turned towards surreptitiously moving vast quantities of fake goods, with smugglers able to make more money in transporting phony DVDs than they can for the equivalent weight of marijuana.

ORGANIZED CRIME
IN SOUTH AFRICA

AIDS has decimated communities across Africa and made many orphans in South Africa vulnerable to exploitation by child trafficking and prostitution gangs.

India is not the only country whose future economic success is jeopardized by an international reputation for corruption and widespread organized crime. Once apartheid started to be abolished in 1990, South Africa was able to fully integrate into the global economy. The full financial power of Africa's wealthiest nation made it a magnet for organized crime groups. With its riches, under-resourced police and many politicians willing to collude in illicit enterprise, within a decade, it was home to over 200 organized crime groups.

The international perception of organized crime's penetration of the highest echelons of the political and business community in South Africa was such a significant problem that, by 1999, it had cost the country billions in lost investment. In June 1999, President Thabo Mbeki created the Directorate of Special Operations (DSO), nicknamed the Scorpions, who took the lead in the fight against organized crime and corruption.

Despite high-profile raids on the homes of politicians within the ruling African National Congress Party, including that of Deputy President Jacob Zuma, few believe that the DSO have dented the well-established links between the crime syndicates and South Africa's ruling elite in the police, judiciary and political spheres. It is claimed that the Scorpions have been successful in hurting the Nigerian crime syndicates, Triads and Indian-based criminal networks that have proliferated in South Africa post-apartheid, but few on the ground have seen solid evidence of this.

The DSO acknowledges that Nigerian crime syndicates, who have made the country a major part of their trans-national drug trafficking operations, have heavily penetrated South Africa. The Nigerian groups have become the dominant players in fraud and identity theft within the country. They often employ white South Africans to front international scams for them, as they

believe this is an effective way to escape the higher scrutiny Nigerian groups have been subject to by bodies such as the FBI. Through connections with local gangs, they have also established a car theft network where cars that are stolen in South Africa are quickly available for resale elsewhere in Africa.

There has been a Chinese community in South Africa since 1904, when Chinese workers came to work in the Transvaal gold mines. Recent years have seen a large increase in immigrants and investment coming from Taiwan and China. This has also led to an increased Triad presence in the country. Many in the Chinese business community have actually welcomed the Triads as protectors from South Africa's constant crime problems of robbery and violence. The Asian groups have used the Johannesburg Stock Exchange, the tenth largest in the world, for money laundering, and have taken a key role in the smuggling of illegal aliens to and from the country. They now also rival the Nigerians for control of the devasting trade in endangered wildlife.

South Africa's longstanding role in the global diamond trade has made it a base of operations for what is called the "Israeli Mafiya", which features a mix of gangsters from Israel and members of the Russian Mafiya. Specializing in gem smuggling and the extortion of businessmen, it has been responsible for several high-profile murders in South Africa, such as the killing of diamond trader Shai Avissar in 1999.

The legacy of South Africa's role in the Mozambique civil war has meant a steady flow of arms into South Africa organized by ex-guerrilla fighters who now control highly organized smuggling networks. The dire political and economic situation in Zimbabwe has lead to a massive flow of illegal migrants into South Africa whose vulnerability has been exploited by organized crime gangs involved in child trafficking and prostitution. The same gangs also take advantage of the large number of children in South Africa who were made orphans by the ravages of AIDS. Major sporting events, such as the 2010 FIFA World Cup which was held in South Africa, are notorious for encouraging foreign organized crime groups to flood a country with prostitutes, but as one Russian Mafiya member told me: "We did very little of that. We found the local market too saturated by all the children and teenagers run by the local gangs."

One investigator into child slavery working in the country told me, "South Africa is like a woman beaten by her husband. She has two faces. The one she shows to the outside world, and the true face of terror and shame. The true face is not that of winning cricket and rugby teams. It is not wildlife safaris or the Johannesburg Stock Exchange. The true, hidden face of South Africa is seen in the children and other victims of organized crime whose lives are ruined for greed".

Johannesburg's Flying Squad apprehends a member of one of the city's many crime syndicates that specialize in car theft, narcotics and people smuggling.

THE VICTIMS OF ORGANIZED CRIME

10

"Of course there is no such thing as a 'victimless crime'. I just don't feel sorry for my victims."

Zef Nano, Albanian mobster

There has always been an element of romance attached to crime. It is not just the English who populate their culture with stories of bandits who rob from the rich to help feed the poor or of thieves who live by a code of honour. Hollywood cinema – the cultural jugular of America – shows no sign of ending its 80-year love affair with the gangster. Japanese manga celebrates legendary Otokodate and the Yakuza who claim to be descended from them, and Indian gangsters, such as Dawood Ibrahim, are also seen by some as heroes.

The glamour that has attached itself to organized crime has become a danger in itself. It can blind us from a simple truth that we ignore at our peril. Nothing should obscure the fact that each year, ruthless criminal networks exploit millions of vulnerable people and merely add to human misery in the world.

The vast majority of victims of organized crime remain nameless. Ironically, the best reported victims tend to be infamous criminals themselves – their violent deaths splashed across the headlines. Reporting the murder of smaller underworld players is uncommon, unless their deaths have been spectacularly brutal. The media often capture the impact of crime on the rich and famous, but for many other innocent victims their innocuousness ensures their tragedies remain untold.

However, the story of every victim – whatever their background – can tell us something important about how organized crime operates. It can also show us crime's true nature when stripped of the illusive charm created by the manufactured mythology it has conjured around it in the twenty-first century.

ALBERT ANASTASIA

Albert Anastasia was regarded by fellow Mafia bosses as Cosa Nostra's "Lord High Executioner". However, his proven record as a killer did not prevent his own brutal murder.

It is hard to have empathy for the brutal gangland slaying of Albert Anastasia. Among members of Cosa Nostra, Anastasia was known as the "Mad Hatter". This was due to his erratic behaviour and tendency to have anyone killed at the "drop of a hat". He also had another nickname, given to him by gang bosses Frank Costello and Meyer Lansky – "Lord High Executioner".

Born Umberto Anastasio in Italy in 1903, the Mad Hatter stowed away on a ship that brought him to New York in 1917. By 19, he was already in Sing Sing correctional facility for killing a longshoreman. However, he was granted a second trial when four witnesses who had testified against him disavowed their evidence after visits from his brother Anthony "Tough Tony" Anastasio. Beating the murder rap, Umberto changed his first name to Albert and the last letter of his surname to spare his family in Italy from having to read about him.

In the early years of Prohibition, Anastasia found work with Frankie Yale's booming bootlegging outfit. Anastasia was soon notorious for knocking off truckloads of alcohol from rival operations. He also earned a reputation as a brutal man who got pleasure from any job that involved shooting someone. His enthusiasm for murder worried many of his colleagues and earned him his nickname.

When Lucky Luciano made the first of his audacious moves to end the war between rival bosses "Joe the Boss" Masseria and Salvatore Maranzano, and assume power by killing Masseria, he asked Anastasia to be one of the hitmen. Albert responded by bear-hugging Luciano and promising, "You're going to be on top if I have to kill everybody for you". His loyalty to Lucky and love of killing saw Luciano and Meyer Lansky make Anastasia second-in-command of the National Syndicate's enforcement arm – Murder Incorporated.

Anastasia personally took part in many of the nearly 500 hits against fellow Mafia members undertaken by Murder Inc., becoming the organization's Lord High Executioner. With the support of his close friend and established Mafia boss Frank Costello and the nod of Luciano, Anastasia killed Phil Mangano, the brother of Mafia boss Vince Mangano in April 1951. A few weeks later, Anastasia also made Vince do a permanent disappearing act and took over as boss of Vince's old crime family.

In 1952, Anastasia saw salesman Arnold Schuster give a television interview about how he had tipped police off about the whereabouts of wanted bank robber Willie Sutton. Anastasia was so incensed by this innocent member of the public being a "Bastard stoolie", that he ordered him murdered. In doing so he broke one of the Mafia's rules – never needlessly kill a "civilian". Incidents such as this further weakened Anastasia's standing with fellow members of the Mafia and left him open to the power-struggles raging around him. He made his position worse by crossing Meyer Lansky in an attempt to get a slice of the Cuban gambling operation.

By 1957, cunning underboss, Vito Genovese, had decided to try and take Frank Costello's place as boss of the Luciano crime family. In May 1957, Genovese tried to have Costello assassinated. The hitman, Vincent "the Chin" Gigante, only succeeded in wounding Costello, so Genovese decided to try and weaken Costello by removing his loyal supporter, Anastasia.

With Lansky's approval, Genovese put out a hit on Anastasia. On October 25, 1957, Anastasia's bodyguard called in sick, so he drove himself into Manhattan from the suburbs where he lived with his wife and children. He went, as he often did, to the barbershop in the Park Sheraton Hotel. No sooner had he sat back in the barber's chair and closed his eyes to wait for a shave than two gunmen walked in. One of them, Carlo Gambino, shot Anastasia three times in the upper chest. Roaring with pain and anger, the confused Anastasia charged at the reflection of his attackers in the mirror. It took another 10 shots to kill him. Frank Costello got the message and retired, handing his family over to Vito Genovese.

He may have been the victim of a classic mob hit, but there is a faint echo of justice in the execution of the Lord High Executioner. Anastasia, like so many of his victims, died by bullets as he had lived by them.

Before becoming a Mafia boss, Carlo Gambino was one of the two button men who had the tricky job of taking out the Mob's own "Lord High Executioner".

JIMMY HOFFA

Jimmy Riddle Hoffa was the most infamous Mafia-linked union leader in American history, but the full details of his disappearance and murder remain shrouded in the shadows of mystery.

Most times when Cosa Nostra cause someone to disappear, it doesn't make the headlines. However, when they made ex-union leader Jimmy Hoffa vanish off the map it not only made newspapers across the world, but the disappearance entered the halls of fame in urban legend and conspiracy theory.

Since the fateful day on July 30, 1975 when he got into a car with four unknown men, how and why Hoffa was killed, who did the dirty deed and where the final resting place of his body might be have been the subject of constant conjecture. The one thing that everyone is agreed on, except the most extreme conspiracy nuts, is that Jimmy Hoffa was murdered by the Mafia on the day he went missing.

James Riddle Hoffa was charismatic and cunning, and as a result he swiftly rose up the ranks of power in the International Brotherhood of Teamsters – one of the most powerful trade unions in the United States. By the time he became the Teamsters' President in 1957, Hoffa was widely recognized as an associate of several key figures in Cosa Nostra. The Mafia had a number of lucrative rackets running through the Teamsters groups and were quick to use Hoffa to consolidate their grip on the entire union. This made Hoffa a key witness before the Senate's McClellan Committee, which began investigating organized crime's control of America's unions in the late 1950s. Hoffa clashed ferociously with the chief counsel of the Committee, Robert Kennedy.

When JFK became president in 1961, Robert Kennedy became Attorney General and launched a "Get Hoffa Campaign". Within a year, Hoffa was on trial for extorting illegal payments. The jury could not decide on the case, but Hoffa ended up with an eight-year jail sentence for bribing one of his jurors. In 1964, he was found guilty of making illegal loans, worth $1.7 million taken from the Teamsters' pension fund, to Mob figures.

In 1971, President Nixon commuted Hoffa's jail sentence, providing he did not get involved in union activities for 10 years. However by 1975, he was on the verge of overturning his 10-year ban and sweeping back to power. This was the last thing the Mafia wanted. They had replaced Hoffa with the even more compliant Frank Fitzsimmons. If Hoffa was back in charge it would jeopardize their control over the union, generate bad publicity and heighten FBI scrutiny.

It was to discuss the issue of his return that Hoffa was to meet two of the Mafia's main union racketeers, Anthony "Tony Pro" Provenzano and Anthony "Tony Jack" Giacalone, at the Manchus Red Fox restaurant in Detroit at 2pm on July 30, 1975. The men did not turn up and, at 2:30, Hoffa rang his wife to say he was still waiting. At 2:45, Hoffa was seen getting into a car with four men. It was the last time he was seen alive.

There are more suspects to the killing of Hoffa than there are football players on a field. Even by 2005, the only thing the FBI have ever been able to firmly establish was that DNA evidence analysed in 2001 showed that he been in the car that was owned by Mafia member Anthony Giacalone's son and driven at the time by Hoffa's friend Chuckie O'Brien. The brother of one of the prime suspects, Gabriel Briguglio, was shot, in 1978, for talking to the police about the case and since then there has been a shortage of reliable informers.

Just before his death in 2003, Mafia hitman and friend of Hoffa, Frank "the Irishman" Sheeran confessed to his role in the killing. However, law enforcement agencies seemed less than fully convinced by Sheeran's claims. In 2006, more than 30 years after he disappeared, the full FBI "Hoffex" memo giving their view of the case was finally published. It showed that the FBI believed Hoffa was murdered on behalf of organized crime members who feared he posed a threat to their lucrative control over the union's pension funds. The FBI's favoured theory of Hoffa's final resting place is that he was disposed of in a Mafia-owned fat rendering plant. Other theories claim Hoffa's body is at the bottom of Lake St. Clair, under the redeveloped Giants Stadium in New Jersey or below the foundations of General Motors headquarters in Detroit.

Perhaps the darkest element of this story is the betrayal rather than the probable brutality of his killing. He would not have got into the car if it hadn't been in the company of someone he trusted as a loyal friend. Chillingly, when you are marked as a victim of organized crime, concepts such as loyalty and friendship will do nothing to protect you.

JOHN PAUL GETTY JR AND JOHN PAUL GETTY III

The majority of the victims of organized crime across the globe come from the ranks of the poor. Criminal gangs make the bulk of their profits from exploiting human misery at the lower end of the economic order, where their prey does not have the same resources that usually insulates the wealthy from crime. So when one fabulously rich family suffers at the hands of an organized crime group, it is newsworthy enough to hit the headlines. This is exactly what happened with the kidnap of John Paul Getty III by the Sicilian Mafia.

The teenage son of John Paul Getty Jr, John Paul Getty III, was the grandson and one of the potential heirs of oil billionaire John Paul Getty Sr. When his father left Italy in the early 1970s, John Paul Getty III remained behind. In 1973, the 16-year-old was regarded by those knew him as a happy, free-spirited and typically rebellious teenager, who had come through his parents' divorce and his father's alcohol and heroin addiction relatively unscathed. Living the carefree life of a wealthy, good-looking young man, he had no idea that his family name and wealth were about to condemn him to months of misery.

On July 10, 1973, John Paul III was snatched from the streets of Rome, bundled into a van and driven high into the mountains of Calabria. His captors took him to a lair in some mountain caves that had been a bandit hideout for many centuries. He was then chained to a stake and

Oil billionaire, John Paul Getty Sr, was only prepared to loan his son John Paul Getty Jr $2 million to pay the ransom for his kidnapped child at an agreed interest rate of 4%.

Gail Harris is reunited with her son John Paul Getty III after his release by kidnappers who had held him for six months and severed his right ear.

left in the dark while his kidnappers began to try turning their victim into cash.

When his family received the first ransom note for $17 million they thought it was a trick by John Paul III to fool his notoriously tight-fisted grandfather into parting with some of his fortune. The Italian police were not informed and no reply was given to the kidnappers. After several weeks, however, it dawned on the family that this was not a game being played by John Paul III and that he really had been kidnapped. The ransom notes were real and his life was in jeopardy.

By the time the police were involved, the kidnappers' trail was long cold. The Getty wealth and influence ensured a massive police manhunt, but the investigation was hampered by the misapprehension from some detectives that the abduction was the work of Italy's infamous Red Brigade terrorist group. By September, John Paul III's father realized that the only way he was going to see his son alive again was to pay the ransom.

However, despite his wealth, his dissolute life as a drug addict and a socialite had squandered much of his personal fortune and he could not raise the $17 million demanded.

John Paul Getty Jr approached his father and John Paul III's grandfather, John Paul Getty Sr, for the rest of the money needed to free his son. Getty Sr refused, saying "I have 14 other grandchildren. If I pay a penny of ransom, I'll have 14 kidnapped grandchildren".

In October, the severed right ear of John Paul III arrived at the offices of one of Italy's national newspapers. With it was a note that read "This is Paul's ear. If we don't get some money within 10 days, then the other ear will arrive. In other words, he will arrive in little bits".

The letter was delivered three weeks late due to a postal strike, but it persuaded John Paul Getty Sr to help free his grandson. He negotiated a deal with the kidnappers, agreeing to pay them $2 million, which he lent to his son at 4 per cent interest. On 14 December, John Paul Getty III was freed – he was found wandering by a roadside in southern Italy. The teenager never fully recovered from the trauma of his abduction, imprisonment and mutilation. He descended into years of alcohol and drug addiction that eventually left him paralysed and blind.

Most of those involved in the crime were never caught. The whole affair had been masterminded by Luciano Leggio, head of the Corleonesi Mafia family in Sicily. It proved to be just one of many similar crimes that his men carried out in Italy during the 1970s that for once, made the rich and powerful the prime targets of organized crime.

KIDNAPPING

The concept of abducting someone and holding them for ransom dates back to the capture of high-ranking soldiers and members of the nobility during ancient times of war. Those of similar rank were often unwilling to kill those they captured and so ransoming for profit became a common practice.

It did not take long, however, for the practice to spread to anyone with a degree of wealth. Kidnapping, as the name suggests, became focussed on the abduction of children from powerful or rich families. It was particularly popular in Sicily, the Middle East and many parts of Asia from the medieval period onwards.

In the modern era of trans-national organized crime groups, one of the key targets for kidnapping plots is international sports stars. Brazilian and Mexican soccer players Robinho and Jorge Campos, as well as the Georgian basketball player Nikoloz Tskitishvili, have all had family members in their home country kidnapped while gang members in the country where they play attempt to extract a ransom from them or their clubs. Celebrities are also prime targets, though in the kidnapping of Jimi Hendrix, the kidnappers made their money through being paid to abduct the star.

Members of organized crime gangs are also often targets for kidnap themselves, due to their wealth and reluctance to contact the authorities. In the 1930s, Vincent "Mad Dog" Coll financed his ongoing war with leading mobster Dutch Schultz by kidnapping bootleggers and other Mafia associates. Even major Cosa Nostra bosses, such as Carlo Gambino, have had family members kidnapped and held for ransom by elements of other organized crime groups.

CARMINE "THE CIGAR" GALANTE

Even by the brutal standards of Cosa Nostra, the lives of some Mafia men are so steeped in caustic violence and death that you can only ever imagine them ending their days in a hail of gunfire. Carmine "The Cigar" Galante was one such man.

The son of a Sicilian fisherman, Galante emigrated along with his family from Castellammare del Golfo to the tough streets of East Harlem in 1910. By the tender age of 11, Galante was already well known as a skilled wielder of a knife in a fight, among the gangs of New York's Lower East Side. When Prohibition came in 1919, he found work as a bootleg hijacker, making his way quickly from Mafiosi associate to full Mafia soldier, working as an enforcer for the Joseph "Joe Bananas" Bonanno family in Brooklyn. Along the way he acquired his nickname, "Lilo", from the small cigars that he seemed to keep permanently glued to his mouth. Some just referred to him as "The Cigar".

In 1930, Galante was caught by New York police officer Joseph Meenahan, leading a crew that was hijacking a truck packed with illegal drink. Galante was never one for admitting defeat or coming quietly and a shoot-out inevitably ensued. In the resulting blaze of bullets Galante was captured, but not before he had hit Meenahan in the leg and severely wounded a six-year-old girl who was caught in the crossfire. The resulting 12-year sentence was to be the first of his lengthy prison stays.

Paroled in 1939, Galante found he was still in demand as a hitman. In 1943, he assassinated the radical left-wing journalist, Carlo Tresca, whose newspaper for New York's Italian community – *Il Germe* (*The Seed*) – had annoyed Mussolini. Mafia boss Vito Genovese arranged the hit as a favour to the Italian dictator; it was not the last murderous job he put Galante's way.

In 1954, Galante and Giuseppe "Pep" Cotroni were sent by Joe Bonanno himself to take over the running of the Montreal Connection, which was responsible for bringing up to $50-million-worth of heroin into New York each month. Within a few short years, Galante went from being Joe Bananas' chauffeur to the underboss of the Bonanno crime family. Despite his new position of authority and power within the mob, Galante remained a deeply unpopular man. Few of his colleagues were upset therefore when his role in the Montreal Connection meant he was busted and handed a 20-year jail term in 1962.

While Galante was locked away in Lewisburg Federal Penitentiary, the Mafia's National Commission forced Joseph Bonanno into retirement and the Bonanno crime family was taken over by Phil Rastelli. Suddenly, in 1974, Rastelli was put in prison just as Galante

The bloodied body of Carmine Galante lies on the floor of a New York restaurant garden. Even in death, Galante's trademark cigar remains firmly clamped in his mouth.

got back on the streets. This turn of events catapulted him back to where he had always wanted to be – the boss of the Bonanno family.

The Cigar was an old-school throwback. He believed in the Sicilian way of vendettas and he soon made it clear he was going to settle ancient scores with rival crime boss Carlo Gambino. He was also determined to muscle in on other families' territories and make the Bonanno family the most powerful outfit in Cosa Nostra. He brought in new muscle from Sicily to strengthen his position and soon the dead bodies of Genovese family soldiers, and any others that stood in his way, were stacking up.

In 1978, following complaints about his behaviour from Galante's own capos, including Alphonse "Sonny Red" Indelicato, the Commission met about "the Cigar problem". A unanimous vote was taken to have him executed. On July 12, 1979, Galante went into one of his favourite Brooklyn eateries – Joe and Mary's Restaurant. During the meal, one of his men left, complaining of feeling unwell. Moments later the back door to Joe and Mary's outdoor area burst open and three masked men rushed in. One of them, Anthony "Bruno" Indelicato, gave Galante both barrels of a sawn-off shotgun. Galante fell dead to the ground, his cigar stilled clenched firmly between his teeth. A .45 was then used to put the traditional bullet in his left eye.

The trajectory of Galante's life, from Mafia hitman to gangland slaying victim, seems to resonate with a form of karmic justice. The Cigar was a man of blood and bullets, whose history made the nature of his end not only almost inevitable, but fitting.

AVIANCA AIRLINES FLIGHT 203

The innocent rarely have the fame, power or money to have themselves remembered as victims of organized crime in the way that the guilty tend to be. The names of Carmine Galante or Albert Anastasia are remembered whether they deserve to be or not. Yet for the 110 people who died when the Medellin cocaine cartel bombed Avianca Airlines Flight 203, there is no grand memorial. Their names persist sharply only in the memory of those loved ones who miss them to this day.

If it would not convince my publisher that I had finally gone mad, I would spend the next few hundred words giving you the names of all 110 victims of what was just one atrocity in the undeclared war between Pablo Escobar-Gavira and the Medellin cartel, and the people and government of Colombia. I would not just type a list of names, I would try and tell you who they were, what they did and what they meant to the people who loved them. One hundred and ten fathers, mothers, daughters, sons, grandparents, lovers and friends died. One hundred and ten precious, unique lives destroyed in a screaming explosion of metal, jet fuel and dynamite. One hundred and ten innocent people killed in order to protect the cocaine empire of Escobar and his colleagues. Telling the story does not seem like much of memorial, but it is the best I can give them.

On the morning of November 27, 1989, Avianca Airlines Flight 203 took off from the Colombian capital Bogota for an internal flight to Cali. The 107 passengers and crew on board the Boeing 727 were expecting their journey to last around an hour. In fact, it lasted only six minutes before an explosive device on board went off. The plane was ripped apart. As the flaming wreckage hit the ground, three more innocents were also killed. It was the single worst act of violence committed by the Colombian drug cartels in a decade of what many in Colombia simply called "The Terror" – an apt name for the often indiscriminate death caused by the drug barons as they waged war on each other and the state.

Responsibility for the atrocity was claimed by the Medellin cartel, led at the time by Pablo Escobar-Gavira. The reason given for the bombing was that they were trying to kill Cesar Gaviria Trujillo, the leading candidate in the presidential elections that were taking place. Even though Trujillo was not on the plane, it seemed a likely reason, given that the Medellin cartel had orchestrated the assassination in August of Luis Carlos Galan, his predecessor as presidential candidate for the Liberal Party.

However, some suspected the real reason was to silence two police informers who may have been on the plane, or to eradicate a corrupt police chief or member of the rival Cali cartel. Whatever the reasons, it did not alter the fact that 110 people were dead and the organized crime group from Medellin were responsible.

In Colombia, it was believed that the ruthless orders for the bombing had come directly from Pablo Escobar-Gavira and were arranged on his behalf by one of his most feared colleagues – Gonzalo Rodriguez Gacha, "The Mexican". However, American Drug Enforcement Administration agents and members of the United State's secret services, who were present in Colombia as part of the "War on Drugs", believe the murders had been organized by Dandeny Muñoz Mosquera, a man they claimed was the chief assassin for the Medellin Cartel.

According to the Drug Enforcement Administration, 23-year-old Muñoz Mosquera was also responsible for running an "executioner's training camp", where he would teach teenage boys from the slums of Colombia how to be effective sicarios (professional terrorists and hitmen). According to some Drug Enforcement Administration agents, classes taught at the camp included how to skin and castrate victims in order to make them talk.

Despite Colombian Attorney General Gustavo de Greiff writing to US prosecutors telling them, "We have no evidence linking Mr Muñoz Mosquera to that attack", Muñoz Mosquera is currently serving 10 consecutive life sentences for the bombing of a civilian aircraft. He is currently being held at possibly the most secure prison on mainland US – the Federal ADX Supermax prison in Florence, Colorado. Whether he is guilty or the 111th victim of an organized crime atrocity, there is still no fitting memorial for those died on Flight 203.

Emergency services search the wreckage of Flight 203 for the bodies of the 110 people who died as a result of the Medellin Cartel's attempt to remain top dogs in the cocaine business.

THE RETTENDON MURDERS

The image of the metallic-blue Range Rover parked in the snow on an isolated farm track is as sharp in my mind now as it was on the day I saw it on December 7, 1995. The track, called Workhouse Lane, is situated just off the A130 road in Essex, England, near the small village of Rettendon. Inside the Range Rover were three dead bodies. All male. All of them blasted in the head at close range by a shotgun.

The bodies were the reason I, and a rabble of other reporters and photographers, stood in the cold and mud as police forensic experts scrambled around and the blood-soaked vehicle was hoisted onto a truck to be taken away for further examination. We were there not just because of the deaths, but because within hours of the murders the word was out that the shootings were related to the death of Leah Betts.

Leah Betts was a student from Essex, who had taken an ecstasy tablet at her eighteenth birthday party on November 12, 1995. She collapsed, fell into a coma and died four days later. Her parents, Paul and Janet, decided to release a photograph of the comatose Leah to the media as a warning about the potential danger of drugs. The picture made the front pages of national and of local newspapers, such as my own. Leah's death and the publicity generated by her parents instigated a media scrum. I was sent out to buy ecstasy and ketamine on expenses, while some reporters wrote hypocritical stories about the dangers of "party drugs", despite their own regular usage. Everyone knew Leah bought the ecstasy that killed her from someone associated with notorious Essex nightclub Raquels – the hunt among journalists and police alike, was to find that person and the chain of supply behind it.

Within hours, detectives were confirming what local reporters already knew. The three men found dead in the Range Rover, Patrick Tate, Craig Rolfe and Anthony Tucker, had been responsible for a large part of the supply chain – they were part of what was unimaginatively called by some, the "Essex Firm".

Led by Tucker, the "Firm" was a group of bouncers who had gone from small-scale thuggery to running a vast drug distribution network through the clubs they were supposed to be providing security for. Fuelled by steroids, amphetamines and cocaine, bodybuilder Tucker had a reputation for psychotic violence and was one of the most feared men in Essex. They had beaten all the local competition into submission and are suspected of showing their ruthlessness by killing drug dealer Kevin Whitaker, forcing him to overdose on massive quantities of narcotics. They were now playing in the big league, making deals with notorious English gangland figures such as Kenneth Noye, and known to be rubbing up against some of the most dangerous East End gangs around.

The untoward publicity surrounding Leah Betts's death had shaken the foundations of Tucker's drugs empire. The Firm was now under police pressure, in a weakened state and on the wrong side of some heavy duty villains, who were threatened by the attention to their activities.

Tucker and his two associates had turned up at Workhouse Lane late on the night of December 6 in the hope of making a massive, million-pound plus drug deal that would help keep them on top. However, there was no deal. It was a set-up. They were ambushed and savagely shot in an expert, professionally performed gangland execution.

In May 1996 Essex Police arrested Michael Steele and Jack Whomes, two Essex drug smugglers and charged them with the murder. After a long trial at the Old Bailey they were both convicted, largely on the word of police "supergrass" Darren Nichols. Through the tireless campaigning of their families and former Tucker associate turned crime author, Bernard O'Mahoney, new testimony and forensic evidence emerged that appeared to suggest that Steele and Whomes could not have committed the crime. However, both men lost their appeals against their convictions in 2006.

The pair continue to plead their innocence and many of the underworld and sections of the Metropolitan Police privately back their claims, suggesting the murders were actually committed by an East End crime gang. If Steele and Whomes are telling the truth, they can be considered the final victims of a terrible chain of crime that began with the death of Leah Betts.

WILLIE MORETTI

The victims of Cosa Nostra killings are rarely genuinely mourned by the men who order their death or by the "buttonmen" who actually pull the trigger or tighten the garrotte. However, when New Jersey crime boss, Willie Moretti, was "whacked" in 1951, the tears shed by the members of the Mafia who conspired against him were certainly not of the crocodile variety. Their sadness and regret came from the heart. Almost everyone in the mob, including his killers, liked Willie.

Willie Moretti had been a childhood pal of New York Mafia boss Frank Costello. Like his old friend, Willie had made his name and fortune during Prohibition. Starting out as enforcer, he was soon running his own rackets in New Jersey in close co-operation with big name guys such as Lucky Luciano, Joe Adonis, Abner "Longy" Zwillman and, of course, his childhood friend Costello.

By the time Prohibition had ended, Moretti had a string of clubs and betting rooms. It was through these interests that Moretti discovered and gave the first major break to a young Frank Sinatra. He became the singer's close friend and played an influential role in the star's early career. In fact, if it hadn't been for Willie, Sinatra may never have gone to Hollywood. Moretti himself was also regarded as something of an entertainer among his fellow Mafiosi – he was always able to lighten the mood of a killing or a bit of bloody, violent unpleasantness with a well-timed joke or line.

When Frank Costello got his seat on the National Syndicate, he used his position to ensure Moretti got control of New Jersey and Willie made good on Frank's faith in him by turning in great profits from the gambling and other rackets in his control. However, there was a problem that Costello didn't yet know about – Willie had a mental illness.

It was usual for Mafia bosses to use a part of their illicit fortune to maintain high-cost mistresses. Moretti, however, spent a large part of his leisure time with the cheapest African-American prostitutes he could find. As a result, somewhere along the line, he contracted syphilis and the disease eventually affected his brain. Although mental illness doesn't always hamper a career in organized crime, Willie's behaviour started to worry people. He began to try and place huge bets on horses that didn't exist and others with guys who had been dead for years. When it became known he was talking about Cosa Nostra business to outsiders, his fellow bosses became even more worried.

Willie had been best man at Frank Costello's wedding back in the 1920s and it was clear that Frank held him in great affection. In 1949, he arranged for Willie to go on a long vacation to Florida, accompanied by a male nurse. Willie begged to be allowed to come back, but Frank kept him away until the symptoms appeared to subside, but there was one thing that Costello's protection could not prevent. Moretti was called to give evidence before the Senate's Kefauver Committee which was holding a televised hearing into organized crime, in the spring of 1950.

The majority of mob bosses who were called before Senator Kefauver were wise enough to plead the Fifth Amendment, but Moretti wasn't. Instead he co-operated with the Committee. He answered questions. He joked. He mimicked the voice of Curly from the Three Stooges by saying "Soitenly!" He said he wasn't a member of the Mafia only because, "I do not have a membership card". In the end, his ramblings didn't give much away, but were enough to convince his fellow bosses that he was becoming a danger to them.

The Syndicate, pressed by Vito Genovese, who wanted Moretti killed as part of his ongoing power struggle with Costello, decided to have Willie taken care of. Even Willie's friends, such as Albert Anastasia, agreed that killing him would be an act of "mercy". On October 4, 1951, the unsuspecting Moretti went to lunch with three colleagues at one of his favourite restaurants in New Jersey. When the waitress went into the kitchen, they shot him several times in the chest. The fact that they shot him in the front was a mark of respect and fondness.

Willie became a victim because he broke the Mafia rule of omerta (silence). If he had kept his mind, his mouth would have stayed shut, and he might have lived longer.

Mob boss Frank Costello (right) could not prevent fellow Mafia leaders deciding that Willie Moretti needed to be taken out as a "mercy killing" to prevent him exposing the Mob.

BRENDAN CAMPBELL

Nationalist violence and political dissent have been hijacked by elements of the IRA who have used them as a cover for their organized crime activities.

On Monday 10 February, 1998, a man and a woman left a restaurant on the Lisburn Road in Belfast, Northern Ireland. Suddenly the woman was hit in the back of the neck by a bullet and fell injured to the ground. The man was then chased into a nearby alley and shot in the head. He died in Belfast City Hospital less than an hour later. If it had been a random robbery, the man and woman could just as easily have been an ex-partner and myself, as we were in Belfast and in the area at the time. But this was not a casual case of deadly street crime. The man was Brendan Campbell, a small-time drug dealer. He had been murdered by the organized crime element within the Irish Republican Army (IRA). The killing was undertaken to protect their drug empire and to send a clear message to any other minor criminal thinking about defying their authority on the streets they considered their territory.

Responsibility for Campbell's murder was claimed by Direct Action Against Drugs (DAAD). The group was well known to be nothing more than a cover for members of the IRA, who could not take responsibility for the shooting without breaking the ceasefire agreement they had made as part of the political peace process in Northern Ireland a year earlier.

This was not the first time that the DAAD group had been active – during a previous IRA ceasefire, they had been responsible for the murder of eight drug dealers. It had also ordered several other people it labelled "drug scum" to leave Northern Ireland or face "punishment". According to the Royal Ulster Constabulary's Chief Constable, Ronnie Flanagan, DAAD was "Simply a flag of convenience for the IRA".

As a terrorist organization fighting to liberate Northern Ireland from British rule, the IRA had been involved in organized crime to fund its activities since its formation. When the Royal Ulster Constabulary effectively lost the ability to police some of the strongest Republican areas of Belfast, the IRA stepped into the role. It brought its law to the streets – punishment beatings and shootings were handed out to young car thieves and anyone who tried to move in on their moneymaking activities.

Officially anti-drug, the reality was that the IRA was the major importer of drugs into Northern Ireland. No one dared to deal drugs in the communities they controlled without paying a percentage over to the organization. Punishment beatings, knee-capping and forcing people to flee the country was entirely aimed at protecting their operation. The political justification was mere spin.

Campbell was a member of a cross-community Belfast drug syndicate that unified Catholics and Protestants in a profitable organized criminal enterprise. His group did not restrict itself to Republican or Loyalist communities and had no intention of giving the terrorists on either side of the political divide a share of its profits. Campbell was cocky. He survived a previous DAAD shooting in a Belfast bar thanks to a hidden bulletproof vest, and responded by claiming responsibility for shots fired at a solicitors next door to Sinn Fein's Andersonstown HQ. He was killed not only because he was eating into the IRA's drug profits, but also because he openly challenged their authority – how he ever thought he would cheat death given this is unclear.

Like the vast majority of victims murdered by organized crime, Brendan Campbell does not usually feature in books chronicling the activities of drug lords, extortionists and money launderers. Except for those who knew him, the detectives that failed to jail his murderers and those that orchestrated his death, he has been all but forgotten.

Campbell was a relatively petty drug dealer. He never made huge fortunes and he never killed anyone. Despite what he might have liked to imagine, he was not even a major player in the world of Belfast narcotics. Brendan Campbell was strictly small fry, but that, and the fact he was a criminal himself, doesn't make him any less of a victim. He was still someone's son, still someone's beloved. He was killed like many who fall foul of an organized crime group, for one simple reason – greed. If for no other reason than that, he deserves to be remembered.

ROBERTO CALVI

On the morning of June 18, 1982, at 7:30am, a postman walked under Blackfriars Bridge on the north bank of the River Thames in London. It was part of his usual route, the daily repetition dulling his senses to the sights and sounds of the area. It was pure chance, therefore, that he happened to glance up at the underside of the bridge. Hanging from scaffolding that had been erected to check the bridge supports was a dead body.

When the police eventually cut the corpse down, several things stood out as unusual – the quality of the man's clothes, the £15,000 in soggy cash stuffed into his pockets and the bricks that were down the front of his trousers. The identity of the hanged man was quickly established because the police were already looking for him. He was Roberto Calvi, known as "God's banker" because of his close links with the Vatican and the Istituto per le Opere di Religione – the Pope's own bank.

Calvi had fled Italy on June 11, while on bail pending an appeal into a four-year conviction for laundering several billion lire in his role as Chairman of Banco Ambrosiano, Italy's largest private bank. When Banco Ambrosiano collapsed in June with debts of up to $1.5 billion

The body of crooked Vatican banker and Mafia associate, Roberto Calvi, was found hanging under Blackfriars Bridge in London with bricks and £15,000 cash in his pockets.

dollars, he disappeared. This led the police in Rome to alert their colleagues across Europe to be on the watch for him.

Despite protests from his widow that he had been murdered as part of a conspiracy involving the Mafia and a number of other inexplicable elements of evidence, a London coroner ruled at an inquest, on July 23, 1982, that Calvi had committed suicide. This ruling was overturned at a second inquest, in 1983, and the cause of death subsequently left open. It was not until his body was exhumed in 1998, by Italian investigators, that it was officially accepted that Roberto Calvi had not killed himself.

New forensic evidence from the exhumation showed that he had, in fact, been slowly strangled to the point where he had passed out, before the noose was put around his neck. Detectives surmised that he had then been taken to the bridge by boat and attached to the scaffolding, being carefully placed so that the water only came up to his calves. Pathologists determined that with the weight of the bricks and pull of the tide it would have taken Calvi between 30 and 60 minutes to die as the noose slowly tightened.

In Italian, the word suicide can also become "suicided", to suggest a murder disguised as suicide – a major investigation into who suicided Calvi, and why, was launched. Many theories have been advanced over the years due to Calvi's links to the infamous Masonic Lodge, P2, which contained a number of high-ranking Italian politicians, secret service agents, Mafiosi and leading members of the Catholic Church. While the ritualistic elements of his death echoed Masonic oaths against those who tell secrets, it was the Mafia that prosecutors eventually believed was responsible.

In October 2005 a trial began in a specially fortified section of Rome's Rebibbia prison of five people charged with Calvi's murder. Amongst the defendants were Mafia associated businessman Flavio Carboni, one of the Mafia's most important money launderers Giuseppe "Pippo" Calò and

Calvi's former bodyguard Silvano Vittor. However, in June 2007 all five individuals were cleared of the crime after the presiding judge dismissed the charges owing to insufficient evidence. In 2010 the Italian Court of Appeals confirmed the acquittals, leaving Calvi's family claiming that they felt as if: "He has been murdered for a second time". With so many years elapsed between the murder and so many potential witnesses dead, untraceable or unwilling to cooperate, prosecutors admit it is unlikely anyone will now ever be found guilty.

In one of the Calvi case's strange ironies, a highly fictionalized version of his money laundering career, his links to the Mafia and his murder appeared in the 1993 movie *The Godfather III*, in the form of the character Frederick Keinszig. In the few days before Calvi fled from Italy to London, he had taken to carrying around with him a copy of Puzo's original *The Godfather* novel. He read chunks of it repeatedly, almost obsessively, telling everyone who asked why, "The only book you have to read is *The Godfather*. Read it. It is the only one that tells the truth about things. Read it and you will understand the way the world really works". Strangely prophetic words from a man in fear of his life and who would soon become a victim of classic Mafia vengeance.

Italian businessman, Flavio Carboni, was one of five defendants who were accused of conspiracy to murder Calvi by Italian prosecutors in 2005.

ZORAN ĐINĐIĆ

Many organized crime groups have the power to murder politicians who are causing them problems. However, the Zemun Clan of the Serbian Mafia are the only known crime syndicate to have felt so confident about assassinating a premier, that they actually told journalists they were going to do it the day before it happened.

On March 12, 2003 at 12:23pm, the Prime Minister of Serbia, Zoran Đinđić, was walking down the steps outside the main government building in the capital Belgrade when he was shot in the chest. One, high-power bullet penetrated straight into his heart. As he collapsed, tumbling down the steps, a second shot hit his bodyguard in the stomach. Đinđić was rushed to hospital, but by the time he arrived he was dead. The previous day, a Belgrade newspaper with well-known links to one of the leaders of the Zemun Clan, Milorad Luković, had headlined on its front page "Đinđ

ić Target of Sniper!"

The fact that elements of the Serbian Mafia had marked Zoran Đinđić for dead was common knowledge. The previous month, the motorcade taking the Prime Minister to Belgrade airport had been attacked by an Austrian-registered freight truck that repeatedly swerved into the car carrying him. It was only the fast reactions of Đinđić's chauffeur that saved his life. The police captured the truck and discovered it to be driven by Zemun Clan member Dejan Milenković (known as "Bugsy" to his fellow gang members). Milenković fled to Greece and was only returned to Serbia to face trial for his actions in 2005. He had been caught by the Greek police, who had him under surveillance for more than a month before seizing him in the port city of Thessaloniki.

Zoran Đinđić had swept to power in 2000, as one of the key leaders of

The Zemun Clan of the Serbian Mafia thought nothing of planning to kill the Serbian Prime Minister, Zoran Đinđić (centre).

the massive public protests on the streets of Belgrade against the former Serbian dictator Slobodan Milošević. Under the rule of Milošević and the years of turmoil during the Yugoslav wars, the Serbian Mafia had become the country's shadow government. Crime bosses, such as Željko Ražnatović (AKA Arkan), had run vast paramilitary groups and used their military and financial power to become part of the apparatus of the state. The Voždovac and the Zemun groups within the Serbian Mafia, which is known collectively as Naša Stvar, operated openly from mansions in the Belgrade suburbs from which they took their names. Western diplomats talked of the Serbian Mafia as the greatest organized criminals of the twentieth century – the gangs that had "Stolen a whole state".

It was known that the peacefulness of the October street revolution was due to the tacit approval of the Naša Stvar, and that it had been arranged through secret meetings between Đinđić and key underworld figures. However, since he had become Prime Minister, crime syndicate bosses, such as the Zemun Clan's Milorad Luković (better known as "Legija" – literally "Legion", due to his time spent in the French Foreign Legion), felt betrayed by his actions – notably, his sending of Milošević to the Hague to stand trial for war crimes and his attempts to clamp down on the power of the Mafia in Serbia.

Following the massive outpouring of grief by the Serbian people at of Đinđić's slaying, an unparalleled police crackdown on the Zemun Clan swung into action. Their mansion headquaters was bulldozed; 300 of them were questioned and the mansion of Arkan's widow was raided and Zemon underbosses dragged from its secret basement. However, the two most significant arrests were those of specialist police marksman and Zemun Clan member, Zvezdan Jovanović (known as the "Snake") and of Legija.

In May 2007, a Serbian court found 12 men guilty of the murder of Đinđić. Jovanović and Legija both received jail sentences of 40 years for their role in the assassination. Yet of the other ten tried and convicted, only five were in court as the remaining five had evaded capture and were prosecuted in absentia. The trial itself was beset with problems with two witnesses being murdered and its judges receiving death threats. For many in Serbia, instead of the prosecutions bringing a sense of victory over the Zemun Clan, it only indicated how successful they had been at regrouping after the crackdown and how much power they retained.

After surviving the earlier assassination attempt on his motorcade, Zoran Đinđić gave a defiant message to the Serbian Mafia saying: "If someone in Serbia thinks the law and reforms can be stopped by eliminating me, then he is in a huge delusion. Serbia will live on and proceed along that path with or without me." However, despite the initial backlash against the Serbian Mafia caused by his death, many commentators believe that the murder of Zoran Đinđić is an event from which Serbian democracy has never fully recovered. Organized crime continues to thrive in Serbia and no one with the power and status of Đinđić has yet emerged to successfully challenge it.

Hundreds of thousands of Serbians took to the streets of the capital, Belgrade, for the funeral of Zoran Đinđić.

ORGANIZED CRIME FIGHTERS

11

"The criminal's worst nightmare
is an honest cop."
Traditional saying, sometimes also attributed to Frank
Serpico, former New York policeman and heroic testifier
against corruption

It must be clear to anyone reading this book that the power of
organized crime has grown to frightening levels. It is the world's
largest industry – its illicit profits are above the trillion-dollar
mark – and it destroys millions of lives a year. Sometimes, it
is even so secure in its strength that it openly trades in human
misery: buying and selling children for a few dollars or executing
opponents without any fear of action from the alleged legitimate
authorities. In many countries, it has effectively transformed itself
into an alternative form of government and notorious gangsters
worldwide are seen enjoying lives of opulence and luxury.

It often seems that organized criminals have it all their own
way. However, as the menace of organized crime has grown, so
too have the number of dedicated forces and individuals opposed
to it. From seminal, solo "mob-busters", to government and
international agencies, the bravery of certain individuals has often
been all that has protected society against the rising tide of crime.

Just as criminal networks have transformed themselves over
recent years, taking advantage of emerging technologies, forming
fresh global alliances and developing innovative ways of making
dirty money, so the crime fighters have evolved to tackle the new
nature of trans-national crime. Yet the core of crime fighting
remains, ensuring that those living in fear of criminal syndicates
can believe that justice will prevail and provide protection. When
that belief exists and is justified by the actions of the authorities,
organized crime is always the loser.

ELIOT NESS AND THE "UNTOUCHABLES"

One of the things I have heard those who fight organized crime professionally complain about over the years, is that police officers are remembered less than the criminals they catch. From London to New York, I have heard detectives complain about how the media mythologizes the villains instead of lionizing the cops. I've even endured rants from one Scotland Yard detective, complaining that the most famous detective in England was "Sherlock Holmes – a jumped up fictional character who wouldn't be much bloody good investigating Yardie shootings".

However, one legendary law enforcement officer who has been mythologized by the media, both at the time of his fight to bring down Al "Scarface" Capone and his Outfit and in subsequent years, is Eliot Ness. Not that this lionization pleases some bitter detectives, as Eliot Ness was not an actual policeman but rather a Treasury Agent.

When Herbert Hoover became the thirty-first President of the United States in 1929, his personal grudge against Capone soon became apparent. Hoover wanted Capone behind bars, but it was obvious that Capone had the Chicago and state authorities in his control. Following advice from Colonel Frank Knox, whose paper the *Chicago Daily News* had started printing a "Most Wanted" list of criminals in the city, of which Capone was No.1, Hoover was determined to nail him on one of two Federal charges – bootlegging or tax evasion.

To this end, Hoover charged Andrew Mellon, Secretary of the Treasury, with Capone's downfall. Mellon in turn picked 26-year-old graduate Eliot Ness to head up a special unit to bust Capone's bootlegging operations. Ness's first move was to form a squad of agents who would not be susceptible to bribery or blackmail. In addition, he wanted them to be experts in areas he felt would prove invaluable when going up against the bootleggers – wiretapping, sharp-shooting, high-speed pursuit and handling informers. With his team assembled, Ness went to war with the bootlegging side of the Chicago Outfit.

Despite the hype of his later biographers and various films and television shows, Eliot Ness and his men never succeeded in making Chicago a "dry" city. However, their constant raids certainly hit Capone in the pocket. Ness was one of the first lawmen to really understand how to get the full benefit from publicity. Every time he made a major raid, he would tip off the photographers so the papers could get a good picture of his men in action – breaking up a distillery, capturing a truck full of whiskey or even uncovering a whole warehouse of booze. As soon as one of his men was approached to take a bribe, Ness sold the papers on the story of how his men were incorruptible and that the Mob had nicknamed them the "Untouchables". Ness knew the criminal folklore he was creating would help to convince the public and Capone's own men that Big Al was vulnerable.

Within six months, Ness claimed to have seized illegal bootlegging assets worth more than $1 million. By 1932, that total had risen to $9 million, with Ness parading captured beer trucks outside Capone's HQ at Chicago's Lexington Hotel in an attempt to humiliate him even further. In the end, Ness and his Untouchables did little more than eat into Capone's profits and cause his operations a load of headaches – eventually it was the Internal Revenue Service Agent Frank Wilson that made President Hoover a happy man, by securing the evidence that finished Capone off.

The reality of what Ness achieved in Chicago is somewhat overshadowed by the media myths and legends that sprang up in later years, thanks to his autobiography and the television show, *The Untouchables*, that began airing two years after his death in 1957. His even more significant success in cleaning up corruption in Ohio, his failure to catch the "Cleveland Torso Murderer", the threats that were made to his life while he was trying to take down the Outfit, and his own drunk driving accident are not included in the films that portray him as an iconic hero and a fearless "mob-buster".

Ness was clever, media savvy and an effective fighter against organized crime. However, his real legacy is as an inspiration: the ideal of the incorruptible man who dares to stand up to power of the Mob.

Eliot Ness has become a legendary figure in crime fighting partly thanks to his clever media manipulation of his own image as a totally incorruptible and honest agent of law enforcement.

THE FEDERAL BUREAU OF INVESTIGATION

The Federal Bureau of Investigation (FBI) is the world's most famous law enforcement agency. There is no denying part of its renown is down to the Hollywood myth-making machine, but it has also earned its prominence by leading the way in developing crime fighting techniques and technology and through some amazing success stories in the fight to uphold the law.

One area where the FBI's record of success is balanced against a history also marked by inaction and massive failure is in the fight against American organized crime. The development of a national police force in the USA ran parallel to the early development of the American Mafia. Whilst the opposing forces on the spectrum of justice should have been natural enemies, it was not until 1957 that the FBI seriously started to fight the forces of Cosa Nostra and other US criminal syndicates.

What was to evolve into the FBI started out, in 1908, as a force of special agents instigated by US Attorney General Charles Joseph Bonaparte. Right from the start it was easy on the organized criminal activity of the Black Hand gangs that plagued the Italian-American community. Originally called the Bureau of Investigation, it did not change its name to the FBI until 1935.

Although many of its signature crime busting techniques, such as wiretapping, infiltration and the pioneering use of cutting edge forensic science, were all in place by the early 1930s, none of them were actually used by the Bureau against the developing network of Mafia crime families.

When President Hoover wanted to bring down Capone's Chicago Outfit, he had to turn to the US Treasury rather than to the FBI. The main reason for this was the other Hoover – J. Edgar Hoover, Director of the FBI from 1924 to his death in 1972. For decades, J. Edgar Hoover insisted there was no organized crime network in the United States. In his view, there was no such thing as the "Mafia". Despite all the blatant evidence to the contrary, despite the protests of his own men who desperately wanted to pursue the big bosses, such as Meyer Lansky and Frank Costello, J. Edgar Hoover claimed there was no Mafia to investigate.

No one has definitively been able to explain Hoover's bizarre position with regard to Mafia. Some believe the Genovese crime family or Meyer Lansky was blackmailing him over his homosexual relationship with Clyde Tolson. Others believe his gambling addiction and association with the Mafia "Prime Minister" Frank Costello compromised him.

The FBI HQ building in Washington is the hub of the FBI's fight against American organized crime, despite it being named after J. Edgar Hoover, who refused to believe the Mafia existed.

Whatever the reasons behind him effectively killing all investigation into organized crime, the situation was blown apart by the public exposure of the Apalachin Conference (1957), the Kefauver and McClellan Committees (1950–1 and 1956–68 respectively) and Robert F. Kennedy's anti-Mafia campaign (1960–3). Once J. Edgar Hoover was forced to face up to the reality of the situation the FBI quickly began to catch-up, after more than three decades of sitting on its hands. It began to hurt the Mafia's operations across the country, hitting it hardest on union rackets.

With the introduction of the Racketeer Influenced and Corrupt Organizations Act in 1970 and J. Edgar Hoover's death in 1972, the FBI's war against the Mafia moved up several gears. With an explosion of electronic surveillance, federally protected witnesses and stool pigeon Mafiosi cutting deals for lighter sentences, by the late 1980s the FBI had put away a lot of Cosa Nostra's top men and claimed to have made massive inroads against organized crime's power in the US.

In the 1990s the FBI's image of tackling organized crime was blighted by revelations of collusion between its agents in Boston and the city's notorious Irish organized crime outfit, the Winter Hill Gang. One agent, John J.

Connolly Jr. was sentenced in 2002 for ten years in prison for tipping off and abetting gang boss James "Whitey" Bulger. Many were worried that with growing internal corruption and a focus on terrorism, the FBI's gangster fighting days were waning. However, these fears have not manifested themselves and the Bureau has continued to hit the Mob hard.

In January 2011, the FBI led what they described as "the largest Mob round-up in our history". More than 800 agents working with police forces in several states made a dawn swoop, arresting over 120 suspects for crimes relating to murder, extortion, racketeering and money laundering. Amongst those arrested was the legendary 83-year-old Luigi Manocchio, the former boss of New England's Patriarca crime family and 34 "made" members of New York's five crime families. Speaking after the arrests, Attorney General Eric H Holder said: "Organized crime remains a top priority for the FBI as long as it continues to be a major threat to the economic well-being of this country."

US Attorney General Eric Holder addresses a press conference detailing the January 2011 operation which saw dawn raids arrest over 120 people.

ROBERT F. KENNEDY

When the names Robert F. Kennedy and Cosa Nostra come together on the page of a book, it is usually the prelude to a conspiracy theory. Given the links between the Kennedy family and leading Mafia figures, such as Carlos Marcelo or Sam Giancana, most of these theories, however, are not entirely unreasonable.

The problem with the conspiracy theories is that they tend to obscure the amazing role that Robert Kennedy played in the fight against the American Mafia. Cynicism and an awareness of the corruption that can occur when the worlds of politics and organized crime meet prevents most of us from thinking of politicians as crime fighters. However, that is exactly what Robert Kennedy was. During his life, he was possibly the single most dangerous man the Mafia had ever come up against.

Robert F. Kennedy first made a name for himself as a man who was willing to go toe-to-toe with the Mafia in his role as Chief Counsel of the Senate Labor Rackets Committee hearings, which began in 1956. The hearings, commonly known as the McClellan Committee, introduced televison viewers to the young Kennedy. Via heated confrontations and bouts of insult-hurling with Teamsters union boss Jimmy Hoffa, Robert Kennedy exposed the links between union leaders and Cosa Nostra members, such as Anthony "Tony Ducks" Corallo. It soon became clear to everyone, especially the Mafia, that Robert Kennedy had good sources of information, knew a lot about them and was going to do everything in his power to destroy their profits and power.

It's well known that there was a collective sigh of relief from Mafiosi nationwide when Robert Kennedy quit the McClellan Committee to help run his brother's presidential election campaign. Their relief was short-lived, however, as the newly elected President John F. Kennedy appointed his brother Bobby as US Attorney General. Within weeks of him taking over the post, it was clear he was going to be the first ever Attorney General to use the job to try and dismantle the organized networks that had been a part of US crime since the 1920s.

J. Edgar Hoover was forced, much against his will, to step up the fight against organized crime. Robert Kennedy, who had recently published his book, *The Enemy Within: The McClellan Committee's Crusade Against Jimmy Hoffa and Corrupt Labor Unions*, made it open knowledge that he was running a "Get Hoffa campaign". Unlike other Attorneys General, who would talk tough about tackling underworld problems and do nothing, Kennedy walked the talk. He knew the identity of all the big bosses and was constantly chasing up agents on what progress they were making against them. He never let up; it was a constant crusade for him. Not unsurprisingly, it did not make him popular with Hoover or the likes of Sam Giancana.

Robert Kennedy's work did have some fans, though, one of whom was Harry J. Anslinger. The first Commissioner of the Federal Bureau of Narcotics, Anslinger was one of the few senior men in US law

Both Robert F. Kennedy (left) and his brother John F. Kennedy tackled the Mob during Senate hearings in the 1950s, but it was RFK's crusade as Attorney General that really hurt the gangsters.

enforcement to tackle organized crime in America, despite J. Edgar Hoover's claims there was "no such thing as the Mafia". In his 1964 book, *The Protectors*, he told how Kennedy travelled the country holding special meetings with his Federal Bureau of Narcotics agents, exhorting them to nail the big drug traffickers and ensuring they had full support from the prosecutors. He claimed that "It was, in large measure, due to his forceful encouragement that we knocked off some of the biggest public enemies".

The irony of Robert Kennedy's determination to battle against organized crime has not been lost on historians. The man who banned Frank Sinatra from the White House because of his Mafia links was also the son of Joseph P. Kennedy, a man who had made a bootlegging fortune during the Prohibition era. Joseph Kennedy also used his associations with Mafia leaders to get them to help swing JFK's presidential election win.

Despite these and other familial links to Cosa Nostra, there is little doubt that before his brother's assassination cut his term as Attorney General short, Robert F. Kennedy was delivering some painful blows to the Mafia. His lasting legacy is that the FBI became feared by the Mob. If an assassin's bullet had not taken his own life five years later, in 1968, he may have become a US president who was willing and capable of actually turning the tide on the constant war against organized crime.

HONG KONG'S ORGANIZED CRIME AND TRIAD BUREAU

On the twenty-first, twenty-second and twenty-third floors of Arsenal House, the building that houses the Hong Kong Police Force, detectives engage in possibly one of the most difficult law enforcement jobs in the world – policing organized crime and Triad activity in Hong Kong. The detectives are members of Hong Kong's Organized Crime and Triad Bureau (OCTB), known all over the world for being at the forefront of tackling Chinese criminal networks. It is arguably also the only police team in the world that has to contend daily with the machinations of ancient secret societies which date back to at least 1352.

Described to me by one of their senior foreign counterparts at Scotland Yard as "The most professional, efficient and knowledgeable police agency I've ever known", the OCTB is formed from a team of detectives and specialists. Its objective is clear – to investigate the complex organized crimes and serious Triad offences that other detectives in Hong Kong do not have the time, resources or expertise to tackle.

Each day, the OCTB is involved a raft of activities that are designed to fight the massive power that the Triads in Hong Kong wield, from street-based crime right up to the boardrooms of major Hong Kong institutions. One OCTB team may be tracking global money laundering operations by feeding illicit cash to Triad chiefs based in Hong Kong, while another co-ordinates criminal intelligence with colleagues on mainland China and as far away as Canada. In one office, a squad of detectives could be being briefed before a major raid on

Triad-controlled vice operations in the Mong Kok district, while next door a review of an extortion case involving a Hong Kong film star is underway.

The Organized Crime and Triad Bureau is part of a tradition of organized crime fighting that dates back to 1841, when the territories' first police force was established after the British seized power in Hong Kong. The irony of establishing a police agency when part of a country has been taken over to control and profit from the opium trade was lost on Captain William Caine, the founder of the Hong Kong Police Force. Starting with a multi-ethnic force of 35 men, the Hong Kong police had a role in combating Triad activity from the very beginning.

By 1931, eight main Triad groups were established in Hong Kong with numerous sub-societies and public fronts. They were split along ethnic Chinese and regional lines, operating mainly from different areas of Hong Kong Island, Kowloon and the New Territories. During the Second World War, the Triads co-operated with the Japanese invaders. They effectively replaced the police and saw their prostitution, gambling and black market rackets boom. When British colonial rule was re-established, the Hong Kong Police Force had to deal with a massive influx of Triads fleeing the communist takeover of mainland China in 1949.

The 1950s and 1960s were just as dark a period in the force's history. Activity against organized crime diminished and the police entered into deals with the Triads to keep the peace. Police corruption became rampant, eventually being publicly exposed in 1973, when the Chief Superintendent of Police, Peter Fitzroy Godber, was found to have nearly 5 million Hong Kong dollars (almost $650,000) in his bank account. Godber fled the country, but was eventually extradited and spent four years in prison for colluding with organized crime. A radical shake-up in the wake of this led to the creation of the OCTB.

There are now around 50 Triads operating in Hong Kong for the OCTB to tackle. Although some are little more than organized street gangs, two of the biggest Triad global networks – Wo Sing Wo and 14K – are based in the territory. Since the British handed Hong Kong back to China in 1997, neither the OCTB's daily crime fighting challenges nor its globally recognized role as possibly the best source of Triad information, has diminished. Its current focus on covert intelligence and tracing laundered money yielded some big hits against the Triads in the early years of the twenty-first century, further establishing its reputation as an effective organized crime fighting operation. However, its success is now challenged by high-level penetration by Triads of the political system, especially in mainland China. As one ex-OCTB officer told me, "What's the point of catching them if they've the powerful friends needed to get released within a few days?"

The Organized Crime and Triad Bureau swoop on a Triad gathering in Hong Kong, making a dramatic mass arrest. Such events are commonplace for OCTB detectives in their ongoing war against Triad crime.

THE ROYAL CANADIAN MOUNTED POLICE

One police force that has co-operated closely in recent years with Hong Kong's Organized Crime and Triad Bureau is the Royal Canadian Mounted Police (RCMP). These days, the growing Triad presence in Canada is just one of the many foreign-based crime networks the RCMP has to face as part of its remit to "reduce the threat and impact of organized crime".

Since its creation in 1920, the RCMP has continually faced organized crime problems emanating from outside the Canadian border. This was first strongly witnessed during American Prohibition in the 1920s. As Canada did not stop the production of beer, wine or whiskey for export purposes, and owing to its long border with the US, it was inevitable it would become one of the main supply sources for the bootleggers.

Customs officials on both sides of the border colluded with the bootleggers who built up massive operations in Quebec and Ontario. The RCMP fought a constant, and losing, battle against the smugglers. The level of the corruption, that went all the way up to Jacques Bureau, the Minister for Customs, made their work virtually impossible. Bureau withdrew the RCMP from the borders of British Columbia and Quebec, and even appointed a notorious bootlegger – J. A. E. Bisaillon – as Chief Customs Officer for Montreal. Smuggling remains a headache for the RCMP today, whether it is trying to tackle First Nation groups trafficking tobacco or the Cotroni Gang importing cocaine.

The legacy of the bootlegging that the RCMP failed to prevent was the massive profits that were generated both sides of the border. These were used to establish a wide range of other rackets that continued long after Prohibition ended in 1933. The liquor that had flowed from Ontario created the Buffalo Mafia under the Magaddino crime family. They expanded across the border and still control much of the underworld in Toronto and Ontario today. In Quebec, the same situation led to the creation of the powerful Montreal Mafia, linked to New York's Bonanno crime family.

Montreal also became the centre for organized crime in Canada. At the end of the 1950s, it was the focus for the RCMP's groundbreaking surveillance work that led to the biggest setback the Mafia in Canada have ever endured. Two years of wiretaps, intelligence gathering and covert surveillance by the RCMP uncovered the "Montreal Connection" which was importing heroin from France and sending $50-million-worth of street heroin to New York each month. In 1961, working alongside the US Federal Bureau of Narcotics, the RCMP smashed the operation wide open and helped give leading Mob figures, such as Carmine "The Cigar" Galante, lengthy spells in jail.

Ironically, the RCMP's success in hurting the Montreal Mafia, alongside a vicious war for control between Sicilian and Calabrian

Forensic experts examine the aftermath of the Rochfort Bridge shooting in Alberta where four RCMP officers were brutally shot while investigating an organized criminal group's cannabis-growing operation.

factions, gave a boost to Montreal's Irish-dominated organized crime group, the West End Gang. Currently operating with around 150 members, the West End Gang is estimated to have been responsible, between the mid-1960s and the mid-1990s, for dealing up to 10,000kg (22,050lb) of cocaine and 500 tonnes (551 tons) of hashish, with a street value of billions of dollars. The problems the RCMP caused for the Montreal Mafia also provided an unexpected opportunity for the outlaw biker gangs, who are currently the RCMPs biggest organized crime headache.

The open warfare between the Hells Angels, Satan's Choice and Rock Machine outlaw motorcycle gangs began as a fight for control over the lucrative Montreal narcotics trade. Decades later, it has grown into a nationwide battle as the bikers have assumed control over the majority of drug distribution in Canada. The RCMP's role in combating terrorism as well as organized crime has blurred as the war has spiralled out of control to include bombings that have killed innocent civilians. Efforts to control the drugs within Canada have also cost the lives of many RCMP officers – notably in 2005, when four RCMP members were gunned down while investigating a cannabis growing operation in Rochfort Bridge, Alberta.

The increasing presence of Nigerian organized crime syndicates, Jamaican Posses and Triad and other Asian criminal networks in Canada has seen the RCMP leading the way in international co-operation and criminal intelligence sharing. However, it is clear to any expert that the power of organized crime in Canada now outpaces the RCMP's legendary ability to "always get their man".

DIREZIONE INVESTIGATIVA ANTIMAFIA

Some people may be surprised that many law enforcement experts believe the Royal Canadian Mounted Police to be under-resourced and therefore struggling with a rising tide of organized crime in Canada. However, it would be less of a surprise if that accusation were made over the fight against organized crime in Italy.

Survey after survey suggests that citizens in other countries believe the Italian legal authorities to be prone to corruption and ineffectual against the Mafia. The trials of seven-times Prime Minister, Giulio Andreotti, over his Mafia links, the car bombings of anti-Mafia judges and the fact that the one-time head of the Mafia in Sicily, Bernado Provenzano, evaded capture for

decades, do little to create an image of an incorruptible government and strong law enforcement.

It was partly to address the external economic problems that such beliefs about organized crime in Italy created, that the Direzione Investigativa Antimafia (DIA) was established in 1992. Reporting to the Interior Ministry, the DIA was created to become the Italian body responsible for co-ordinating investigations into organized crime and to ensure the successful prosecution of those it had evidence about. It is made up of a central co-ordinating force in Rome and 12 regional command centres in areas and cities across Italy that are notorious for Mafia activity. The DIA draws its forces primarily from the State Police, Treasury Department and Carabinieri (the arm of the Italian army with policing duties).

Former Italian Prime Minister and media mogul Silvio Berlusconi in court facing bribery charges.

It was the 1992 murders of anti-Mafia Judges Giovanni Falcone and Paolo Borsellino, who had supported the creation of the DIA, that provided the immediate catalyst for its rapid growth. The massive wave of Italian public outrage against organized crime after these killings led to a government crackdown on the Mafia's apparent power to kill anyone who threatened them. More than 7,000 troops were sent to Sicily and a widespread shake-up of how the police tackled organized crime was undertaken.

The DIA hit the ground running, helping to tackle the terrorist bombings that occurred across Italy in 1993, conducted by the Mafia in the wake of the government moves against them. In what was seen as a declaration of war by the Mafia against the state, the DIA quickly secured a major victory for the authorities. DIA surveillance and monitoring helped ensure the capture and prosecution of Toto "The Beast" Riina. A leader of the Corleonesi Sicilian Mafia clan, Riina (also known as "The Short One" owing to his diminutive size) had been on the run for more than 20 years and had personally ordered the deaths of Falcone and Borsellino.

Building on this success and a public mood that wanted organized crime broken and decades of political corruption tackled, the DIA continued to wage war on the Mafia using the latest investigative procedures and technology. Within a decade of being formed it had broken the "Fire Group" responsible for the Mafia bombings, captured dozens of the most wanted Mafia fugitives, seized tens of millions of dollars of 'Ndrangheta and Camorra assets and could even claim to have entirely dismantled some Sacra Corona Unita trafficking groups. The age of any weakness in Italian law enforcement against organized crime was well and truly over.

Although the word Antimafia implies a purely Italian remit, the international alliances and operations of the Sicilian and other Italian Mafia networks means the DIA also plays a key role in intelligence sharing at a global level. Successful DIA operations have disproved the idea that the only underworld groups operating in Italy are the Mafia. In 1993, they broke up a Triad-related gang that was running a people smuggling network bringing illegal Chinese immigrants into the country. By the late 1990s, it was also regularly tackling Albanian and Russian Mafiya rackets within Italy.

Despite having an avowed aim of tackling the Mafia's penetration of the Italian economy and its political infrastructure, the majority of commentators believe that the DIA has failed to make any significant impact in these crucial areas. In a country where former Prime Ministers such as Silvio Berlusconi have stood trial for Mafia associations, there exists a culture of corruption so ingrained it may be impossible for one agency – even a powerful and effective one such as the DIA – to make a dent.

However, even if the DIA is losing the overall war against organized criminality at the highest level in Italy, it still has continued to score some impressive victories. In 2008 it seized more than 1 billion euros worth of criminal assets, a figure it has increased in recent years to more than 3.2 billion. It has spearheaded successful crackdowns on several Camora clans and actions against the Sicilian Mafia saw it break apart gangs in Etna and Messina in 2010. The most powerful sign that the DIA is still a major threat to Italy's crime gangs is the acknowledged hatred it generates amongst them.

SCOTLAND YARD'S SERIOUS AND ORGANIZED CRIME GROUP

London's Metropolitan Police officers, working out of their head-quarters at New Scotland Yard, have a history of wearing unusual tiepins. Not officially part of the uniform, the Flying Squad tiepin at one time was a winged pig, while Drug Squad members could be seen wearing one with a syringe design

Recently I was drinking with a senior detective, who had acquired a new tiepin thanks to the role he played in Operation Cartwright – a successful police swoop that caught eight robbers who planned to steal £33 million in gold, cash and gems from Heathrow Airport in May 2004. After explaining about some of the newer tiepins his colleagues were wearing he turned to me and said, "We ought to have one with the UN logo on it, given that London's home to every bloody organized crime group on the planet".

His comment was not much of an exaggeration. London is one of the most multi-ethnic and culturally diverse cities in the world, and this is reflected accordingly in its organized crime. The amazing range of foreign organized crime syndicates present in London can also be attributed to the city's size, wealth and role as one of the world's major financial, communications and travel hubs. Consequently, Scotland Yard's Serious and Organized Crime Group's list of organized crime gangs operating in London, but originating from abroad, is staggeringly large.

It includes the Serbian Mafia; Italian organized crime groups from the Sicilian Mafia to the Venetian Mala del Brenta; the Albanian Mafiya; crime

Commander Mike Fuller was the head of Operation Trident which tackled the rising tide of gun crime on London's streets.

gangs with links to organizations in India and Pakistan; Nigerian crime syndicates; Japanese Yakuza; at least five Russian organized crime gangs; Jamaican Posses; Thai crime syndicates; several Turkish gangs; numerous Colombian drug cartels; and elements from every major Triad and Asian crime gang. And of course, the Serious and Organized Crime Group also has to deal with plenty of home-grown organized villainy as well.

Trying not only to monitor, but also to police and proactively put out of operation the organized crime groups in London is an incredible challenge. In order to meet this challenge, Scotland Yard formed the Serious and Organized Crime Group. It is seen as giving a collective identity and focus to a number of well-established police teams, that between them have an illustrious history of fighting London's top criminal gangs. The most famous of these teams is the Flying Squad (known in criminal rhyming slang as "the Sweeney Todd"). Scotland Yard's specialist "thief takers", the team has decades of experience in capturing armed gangs as they attempted daring robberies, such as the foiled £200m diamond grab from London's Millennium Dome in November 2000.

The Central Task Force of the Serious and Organized Crime Group is responsible for proactively targeting serious crime, with a focus on drug and arms traffickers, while the Group's Projects Team conducts actual operations both in the UK and across international boundaries. The Intelligence Support Unit of specialist researchers and crime analysts feeds intelligence on organized crime to all other elements of the Serious and Organized Crime Group and Scotland Yard's wider Specialist Crime Directorate. This includes departments that focus on areas such as covert policing, cyber-crime, fraud and wildlife crime.

The formidable reputation and success rate of the Serious and Organized Crime Group in tackling organized crime in London and across Britain has occasionally been marred, however, by links to organized crime that have put some of its officers on the same side as the villains. Flying Squad head, Commander Kenneth Drury, brought shame on the force with his conviction for colluding with the London underworld in 1976. More recently, in 2003, Flying Squad detectives were jailed for syphoning off hundreds of thousands of pounds from the proceeds of robberies. Former Metropolitan Police Commissioner Sir Paul Condon once claimed his force contained, "250 bent officers".

Despite such problems and the massive task facing them, the SOCG developed a reputation for intelligence-led policing envied by most of its international equivalents. However, the recent history of Scotland Yard has once again become dogged by allegations of racism and corruption linked to elements of the UK media. Alongside budgetary cuts, this has created a difficult working environment for many detectives. One officer confessed to me: "The Met feels so embattled [that] our priorities have got lost. The focus needed on organized crime is not there at the top levels and we are losing ground." Other officers remain more positive, one claiming: "We have every sort of organized crime in London carried out by gangs from almost every country on the planet, but as long as our intelligence remains strong, we have a chance of taking them down."

INTERPOL

Like Scotland Yard, the mention of the name Interpol instantly brings to mind an association with expert crime fighting. The organization has developed an aura that makes it instinctively feared by criminals, even if they have little appreciation for the organization's history, structure and role in the twenty-first century fight against organized crime.

The name Interpol derives from the contraction of the phrase "international police", which it began using as its telegraphic address in 1946. This quickly became preferred shorthand, and was used by police forces across the world instead of the actual name – the International Criminal Police Commission. In 1956, the organization responded to this by changing its name to the International Criminal Police Organization – Interpol.

The actual origins of the global crime fighting body date back to 1914, when the first ever International Criminal Congress, held in Monaco, floated the idea that an international police body was needed to fight the increasing international mobility of criminals and an emerging culture of crime groups operating outside of their country of origin. Acting on this idea in 1923, Dr Johannes Schober, President of the Vienna Police, set up the International Criminal Police Commission (ICPC) and provided them with a headquarters in Vienna.

Unfortunately, there followed a dark period in Interpol's history that the organization is reluctant to mention. In 1938, it was taken over by the Nazis, after the Anschluss of Austria, and came under the control of the Gestapo – the Nazi secret police run by the SS. During the Second World War, it was used to expose anti-Nazi agents and anyone who posed a threat to the German domination of Europe.

When the ICPC was reformed after the Second World War, in 1946, its aims were exactly the same as they are today – to facilitate cross-border police co-operation and to support all authorities whose mission is to combat international crime. Interpol has now grown to become the second largest international body after the United Nations with 184 member countries. Contrary to Hollywood mythology, Interpol fights crime not by sending out its own staff to conduct inquiries, but by pooling knowledge and expertise from police forces across the world and running a global database of the latest information about criminals and organized crime groups. It also issues its famous Red, Green and Blue Notices.

Dating from a time way before the Internet was available, the colour coding of the Interpol Notice System is derived from when sheets of paper with different coloured corners would be sent out across the globe from its old headquarters outside of Paris. These days the Notice System is applied via email, with the principle remaining unchanged. Red Notices are sent by Interpol to the police force in the receiving country to ask them to immediately seek out and hold a named suspect. Blue Notices are requests for more information about a suspect's current location or activities and Green Notices are those requesting that the police in the receiving country watch the movements of a particular individual.

The Notice System is incredibly effective. Every year it catches hundreds of members of trans-national criminal networks, who have fled arrest in one country and who are hiding or have begun working in another territory. A good example of this is the case of Ryszard Niemczyk – the Polish crime baron known as "Pershing", and kingpin of the notorious Pruszkow mafia. Through the Interpol Notice System and database, he was tracked across Europe and arrested in Germany for the murder of a Polish Police General.

Interpol's role in the fight against international organized crime goes far deeper than chasing gangsters on the run. As organized crime now spans the globe, Interpol is often the only police body to have a clear view of emerging global trends, complex trafficking routes from the country of origin to the final destination, and the fresh alliances between groups thousands of miles apart. By linking police forces in 184 countries into one store of intelligence on crime, it has become the eyes and ears for hundreds of thousands of disparate detectives fighting the menace of trans-national crime.

Hitler shakes hands with members of an elite SS unit, while their commander, Heinrich Himmler, looks on. During the Nazi period, Interpol became an instrument of the Gestapo, Himmler's secret police force.

PEOPLE TRAFFICKING

According to the United Nations, the unlawful trafficking of people across international borders is now the second biggest global revenue stream for organized crime. The nature of this illicit activity falls into two categories: the smuggling of willing illegal immigrants across international borders and the transportation of men, women and children into foreign countries for use in involuntary activity – whether it is sexual exploitation or another form of slavery.

The smuggling of people voluntarily is a relatively new crime in historical terms, having only become a major worldwide criminal business activity during the twentieth century. According to Interpol, "People smuggling has become the preferred trade of a growing number of criminal networks that are showing an increasing sophistication in regard to moving larger numbers of people at higher profits than ever". Currently there are more than 20 million illegal immigrants on the move at any given time. Each of these can pay organized crime gangs anything up to $30,000 a time to be transported from poorer countries to Europe and North America.

Alongside this booming business is the trafficking of people who have been sold, tricked or coerced into virtual slavery. Their criminal masters will then sell them on to others who will exploit them as bonded or forced labourers in industries ranging from agriculture, domestic servitude, industrial sweat shops and the sex trade. This form of organized criminal activity is as old as mankind, but it has become increasingly profitable and sophisticated in the twenty-first century, where children and the vulnerable in impoverished territories have become a common criminal commodity.

RAUL GIBB GUERRERO

Not everyone who fights against organized crime is a member of a police force. Nor are they necessarily experts in criminology or even crusading politicians. Some of the bravest and most effective people combating organized criminality are ordinary citizens who are willing to put everything on the line by standing up and saying, "I can see what organized crime is doing in my community. It is wrong and it has to stop".

Raul Gibb Guerrero was one such person. He did not have the protection that being part a police force usually brings, nor was he politically powerful or wealthy enough to have bodyguards, but when he saw what the Mexican organized crime group, the Gulf Cartel, was doing, he tried his best to make people aware of it. Unfortunately, his incredible courage saw him pay the ultimate price.

Guerrero was the Editorial Director of the regional daily newspaper *La Opinion*, published in the north of the Mexican state of Veracruz. Working for a regional newspaper is mostly unglamorous and tends to involve long hours. In certain areas of Mexico, if you are not careful about what you write, the job can also carry the risk of assassination. The reason for this is the incredible power the Mexican drug cartels now have through cocaine smuggling.

The massive profits their drug trafficking activities have earned them have been used to create vast empires of police and political corruption, backed up by their own private armies of hitmen and former Special Forces soldiers from the Mexican army. The fear the Cartel's gunmen create in most law-abiding people has placed the organized crime gangs almost above the reach of the law. Few are brave enough to speak out, especially when they have good reason to believe that those who are meant to ensure justice are actually on the drug barons' payroll.

Raul Gibb Guerrero was not afraid to write the sort of stories that organized crimes group did not want reported. He was very good at obtaining accurate information about exactly what the criminals were doing and was able to piece together what he knew to form a complex picture of the web of corruption and criminality that existed in Veracruz. He also believed in the journalistic code of ethics that compelled him not only to tell the truth, but also to turn down bribes from gangsters, who were starting to get concerned about him revealing their business dealings in his paper.

At around 10pm, on April 8, 2005, after a long day at work, 53-year-old Guerrero was driving home to his family's apartment in the city of Poza Rica. As he got close to home, four unidentified gunmen fired a volley of 15 shots into his car. Eight bullets struck his body, three of them to the head. Guerrero's car spun out of control and crashed. By the time paramedics arrived at the scene, he was dead. Experts believe ex-members of the Mexican Special Air Mobile Force Group may have fired the shots.

In the days before his death, Guerrero had received anonymous death threats. He suspected they came from one of two sources. He had recently refused bribes from Martin Rojas, the leader of the organized crime gang Los Chupaductos, that were intended to stop him printing a series of reports about a gasoline smuggling racket they were running. Guerrero had also just run a number of hard-hitting editorials exposing the activities of the Gulf Cartels in Veracruz and their alleged links to top politicians.

No one has ever been successfully prosecuted over Guerrero's murder. Nor has anyone been put behind bars for the kidnap, torture and murder of reporter Alfredo Jimenez, on April 2, 2005, by drug-traffickers in the north-western Mexican state of Sonora. The gunman who shot radio reporter Dolores Guadalupe Garcia Escamilla across the border in Laredo, Texas, on April 6, 2005, for the Gulf Cartel, is also still at large.

That reporters continue to fight organized crime syndicates in Mexico by telling the truth when three of their colleagues are gunned down within the space of few days is a demonstration of the power of human spirit that not even the barrels of organized crime's guns can silence.

Mourners pay their respects to Raul Gibb Guerrero, who died at the hand of assassins hired to silence him from speaking out against either the Gulf Cartel or Los Chupaductos organized crime gang.

NEW YORK ORGANIZED CRIME CONTROL BUREAU

It seems that most police forces in the western world that are fighting organized crime have a mission statement. Most of them read like typical management-speak and none of them I have ever come across is as simple and straightforward as, "We try to catch those involved in organized crime". Thankfully, by these standards, the mission statement of New York City's Organized Crime Control Bureau (OCCB) is fairly easy to understand. It reads, "Our mission is to improve the quality of life in New York City by combating all aspects of organized crime: narcotics, vice, traditional/non-traditional organized crime and auto theft, while maintaining high standards of safety and integrity".

The Organized Crime Control Bureau is one of the nine bureaux that form the New York Police Department. The fact that the Bureau exists in its current format and that its mission statement contains the phrase "high standards of safety and integrity" is largely down to the bravery of just one man – Frank Serpico.

In 1971, Frank Serpico became the first New York City policeman to testify against his fellow officers. He gave evidence of widespread corruption and collusion by detectives with organized crime networks within New York City. Seen as something of a counterculture freak by his fellow officers, Serpico's career problems as a plainclothes detective were not just restricted to his colleagues' view of him as a "goddamn anti-war hippy". He concerned many of them because he was ruthlessly honest and refused to look the other way and accept bribes. When his superiors did not act on the evidence he had collected of officers' corruption, he went to the *New York Times* with the story, which they then ran as an exposé. The media uproar forced New York's Mayor, John Lindsay, to establish the Knapp Commission in 1970, in order to investigate the claims.

Ahead of his giving evidence to the Commission, Serpico received a number of death threats; then, during a routine drug bust in February, 1971, that may have been a set-up, he was shot point blank in the face. His fellow detectives failed to call in the shooting and left him bleeding to death on a tenement-building stairwell – his life was only saved by the assistance of a member of the public. It emerged that the Mafia had placed a contract on his life, but despite being deafened by the bullet that severed an auditory nerve and left fragments embedded in his brain, he recovered enough to give an explosive testimony to the Knapp Commission.

Actor Al Pacino's portrayal of Frank Serpico in 1973 movie *Serpico* highlighted why many of Serpico's fellow officers considered him "The most dangerous man alive – an honest cop".

Acknowledging that the picture Serpico painted, of a police force systematically corrupted by organized crime that had paid police officers millions of dollars in bribes over the course of several years, was accurate, the Knapp Commission recommended the creation of the OCCB in November, 1971. All NYC police operations viewed as prone to corruption, including vice, narcotics and organized crime, were unified under the command of the OCCB. Officers were split into specially-structured working teams, typically consisting of one sergeant, six investigators and two undercover officers. This led to high accountability and much less room for rogue detectives to collude with criminals. It also proved very effective in investigation terms.

Since its establishment, the OCCB has scored victory after victory against New York's famous five Cosa Nostra crime families. In the 1980s, its Organized Crime Investigation Division played a leading role in spearheading Rudolph Giuliani's campaign against Cosa Nostra, when he was US Attorney for the Southern District of New York. During this period, it won convictions against the Colombo and Genovese families for construction industry rackets and cartels. It also broke apart the massive Mafia theft operation that had been running for years at JFK Airport.

The OCCB has rivalled the FBI for its effective use of the Racketeer Influence Corrupt Organizations Act (commonly called RICO), using it to squeeze the Mafia out of the waste disposal industry and tackle the Mob's hold on union activities. However, whilst the OCCB is seen as strong on Cosa Nostra, Triad and Irish-American crime gang activity, it has been criticized for being weak on Russian, African and Indian controlled gangs operating in New York. Despite the existence of a Joint Organized Crime Task Force working with the FBI, much of the denigration of the OCCB made to journalists comes privately from agents working in the FBI's New York Field Division.

The brave honesty of Frank Serpico helped bring the OCCB into existence. It remains a fitting testimony to one man's integrity that its officers are now seen as a major headache for organized criminality in the Big Apple.

After years of corruption and ineffectual policing against the five Cosa Nostra families in NYC, the OCCB has begun to start causing the Mob some pain.

FRIENDS IN HIGH PLACES

12

"A word in the right ear can make or murder a man."
Traditional Sicilian saying

Organized criminals have always attempted to link themselves with the rich, famous and powerful. Having friends in high places is one of the best ways to stay out of jail and to boost your criminal network.

In most cases it is obvious what both sides get out of the friendship. A senior judge who spends time with Mob bosses is unlikely to be discussing a mutual interest in legal reform. The majority of relationships between the judiciary, police and gangsters are purely financial. It is usually a matter of straightforward bribery and corruption: justice perverted by crime's financial muscle and the greed of man.

When it comes to criminal links to politicians, the stake is often power. Organized criminals can use their power of intimidation to deliver votes – the lifeblood of most politics. In return, they often expect the official they helped elect to use his position to deliver them anything from tax breaks to immunity or government contracts.

It is often harder to fathom the nature of the relationship between high echelon espionage agents and assorted illicit groups; both sides tend to be expert at keeping secrets. The same can be said of the contact between higher-ranking churchmen and the Mafia, where the reasons for either side cultivating powerful allies in the other camp are often shrouded in mystery.

Perhaps the most authentic friendships between the underworld and the rich and famous are those forged with certain celebrities. Gangsters can hunger after glamour as much as anyone and even the bright lights of show-business has shadows, where well-built, well-armed friends do not go amiss. At least here, when two worlds meet, there is often genuine respect and fondness, alongside the money of course.

FULGENCIO BATISTA – CUBAN DICTATOR

Revolutions that sweep dictators from power tend to be chaotic. There are usually a few hours when no one is entirely sure who is in control, and confusion reigns. When the revolution comes during New Year's Eve celebrations, gunshots mixing with the fireworks, it can be impossible to know whether some of the street parties are celebrating liberation or simply the dawn of another year.

However, when soldiers arrived at the New Year's Eve party of Cuban dictator Fulgencio Batista in 1958/1959, he knew they represented the end of his time in power. The guerrillas of Fidel Castro's 26th of July Movement, under the direction of Che Guevara, had taken all but the Cuban capital, Havana. His own loyal soldiers had arrived to tell him that Che would soon have control of Camp Colombia military airbase – if they were to escape, they would have to leave now. As his supporters began a headlong tilt towards panic at the prospect of a hurried evacuation, Batista made a phone call. He did not ring one of his generals to check the situation, his first priority was to call American Mafia boss Meyer Lansky.

Batista wanted Lansky to know that Castro had won, that he was leaving for the Dominican Republic and that he too should escape. Although the two men had known each other for more than 20 years, the reason why Batista had tipped off Lansky first could be explained by what Batista's soldiers were now busy loading into seven cars – millions of US dollars. Lansky had given the money to Batista in return for the Cuban leader's co-operation in allowing Cosa Nostra to run the island's gambling, dominate its nightlife and use it as a drug trafficking and money laundering haven.

Between 1933 and 1940, Batista was the puppet-master of a series of figurehead leaders, before becoming Cuban President himself, in 1940. Some have suggested that Lansky and Batista first became friends when Lansky travelled to Cuba during the American Prohibition, but this is unlikely. Batista spent Cuba's prime rum-running years in the army as a lowly sergeant. It was not until he led the Sergeants' Revolt, that overthrew the Government of Carlos Manuel de Cespedes in 1933, that he began to wield the sort of power that made him someone that Mafia men would want to know.

It was during Batista's official presidency of 1940–1944 that he and Lansky began their first financial arrangements. In return, the Mafia boss was allowed to take an interest in the Cuban casino sector. Even when he was not President, Batista still controlled Cuba, so when boss of the Tampa crime family Santo Trafficante Jr wanted to emulate Meyer and begin operating in Havana, in 1946, he approached Batista for his permission. In return he was told: "You have to clear it with the Little Man first". The Little Man was Batista's affectionate name for Lansky, and such loyalty was rewarded by the Little Man – he allowed Trafficante a cut of the Havana action, but ensured a good percentage of the profits was fed back to Batista.

When Batista returned to power in Cuba in 1952, after a *coup d'état*, Meyer approached him with a plan to transform the island into a major tourist destination. Meyer and his Mafia friends would take over all the casinos and racetracks in Cuba, clean them up and

When the dictatorship of Fulgencio Batista collapsed on New Year's Eve in 1958, his demise signalled not only the rise of Castro, but the loss of Cosa Nostra's Cuban casino empire.

promote them as a gambling Mecca to Americans. In return for a free rein in this and other rackets, they would pump money into building luxury hotels and modernizing Havana. Then Meyer opened a suitcase containing $6 million in cash for Batista.

For the next seven years, Lansky kept up his end of the bargain. His scheme transformed Havana. He also arranged for his "bagman", Doc Stacher, to courier millions of dollars direct to Batista or into his Swiss bank account in Geneva. Lansky could afford it – the control over gambling in Cuba generated fabulous profits and also allowed him to launder vast sums of Cosa Nostra money from the USA.

Unfortunately, Batista could not hold up his end of the bargain and he was unable to quell Castro's growing rebellion against his corrupt rule. When his regime collapsed, Lansky, Trafficante and many other Mob bosses lost millions in investments as Castro closed the casinos and the residents of Havana went on a slot machine smashing rampage in revenge against those known for being good friends of Batista.

GENERAL NORIEGA – LEADER OF PANAMA

Being a dictator is a perilous position. While politics in a democracy is viciously treacherous, in a dictatorship, when one of your rivals knifes you in the back, you can expect more than a hostile, off-the-record briefing to journalists. Aside from making dictators exceptionally paranoid, this fact of life often encourages them to seek out alliances with those that, for even an absolute ruler, qualify as powerful friends.

General Manuel Noriega of Panama had two groups of exceptionally powerful friends, but both of them happened to be involved in the cocaine business – the drugs barons of the Colombian cartels and the Central Intelligence Agency (CIA) of the United States of America. Between the massive financial muscle of the Colombians and the covert assistance of the CIA, Noriega's pals in narcotics were certainly able to help keep Panama firmly in his grip.

Noriega, also known as Cara de Piña (Pineapple Face), due to his pockmarked complexion, had started his path to power in 1969. A military coup in 1968 saw him promoted to Lieutenant Colonel and put in charge of Panama's military intelligence by the then military dictator, Brigadier General Omar Torrijos. Despite a total conflict of

Despite having been a loyal employee of the CIA, receiving kickbacks from the Agency's drug running operations, when America turned on General Noriega his fate was sealed.

interests, Noriega began accepting a second salary from the CIA – this was confirmed years later by former CIA Director Admiral Stansfield Turner. When Noriega finally decided to oust Torrijos and place himself in control of Panama, his friends in the CIA helped out. In 1981, they put a bomb on a plane carrying Torrijos, leading to his death and Noreiga's ascent to dictator.

In return for this, Noriega happily turned a blind eye to the illegal CIA actions that were taking place that involved using Panama as a base. Among these were CIA collaborations with Colombian drug barons that saw CIA operatives transport cocaine into the USA in return for a share of the illicit profits. These were then used to fund a clandestine war against the left-wing Nicaraguan forces known as the Sandinistas. For his continuing co-operation, the CIA rewarded him with kickbacks from the drug running operation on top of his secret CIA salary.

Noriega's involvement with illicit cocaine money deepened in 1984, when he agreed to provide sanctuary and protection to members of the Medellin cartel, including one of its bosses, Carlos Enrique Lehder Rivas. In return for payments of more than $5 million dollars Noriega allowed cartel fugitives from both Colombia and the United States to continue their business from Panama without fear of capture. Given that elements of the CIA and the cartels were working together at this point, Noriega foresaw no problems with the arrangement.

However, times changed, and Noriega's refusal to provide full military support against the Sandinistas lost him American political allies and the activities of the CIA were curtailed by the Iran-Contra scandal in 1986. In 1988, Senator John Kerry's subcommittee on terrorism, narcotics and international operations concluded, "The saga of Panama's General Manuel Noriega represents one of the most serious foreign policy failures for the United States. Noriega was able to manipulate US policy toward his country, while skillfully accumulating near-absolute power in Panama. It is clear that each US government agency which had a relationship with Noriega turned a blind eye to his corruption and drug dealing, even as he was emerging as a key player on behalf of the Medellin cartel". This exposure in the US made it inevitable that his CIA friends would have to turn against him.

When a US Marine was shot in Panama, in 1989, President George Bush used it as an excuse to launch Operation Just Cause, the aim of which was to oust Noriega from power and return him to the US to face drugs and money laundering charges. When the US military invaded, Noriega sought sanctuary in the Vatican Embassy in Panama. US forces besieged the compound and tried to force Noriega out by blasting rock group Metallica's *Enter the Sandman* at building-shaking decibels, 24 hours a day. After several days of this, Noriega surrendered and was taken to the US, where he was tried in 1992. Carlos Lehder Rivas cut a deal with his US captors to receive a lighter sentence and retain a larger share of his illicit fortune in return for providing evidence against his former friend, Noriega. With no remaining allies, Noriega was sentenced to 40 years in prison – he becomes eligible for parole in 2029.

JOSEPH KENNEDY – POLITICAL PATRIARCH

Prohibition transformed the face of the United States. It also transformed the economic circumstances of many of those who became involved in bootlegging. Not everyone who profited was a direct member of the American Mafia, but if you made money from illegal alcohol between 1920 and 1933, at some point you had to do business with the Mob.

One family whose financial situation was radically improved by bootlegging was that of Joseph Kennedy. The original patriarch of the political dynasty may not be everybody's idea of a successful player in the illegal drink business, but he made as much money from Prohibition as many infamous racketeers.

While it seems incongruous that a respected Irish-Catholic community leader and successful businessman could also be a bootlegger, it needs to be remembered that, away from the killings, hijacking and gang wars, merely supplying alcohol to various bootlegging gangs could be a highly profitable and low risk occupation. This was especially true if you had the political and judicial contacts of Joe Kennedy to keep the authorities off your back.

Kennedy had made his first fortune through insider trading and stock manipulation, but Prohibition provided him with an opportunity too good to miss. His father had owned a series of saloons and, as America went dry, the family business – Somerset Importers – became the exclusive agents for Gordon's Dry Gin and Dewar's Scotch. They were allowed to import gin and scotch for medicinal purposes, but much of it made its way straight to the various Irish-American gangs that dominated Boston at the time.

Seeing the money that could be made, Kennedy financed the regular rum-running of alcohol from the Caribbean to Massachusetts. The large profits that began rolling in from this allowed him to branch out into buying Hollywood Studios. His illegal alcohol importation also brought him into contact with Frank Costello, the man known as "the Prime Minister of the underworld". Costello was quick to cultivate such a prominent, apparently legitimate businessman with a range of high-powered political contacts. Costello and Kennedy did business with each other and Costello occasionally helped Kennedy obtain leverage over his business partners in Hollywood through less than ethical means.

Kennedy's relationship with Costello cooled, however, when Prohibition ended and he began to grow in political prominence, including an appointment as United States Ambassador to the Court of St James (in the United Kingdom) in 1938. However, it was through Costello that Kennedy became an associate of Mafia boss Meyer Lansky. A regular visitor to Lansky's illegal Florida gambling club – the

Colonial Inn – Kennedy, along with Lanksy, eventually invested money in the Hialeah Race Track in Florida. It was in this social milieu that Kennedy first came into contact with Sam "Momo" Giancana – leader of the Chicago Syndicate.

Joe Kennedy knew what line of business his friends were in. This is why he asked Giancana to help use his control over the Teamsters and other unions to support his son, John F. Kennedy, in the crucial West Virginia presidential primary campaign in 1960. He also persuaded them to help in the Texas and Chicago vote frauds that resulted in JFK beating Richard Nixon in the presidential election in the same year.

It had taken all of Kennedy's persuasive power to get Giancana and other mobsters to back his son, due to Robert F. Kennedy's prominent

anti-Mafia crusade. At one point during the McClellan Committee hearings into racketeering, RFK had mocked Giancana, saying "I thought only little girls giggled, Mr. Giancana?" Joe Kennedy had told Giancana that with JFK in the White House, RFK would lay off his pals. Suddenly, the prospect of having a friend's son in the absolute highest of places seemed like a very good idea.

However, when JFK became President, he no longer needed his father's background political manoeuvring and was in no mood to listen to him over the Mafia. JFK appointed his brother, Bobby Kennedy, as Attorney General, and he used the postion to become the biggest problem Cosa Nostra had ever encountered. This left Giancana complaining, "We broke our balls for him and gave him the election and he gets his brother to hound us to death". Further insult was added when Giancana's emissary to Joe Kennedy – Frank Sinatra – was banned by RFK from both the White House and Kennedy family social gatherings, leaving Joe's old pals out in the cold.

Friend of the Mob, Joseph Kennedy, with two of his sons – the future US President John F. Kennedy and his eldest son Joseph, who was killed in action in the Second World War.

FRANK SINATRA – HOLLYWOOD SINGER

Frank Sinatra was not a member of the Mafia, although you could be forgiven for thinking he was. The publicity his links to Cosa Nostra received was enough to make his fans suspicious. Director of the FBI, J. Edgar Hoover, was so convinced Sinatra was linked to organized crime that he authorised hundreds of hours of investigation into the star's life. Although no charges were ever brought against him, Sinatra's 2,403-page FBI report almost saw Old Blue Eyes prosecuted for extortion.

A reading of the file makes it clear that Sinatra had the right connections to become a "made man" and could have had his pick of joining several Mafia families. However, if Frank had joined, it would have been purely honorary – he was an entertainer, not a killer. Alongside his associations with top Cosa Nostra leaders, Sinatra also had the required Italian-American pedigree for membership and an established family link. Sinatra's uncle, Babe Gavarante, had been an associate of New Jersey crime boss Willie Moretti, before Babe had been convicted of murder in 1921.

Strangely enough it was Willie Moretti who became the star's first major Mafioso friend. Moretti had spotted the young Sinatra singing in his New Jersey clubs in the 1930s and always gave him work. The former hitman and the struggling singer forged a bond of genuine friendship. When Frank ran into his first major professional problem, he asked Moretti to help him out. Frank had signed a contract with band leader Tommy Dorsey, but Dorsey refused to let Sinatra go as the singer's career began to rocket. In 1943, after he had offered Dorsey more than $60,000 to rip up the contract, Frank's friend Willie began "negotiating". This involved Moretti jamming the barrel of a gun in Dorsey's mouth to encourage him to sign away his interest in Sinatra for a mere $1.

This incident became a well-known show-business tale and Mario Puzo included it in his best-selling novel, *The Godfather*, where Sinatra became singer Johnny Fontaine. When Sinatra saw Puzo in a restaurant he verbally attacked the author, made serious threats and used words that certainly never featured on any of his records. Frank had a habit of threatening people who wrote things he didn't like about the Mafia. In 1960, again in a restaurant, he attacked Desi Arnaz, whose production company with his wife Lucille Ball made the hit TV show, *The Untouchables*.

If Old Blue Eyes was so concerned about the publicity his Mafia links attracted, he should have reconsidered acts such as flying to Havana in 1946 to sing for his friend, Charles "Lucky" Luciano, at a Commission meeting and giving him a gold lighter inscribed "To my dear pal Charlie, from his friend Frank". It may also have been wiser not to give Chicago Syndicate boss, Sam Giancana, a sapphire friendship ring, and he should have known better than to be photographed in the company of gangsters, such as Carlo Gambino. When the Kefauver investigations into Mob activities questioned Sinatra, in 1950, he admitted to knowing Luciano, Moretti, Joe Adonis, "Bugsy" Siegel, Frank Costello and Meyer Lansky.

When Lansky was building up Las Vegas and needed to pull in the punters, he gave Sinatra a 9 per cent stake in the Sands Hotel in return for the Rat Pack performing there. Sinatra and crew gave Las Vegas a big boost and the Mafia looked after Frank and his Hollywood pals well while they were in the desert. When comedian Jackie Mason was in Vegas, in 1966, and made a couple of anti-Frank jokes in his nightclub routine, his hotel room was shot up and he suddenly found he could no longer get work in the town.

Amongst Sinatra's Rat Pack pals was Peter Lawford, the actor and husband of John F. Kennedy's sister Patricia. This gave Sinatra access to the Kennedy family that Sam Giancana tried to exploit. At one point, through Sinatra introducing them both to the same woman – Judy Campbell – JFK and Giancana even became points in a bizarre love triangle. However, anti-Mafia campaigner Robert F. Kennedy eventually banned Sinatra from seeing any of the Kennedy family.

Cosa Nostra loved Frank and he loved them right back. They had always been there for him in both the highs and lows of his career. The Mafiosi who called him a friend were proud of the talented Italian-American who had made good, and they loved the opportunity to rub shoulders with one of show-business's legendary names.

Old Blue Eyes once flew to Havana to sing for Cosa Nostra boss "Lucky" Luciano, who was in exile at the time.

THE KRAYS – THE LONDON GANGSTERS WHO MIXED CRIME WITH POLITICS

Many people crave the company of celebrities and ache to bathe in the perceived projection of glamour they generate. Those in the upper echelons of organized crime rarely have problems rubbing shoulders with the rich and famous. Not only do they have the money to mix in the best places and be seen with the "right people", they often have more wealth than the stars and actually own the spots the famed want to visit. This was certainly the case with the Kray twins, London's most infamous 1960s gangsters.

In using their reputation for psychotic violence to take over

Esmeralda's Barn – a nightclub in London's exclusive Knightsbridge area – in 1960, Ronnie and Reggie Kray found themselves the owners of a venue that was frequented by the wealthy, well-known and powerful. This was a source of great joy to Ronnie. He tried to live much of his life based on the 1930s Hollywood gangster films he adored, and the chance to play the gracious host to those regularly photographed for society magazines and the newspapers became a vital part of his real-world fantasy.

It was by providing entertainment and protection to American stars, such as Judy Garland and George Raft, that the Krays came into contact with the American Mafia. George Raft was the front man for Meyer Lansky's London casino, The Colony. He introduced the twins

As well as mixing with celebrities, the Krays forged friendships with MPs and members of the House of Lords in an attempt to gain political protection from police investigation.

to his Cosa Nostra pals and this led to some limited business dealing between the American and English mobsters.

Ronnie's younger twin Reggie, the more astute of the pair, could see that mixing with celebrities gave their string of London clubs a patina of credibility. The cynicism their attempts to gain good publicity, by making donations to charity, met in the press could be subverted if a showbiz name was attached. While Ronnie enjoyed the company of actresses, such as Diana Dors and Barbara Windsor, because he wanted to be a celebrity himself, to Reggie it was just clever marketing. One thing both brothers agreed on, however, was that in England, courting the upper classes and those with political clout was an even better way of gaining standing and influence in society.

Their first major step in this process was hiring hereditary peer and member of the House of Lords, the Sixth Earl of Effingham, as a director of Esmeralda's Barn. His job was to bring "class" to the club's front of house, he also became the butt of the twins' jokes – they would constantly torment him with quips such as "Bring us some effing tea Effy". The Krays' names even became known to established Labour peer "Manny" Shinwell, during the period in the gangsters' career when they were trying to involve several politicians in their failed attempt to create a property, tourist and retail business in Nigeria.

However, the best political contacts the twins made were through Ronnie's homosexual parties. Providing young men like some hosts serve canapes, these sordid affairs brought Labour Member of Parliament, Tom Driberg, and leading Conservative peer, Lord Boothby, into the Krays' circle. Driberg was persuaded to ask questions in the House of Commons in order to pressurize the Home Office into looking into the cases of associates of the Krays who were behind bars. Boothby was readily prepared to ask questions in the House of Lords and apply political pressure when the Krays were imprisoned in 1965, ahead of their trial for demanding money with menaces from Hew McGowan, the son of a fellow peer.

Boothby's association with the known gangland bosses had become knowledge in 1964, when the *Sunday Mirror* newspaper ran a story about "The Peer and the Gangster" while the *Daily Mirror* newspaper followed up with the headline "The Picture We Dare Not Print", referring to a picture of Boothby taken with Ronnie Kray and cat burglar Leslie Holt – whom both men shared as a lover. Boothby sued the *Daily Mirror* over the story and won £40,000 in damages. While this helped scare off other papers from writing about the Krays, it also helped bring about their downfall.

Extreme concern at high levels of government over the political linkage the twins were building up led to renewed pressure on the police to put them behind bars for a significant period. Not surprisingly, when the Krays were eventually jailed for murder in 1968, support from peers and politicians soon vanished. Former friends in high places could do nothing now to save them from spending the rest of their lives at Her Majesty's pleasure.

GIULIO ANDREOTTI – ITALIAN PRIME MINISTER

Seven-times Italian Prime Minister Giulio Andreotti, known to his countrymen as "Uncle Giulio", was eventually tried and convicted of being a "component of the Sicilian Mafia".

When it comes to organized crime claiming friends in high places, few stories can top that of Giulio Andreotti's relationship with the Sicilian Mafia.

Giulio Andreotti bestrides the history of post-Second World War Italian politics like no other figure. After entering Parliament in 1946, he played a key role in shaping the country's destiny right up until 1992, when he served his final term as Prime Minister. Andreotti served as a Deputy Minister in government in the early 1950s, as Italy's foreign minister between 1983 and 1989, and as Prime Minister he served no less than seven times.

Throughout his career, he wielded immense power over both the Italian government and the Christian Democratic Party to which he belonged. Only media mogul and multi-time Italian Prime Minister Silvio Berlusconi has come close to the type of influence Andreotti once possessed. Yet incredibly, Andreotti was eventually tried and found guilty of being a "component of the Sicilian Mafia".

It was not until 1968 that rumours of Andreotti's links to the Mafia began to emerge. This was the year he entered into a deal with the Sicilian Christian Democrat politician, Salvatore Lima. It was with Lima's support that Andreotti's faction of the Christian Democrats took control of the party. Lima had long acted as a conduit between Italian politics and leading crime bosses so through his ties to the

Mafia he was able to guarantee that Andreotti received the bulk of Sicilian votes in any Italian election.

Within Mafia circles Andreotti became known as "Uncle Giulio" – a trusted friend and ally, who could be relied upon to perform favours and look after his pals. As it became clear at his later trials, between 1970 and 1980, Andreotti had face-to-face business dealings with several top Sicilian Mafia leaders, including Stefano Bonatate, Tano "Sitting Bull" Badalamenti and Michele "the Pope" Greco. It even emerged that during this period he had given the special kiss of respect between two Mafia members to Toto "The Beast" Riina, leader of the dominant Corleonesi clan, while its head Luciano Leggio was in jail. At the time of the kiss, Riina was on the run and the Italian police's most wanted organized criminal.

In 1979, the journalist Mino Pecorelli uncovered most of this information. He obtained photographic proof and attempted to blackmail Andreotti. Pecorelli, a former member of the P2 Masonic lodge containing many prominent politicians, Mafiosi, churchmen and members of the Italian secret service, should have known he was playing with fire. Within weeks of his first demands, his body was discovered; he had been executed in one of the traditional Mafia styles for traitors – with a bullet through the back of the head.

It seems to have been this incident and the Mafia ignoring Andreotti's request, in 1980, not to go ahead with plans to assassinate Piersanti Mattarella – a Christian Democrat who was trying to distance his party from organized crime – that caused "Uncle Giulio" to back away from his murderous friends. However, he still used his position to give them assistance, such as appointing a "verdict-killing" judge to overturn many of the convictions against Mafiosi that were obtained at the 1986 Mafia Maxi trial, thanks to the evidence of Sicilian Mafia supergrass Tommaso Buscetta (who a decade later would go on to give evidence against Andreotti himself).

When the "Clean Hands" campaign against government corruption and links to the Mafia began to gather force in 1991, Andreotti, as Prime Minister at the time, was forced into a more anti-Mafia stance. This led to Riina's campaign of "eminent corpses" to try and change government policy. One of the first corpses was that of Salvatore Lima. By 1993, the extent of Andreotti's and the Christian Democrats' ties to the Mafia had become clear. The party disbanded and Andreotti's decade-spanning political power was finished.

In 2002, Andreotti was tried and convicted of ordering the Mafia to murder Mino Pecorelli. In the aftermath of the sentencing, Andreotti joked that "A 24-year sentence for an 83-year-old is a form of good wishes for a long life". In 2003, his appeal against the conviction was upheld, but the Court also upheld charges that he was guilty of enjoying strong ties to the Mafia and that he used them to further his political carreer. He only escaped prison because the Italian statute of limitations for his crimes had expired. In Italy, Andreotti's most famous one-liner remains: "To think the worst of a person is a sin, but you usually guess right".

SUN YAT-SEN – FOUNDER OF MODERN CHINA

Chinese national hero Yat-sen was not only a member of a Triad, but used alliances with Triad leaders to bring about the end of thousands of years of Imperial rule.

Sun Yat-sen is unique in modern Chinese history. He is the only figure revered by both Communists on mainland China and Nationalists in Taiwan, even to this day. It was Sun who brought about the final end of the Qing Dynasty and laid the foundations for the emergence of the post-Imperial China that exists today.

In Taiwan, he is known as "National Father Mr Sun Chungsan". On mainland China, his official title is "The Forerunner of the Revoution". Statues of him grace parks in both countries and his mausoleum in Nanjing is a national monument. There is never any official mention, however, that the founder of modern China was also a Triad member.

Sun was born in 1866 to a poor peasant family who lived in the Guangzhou prefecture, Guangdong province, 16 miles north of Macao. As a teenager, Sun joined the Three Harmonies Triad society. While studying martial arts with his fellow Triad brothers, he desecrated a local temple, smashing the hand off one of the holy statues. Forced to flee his local community, he went to Hawaii where he joined Kwok On Wui Triad society, which had a heavy presence on the island.

With loans from his Triad brothers, Sun was able, against his family's wishes, to study to become a doctor. Over the years, Sun became increasingly political, resenting the Imperial system and its heavy taxation on the poor of China. The core political purpose for the existence of the Triads had always been best expressed by their motto Fan Qing – Fuk Ming (Overthrow Qing – Restore Ming). Through this belief, Sun felt the Triads could play a role in his vision of China becoming a democratic, republican state. Their criminal activities did not worry him – in fact quite the opposite: it merely meant that they had the funds necessary to support his proposals for revolution.

Reasoning that there were millions of Triad members in China, and across the world, who could become a revolutionary force, he formed his first group, a secret society dedicated to the overthrow of the Qing Dynasty and following the 36 Triad oaths. Called the Hsing Chung Hui (Revitalize China Society), they changed the words of the thirty-sixth oath to: "Our common aim is to avenge the Five Ancestors and establish a democratic government". Sun quickly made alliances with major Triad leaders, such as Charlie Soong, who ran the Huang Pang (Red Gang) that controlled the Shanghai underworld in the 1890s. It was Triad members who made up the majority of Sun's force in his first failed rebellion attempt to overthrow the Qing Dynasty, in 1895.

In the aftermath of his failure, Sun became a Red Pole (a Triad rank equivalent to gang leader) in the Che Kung Tong society in America. Touring the world and amassing support, Sun encouraged his supporters to join Triad groups and bring them into the eventual revolution he was planning. With aid and support from the Japanese Black Dragon society (who had their own reasons for wishing to foment political upheaval in China), by the 1900s Sun had widespread Triad backing. In 1899, a group of major Dragon Heads (overall leaders of Triad societies) pledged support to Sun and the Hsing Chung Hui, in a traditional Triad ritual involving cock's blood and spiced wine. From this moment on, most of Sun's funding and intelligence came directly from the Triads.

Despite years of joint plotting and rebellions, neither the Triads nor Sun played an extensive or direct role in the 1911 military uprising at Wuchang that eventually led to the overthrow of the Qing Dynasty and saw Sun elected as provisional President of the Republic of China. During the next 14 years of his rule as President and his attempts to wrest control of the country from powerful warlords, Triad support for Sun fell away. Now that the Qing were defeated, they were more intent on pursuing their criminal ambitions. However, Sun's successor, Chiang Kai-shek, brought the Triads into an alliance with Sun's Nationalists against Mao Zedong's Communist forces during the Chinese Civil War of 1927–1949.

To this day, school history books in China and Taiwan not only fail to mention Sun's Triad membership, but also how the "National Father" and "Forerunner of the Revolution" only brought about a republic in China after thousands of years of Imperial rule with the direct assistance of the Triads.

NOBUSUKE KISHI – JAPANESE PRIME MINISTER

From the Sicilian Mafia to the 14K Triad, the Cold War had the West turning to some strange allies to combat Communism. There were many in American government and intelligence who were prepared to enter into partnerships with, and give money to, organized crime, if they could help them in the fight against the perceived "Red Menace". However, the fact that the US was prepared to support a Class A war criminal and known associate of the Yakuza as Prime Minister of Japan, and give him control of a multi-billion dollar secret fund, still retains its power to shock more than half a century after some of the events transpired.

Nobusuke Satō was born in Japan's Yamaguchi Prefecture, in 1896. As a young boy, Nobusuke was sent from his home to move in with the more affluent Kishi family and eventually adopted their name. With his new family's support, Nobusuke Kishi found a good position in the Japanese civil service. In 1932, Japan invaded and occupied Manchuria in China. They placed Puyi, the former Child Emperor of China and last of the Qing Dynasty, on the throne of the puppet state, which it called Manchuko. Kishi found himself put in charge of utilizing the occupied country's mineral wealth and developing its industrial base.

His new position brought Kishi into contact with many major Yakuza figures who also shared an interest in exploiting Manchuria through stealing anything of value, sending its men as virtual slaves to work as labourers in Japan and trafficking its women into forced prostitution. One of the key Yakuza members that Kishi formed a relationship with during this period was Yoshio Kodama, who ran a massive drugs operation in the subjugated territory. Kishi helped many of the Yakuza plunder Manchuria and so successful was his own pillaging of the country's natural resources that he was appointed Minister of Commerce and Industry, between 1941 and 1945, and even co-signed Japan's declaration of war against the United States of America and the United Kingdom.

After the war, Kishi was accused of being a Class A war criminal and sentenced to imprisonment in Tokyo's Sugamo Jail. Behind bars he renewed his friendship with Yoshio Kodama and major Yakuza associate Ryōichi Sasakawa, who were also both classified as war criminals. When he was released in 1948, Kishi's right wing, anti-Communist views meant he found support from his former American captors and returned to politics within the new Democratic Party.

When Kishi's party merged with the Liberal Party in 1955 to form the ruling Liberal Democratic Party (LDP), he was put back in government and, by 1957, Kishi was Prime Minister of Japan. Instead of cutting all ties with organized crime at this point, Kishi used the power of his office to further the influence of his Yakuza friends and

Class A war criminal and Yakuza associate Nobusuke Kishi used his position as Prime Minister of Japan to advance the fortunes of leading members of organized crime.

use for "security purposes". It was called the M-Fund after its first overseer, General William Marquat, but it soon passed completely into the control of Kishi and other senior Japanese politicians. The Anpo treaty that Kishi presented to his country led to widespread anti-American and anti-government feeling in Japan. Left-wing protestors rioted, clashing with police on the steps of the National Diet Building, and White House Press Secretary, James Hagerty, was besieged on his way to the airport and had to be evacuated by military helicopter. Kishi, meanwhile, gave more than $50 million from the M-Fund to Yoshio Kodama to bring a force of more than 36,000 Yakuza onto the streets to combat the dissent and assist the police. Yakuza thuggery soon restored order, but Kishi resigned as Prime Minister.

Nobusuke Kishi remained a powerful figure in Japanese politics, especially when his brother, Eisaku Satō became Prime Minister between 1964 and 1972. He also maintained his close connections to the Yakuza, demonstrating his visible support for them by being one of the LDP politicians who stood bail for a senior member of the Yamaguchi-gumi criminal clan when he was charged with murder in 1973. With friends like Kishi, it is no wonder that organized crime became such an entwined part of Japanese society.

JAMES JESUS ANGLETON – CIA DIRECTOR

When it comes to aliases and nicknames, it is hard to beat the sheer number that some criminals manage to acquire during their careers in organized crime. However, one man that could match even the most titled gangster was James Jesus Angleton, the long-serving CIA director of counter-intelligence. Although his official CIA cover name was Hugh Ashmead and his code designation was KU/Mother, Angleton clocked up more than 50 other names during more than three decades of espionage work. At CIA headquarters many referred to him as "the Grey Ghost of Langley", a coincidental echo of the name the Sicilian Mafia gave him – "the Ghost".

Angleton is a giant figure in the annals of spying. The orchid growing, fly-fishing, poetry reading, chess playing agent began work for the Office of Strategic Services (OSS) in 1943. The OSS was the wartime forerunner of the Central Intelligence Agency and continued to control US intelligence until the CIA was established in 1947 – the year that Angleton started working with the Mafia. As he had spent much of his childhood and teenage years in Rome, it was felt Angleton was the perfect agent to establish an underground, anti-Communist network to ensure that Italy remained closely aligned to the US and free from Soviet influence.

their allies. He not only awarded billions-of-yen-worth of contracts to them, he even gave some Yakuza roles within government itself.

As part of the 1959 negotiations over the Treaty of Mutual Co-operation and Security between Japan and the United States of America (known as Anpo in Japan), Kishi obtained from Vice-President Richard Nixon a secret fund of several billion dollars to

CIA Counter Intelligence Director, James Jesus Angleton, was happy to use the Sicilian Mafia as part of his grand plan to keep Italy in a state of fear and free from communist control.

Angleton's creation was called Gladio. Utilizing former SS intelligence officers and Italian fascists, it was secretly funded with millions of dollars from the CIA. Part of its purpose was to ensure that at Italian elections, the results tilted towards the right. This led Angleton to devise what would later be called the strategia della tensione (strategy of tension). Its aim was to manipulate public opinion, not only through disinformation and propaganda, but also through acts of terrorism that could be blamed on the left. It was not surprising, therefore, that Angleton brought elements of the Sicilian Mafia into Gladio.

The OSS and the Mafia had begun working together during the Second World War. In 1941, worried over acts of sabotage in American ports by German or Italian agents and an increasing number of strikes, US intelligence brokered a deal with Cosa Nostra via Meyer Lansky. Acknowledging their virtual control over the dockyard unions, in return for moving "Lucky" Luciano (who was behind bars for life on prostitution charges) to a more comfortable prison, the OSS expected the Mafia to end worker dissent in the docks and assist in anti-saboteur operations.

The American Mafia complied and when the US military began planning to invade Italy in 1943, a new arrangement was brokered. Luciano would be freed and deported at the end of the war if Cosa Nostra would guarantee its colleagues in the Sicilian Mafia would assist with the American invasion of Sicily and its peaceful occupation. Leading Cosa Nostra figure Vito Genovese, who had fled the US in 1937, and was now linked to Mussolini, also agreed to switch allegiance, provide intelligence and help OSS operations in Italy.

Angleton built on these wartime links with the Sicilian Mafia for Gladio. Mafiosi recruited by Angleton committed terrorism under the banner of left wing groups and joined the P2 Masonic lodge that Gladio established as a way of controlling leading Italian politicians, journalists and even churchmen. Through Gladio funds and protection, the Mafia path to dominant political corruption within Italy was greatly smoothed. Unfortunately for Gladio, Mafia involvement in P2 eventually led to the Banco Ambrosiano scandal in 1981. This exposed the links between high-ranking members of the Vatican and leading Italian gangsters, and even put Gladio itself under the spotlight of public scrutiny.

Angleton also made friends amongst leading members of the American Mafia. Following the revolution in Cuba, in 1959, he knew that leading Mob figures, such as Sam Giancana and Santo Trafficante Jr, had lost millions of dollars, so he suggested recruiting them to help assassinate Fidel Castro. This led to a long period of CIA funding of various Cosa Nostra plots to kill the Cuban leader, all of which failed – including the attempt to kill him with an exploding cigar.

When Congress investigated CIA wrongdoing through the Church Committee, in 1975, they discovered not only Angleton's illegal campaigns against American citizens within America, but also his work with the Mafia. As the details of the Mob-CIA relationship came out, both sides began to reflect on the wisdom of having high-placed friends in such notorious professional murder organizations.

PAUL "THE GORILLA" MARCINKUS – CATHOLIC ARCHBISHOP

There can't be many members of the clergy with such criminal sounding nicknames as "The Gorilla". Then again it can only be hoped that there are not too many churchmen like Archbishop Paul "The Gorilla" Marcinkus, who not only counted leading Mafiosi as his close friends but also became intrinsically involved in their criminal activities.

Paul Marcinkus was born in the Chicago suburb of Cicero, in 1922. As a young boy he grew up hearing tales of infamous Cicero neighbours, including Al Capone, Jake "Greasy Thumb" Guzik and Frank "The Enforcer" Nitti. Yet these stories had no impact on

Marcinkus's chosen career. As a teenager he entered the seminary to study for the priesthood. It was his friends during this period that nicknamed him "the Gorilla", due to his impressive 6ft 3in (1.92m), 200lb (91kg) frame. The name stuck. Everyone at the seminary remembered him as a "gentle giant" and a "man without malice". After his ordination in 1947, Marcinkus eventually found himself sent to Rome, where he was part of the security team for two Popes.

Marcinkus's devotion to service and charm won him many friends within the Vatican and he was ordained to the episcopate as Titular Archbishop of Horta and Secretary of the Roman Curia in 1969. This role acted as a stepping-stone to his appointment as the President of the Istituto per le Opere di Religione – the Institute of Religious Works (IOR) – in 1971. The IOR acts as both the Pope's personally owned

Archbishop Paul "The Gorilla" Marcinkus (far left) acted as a bodyguard to the Pope before obtaining a position of power in the Vatican that he used for criminal purposes.

bank and the national bank of the Vatican City, in its role as an independent state. Maintaining accounts for clerics and religious organizations across the world, it controls and has access to billions of dollars of funds.

It was in 1971 that Marcinkus also became a member of the P2 Freemasonry lodge (also known as the Propaganda Due Lodge) that had been set up as part of CIA director James Jesus Angleton's secret Gladio network in Italy. Despite the fact that his faith expressly forbade him from becoming a Freemason, it was through P2 that Marcinkus met fellow Mason, Michele "The Shark" Sindona. Renowned as a major Sicilian Mafia banker and lawyer, Sindona began to advise Marcinkus on Vatican investments.

In 1972, Sindona purchased a controlling interest in New York's Franklin National Bank and used it to begin laundering Mafia money. As the bank began to collapse, due to fraud and bad foreign currency speculation, Sindona entered into a deal with the American and Italian Mafias to distribute $950 million of counterfeit stock certificates. It emerged that Marcinkus, acting for the IOR, had purchased nearly $100 million of the worthless stock. As evidence of the scandal surfaced, New York District Attorney Frank Hogan tried to extradite Marcinkus to the US to face charges over the fraud. The Vatican used political pressure to block the extradition request and refused to remove Marcinkus as President of the IOR.

Being involved in one Mafia banking plot should have made Marcinkus more careful about the friends he made in P2. Unfortunately for the Vatican he was not. Marcinkus made IOR the major shareholder in the Banco Ambrosiano, run by Roberto Calvi. The Archbishop also became the co-owner, with Calvi, of the Cisalpine Bank in the Bahamas that Calvi used to launder Italian Mafia drug profits. It was just one of a number of "ghost banks" set up by both men to handle millions of dollars of illicit money. By the time it was discovered, in 1982, the Banco Ambrosiano could not account for more than $1.287 billion. Calvi fled Italy, only to be found dead within weeks in London.

Despite having embroiled the Vatican in the biggest banking scandal of the twentieth century and made it responsible for hundreds of millions of dollars' worth of Banco Ambrosiano's debts, Marcinkus remained president of the IOR until 1989. When authorities again tried to extradite the Archbishop for questioning, Pope John Paul II made him Pro-President of the Vatican City (effectively both Mayor of Vatican City and its Prime Minister), a position equivalent to that of many heads of state and therefore exempt from legal proceedings.

Marcinkus had proven a useful friend to the Mafia, but it is unclear whether he actually benefited from the relationship. His own friends in high places, however, prevented any harm from coming to him – possibly their actions were tempered by remembering Marcinkus's own words: "You can't run the Church on Hail Marys alone".

MONEY LAUNDERING

Money laundering is often defined in law as "engaging in financial transactions in order to conceal the source or destination of illegitimately acquired money" – in short, the method of legitimizing ill-gotten gains. With hundreds of billions a year in illicit profits to legitimize, money laundering has become a central operation for most modern criminal groups.

Money laundering is usually a three-stage process involving placement, layering and integration. Placement is the initial point of entry for funds that are derived from criminal activities. Layering is the creation of complex networks of transactions to obscure the link between the initial funds and the end of the laundering cycle. Integration is the return of funds to the legitimate economy for extraction.

There is some debate as to whether the term "laundering" comes simply from describing the process of making "dirty cash" clean, or if it relates to the Chicago Syndicate's 1930s use of Laundromats to transform proceeds from its criminal activities into legitimate income. Laundromats were used because all the money entering them was in coins so it was easy to add additional cash to the takings, thus disguising the original source of the income.

Many of the money laundering practices in use today originated with National Crime Syndicate boss Meyer Lansky. He took advantage of 1934 changes in Swiss banking laws to move millions of dollars worth of his and Cosa Nostra money through a chain of holding companies into a Swiss bank he secretly controlled. These days, one of the more recent, innovative ways for global gangs to launder funds is through football clubs and its lucrative player transfer market.

KEY FIGURES

13

"There's no such thing as the underworld – just known criminals."

Tommy Wisbey, Great Train Robber

According to most of the detectives I have spoken to in the last 15 years, the best criminals are the ones the public never get to know about. After all, if you are involved in organized crime, it pays to try and hide your identity and activities from the authorities and the press. As one of the villains I interviewed while researching this book, Zef Nano, said, "If they know you, they can catch you". If you become a "face", the chances of spending time behind bars escalates.

The majority of criminals know the benefit of a low profile. They succeed in remaining invisible to those who lack an intimate knowledge of the underworld. Those with true criminal power and wealth rarely feel the need to flaunt it and attract attention. There have always been villains, however, who lack this bit of basic common sense. American organized crime's "Gangsta" style is not new; it has just evolved from the silk shirts, sharp suits and rings of the Chicago Mob in the 1920s to the designer labels and flashy jewellery of the early twenty-first century. Ironically, it is often this type of attention-seeking criminal that is most quickly forgotten by the public.

Yet there remain some organized criminals whose outrageous activities, flamboyant lifestyles and historical importance end up legendary, not only to the police and other gangsters, but to the world at large. They escape the confines of the criminal fraternity to become iconic, internationally known figures. The villains remembered through the decades are those whose deeds make them important rather than the expensive clothes they wear. They are known not because they wished to be, but because their crimes made them key figures in the times they lived.

AL CAPONE

Al Capone is possibly the most famous organized crime figure of the twentieth century. Beyond defining the ideas of gangster and Mafia in the minds of most Americans (despite the fact that he was never a member of the Mafia), Capone's infamy has spread worldwide. From the streets of London's East End, to the Trenchtown neighbourhood of Kingston, Jamaica, he has acted as an inspiration to aspiring villains while his criminal legacy still echoes decades after his death.

Yet Capone's iconic status has led to most people holding a rather two-dimensional view of him. He is Al "Scarface" Capone, the unruly killer and Mob boss of countless 1930s gangster movies and later television shows, such *The Untouchables*. He is the cigar smoking, fedora- and overcoat-wearing Capone from hundreds of archive photographs of Chicago in the Roaring Twenties. He is the definitive symbol of Prohibition America, the epitome of thuggery. With all these second-hand perceptions, the real Capone gets lost and the mythic being is often all that remains.

Aphonsus Gabriel Capone was born in Brooklyn, New York, in 1899. His father was a barber from a village near Naples and his mother was a seamstress from the province of Salerno. Capone would fly into a rage if anyone called him Italian, bellowing, "I'm a goddamn American". This is significant, as is the fact he did not join the Camorra gangs he was entitled to with his Neapolitan heritage. When he formed his Outfit in Chicago there were no initiation rituals or even a whiff of a secret society. Capone did not look to the past to legitimize the present, he did not trade off his Italian ancestry. Capone was a product of the United States and his brand of organized crime was a product of its time.

Capone was born into the harsh conditions of immigrant poverty. At one point his parents and 11 brothers and sisters shared a tenement flat with no indoor toilet or furniture. He grew up in a multi-ethnic neighbourhood and married an Irish girl. Dropping the various swindles he worked after leaving school at 14, Capone tried a legitimate life for the sake of his wife and young son. For a while he prospered as a bookkeeper, a role that made the most of his skill with figures. His return to crime was largely a result of having to support his family as his father's health failed from 1916 onwards.

Capone earned his famous scar in a fight that resulted from insulting the sister of fellow hood Frank Gallucio by saying, "Honey, you have a nice ass". Capone hated the nickname (he preferred "Snorky", a slang term meaning well-dressed) and claimed he learnt much about controlling his temper through the incident. He also demonstrated his magnanimity by making Gallucio his bodyguard in later years. Despite deserving his reputation as a vicious killer, Capone was unusual for a Mob boss of that age, as he did not believe in vendettas. He offered everyone forgiveness and a second chance, but to cross him more than once was a guarantee of death. He preferred peace to war, but if it came he would always win through well-planned, well-executed butchery.

Capone was also the American underworld's first equal opportunities employer. He never discriminated on ethnicity or religion – he saw organized crime in business terms and anyone who made money and was loyal to him was welcomed into his family. Capone understood politics, publicity and popularity as well as any politician and prospered through skilful manipulation as well as bribery. So powerful was his criminal empire, Cosa Nostra had to recognize his independent, non-Sicilian American operation. Capone's official contribution to organized crime ended when he was jailed for tax evasion, in 1931, but the American Mafia learnt much from

Despite his fearsome reputation, Al Capone preferred to be called by the nickname "Snorky" rather the sobriquet "Scarface" that was earned during his early years as a New York tough guy.

the way he conducted his affairs that can still be seen today.

If Capone had left prison a sane and well man, his impact may have directly shaped the Mob post-Prohibition, but it was not to be – syphilis, not imprisonment, destroyed Capone. In his final years of decline, with his mental condition deteriorating, he was racked by guilt for giving congenital syphilis to his son and constantly "saw" the ghost of James Clark, one of the victims of the St Valentine's Day Massacre. A

hollow wreck of a man by the time of his death in 1947, Capone's biggest personal tragedy may have been that he was oblivious to the fact that his legacy and legend would endure.

Capone leaves the Federal Building in Chicago after being convicted of evading income tax in December 1931. Imprisonment marked the start of his decline in power and sanity.

"LUCKY" LUCIANO

There has never been a more powerful and infamous crime boss in the history of Cosa Nostra than Charles "Lucky" Luciano. If anyone can claim to have created the modern Mafia in America, it was Lucky.

Arriving in the US as a child of nine, he was born in 1897, in Lercara Friddi, Sicily, as Salvatore Lucania (he changed his name to Charles Luciano to spare his family the shame of reading about him in the press). In 1915, at the age of 18, Luciano was arrested for the first time for running a heroin ring. Within the next year, he had established himself not only as a major drug dealer, but also as a powerful pimp. His drug dealing brought him into contact with the Jewish gangs who dominated narcotics in New York at the time and he forged friendships with members such as Meyer Lansky and Benjamin "Bugsy" Siegel.

When the Eighteenth Amendment came into force in 1920, and Prohibition began, Luciano diversified into bootlegging. Working first with Jacob "Little Augie" Orgen, he later began working for the Mafia family of Giuseppe "Joe The Boss" Masseria. He quickly became Masseria's right-hand man, running his alcohol, narcotics and prostitution operations.

In the late 1920s, Masseria fought a bitter turf war against Salvatore Maranzano, who had been sent from Sicily to manage the American-based crime families. As Masseria's lieutenant, Luciano found himself right in the middle of the bloody conflict that became known as the Castellammarese War (after Maranzano's Sicilian hometown).

One night, in 1929, Maranzano sent four of his men to kill Luciano. They grabbed him from the docks where he was inspecting a shipment

of heroin. He was driven to Staten Island where he was beaten to a pulp, had his throat cut and his cheek slashed, before they dumped him in a ditch and left him for dead. Luciano, however, survived the death trip and earned his legendary nickname of "Lucky".

In order to convince the younger gang members on all sides of the bitter conflict (which had already claimed the lives of 50 men) that the war was pointless and should be brought to a swift end, Luciano set up his own boss. On April 15, 1931, he arranged to play cards with Masseria in a Coney Island restaurant. When Luciano went to the bathroom, he gave the signal for his allies – Albert Anastastia, Joe Adonis, Vito Genovese, Meyer Lansky and Benjamin Siegel – to burst in and kill Masseria in a hail of bullets.

Luciano assumed control of Masseria's empire and quickly arranged peace with Maranzano, who got the bootlegging action while Luciano kept the girls and the narcotics. In return, Luciano was made his second in command, while Maranzano announced that he was now the Capo di Tutti Capi (the Boss of Bosses) of the New York Sicilian Mafia. Within four months, using four Jewish hitmen posing as policemen, Luciano had had Maranzano murdered, thus ending Sicilian control of the US Mafia. He then assumed control of Maranzano's empire and used it as his power base to create the National Crime Syndicate and bring the Jewish gangs into a formal alliance with the Cosa Nostra.

The next five years saw Luciano live a life of unparalleled excess and power, as the head of a consolidated national criminal network. With the brains of Lansky behind him and the muscle of Siegel and Murder Inc. (the enforcement arm of the National Crime Syndicate), his grip on power was secure. However, in 1936, mob-busting Special Prosecutor Thomas E. Dewey bribed more than 30 prostitutes to testify and managed to ensure that Luciano received a 30-year sentence for pandering.

Luciano continued to run his empire from prison and, in 1946, in return for services provided to the US military and intelligence service during the invasion of Sicily, he was paroled and deported to Italy. Later that year he attended the meeting of the National Crime Syndicate bosses in Havana. When Vito Genovese suggested that he was past it and should step down from power, Luciano leapt on him and beat him so severely that three of his ribs were broken.

In 1957, when Luciano discovered Genovese was arranging to have him killed, he ensured that Vito was convicted on selling drugs and put in prison. However, his failing health, combined with his exile in Italy, saw him gradually losing power. Ironically for a man who had arranged the brutal deaths of hundreds of men, Lucky died not from an assassin's bullet, but from a heart attack, in 1962.

Charles "Lucky" Luciano (centre), accompanied by a number of close associates, enjoys a walk in Palermo, Sicily during his enforced exile after being deported from America.

MEYER LANSKY

It may have been "Lucky" Luciano who has gone down in crime history as the godfather of the American Mafia, but Cosa Nostra would not exist in the form it does today if Luciano had not had the brains of Meyer Lansky behind him.

It is impossible to overstate Lansky's contribution. From the current rituals of Cosa Nostra to the structure of the National Crime Syndicate and the creation of Murder Inc., there is not a single major element of the American Mafia he did not influence. His fellow senior Mob bosses called him "the Little Man", but there was no disparagement in the nickname. They always listened to Lansky's advice. He may not have been a Sicilian, or even an Italian, but throughout his entire criminal career, Lansky was never excluded from any significant Cosa Nostra decision for being a Polish American Jew – his input was too valuable to miss.

Meyer Lansky was born Maier Suchowliński in Grodno, Russian-occupied Poland in 1902. His family emigrated to the US in 1911, anglicising their name to Lansky and moving into the tough Lower East Side of Manhattan. As a teenager he supplemented his meagre wages by taking part in the street gambling scene. By the age of 16, he was already known as a shtarke – a strong arm man who looked after the craps games and who was willing to commit violence for a price.

It was in a fight over a craps game that Lansky first met his lifelong friend, Benjamin "Bugsy" Siegel. Despite being opposites in many ways, the flash and brawn of Siegel gelled with the studious, low-key approach of Lansky, and they became inseparable partners in crime. Even before Prohibition, the Bugs and Meyer gang was already extorting money from Jewish, Italian and Irish businesses on the Lower East Side, distributing drugs and running a car theft ring.

When Prohibition came in, Lansky could see that transporting illegal alcohol was going to be a major money maker, so he approached Albert "the Fixer" Rothstein for a loan to buy a trucking company and warehouse. Bugs and Meyer soon established themselves as the best hijackers and transporters in New York. They also had a profitable sideline in "slammings" – murdering for a fee. Rothstein took Lansky under his wing, introducing him to his idea of a united national organized crime body. At the same time, Rothstein was also imparting his wisdom to "Lucky" Luciano, whom Meyer and Siegel had already encountered and become close friends with.

After Rothstein's murder in 1928, it was Luciano and Lansky who, together, were able to make his vision a reality. Yet it was Lansky alone who developed many of the key systems and details that made it work. It was Lansky who brought the major Jewish organized crime operations, such as Detroit's Purple Gang, into the National Crime Syndicate and who insisted that Luciano keep its name and retain some of the Sicilian trappings, pointing out, "No one goes into a showroom and asks for the car made by the company with no name, you got to give people something to hold onto". Lansky also developed Murder Inc. to help them retain their hold on power.

Luciano credited Lansky as "the biggest brain" and the man who could "look around corners". Lansky helped lead the American Mafia into gambling and drugs, foreseeing the profits from Prohibition drying up. His ability to think and plan also saw him advising his fellow gang bosses on how to launder their money post-Capone's imprisonment for tax evasion. He was the first Mobster to open a Swiss bank account, in 1934, and the first to actually own a foreign bank. Lansky's key status and ultimate legacy rests on the fact that he helped the Syndicate make more money after 1933 than anyone else.

Lansky maintained a key role in running the National Crime Syndicate until he "retired" in 1970. Ironically, having kept a low profile during his prime crime years, it was only in 1972, when he was extradited from Israel, that Lansky faced criminal charges. After he was found not guilty of tax evasion in 1974, the FBI gave up on its attempts to put him behind bars, with one agent commenting, "He's a genius. He would have been chairman of General Motors if he had gone legitimate". By the time he died in 1983, Lansky's legitimate business holdings were worth more than $400 million. No one knows how much he had in his Swiss banks accounts.

A relaxed looking Meyer Lansky (right) turns up to a Florida court with his attorney in 1978. The man who "looked around corners" may have been America's all-time most successful mobster.

DUTCH SCHULTZ

One of the Jewish mobsters Meyer Lansky brought into the National Crime Syndicate was Dutch Schultz. Some claim it was the only mistake Meyer ever made in his criminal career. However, given the power that Dutch Schultz wielded in New York in the early 1930s, Lansky, Luciano and the other organized crime bosses had little choice, unless they wanted war with possibly the most brutal killer in American criminal history.

Schultz was born Arthur Flegenheimer, in 1902, to Jewish German American parents living in the Bronx. When he was 14, his father deserted the family and Schultz took to crime to support himself and his beloved mother. He started out by robbing craps games before turning to burglary. At 17, he received his only prison sentence for breaking into a Bronx apartment. When his violent behaviour saw him transferred to a higher security prison, he quickly escaped and went on the run.

After he had been recaptured and served his time, Flegenheimer found his tough guy antics had earned him the moniker of a legendary dead Bronx tough guy, Dutch Schultz. He joked that he stuck with the name because, "Flegenheimer wouldn't have fitted in the newspaper headlines". Schultz's later crimes certainly made those headlines.

During the start of Prohibition, Dutch started out driving a truck for Albert Rothstein and working for club owner and bootlegger Jack "Legs" Diamond, before striking out on his own. By 1928, Schultz had put together a gang of Jewish and Irish hoods that brought him complete control of the Bronx beer distribution. If you ran a speakeasy in his territory, you bought your beer from Dutch or you did not breathe any more. When his old boss Diamond crossed him, Schultz had him blown away, commenting to journalists, "He was just another punk with his hands in my pockets".

Known as psychotic, even by the Mafia's standards, being one of his 100-plus shooting victims was preferable to suffering any of Schultz's more exotic retributions. In 1929, Schultz punished one speakeasy owner who stood up to him – Joe Rock – by kidnapping him, hanging him from his thumbs by meat hooks and then smearing his face with a piece of cloth covered in gonorrhoea discharge, thus causing Rock to go blind. Strangely, Schultz claimed his crime career was part of a "spiritual quest".

Sensing that Prohibition would not be around forever, Schultz expanded into gambling. He forced clubs to take his slot machines and took over the numbers racket in Harlem, forcing the local hoods to act as his agents. With the aid of disgraced accountant and mathematical genius Otto "Abbadabba" Berman, he found a way to ensure he almost never had to pay out to any suckers that gambled on the numbers.

By the end of Prohibition, Schultz was worth more than $12 million. He was notoriously mean, though, commenting, "I think only

queers wear silk shirts. A guy's a sucker if he spends $15 on a shirt when he could get a good one for a buck". His inability to share his profits with his men led to a bitter, bloody war against former gang member Vincent "Mad Dog" Coll, who formed his own group against his former boss. In 1932, after two years and numerous shoot-outs, including one in which a five-year-old child died in the crossfire, Schultz's gunmen caught Coll in a phone booth and let rip with a hail of fire that cut his body in half.

Facing constant harassment from Special Prosecutor Thomas E. Dewey, Schultz went to the National Crime Syndicate, in 1935, to ask for permission to assassinate Dewey. They refused, fearing the heat it would generate. When it became clear that Schultz was going to ignore them, however, they ordered a Murder Inc. team to take care of him. Surprised, he was shot while using the washroom at the Palace Chop

Despite being shot by a Murder Inc. team while he was using the toilets in a restaurant, Schultz managed to pull up his trousers, call for help and stagger back to his table before collapsing.

House in Newark, in October, 1935. Schultz staggered to his feet, did up his trousers and then made it to a table before collapsing.

Running a fever and delirious on morphine, Schultz hovered between life and death for two days. Undergoing a deathbed conversion to Catholicism, his bizarre ramblings later formed the inspiration for works by Beat poets and the writer William S. Burroughs. Among Schultz's last words before he died were, "Please crack down on the Chinaman's friends and Hitler's commander… The Baron does these things… The Chimney Sweeps. Talk to the Sword… French Canadian bean soup".

"BUGSY" SIEGEL

Before his death at the hands of Murder Inc., Dutch Schultz had hired the services of the National Crime Syndicate's killers to take care of gangster Bo Weinburg, who was attempting to move onto his turf. Murder Inc., gave the job to their most sure-fire killer – "Bugsy" Siegel.

Within hours of getting the order, Siegel pistol-whipped Weinburg to unconsciousness, placed his body in a stolen car and then pushed the vehicle into New York's East River. Schultz let Siegel know he was impressed, little knowing that a few months later Siegel would be planning his execution with similar efficiency.

Although fixed somewhat erroneously in popular consciousness as the Mafia man who single-handedly created Las Vegas, Bugsy Siegel's key role in the history of American organized crime is as its most important hitman. While others killed in higher numbers and more viciously, it was the murders Siegel committed and arranged on behalf of his good friends, "Lucky" Luciano and Meyer Lansky, that allowed the pair to create the National Crime Syndicate. It was Siegel's work that rubbed out both Giuseppe "Joe The Boss" Masseria and Salvatore Maranzano in order to clear the path for Luciano to become de facto Boss of Bosses. It was Siegel's team of killers that became the core of the Syndicate's guarantee of power in the early years – Murder Inc..

Born Benjamin Hymen Siegelbaum, in 1906, to Austrian émigrés living in the Bronx, Siegel earned his nickname "Bugsy" (meaning totally crazed) by the age of ten. He and another precocious ten-year-old hoodlum ran an extortion racket, where they threatened to set fire to street vendors' carts unless they were paid a dollar each. The name came when Siegel proved that he was willing to do it right in front of those who did not cough up. Siegel, however, hated the moniker and would beat up anyone who said it to his face, thereby undermining his lifelong attempt to shake it.

It was Siegel's propensity for violence and coolness when killing, teamed with longstanding friend Meyer Lansky's criminal brainpower, that propelled their jointly controlled gang to its powerful position in Prohibition New York. Throughout the 1920s, both men saved each other's lives dozens of times though it remains unclear who saved whom when they became involved in the altercation with Luciano that eventually led to all three becoming pals.

A fear of Siegel's tendency to "go bugs" and a desire not to give Lansky too much power meant that the National Crime Syndicate baulked at him being put in charge of Murder Inc.. However, in its early days, Siegel remained one of the key planners and gunmen, before Luciano and Lansky decided to send their friend out west, in 1937, to take control of Syndicate gambling operations in California. The boss of the LA Mafia, Jack Dragna, did not object too strongly, figuring it was unwise to go against someone of Siegel's reputation, especially when he was backed by Luciano.

Siegel soon ensured that money was rolling in for the Mob back east and got on with living the LA highlife. His charm, good looks and wealth soon saw him surrounded by a circle of Hollywood friends, including stars like Clark Gable, Jean Harlow and George Raft. Alongside his long-term mistress, Virginia Hill (who had once been Capone's accountant), he simultaneously dated actress Wendy Barrie and Italian aristocrat Countess Dorothy diFrasso. It was through diFrasso that Siegel met Hermann Goering and Joseph Goebbels, while

"Bugsy" Siegel was the archetypal glamorous gangster. With Hollywood screen tests, film star and aristocratic girlfriends, the cold-blooded killer earned a reputation as one of the Mob's ladies' men.

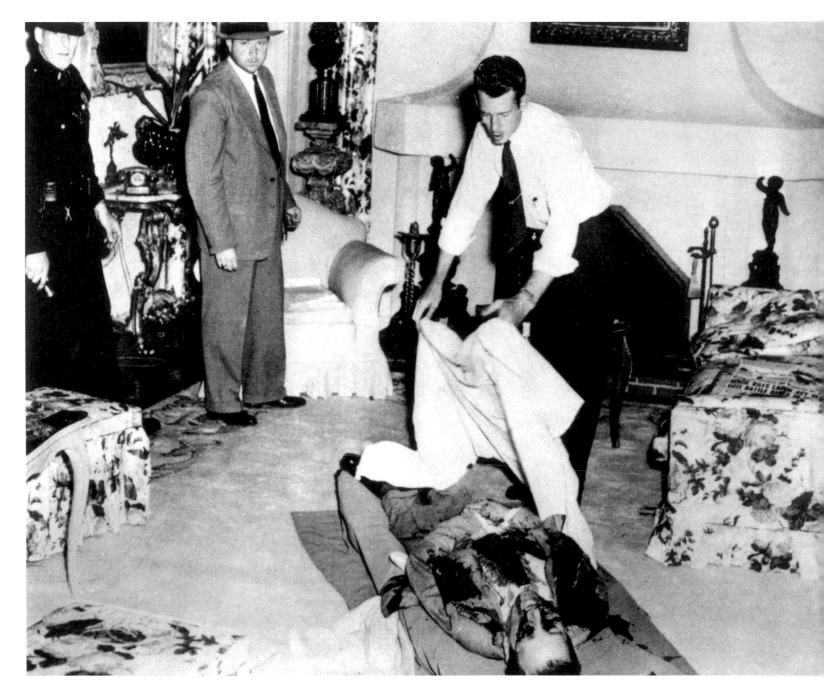

in Italy in the 1930s. He was only restrained from killing them by a pleading Countess and because he had a larger plan to kill Mussolini.

It was Siegel's plans for Las Vegas that led to the sequence of falling dominos that saw both Lansky and Luciano turn against him and order his death. Siegel persuaded Mob bosses to invest more than $6 million in his luxury hotel and casino, The Flamingo. Its poor performance in the first few months of operation in 1947, and the suspicion that Siegel had skimmed more than a million from its construction costs, led to Lansky himself ordering Murder, Inc. to carry out a hit on his old friend.

When Siegel's Mob bosses and old friends turned on him, his fate was sealed and nothing could prevent one of the Mafia's key killers from suffering a similar fate to his many victims.

Believing he had more time to sort things out, on June 20, 1947, Siegel was relaxing in the living room of his Beverly Hills mansion when two bullets tore through a window. They caught him in the face with such force that his left eye was found 15ft (4.5m) away in another room. The Mafia's key killer was dead.

SAM GIANCANA

"Bugsy" Siegel was not the only senior American Mafia figure who hated his nickname because it suggested he was not entirely mentally stable. Chicago Syndicate boss Sam Giancana earned the moniker "Mooney" because his fellow gangsters considered him to be "a total lunatic", and they were not the only ones who felt that way. During one of the 70 arrests in his career in organized crime, a detective in a police report described Giancana as "A snarling, sarcastic, ill-tempered psychopath". Not surprisingly, Giancana preferred the alternative nickname "Momo".

Giancana was born Salvatore Giancana, in Chicago's Little Italy, in 1908. In and out of reform school throughout his teenage years, in 1921 he joined the notorious street gang, The 42s. By the time he was 20, Giancana had been the prime suspect in three murders and spent time in prison for auto theft, assault and burglary. Like most members of The 42s, he hoped to graduate to a role in Capone's Outfit and took every opportunity possible to do criminal jobs for those in the organization.

Most of the time, the only jobs Giancana got were stealing cars to be used in hits, but he eventually began to be used as a getaway driver and hitman himself. Giancana earned a reputation as an unstoppable "wheel man" and a ruthless killer, alongside the "Mooney" moniker, and he

came to the attention of trusted Capone lieutenants Paul Ricca and Tony Accardo. As Giancana advanced through the ranks, with the help of mentors Accardo and Ricca, he brought old colleagues from The 42s into his operations to ensure that he had a strong base of loyal supporters.

As Capone's old guard fell away in the 1950s, Giancana was able to take control of the Outfit. He had support, both from the young blood he brought into it through The 42s and from key elder statesmen who felt that, as long as Accardo and Ricca were around as advisers to keep his craziness in line, he was the best bet for boss. The first few years of his reign were good for the Outfit. He expanded their gambling operations in Las Vegas, Cuba and Mexico; took control of the Chicago rackets that had been in the hands of black gangs; and expanded the Outfit's union and loan sharking operations.

However, Giancana's "Mooney" side soon started to come to the fore. He ordered a hit on Desi Arnaz for producing the TV show *The Untouchables* (Accardo ensured the killing did not go ahead), and began working with the CIA on harebrained schemes to assassinate Fidel Castro. Giancana also developed an obsession with the Kennedys. The Outfit had helped JFK to gain the Democratic Party Presidential candidacy and had helped steal the election for Kennedy over Nixon in 1960, through widespread electoral fraud in Illinois. Giancana had hoped this would mean Robert F. Kennedy would drop his anti-Mafia crusade. Instead, one of the first things RFK did when his brother made him Attorney General was tell senior Justice Department aides, "I want that dago Sam Giancana put away for good".

Giancana may also have had personal reasons for hating both of the Kennedy brothers. At one point he was sleeping with Kennedy's mistress Judith Campbell and also enjoying a relationship with Marilyn Monroe, who had been close to both JFK and RFK. His fellow gangsters began to worry about Giancana's high profile friendships with celebrities, such as Frank Sinatra and Phyllis McGuire, as well as his attempts to pursue a campaign against both the President and Attorney General. In 1965, after serving a year in prison for refusing to testify to a Grand Jury, Accardo made Giancana resign and retire to Mexico.

In 1974, he was captured by the Mexican police and returned to the United States to give evidence to the US Senate Intelligence Committee concerning CIA plots against Castro. Once again he was becoming a key figure for the wrong reasons. The CIA and the Mob were both worried he would "pull a Mooney" and spill secrets. On June 19, 1975, someone made sure that this did not happen and Giancana was shot six times at point blank range in his own home. As the news broke, sources in the Chicago Outfit close to its then boss Joseph "Joey Doves" Aiuppa and CIA Director William Colby both claimed, "We had nothing to do with it".

Despite his reputation as a "psychopath", Sam Giancana was able to run the Chicago Outfit, survive Robert F. Kennedy's attempts to destroy him and engineer an alliance between the Mob and the CIA.

LOAN SHARKING

Loan sharking, defined as the lending of money at inflated and illegal rates of interest, is a common source of income for organized crime groups across the world. From the Yakuza to the crime gangs that are associated with Republican and Loyalist terrorist groups in Northern Ireland, there is barely a criminal network that does not derive a steady income from the practice.

Loan sharking needs three things in order to work – money, borrowers who have no other access to credit, and the ability to enforce the debt without recourse to the legal system. It is not uncommon for rates of more than 500% interest to be charged, so a simple $20 debt can lead to a decade of repayments totalling more than $1250.

Gangsters, who are rarely short of money, have little problem in finding borrowers from among the impoverished, who cannot obtain credit from legitimate financial bodies. Those borrowing money put themselves up as collateral. If the gangster's threat of violence does not produce payment, brutal reminders – often the wounding of the debtor's family – usually produce the cash.

Despite its other, more sophisticated, illicit operations, Cosa Nostra still obtains huge sums from loan sharking and leading figures, such as Vincent "Chin" Gigante and Alphonse "Allie" Persico, have been prosecuted for receiving millions in usurious profits. However, not all loan sharking is aimed at the poor. In Italy, in 1999, Cardinal Michele Giordano faced charges over links to organized crime and for charging interest at 300% to Neapolitan businesses.

SANTO TRAFFICANTE JR

Santo Trafficante Jr has many Cosa Nostra claims to fame. Despite being one of the authorities most targeted Mob figures in the last 60 years, he has never served time in a US prison. Trafficante Jr was one of the few American Mafia bosses to inherit the role from his father and yet still have the cunning and force of personality to make a success of his time as an organized godfather. Junior was also the last of the old style dons still active in the game as late as the 1980s.

However, the thing that makes him such a key figure in the history of American organized crime is the bad publicity he attracted during his three decades as boss of the Tampa Mafia family. The constant press, political and FBI scrutiny meant that he became fixed in the public's mind as one of the major Cosa Nostra players in a raft of real and alleged crimes. From control of Florida's gambling and heroin smuggling to the assassination of President Kennedy, Trafficante Jr is the name that has consistently been placed in the frame.

Organized crime in Tampa and Florida benefited more than most from Prohibition. Rum-running from Cuba and the Bahamas made the state an illicit goldmine for gangs during the 1920s and early 1930s. As the National Crime Syndicate came to power and Prohibition ended, Florida became home to the gambling interests of many New York mobsters, including Lucky Luciano and Meyer Lansky. However, the Tampa crime family was not eased entirely out of the picture – it had its own gambling empire and other rackets, and was already heavily involved with drug trafficking.

While his father, Santo Trafficante Sr, was running the Tampa family between 1940 and 1954, Junior was sent to Havana to develop casino, nightclub and smuggling interest on the island. Trafficante Jr was his father's representative at the legendary Havana Syndicate conference of 1946, and ensured a steady stream of profits back to the mainland. When his father died in 1954, he was a popular choice to step into the role of boss. Despite several attempts to prosecute him for running illegal lotteries and bribery in Florida, it was not until 1957 that Junior had his first brush with bad publicity at a national level. Arrested at the Apalachin conference fiasco, he was subsequently questioned over the murder of Albert Anastasia.

In 1959, when Castro overthrew Batista, Trafficante found himself thrown into a Cuban jail. He was not there long. Within weeks, he had a personal meeting with Castro and, uniquely, was allowed to leave Cuba and even take with him the considerable amounts of cash that he had held in Cuban banks. Although taking a massive loss on a now worthless Cuban casino and other investments, Trafficante and the Tampa family bounced back. Within a decade, their fortunes had been revived, thanks to Trafficante making them one of the largest importers of heroin into the US.

Trafficante enjoyed notoriety throughout the 1960s by being profiled in *Life* magazine as one of America's top mobsters and being publicly named by Mafia member and FBI informer Joe Valachi. In 1966, he was even photographed having dinner with New Orleans Mafia boss Carlos Marcello in a New York restaurant. However, he rocketed in the infamy stakes, in 1975, when he was called to give evidence to Senate hearings on CIA attempts to assassinate Castro. While admitting his role under questioning, others suspect Trafficante did nothing more than take money for plots he never attempted and actually informed Castro what was going on. These revelations were followed up by a further scandal, in 1978, when he was called before the House Select Committee on Assassinations about his possible role in the murder of President Kennedy. Trafficante explained his 1962 comment that "Kennedy was going to get hit" to another Mafia member was merely speculation about Kennedy's re-election chances in 1964.

Despite revelations about his work with the CIA in the Iran-Contra scandal and being summoned to court in New York, in 1986, to testify about his involvement with the Bonanno crime family, Trafficante continued to stay in charge of his family and evade prison. The FBI continued sting operations and investigations right up until his death in 1987, but was never able to catch the man the American public believed was blatantly guilty of running organized crime.

Santo Trafficante Junior entering court, in 1966. Trafficante seemed to have a magical "get out of jail free" card, despite being involved in some of the Mafia's most notorious crimes.

JOHN GOTTI

The success of the FBI and other law enforcement agencies against the American Mafia from the 1980s onwards has revealed hundreds of names of more major Mafiosi. Yet in this wealth of exposed information and successfully charged bosses and underbosses, only one key figure seemed to emerge in the public's imagination – John Gotti, head of New York's Gambino crime family.

The sobriquets given to Gotti by the press and public have turned him into an almost mythical Mafia figure. To headline writers he was "The Dapper Don" and "The Teflon Don". To the many ordinary citizens he was simply "the King of New York". However, beyond the suave appearance and savvy media tactics, many innately sensed what his organized crime colleagues already knew as harsh fact – Gotti was a true throwback to the old style Cosa Nostra bosses.

The man whose underworld role model was Albert Anastasia came through the Cosa Nostra ranks the traditional way – wading through blood and dealing bullets as a hitman. When he seized control of the Gambino gang, it was through an old fashioned, bloody coup and he controlled his crime family with an iron fist. Gambino members knew Gotti was not joking when he told one of his men, who did not return his telephone calls quickly enough, "Follow orders or I'll blow your house up".

As a wild Bronx teenager in the 1950s, Gotti began his life in organized crime by running errands for local mobsters. He became part of a group of hoods reporting to Gambino capo Aniello "Neil" Dellacroce, who operated out of the Ozone Park neighbourhood of Queens. Gotti became a Dellacroce favourite thanks to successful hijacks of trucks leaving Kennedy International Airport packed with expensive goods.

However, Gotti's real rise in status came when he avenged the death of boss Carlo Gambino's murdered nephew in 1972. The boy had been kidnapped by Irish gangster James McBratney who had killed the boy despite receiving a ransom of $350,000. Gotti pulled the trigger on McBratney himself when he cornered him in a Staten Island bar. Gotti was arrested and served seven years for the killing, but on his release, in 1979, was rewarded by being named as a capo.

Throughout the reign of Gambino boss Paul Castellano, Gotti was constantly threatening to take over the family. Only underboss and old friend Dellacroce held him back. Within days of Dellacroce's death, in December, 1985, Gotti personally led an 11-man hit squad that wiped out Castellano and, in one bloody swoop, made him boss. Gotti survived an attempted revenge bombing carried out by Genovese boss Vincent "Chin" Gigante and was soon in firm control of the Gambino family.

In 1987, Gotti became the first Cosa Nostra boss to successfully beat racketeering charges brought through the 1970 RICO Act, earning him the title of "The Teflon Don", as the charges never stuck. At his court appearances he always held doors open for lady journalists, wore $2,000 hand-tailored suits and gave snappy sound bites. This turned him into a media star. The

John Gotti was one of the most high profile Mafia bosses seen since the days of Prohibition and became a folk hero to many people.

large, free street parties and festivals he arranged in Queens, along with keeping down street crime in his neighbourhood, made him a folk hero. However, he was less popular with his men, who were worried about his arrogance in the face of FBI surveillance.

In 1992, the Feds prosecuted Gotti on 13 counts of murder, conspiracy to commit murder, loansharking, racketeering, obstruction of justice, illegal gambling, and tax evasion. The Teflon coating started to peel off when the FBI persuaded Gotti's underboss, Salvatore "Sammy The Bull" Gravano, to testify against him. They also rolled out hundreds of hours of incriminating audio surveillance tapes.

The jurors and judge were unimpressed by the daily protests by the "John Gotti" fan club – members of the public who felt the Don was a persecuted hero. They were also not swayed by a bizarre array of character witnesses who came forward for Gotti, including actor Al Lewis (best known for his role as Grandpa in *The Munsters*). The Don was sentenced to life imprisonment without possibility of parole.

Gotti's mental health quickly declined as he endured 23 hours of solitary confinement every day. Within two years of imprisonment, Gotti was no longer a key player in his family, or in fact anywhere else outside of his disintegrating mind. When death from throat cancer claimed him in 2002, many of those attending his lavish, celebrity-style funeral felt it had come as a kindness to the former King of New York.

CARLOS ENRIQUE LEHDER RIVAS

Calling Carlos Enrique Lehder Rivas a significant figure in the history of twentieth-century organized crime is like saying Muhammad Ali is slightly famous for boxing or the President of the United States is mildly powerful. Lehder was key to the 1970s' US cocaine boom: without him it is possible the Colombian cartels would not have emerged as significant criminal networks and players in the global drug trade.

Born in the USA, in 1949, of Colombian and German parents, Lehder started as a strictly small-time criminal. Dealing in tiny quantities of marijuana and smuggling stolen vehicles between America and Canada, his main source of income came from his legitimate business as a used car dealer. In 1973, while serving time for car theft in a federal prison in Danbury, Connecticut, Lehder shared a cell with marijuana smuggler George Jung.

Being cellmates, they swapped stories to pass the time. Jung related how he had made $100,000 a time smuggling marijuana from Mexico by piloting a small plane below radar levels and had been caught delivering more than 100lbs (45kg) of it to the Playboy Mansion. Lehder had the idea of applying Jung's method of narcotics transportation to cocaine, which traditionally was brought into the US via human "mules", or Cosa Nostra controlled shipments. When both men were paroled they began a partnership that began to revolutionize cocaine trafficking and Colombian organized crime.

Within months, they owned several planes and were regularly smuggling more cocaine into the US than most Colombian drug distributors could smuggle in several years with their mules. The quality and quantity of the cocaine they imported led to the drug's price falling as its popularity and accessibility grew. Previously, the Cali Cartel, under Gilberto Orejuela, had dominated Colombian cocaine production and distribution through its links with the American Mafia. Now Jung and Lehder's smuggling route opened up the market to those being held back by Orejuela.

Lehder and Jung teamed up with Pablo Escobar Gavira and others to establish the Medellin Cartel. Escobar and his colleagues took care of production and the Colombian end of the operation, as well as providing security in the US for Lehder and Jung's distribution network. By 1978, their cartel was making hundreds of millions of dollars, but Lehder and Jung's

partnership was over. Although Jung remained part of the cartel, he kept out of the way of his increasingly ambitious and violent former partner.

Lehder had decided that in order to expand, he needed his own Caribbean island and so he began to take over Norman's Cay in the Bahamas. Through buying all the property on the island, and threatening or "disappearing" other residents, he soon had his own tropical hideout. By 1982, he had built a 3,300ft (1,006m) runway on Norman's Cay, with its own radar and protection by armed guards. This allowed him to transport more than 300lbs (136kg) of cocaine per day. Not surprisingly, he soon achieved billionaire status.

However, in 1984, as political power in Colombia turned against the Medellin Cartel and the US authorities began to actively pursue Lehder, he was forced to flee to the protection of General Manuel Noriega in Panama. The next year, Lehder travelled back to Colombia and began to fund the Quintin Lame Movement, an indigenous rebel movement linked to the 19th of April Movement and FARC guerrillas, who continue to fight against the Colombian government to this day.

At the end of 1985, Lehder appeared on television to deliver an anti-American imperialism, anti-extradition speech, before slipping back into his Colombian jungle hideout. He continued to run his multi-billion dollar drug empire in hiding until he was seized by government troops, in 1987, and extradited to Florida to face trial for his organized crime activities. He was found guilty and sentenced to life without parole and an additional 135 years. This was reduced to a 55-year sentence and a large proportion of his seized $2.5 billion assets were returned to him, in 1992, in return for providing testimony at the trial of General Noriega.

One night in 1995 Lehder was whisked away from his prison cell. No one was able to find out from the US Justice Department where he was taken or what happened to him. This led to speculation he had been released or placed in a witness protection programme. Credible reports were made to journalists following the case that Lehder had been seen overseas. Conspiracy theories flourished on the Internet, most suggesting Lehder had inside knowledge on the CIA's role in drug smuggling which had gained him his freedom.

However, in July 2005 most of the speculation was crushed when Lehder appeared in the US Appeal Court. Representing himself, he contested his sentence and accused the United States Attorney General's Office of failing to have kept promises made to him in a co-operation agreement he had entered into with it. His appeal failed and two years later he unsuccessfully attempted to gain an order in the Colombian Supreme Court to get the Colombian government to request his release from the US.

Although it is impossible to obtain official confirmation from the US Justice Department about exactly where Lehder is today, sources from within the organization claim he remains held in the Bureau of Prison's version of a witness protection programme in a US jail. Despite the continuing mysteries surrounding Lehder, there is no doubting his key role in shaping the history of cocaine trafficking and Colombian organized crime.

The Medellin Cartel's most infamous member, Carlos Enrique Lehder Rivas, took control of a Caribbean island before his arrest in 1987.

PABLO ESCOBAR

It may have been the prison cell vision of Carlos Enrique Lehder Rivas that set the Colombian cocaine revolution in motion, but it was Pablo Escobar-Gavira who was key to turning the idea into a multi-billion dollar organized criminal network. In the process of establishing the Medellin Cartel as one of the globe's dominant drug trafficking syndicates, Escobar also transformed himself into one of the planet's richest men, the most infamous drug lord in the world and one of recorded history's most successful organized criminals.

Often called "the world's greatest outlaw", Escobar's criminal origins lay not in drugs, but tombstones. Born in 1949, in the small village of Rionegro close to his eventual base in the town Medellin, Escobar began his career in crime by stealing gravestones, sandblasting the inscriptions off them and reselling them to undertakers. In his 20s he turned his hand to whatever illegal activity could make him money – from car theft to selling fake lottery tickets. Escobar hustled at the level of a small-time hood until he moved into contract killing and kidnapping. Pablo's victims all bore his horrific trademark – known in later years as the Colombian necktie – where he would slash a person's throat and pull their tongue through the wound.

In 1971, Escobar moved into the drugs business. At that point, Colombian cocaine production was small-scale. After supplying a limited domestic market, farmers sent their coca leaf crop across the border to Panama where the leaves were refined before the cocaine made its way into the hands of the American Mafia. Following the lead of Gilberto Rodriguez Orejuela, the founder of the Cali Cartel, Escobar saw the potential for refining the product in Colombia and arranging its direct export to the US.

Escobar paid all the coca farmers in the Medellin area double what they got for sending their product abroad and began to process the drug himself. Within two years, he had joined forces with fellow drug producers, the Ochoa brothers and Jorge Luis Ochoa and Gonzalo Rodriguez Gacha. Between them they controlled a large proportion of all the cocaine produced in Colombia. When George Jung and Carlos Enrique Lehder Rivas presented them with the perfect smuggling and American distribution network, El Cartel de Medellin was created.

By 1980, the Medellin Cartel was sending more than 100 tonnes of cocaine to America and the rest of the world, and Escobar was personally making more than $1 million dollars per day. Through his strategy of "plata o plomo" (silver or lead), which meant accept a bribe or be shot, Escobar dominated the police, army, judiciary and political elite of Colombia. In this way his operations went untouched for several years and, in 1982, he was even elected to Congress.

However, as official opposition began to gather, Escobar changed tack. He began to fund the M-19 guerillas, paying them to guard his jungle laboratories and plantations. The Medellin Cartel began a terrorist war against the Colombian government through a series of bombings, the storming of the Colombian High Court and the murder of half the country's top judges. Escobar went into hiding, but remained incredibly popular with many Colombians – he had spent much of the millions he had made on the country's poor, building sports facilities, hospitals, housing and even introducing the country's first welfare payments.

In 1991, after years on the run, Escobar surrendered to the authorities on condition that he could choose and refit his own prison. It was a wise move. It prevented his extradition to America and allowed him a secure base to run his empire, free from fear of assassination by the rival Cali Cartel, and all in return for serving a five-year prison sentence. His prison, known as La Catedral (the Cathedral), was effectively a fortified mansion and a fitting home for the world's seventh richest man. The guards were more for Escobar's protection than anything else.

After a year of "imprisonment", Escobar began to worry that a change of government could end his deal and he went on the run again. Pursued by a special Colombian security team known as Search Bloc and US Delta Force and Navy SEAL teams, Escobar evaded capture for 17 months. However, on December 2, 1993, he made a fatal mistake – a call from his cell phone was traced. Troops took up positions outside his apartment and, as Escobar tried to escape across the rooftops, he was shot in the back, left knee and the back of the head. The "world's greatest outlaw" was dead, but his legacy of global cocaine distribution lives on to this day.

Pablo Escobar and his bodyguard watching a football game in 1983. Before his death in 1991, Escobar poured millions into building sports facilities and hospitals for the poor.

INDEX

PICTURE CREDITS

The publishers would like to thank the following sources for their kind permission to reproduce the photographs in this book.

Key: t = Top, b = Bottom, c = Centre, l = Left and r = Right

Alinari Picture Library: 14; /ANSA: 17

Corbis: 4–5. 71r, 74, 177; /Pizzoli Alberto: 19; /Babu/Reuters: 148b; /Bettmann: 22, 29, 30, 31r, 34r, 34l, 35, 35r, 37b, 37t, 38, 40b, 41l, 44t, 44b, 47b, 47t, 48l, 51l, 51r, 52t, 68, 72–73, 80t, 82, 163, 210, 211, 216, 219; /Horace Bristol: 61; /Cliff Doerzbacher: 46; /Sophie Elbaz/Sygma: 98; /Peret Franck: 64; /Grzegorz Galazka: 215; /Farrell Grehan: 41r; /E.O. Hoppé: 75t; /Hulton-Deutsch Collection: 58, 195; /Lee Jae-Won /Reuters: 65b; /Sergei Karpukhin/Reuters: 99; /Earl & Nazima Kowall: 79b; /Jacques Langevin: 178; /James Leynse: 140t; /Christian Liewig: 161b; /Rick Maiman: 62; /Gideon Mendel: 155t; /Franco Lannino-Michele Naccari/epa: 21; /Mark Peterson: 52b; /Ongaro Pier Silvio: 25; /Reuters: 16, 83b, 191, 203; /Dan Riedlhulber/Reuters: 179; /Robert Harding Picture Library: 48t; /Sygma: 93; /Tom Wagner: 59, 66, 67.

Getty Images: 175; /AFP: 138, 139, 167, 183, 197; /AFP/Torsten Blackwood: 81t; /AFP/Adrian Dennis: 120–121; /AFP/Emmanuel Dunand: 176; /AFP/Mogens Flindt: 141b; /AFP/Nilton Fukuda: 18b; /AFP/Kim Jae-Hwan: 65t; /AFP/Toshifumi Kitamura: 56–57, 63; /AFP/Tom Kutz: 145; /AFP/Olivier Laban-Matteil: 130b; / AFP/Petras Malukas: 140b; /AFP/Shah Marai: 134; /AFP/Peter Muhly: 126l; /AFP/ Indranil Mukherjee: 154t; /AFP/Orlando Sierra; 106–107, 109t; /AFP/STR: 83t; / AFP/Koca Sulejmanovic; 133; /AFP/Shawn Thew: 113, 169; /AFP/Tark Tinazay: 45r; /AFP/Ernst Van Norde: 141t; /AFP/Jeff Vinnick: 150; /Slim Aarons: 204–205, 208; /Kael Alford/Newsmakers: 132; /Natalie Behring: 78; /Jack Birns/Time Life Pictures: 85; /Patrick A. Burns/New York Times Co.; 214/Giuseppe Cacace/AFP: 172–173, 180; /Central Press: 123bl; /Cancan Chu: 75b; /Ed Clark/Time Life Pictures: 50, 39l; /Marco Di Lauro: 184; /John Dominis/Time Life Pictures: 200; / Evening Standard: 119t, 121b; /Fox Photos: 114–115, 120; /Alan Grant/Time Life Pictures: 42t; /HBO: 54; /Bob Haswell: 119b; /Yvonne Hemsey: 40t; /Hulton Archive: 10, 12, 32b, 116, 130t, 174, 206; /The Image Bank: 136b; /Imagno: 84; / Keystone: 31l, 188–189, 193; /Chuck Konig/Keystone Features: 117b; /Pascal Le Segretain: 128–129, 136t; /Christopher Lee: 13t; /Edwin Levick: 28; /London Express: 117t; /William Lovelace: 196; /Jack Manning/New York Times Co.: 45l; /David McNew: 137l; /Chuck Nacke/Timepix/Time Life Pictures: 7; /Oleg Nikishin: 100, 170–171; /Mark Nilstein: 103; /NY Daily News Archive/Andrew Theodorakis: 55; /Paramount Pictures: 186; /Bob Parent/Hulton Archive: 112; / Per-Anders Pettersson: 155b; /Graeme Robertson: 147; /Robert Harding World Imagery: 127; /Walter Sanders/Time Life Pictures: 137r; /Santi Visalli Inc.: 39r; / Joseph Scherschel/ Time Life Pictures: 190; /Henri Szwarc/Bongarts: 101; /Mario Tama: 186–187; /Time Life Pictures: 217; /Hugh Thomas/BWP Media: 156–157, 166; /Topical Press Agency: 26–27, 32t, 118, 198; /U.S. Attorney South District of New York: 135; /Ami Vitale: 131; /Diana Walker/Time Life Pictures: 201; /Hank Walker/Time Life Pictures: 36; /Natasja Weltsz: 105.

Igor Sherman: 96.

Newspix: 151, 152.

Press Association Images: AP Photo: 33, 42b, 43t, 92, 95, 148t, 159b, 159t, 162; /AP Photo/Giuseppe Anastasi: 161t; /AP Photo/Colombian National Police /HO: 144l; / AP Photo/EL Colombiano: 144r; /AP Photo/Francisco Abreu, O Globo: 149; /Josh Fisttick: 20; /AP Photo/Alessandro Fucarini: 23; /AP Photo/Anton Givon: 81b; /AP Photo/Ricardo Gonzalez-El Debate de Mazatlan: 146; /AP Photo/Eitan Hess-Asjkenzai: 97; /AP Photo/Itsuo Inouye: 109b; /AP Photo/Press Photo: 18t; /AP Photo/RAS: 49; /AP Photo/Alexander Salukov: 91; /AP Photo/Adriana Sapone: 15; /AP Photo/stf: 165; /AP Photo/str: 154b; /AP Photo/Donald Stampfli: 102; /AP Photo/Sunday Alamba: 148c; /AP Photo/Alessandro Tarantino; /AP Photo/Macau Jornar va Kio: 76; /AP Photo/US Attorneys Office: 43b; /AP Photo/Xinhua, Yang Jinzhi: 77; /Andy Eames: 80b; /PA: 123r, 125, 160; /PA/Sean Dempsey: 164; /PA/Sean Nicholson: 181; /PA/Phil Noble:

79; / SMG: 124; /Jeff Widener: 87.

PressPix: 142–143, 153.

Reuters Ltd.: 86; /Stringer Mexico: 185.

Rex Features: Action Press: 24

Topfoto.co.uk: 8–9, 13, 69, 88–89, 94, 122, 158, 202, 212, 213; AP: 2–3, 207; /ImageWorks: 90, 112.

© Collection Dr Walter Wood: 71l.

Every effort has been made to acknowledge correctly and contact the source and/or copyright holder of each picture, and Carlton Books Limited apologizes for any unintentional errors or omissions which will be corrected in future editions of this book.

ACKNOWLEDGEMENTS

Boat drinks to:

April Cole who, like the true friend she is, gave help and support from day one – even when she did not think writing this book was a good idea; Richard "Swiss Tony" Ali; Mary Ann Blau, the HTML fairy; Antoine Catry; Andrew and Sue Collins; Tim "Just a Jack-knife" Dedopulos; J – for keeping me in Milka and digging around for bits of missing ear for me; James "Jimmy the Saint" Harborne; Jick, Skullhead and others at KoL, especially those in the Bandits Outpost; Dan and Kyomi; Mark Lester; Dickon Springate; The Mighty Twists; Sean "FTH" York; Richard Ward; Brendan and Lesley Wilson; Richard Wood. Deepest thanks to my Nanna and Granddad for their constant backing and love.

Professional thanks to:

Carlton Books Limited; Arma dei Carabinieri; Capitano "S"; DIA; DCI "X"; Europol; FBI; "Harry of the Yard"; Interpol; Bernard O'Mahoney; National Institute of Police Science, Japan; The Nathanson Centre for the Study of Organized Crime and Corruption; Zef Nano; OCCB; OCTB; Max Plank Institute of Foreign and International Criminal Law; Scotland Yard; many others such as my Organizatsiya, Mala del Brenta, Voždovac and 14K interviewees who wish to remain nameless.

Inspirational thanks to:

Brian Michael Bendis, one of the best storytellers around; David Benson for Conspiracy Cabaret and who probably thinks I have forgotten all about his very kind email; Duncan Campbell, a journalist who keeps me constantly inspired; J.J. Connolly and Matthew Vaughn for the only decent crime film of the twenty-first century – "Always remember that one day all this drug monkey business will be legal"; Dave Courtney who can recognize a conspiracy when there is one and who showed me that good crime books are always about much more than just naughtiness; Noel Fielding and Julian Barratt for hours of laughter; Raúl Gibb Guerrero, the very spirit of journalistic bravery; Hamell On Trial for the soundtrack; Gary Russell for ensuring there were countless better worlds for me to visit in the evenings after a day in the underworld; Michael Schuck; Frank Serpico; Tony York for introducing me to the world of criminal tattoos.